THE AUTOBIOGRAPHY

OF

JOHANN WOLFGANG VON GOETHE

Translated by

John Oxenford

And with an Introduction by

Karl J. Weintraub

VOLUME TWO

The University of Chicago Press
Chicago and London

When first published, Goethe's autobiography carried the title *Aus meinem Leben: Dichtung und Wahrheit*. As pointed out in the Introduction to the present edition, however, the work has commonly been known by the subtitle alone, *Dichtung und Wahrheit*.

The University of Chicago Press, Chicago 60637
The University of Chicago Press, Ltd., London

© 1974 by The University of Chicago. All rights reserved
Phoenix edition published 1974
Printed in the United States of America
88 87 86 85 84 83 82 81   2 3 4 5 6

ISBN: 0-226-30057-9 (vol. 1), 0-226-30058-7 (vol. 2)
Library of Congress Catalog Card Number: 74-10339

CONTENTS

VOLUME II

PART THREE
Es ist dafür gesorgt, dass die Bäume
nicht in den Himmel wachsen.
Care is taken that the trees
don't grow into the sky.—PROVERB

v

Part Four
Nemo contra deum nisi deus ipse.

World affairs; Benjamin Franklin and George Washington; the privileged classes in Germany – 348. A letter of Ulrich von Hutten – 354. Frankfurt and its government – 356.

Kraus, increase Goethe's desire to join the duke's circle – 420. On the "demonic"; Egmont as an example of it; the "demonic principle": *Nemo contra Deum* – 423. Goethe decides to break away from Lili and to go to Weimar – 425. Unexpected complications; Goethe hides at home, finishes *Egmont* – 428. The Duke's envoy fails to arrive, Goethe decides under pressure to go to Italy – 431; he makes a long stop in Heidelberg where Mademoiselle Delf has different plans for his career and marriage – 432. At the last moment, a letter from Frankfurt explains the delay of the gentleman from Weimar – 435. Goethe decides at once; he takes the stage coach back to Frankfurt, headed for Weimar – 436.

THE AUTOBIOGRAPHY

OF

JOHANN WOLFGANG VON GOETHE

TENTH BOOK.

When the German poets, as members of a corporation, were no longer standing as one man, they did not enjoy the smallest advantages among their fellow citizens. They had neither support, standing, nor respectability, except in so far as their other position was favourable to them; and therefore it was a matter of mere chance whether talent was born to honour or to disgrace. A poor son of earth, with a consciousness of mind and faculties, was forced to crawl along painfully through life, and, from the pressure of momentary necessities, to squander the gifts which perchance he had received from the Muses. Occasional poems, the first and most genuine of all kinds of poetry, had become despicable to such a degree, that the nation even now cannot attain a conception of their high value: and a poet, if he did not strike altogether into Günther's path, appeared in the world in the most melancholy state of subserviency, as a jester and parasite; so that both on the theatre and on the stage of life he represented a character which any one and every one could abuse at pleasure.

If, on the contrary, the Muse associated herself with

3

men of respectability, these received thereby a lustre which was reflected back to the donor. Noblemen well versed in life, like Hagedorn; dignified citizens, like Brockes; distinguished men of science, like Haller, — appeared among the first in the nation, to be equal with the most eminent and the most prized. Those persons, too, were specially honoured, who, together with this pleasing talent, distinguished themselves as active, faithful men of business. In this way Uz, Rabener, and Weisse enjoyed a respect of quite a peculiar kind: people had here to value, when combined, those most heterogeneous qualities which are seldom found united.

But now the time was to come for poetic genius to become self-conscious, to create for itself its own circumstances, and understand how to lay the foundation of an independent dignity. Everything requisite for founding such an epoch was combined in Klopstock. Considered, both from the sensual and moral side, he was a pure young man. Seriously and thoroughly educated, he places from his youth upwards a great value upon himself and upon whatever he does, and, while considerately measuring out beforehand the steps of his life, turns, with a presentiment of the whole strength of his internal nature, toward the loftiest and most grateful theme. The *Messiah*, a name which betokens infinite attributes, was to be glorified afresh by him. The Redeemer was to be the hero whom the poet thought to accompany through earthly lowliness and sorrows to the highest heavenly triumphs. Everything Godlike, angelic, and human that lay in the young soul was here called into requisition. Brought up by the Bible and nourished by its strength, he now lives with patriarchs, prophets, and forerunners, as if they were present; yet all these are only evoked from ages to draw a bright halo round the One whose humiliation they behold with astonishment, and in whose exaltation they are gloriously to bear a part. For at last, after gloomy and horrible hours, the everlasting Judge will uncloud his face, again acknowledge his Son and fellow God, who, on the other hand, will again lead to him alienated men, — nay, even a fallen spirit. The living heavens shout with a thousand angel voices round the throne, and a radiance of love gushes out over the universe, which shortly before had fastened its looks upon a fearful place of sacrifice. The heavenly peace which Klopstock felt in the conception and execution of this poem communicates itself even now to every one who reads the first ten cantos, without allowing certain requisitions to be brought forward, which an advancing cultivation does not willingly abandon.

The dignity of the subject elevated in the poet the feeling of his own personality. That he himself would enter hereafter into those choirs, that the God-Man would distinguish him, nay, give him face to face the reward for his labours, which even here every feeling, pious heart had fondly paid in many a pure tear, — these were such innocent, childlike thoughts and hopes, as only a well-constituted mind can conceive and cherish. Thus Klopstock gained the perfect right to regard himself as a consecrated person, and thus in his actions he studied the most scrupulous purity. Even in his old age it troubled him exceedingly that he had given his earliest love to a lady who, by marrying another, left him in uncertainty whether she had really loved or been worthy of him. The sentiments which bound him to Meta; their hearty, tranquil affection; their short, sacred married life; the aversion of the surviving husband from a second union, — all is of that kind which may well be remembered hereafter in the circle of the blessed.

This honourable conduct toward himself was still further enhanced by his being favourably received for

a long time in well-minded Denmark, in the house of
a great, and, humanly speaking, excellent statesman.
Here, in a higher circle, which was exclusive indeed,
but, at the same time, devoted to external manners
and attention toward the world, his tendency became
still more decided. A composed demeanour, a measured speech, and a laconism even when he spoke
openly and decidedly, gave him, through his whole
life, a certain diplomatic ministerial consequence, which
seemed to be at variance with his tender natural feelings, although both sprang from one source. Of all
this, his first works give a clear transcript and type;
and they thus could not but gain an incredible influence. That, however, he personally assisted others
who were struggling in life and poetry, has scarcely
been mentioned, as one of his most decided characteristics.

But just such a furtherance of young people in
literary action and pursuit, a hopeful pleasure in bringing forward men not favoured by fortune, and making
the way easy to them, has rendered illustrious one
German, who, in respect to the dignity which he gave
himself, may be named as the second, but, in regard to
his living influence, as the first. It will escape no one
that Gleim is here meant. Holding an obscure, but
lucrative, office, residing in a pleasantly situated spot,
not too large, and enlivened by military, civic, and
literary activity, whence proceeded the revenues of a
great and wealthy institution, not without a part of
them remaining behind for the advantage of the place,
he felt within himself also a lively productive impulse,
which, however, with all its strength, was not quite
enough for him; and therefore he gave himself up to
another, perhaps stronger, impulse, namely, that of
making others produce something. Both these activities were intertwined incessantly during his whole
long life. He could as easily have lived without

taking breath as without writing poetry and making presents; and, by helping needy talents of all kinds through earlier or later embarrassments, contributing to the honour of literature, he gained so many friends, debtors, and dependents, that they willingly allowed his diffuse verses to pass, since they could give him nothing in return for his rich benefits but endurance of his poetry.

Now, the high idea which these two men might well form of their own worth, and by which others were induced also to think well of themselves, has produced very great and beautiful results, both in public and private. But this consciousness, honourable as it is, called a peculiar evil down upon themselves, on those around them, and on their time. If, judging from their intellectual effects, both these men may without hesitation be called great, with respect to the world they remained but small, and, considered in comparison with a more stirring life, their external position was nought. The day is long, and so is the night; one cannot be always writing poetry, or doing, or giving; their time could not be filled up like that of people of the world, and men of rank and wealth; they therefore set too high a value on their particular limited situations, attached an importance to their daily affairs which they should only have allowed themselves amongst each other, and took more than reasonable delight in their own jokes, which, though they' made the moment agreeable, could be of no consequence in the end. They received praise and honour from others, as they deserved; they gave it back, with measure indeed, but always too profusely; and, because they felt that their friendship was worth much, they were pleased to express it repeatedly, and in this spared neither paper nor ink. Thus arose those correspondences, at the deficiency of which in solid contents the modern world wonders; nor can it be blamed, when it hardly sees the possibility of eminent men delighting themselves in such an interchange of nothing, or when it expresses the wish that such leaves might have remained unprinted. But we may suffer these few volumes always to stand along with so many others upon our book-shelves, if we have learned from them the fact, that even the most eminent man lives only by the day, and enjoys but a sorry entertainment when he throws himself too much back upon himself, and neglects to grasp into the fulness of the external world, where alone he can find nourishment for his growth, and at the same time a standard for its measurement.

The activity of these men was in its finest bloom, when we young folks also began to stir in our own circle; and with my younger friends, if not with older persons too, I was pretty much in the way of falling into this sort of mutual flattery, forbearance, raising and supporting. In my immediate sphere, whatever I produced could always be reckoned good. Ladies, friends, and patrons will not consider bad that which is undertaken and written out of affection for them. From such obligations at last arises the expression of an empty satisfaction with each other, in the phrases of which a character is easily lost if it is not from time to time steeled to higher excellence.

And thus I had the happiness to say, that, by means of an unexpected acquaintance, all the self-complacency, love of the looking-glass, vanity, pride, and haughtiness that might have been resting or working within me, were exposed to a very severe trial, which was unique in its kind, by no means in accordance with the time, and therefore so much the more searching and more sorely felt.

For the most important event, one that was to have the weightiest consequences for me, was my acquaintance with Herder, and the nearer connection with him which sprung from it. He accompanied the travels of the Prince of Holstein-Eutin, who was in a melancholy state of mind, and had come with him to Strasburg. Our society, as soon as it knew of his arrival, was seized with a great longing to approach him; and this good fortune happened to me first, quite unexpectedly and by chance. I had gone to the Ghost tavern to inquire after some distinguished stranger or other. Just at the bottom of the staircase I found a man who was on the point of ascending, and whom I might have taken for a clergyman. His powdered hair was put up in a cue, his black clothes likewise distinguished him, but still more a long black silk mantle, the skirts of which he had gathered up and stuck into his pocket. This somewhat striking, but yet, on the whole, polite and pleasing, figure, of which I had already been told, left me not the least doubt that he was the celebrated newcomer; and my address was to convince him at once that I knew him. He asked my name, which could be of no consequence to him; but my frankness seemed to please him, since he returned it with great friendliness, and, as we mounted the stairs, showed himself ready immediately for animated communication. I have forgotten whom we visited then: it is sufficient to say, that at parting I begged permission to wait on him at his own residence, which he granted me kindly enough. I did not neglect to avail myself repeatedly of this favour, and was more and more attracted by him. He had a certain gentleness in his manner, which was very suitable and becoming, without being exactly easy. A round face; an imposing forehead; a somewhat puggish nose; a mouth somewhat prominent, but highly characteristic, pleasing, and amiable; a pair of coal-black eyes under black eyebrows, which did not fail of their effect, although one of them used to be red and inflamed. By various questions he tried to make himself acquainted with me and my situation, and his power of attraction operated on me with growing strength. I was, generally speaking, of a very confiding disposition; and with him especially I had no secrets. It was not long, however, before the repelling pulse of his nature began to appear, and placed me in no small uneasiness. I related to him many things of my youthful occupation and taste, and among others, of a collection of seals, which I had principally gotten together through the assistance of our family friend, who had an extensive correspondence. I had arranged them according to the "State Calendar," and by this means had become well acquainted with the whole of the potentates, the greater and lesser mightinesses and powers, even down to the nobility under them. These heraldic insignia had often, and in particular at the ceremonies of the coronation, been of use to my memory. I spoke of these things with some complacency; but he was of another opinion, and not only stripped the subject of all interest, but also contrived to make it ridiculous and nearly disgusting.

From this his spirit of contradiction I had much to endure; for he had resolved, partly because he wished to separate from the prince, partly on account of a complaint in his eye, to remain in Strasburg. This complaint is one of the most inconvenient and unpleasant, and the more troublesome as it can be cured only by a painful, highly irritating, and uncertain operation. The tear-bag is closed below, so that the moisture contained in it cannot flow off to the nose, and so much the less as the adjacent bone is deficient in the aperture by which this secretion should naturally take place. The bottom of the tear-bag must therefore be cut open, and the bone bored through, when a horsehair is drawn through the lacrimal point, then down through the opened bag, and the new canal thus put into connection with it; and this hair is moved backwards and forwards every day, in order to restore the communication between the two parts, — all which cannot be done or attained, if an incision is not first made externally in that place.

Herder was now separated from the prince, had moved into lodgings of his own, and resolved to have himself operated upon by Lobstein. Here those exercises by which I had sought to blunt my sensibility did me good service: I was able to be present at the operation, and to be serviceable and helpful in many ways to so worthy a man. I found here every reason to admire his great firmness and endurance: for neither during the numerous surgical operations, nor at the oft-repeated painful dressings, did he show himself in any degree irritable; and of all of us he seemed to be the one who suffered least. But in the intervals, indeed, we had to endure the change of his temper in many ways. I say *we;* for, besides myself, a pleasant Russian named Peglow was mostly with him. This man had been an early acquaintance of Herder's in Riga, and, though no longer a youth, was trying to perfect himself in surgery under Lobstein's guidance. Herder could be charmingly prepossessing and brilliant, but he could just as easily turn an ill-humoured side foremost. All men, indeed, have this attraction and repulsion, according to their natures, some more, some less, some in longer, some in shorter, pulsations: few can really control their peculiarities in this respect, many in appearance. As for Herder, the preponderance of his contradictory, bitter, biting humour was certainly derived from his disease and the sufferings arising from it. This case often occurs in life: one does not sufficiently take into consideration the moral effect of sickly conditions; and one therefore judges many characters very unjustly, because it is assumed that all men are healthy, and required of them that they shall conduct themselves accordingly.

During the whole time of this cure I visited Herder

morning and evening: I even remained whole days with him, and in a short time accustomed myself so much the more to his chiding and faultfinding, as I daily learned to appreciate his beautiful and great qualities, his extensive knowledge, and his profound views. The influence of this good-natured blusterer was great and important. He was five years older than myself, which in younger days makes a great difference to begin with; and as I acknowledged him for what he was, and tried to value that which he had already produced, he necessarily gained a great superiority over me. But the situation was not comfortable; for older persons, with whom I had associated hitherto, had sought to form me with indulgence, perhaps had even spoiled me by their lenity: but from Herder, behave as one might, one could never expect approval. As now, on the one side, my great affection and reverence for him, and, on the other, the discontent which he excited in me, were continually at strife with each other, there arose within me an inward struggle, the first of its kind which I had experienced in my life. Since his conversations were at all times important, whether he asked, answered, or communicated his opinions in any other manner, he could not but advance me daily, nay, hourly, to new views. At Leipzig I had accustomed myself to a narrow and circumscribed existence, and my general knowledge of German literature could not be extended by my situation in Frankfort; nay, those mystico-religio-chemical occupations had led me into obscure regions, and what had been passing for some years back in the wide literary world had, for the most part, remained unknown to me. Now I was at once made acquainted by Herder with all the new aspiration and all the tendencies which it seemed to be taking. He had already made himself sufficiently known; and by his " Fragments," his " Kritische Wälder " (" Critical

Woods "), and other works, had immediately placed himself by the side of the most eminent men who had for a long time drawn toward them the eyes of their country. What an agitation there must have been in such a mind, what a fermentation there must have been in such a nature, can neither be conceived nor described. But great was certainly the concealed effort, as will be easily admitted when one reflects for how many years afterward, and how much, he has done and produced.

We had not lived together long in this manner when he confided to me that he meant to be a competitor for the prize which was offered at Berlin for the best treatise on the origin of language. His work was already nearly completed; and, as he wrote a very neat hand, he could soon communicate to me, in part, a legible manuscript. I had never reflected on such subjects, for I was yet too deeply involved in the midst of things to have thought about their beginning and end. The question, too, seemed to me idle in some measure; for, if God had created man as man, language was just as innate in him as walking erect: he must have just as well perceived that he could sing with his throat, and modify the tones in various ways with tongue, palate, and lips, as he must have remarked that he could walk, and take hold of things. If man was of divine origin, so was also language; and if man, considered in the circle of nature, was a natural being, language was likewise natural. These two things, like soul and body, I could never separate. Süssmilch, with a realism crude, yet somewhat fantastically devised, had declared himself for the divine origin; that is, that God had played the schoolmaster to the first men. Herder's treatise went to show that man as man could and must have attained to language by his own powers. I read the treatise with much pleasure, and it was of special aid in strengthening my mind; but I did not stand high enough, either in knowledge or thought, to form a solid judgment upon it. I therefore gave the author my applause, adding only a few remarks which flowed from my way of viewing the subject. But one was received just like the other : there was scolding and blaming whether one agreed with him conditionally or unconditionally. The fat surgeon had less patience than I : he humourously declined the communication of this prize-essay, and affirmed that he was not prepared to meditate on such abstract topics. He urged us in preference to a game of ombre, which we commonly played together in the evening.

During so troublesome and painful a cure, Herder lost nothing of his vivacity ; but it became less and less amiable. He could not write a note to ask for anything that would not be spiced with some scoff or other. Once, for instance, he wrote to me thus :

" If those letters of Brutus thou hast in thy Cicero's letters,
Thou, whom consolers of schools, decked out in magnificent
    bindings,
Soothe from their well-planned shelves, — yet more by the
    outside than inside, —
Thou, who from gods art descended, or Goths, or from origin
    filthy,[1]
Göthe, send them to me."

It was not polite, indeed, that he should have permitted himself this jest on my name ; for a man's name is not like a mantle, which merely hangs about him, and which, perchance, may be safely twitched and pulled, but is a perfectly fitting garment, which has grown over and over him like his very skin, at which one cannot scratch and scrape without wounding the man himself.

[1] The German word is " Koth ; " and the whole object of the line is, to introduce a play on the words " Göthe," " Götter," " Gothen " and " Koth." — TRANS.

The first reproach, on the contrary, was better founded. I had brought with me to Strasburg the authors I had obtained, by exchange, from Langer, together with various fine editions from my father's collection besides, and had set them up on a neat bookcase, with the best intentions of using them. But how should my time, which I split up into a hundred different activities, suffice for that? Herder, who was most attentive to books, since he had need of them every moment, perceived my fine collection at his first visit, but soon saw, too, that I made no use of them. He, therefore, as the greatest enemy to all semblance and ostentation, was accustomed, on occasion, to rally me upon the subject.

Another sarcastic poem occurs to me, which he sent me one evening, when I had been telling him a great deal about the Dresden gallery. I had, indeed, not penetrated into the higher meaning of the Italian school; but Dominico Feti, an excellent artist, although a humourist, and therefore not of the first rank, had interested me much. Scripture subjects had to be painted. He confined himself to the New Testament parables, and was fond of representing them with much originality, taste, and good humour. He brought them altogether into every-day life; and the spirited and naïve details of his compositions, recommended by a free pencil, had made a vivid impression upon me. At this, my childish enthusiasm for art, Herder sneered in the following fashion:

> " From sympathy,
> The master I like best of all
> Dominico Feti they call.
> A parable from Scripture he is able
> Neatly to turn into a crazy fable
> From sympathy : — thou crazy parable ! "

I could mention many jokes of the kind, more or less clear or abstruse, cheerful or bitter. They did not vex me, but made me feel uncomfortable. Yet since I knew how to value highly everything that contributed to my own cultivation, and as I had often given up former opinions and inclinations, I soon accommodated myself, and only sought, as far as it was possible for me from my point of view, to distinguish just blame from unjust invectives. And thus no day passed that had not been, in the most fruitful manner, instructive to me.

I was made acquainted by him with poetry from quite a different side, in another light than heretofore, and one, too, which suited me well. The poetic art of the Hebrews, which he treated ingeniously after his predecessor Lowth, — popular poetry, the traditions of which in Alsace he urged us to search after; and the oldest records existing as poetry, — all bore witness that poetry in general was a gift to the world and to nations, and not the private inheritance of a few refined, cultivated men. I swallowed all this; and the more eager I was in receiving, the more liberal was he in giving, so that we spent the most interesting hours together. The other natural studies which I had begun, I endeavoured to continue; and as one always has time enough, if one will apply it well, so amongst them all I succeeded in doing twice or thrice as much as usual. As to the fulness of those few weeks during which we lived together, I can well say, that all which Herder has gradually produced since was then announced in the germ, and that I thereby fell into the fortunate condition that I could completely attach to something higher, and expand all that I had hitherto thought, learned, and made my own. Had Herder been methodical, I should have found the most precious guide for giving a durable tendency to my cultivation; but he was more inclined to examine and stimulate than to lead and conduct. Thus he at first made me acquainted with Hamann's writings, upon which he set a very great value. But instead of instructing me as to these, and making the bias and drift of his extraordinary mind intelligible to me, it generally only served him for amusement when I behaved strangely enough in trying to get at the meaning of such sibylline leaves. However, I could well feel that something in Hamann's writings appealed to me; and to this I gave myself up, without knowing whence it came or whither it was leading me.

After the cure had lasted longer than was reasonable, Lobstein had begun to hesitate, and to repeat himself in his treatment, so that the affair would not come to an end; and Peglow, too, had confided to me in private that a favourable issue was hardly to be expected; the whole position became gloomy: Herder became impatient and out of temper; he could not succeed in continuing his activity as heretofore, and was obliged to restrain himself the more, as they began to lay the blame of the surgical failure upon his too great mental exertion, and his uninterrupted, animated, nay, merry, intercourse with us. It is sufficient to say, that, after so much trouble and suffering, the artificial tear-channel would not form itself, and the communication intended would not take place. It was necessary to let the wound heal over lest the disease should become worse. If, now, during the operation, one could but admire Herder's firmness under such pains, his melancholy and even fierce resignation to the idea that he must bear such a blot about him all his life had about it something truly sublime, by which he gained for ever the reverence of those who saw and loved him. This disease, which disfigured so expressive a countenance, must have been so much the more afflicting to him, as he had become acquainted with an excellent lady in Darmstadt, and had gained her affections. It may have been for this cause principally

that he submitted to the cure, in order, on his return,
to appear more free, more cheerful, and more handsome in the eyes of his half-betrothed, and to unite
himself more certainly and indissolubly with her.
However, he hastened away from Strasburg as soon
as possible; and, since his stay had hitherto been as
expensive as it was unpleasant, I borrowed a sum of
money for him, which he promised to refund by an
appointed day. The time passed without the arrival
of the money. My creditor, indeed, did not dun me;
but I was for several weeks in embarrassment. At
last the letter and money came, and even here he did
not act unlike himself: for, instead of thanks or an
apology, his letter contained nothing but satirical
things in doggerel verse, which would have puzzled, if
not alienated, another; but it did not move me at all,
for I had conceived so great and powerful an idea of
his worth that it absorbed everything of an opposite
nature which could have injured it.

One should never speak, publicly at least, of his
own faults, or those of others, unless he hopes to attain
some useful end thereby: on this account I will here
insert certain remarks which force themselves upon
me.

Gratitude and ingratitude belong to those events
which appear every moment in the moral world, and
about which men can never agree among themselves.
I usually distinguish between non-thankfulness, ingratitude, and aversion from gratitude. The former is
innate with men, nay, created with them; for it arises
from a happy volatile forgetfulness of the repulsive as
well as of the delightful, by which alone the continuation of life is possible. Man needs such an infinite
quantity of previous and concurrent assistances for a
tolerable existence, that if he would always pay to the
sun and the earth, to God and nature, to ancestors
and parents, to friends and companions, the thanks due

to them, he would have neither time nor feeling left
to receive and enjoy new benefits. But, if the natural
man suffers this volatility to get the control in and
over him, a cold indifference gains more and more the
ascendency, and one at last regards one's benefactor as
a stranger, to whose injury, perhaps, anything may be
undertaken, provided it be advantageous to ourselves.
This alone can properly be called ingratitude, which
results from the rudeness into which the uncultivated
nature must necessarily lose itself at last. Aversion
from gratitude, however, the rewarding of a benefit by
ill-natured and sullen conduct, is very rare, and occurs
only in eminent men, such as, with great natural gifts,
and a presentiment of them, being born in a lower
rank of society or in a helpless condition, must, from
their youth upwards, force themselves along step by
step, and receive at every point aids and supports,
which are often embittered and repulsive to them
through the coarseness of their benefactors, since that
which they receive is earthly, while that which, on
the other hand, they give, is of a higher kind; so that
what is, strictly speaking, a compensation, is out of the
question. Lessing, with the fine knowledge of earthly
things which fell to his share in the best years of his
life, has in one place bluntly but cheerfully expressed
himself. Herder, on the contrary, constantly embittered his finest days, both for himself and others,
because he knew not how to moderate, by strength of
mind in later years, that ill-humour which had necessarily seized him in youth.

One may well make this demand of himself; for to
a man's capability of cultivation, comes, with friendly
aid, the light of nature, which is always active in enlightening him about his condition: and generally, in
many moral points of culture, one should not construe
the failings too severely, nor look about after the most
serious and remote means of correcting them; for cer-

tain faults may be easily and even playfully removed. Thus, for instance, by mere habit, we can excite gratitude in ourselves, keep it alive, and even make it necessary to us.

In a biographical attempt, it is proper to speak of one's self. I am, by nature, as little grateful as any man; and, on forgetting the benefit received, the violent feeling of a momentary disagreement could very easily beguile me into ingratitude.

To obviate this, I accustomed myself, in the first place, with everything that I possessed, to call to mind with pleasure how I came by it, from whom I received it, whether it was by way of present, exchange, or purchase, or in any other manner. I have accustomed myself, in showing my collections, to mention the persons by whose means I obtained each article, nay, even to do justice to the occasion, to the accident, to the remotest cause and coincidence, by which things which are dear and of value to me have become mine. That which surrounds us thus receives a life; we see in it a spiritual combination, full of love, reminding us of its origin; and, by thus making past circumstances present to us, our momentary existence is elevated and enriched; the originators of the gifts rise repeatedly before the imagination; we connect with their image a pleasing remembrance; ingratitude becomes impossible; and a return, on occasion, becomes easy and desirable. At the same time, we are led to the consideration of that which is not a possession palpable to the senses; and we love to recapitulate to whom our higher endowments are to be ascribed, and whence they take their date.

Before I turn my attention from my connection with Herder, which was so important and so rich in consequences for me, I find yet something more to adduce. Nothing was more natural than that I should by degrees become more and more reserved toward Herder, in communicating those things which had hitherto contributed to my culture, but especially such as still seriously occupied my attention at the moment. He had destroyed my enjoyment of so much that I had loved before, and had especially blamed me in the strongest manner for the pleasure I took in " Ovid's Metamorphoses." I might defend my favourite as I would ; I might say, that, for a youthful fancy, nothing could be more delightful than to linger in those cheerful and glorious regions with gods and demi-gods, and to be a witness of their deeds and passions; I might circumstantially quote that previously mentioned opinion of a sober-minded man, and corroborate it by my own experience, — all this, according to Herder, went for nothing ; there was no immediate truth, properly so called, to be found in these poems : here was neither Greece nor Italy, neither a primitive world nor a cultivated one ; everything was rather an imitation of what had already existed, and a mannerised representation, such as could be expected only from an over-cultivated man. And if at last I would maintain, that whatever an eminent individual produces is also nature, and that always, in all nations, ancient and modern, the poet alone has been the maker, this was not allowed to pass, and I had to endure much on this account, nay, I was almost disgusted with my Ovid by it ; for there is no affection, no habit so strong, that it can hold out in the long run against the animadversions of eminent men in whom one places confidence. Something always cleaves to us ; and, if one cannot love unconditionally, love is already in a critical condition.

I most carefully concealed from him my interest in certain subjects which had rooted themselves within me, and were, by little and little, moulding themselves into poetic form. These were " Götz von Berlichingen " and " Faust." The biography of the former had seized my inmost heart. The figure of a rough, well-meaning self-helper, in a wild anarchical time, awakened my deepest sympathy. The significant puppet-show fable of the latter resounded and vibrated many-toned within me. I had also wandered about in all sorts of science, and had early enough been led to see its vanity. I had, moreover, tried all sorts of ways in real life, and had always returned more unsatisfied and troubled. Now, these things, as well as many others, I carried about with me, and delighted myself with them during my solitary hours, but without writing anything down. But, most of all, I concealed from Herder my mystico-cabalistical chemistry, and everything relating to it; although, at the same time, I was still very fond of secretly busying myself in working it out more consistently than it had been communicated to me. Of my poetical labours, I believe I laid before him "Die Mitschuldigen;" but I do not recollect that on this account I received either correction or encouragement on his part. Yet, with all this, he remained what he was: whatever proceeded from him had an important, if not a cheering effect; and even his handwriting exercised a magic power over me. I do not remember having ever torn up or thrown away one of his letters, or even a mere envelope from his hand; yet, with my various changes of place and time, not one document of those strange, foreboding, and happy days is left.

That Herder's power of attraction had as much effect on others as on me, I should scarcely mention, had I not to remark that it extended itself particularly to Jung, commonly called Stilling. The true, honest striving of this man could not but deeply interest everybody who had any feeling, and his susceptibility must have charmed into candour every one who was in a condition to impart anything. Even Herder behaved toward him with more forbearance than toward the rest of us, for his counter-action always seemed to stand in relation with the action exerted upon him. Jung's narrowness was accompanied by so much good will, his urgency with so much softness and earnestness, that a man of intelligence could certainly not be severe against him, and a benevolent man could not scoff at him or turn him into ridicule. Jung was also exhilarated to such a degree by Herder, that he felt himself strengthened and advanced in all he did: even his affection for me seemed to lose ground in the same ratio; yet we always remained good companions, made allowances for each other from first to last, and mutually rendered the most friendly services.

Let us now, however, withdraw from the sick-chamber of friendship, and from the general considerations which refer rather to disorder than to health of mind; let us betake ourselves into the open air, to the lofty and broad gallery of the minster, as if the time were still present when we young fellows often appointed an evening meeting to greet the departing sun with brimming goblets. Here all conversation was lost in the contemplation of the country; here sharpness of eyesight was put to the proof, and every one strove to perceive, nay, plainly to distinguish, the most distant objects. Good telescopes were employed to assist us, and one friend after another exactly pointed out the spot which had become the most dear and precious to him: nor did *I* lack such a little spot, which, although it did not come out with importance in the landscape, nevertheless more than all the rest attracted me with an amiable magic. On these occasions the imagination was excited by relating our adventures; and several little jaunts were concerted, nay, often undertaken on the spur of the moment, of which I will circumstantially relate only one instead of a number, since in many respects it was of consequence to me.

With two worthy friends and fellow boarders, Engel-
bach and Weyland, both natives of Lower Alsace, I
repaired on horseback to Zabern, where, in the fine
weather, the friendly little place smiled pleasantly
upon us. The sight of the bishop's castle awakened
our admiration; the extent, height, and splendour of a
new set of stables bore witness to the other comforts
of the owner. The gorgeousness of the staircase surprised us; the chambers and saloons we trod with
reverence; only the person of the cardinal, a little
wreck of a man, whom we saw at table, made a contrast. The view of the garden is splendid; and a
canal, three-quarters of a league long, which leads
straight up to the middle of the castle, gives a high
idea of the taste and resources of the former possessors.
We rambled up and down there, and enjoyed many parts
of this altogether beautifully situated country, skirting
the magnificent plain of Alsace, at the foot of the
Vosges.

After we had enjoyed ourselves at this clerical out-
post of a royal power, and had made ourselves comfortable in its region, we arrived early next morning at
a public work, which most nobly opens the entrance
into a mighty kingdom. Illumined by the beams of
the rising sun, the famous Zabern-stairs, a work of incredible labour, rose before us. A road, built serpen-
tine-wise over the most fearful crags, and wide enough
for three wagons abreast, leads up hill so gently, that
the ascent is scarcely perceptible. The hardness and
smoothness of the way, the flat-topped elevations on
both sides for the foot-passengers, the stone channels to
lead off the mountain-water, all are executed as neatly,
as artistically and durably, so that they afford a satisfactory view. Thus one gradually arrives at Pfalzburg,
a modern fortification. It is situated upon a moderate
hill; the works are elegantly built on blackish rocks,
and of the same kind of stone; and the joinings, being

pointed out with white mortar, show exactly the size of the square stones, and give a striking proof of neat workmanship. We found the place itself, as is proper for a fortress, regular, built of stone, and the church in good taste. When we wandered through the streets, — it was nine o'clock on Sunday morning, — we heard music: they were already waltzing in the tavern to their hearts' content; and as the inhabitants did not suffer themselves to be disturbed in their pleasures by the great scarcity, nay, by the threatened famine; so also our youthful cheerfulness was not at all troubled when the baker on the road refused us some bread, and directed us to the tavern, where perhaps we might procure provisions at the usual place.

We now very gladly rode down the Zabern-stairs again to gaze at this architectural wonder a second time, and to enjoy once more the refreshing prospect over Alsace. We soon reached Buchsweiler, where friend Weyland had prepared for us a good reception. To a fresh, youthful mind the condition of a small town is well suited: family connections are closer and more perceptible; domestic life, which, with moderate activity, moves hither and thither between light official duties, town business, agriculture and gardening, invites us to a friendly participation; sociableness is necessary; and the stranger finds himself very pleasantly situated in the limited circles, if the disputes of the inhabitants, which in such places are more palpable, do not every-where come in contact with him. This little town was the chief place of the county of Hanau-Lichtenberg, belonging to the Landgrave of Darmstadt, under French sovereignty. A regency and board of officers estab-lished here made the place an important centre of a very beautiful and desirable principality. We easily forgot the unequal streets and the irregular architecture of the place when we went out to look at the old castle and the gardens, which are excellently laid out on a hill. Numerous little pleasure-woods, a preserve for tame and wild pheasants, and the relics of many similar arrangements, showed how pleasant this little residence must formerly have been.

Yet all these views were surpassed by the prospect which met the eye, when, from the neighbouring Basch-berg, one looked over the perfectly paradisiacal region. This height, wholly heaped together out of different kinds of shells, attracted my attention for the first time to such documents of antiquity: I had never before seen them together in so great a mass. Yet the curious eye soon turned itself exclusively to the land-scape. You stand on the last landward [1] mountain-point; toward the north lies a fruitful plain, interspersed with little forests, and bounded by a stern row of mountains, that stretches itself westward toward Za-bere, where the episcopal palace and the Abbey of St. John, lying a league beyond it, may be plainly recog-nised. Thence the eye follows the more and more vanishing chain of the Vosges toward the south. If you turn to the northeast, you see the castle of Lich-tenberg upon a rock; and toward the southeast the eye has the boundless plain of Alsace to scrutinise, which, afar off, withdraws itself from the sight in the more and more misty landscape, until at last the Sua-bian mountains melt away like shadows into the ho-rizon.

Already, in my limited wanderings through the world, I had remarked how important it is in travelling to ascertain the course of the waters, and even to ask with respect to the smallest brook, whither in reality it runs. One thus acquires a general survey of every stream-region in which one happens to be, a conception of the heights and depths which bear relation to each other, and by these leading lines, which assist the con-

[1] That is, toward *Germany*. Germany is *the land* by pre-eminence. — *American Note.*

templation as well as the memory, extricates one's self in the surest manner from the geological and political labyrinth. With these observations, I took a solemn farewell of my beloved Alsace, as the next morning we meant to turn our steps toward Lorraine.

The evening passed away in familiar conversation, in which we tried to cheer ourselves up under a joyless present by remembrances of a better past. Here, as in the whole of this small country, the name of the last Count Reinhard von Hanau was blessed above all others: his great understanding and aptitude had appeared in all his actions, and many a beautiful memorial of his existence yet remained. Such men have the advantage of being double benefactors: once to the present, which they make happy, and then to the future, the feeling of which and courage they nourish and sustain.

Now as we turned northwestward into the mountains, passed by Lutzelstein, an old mountain tower, in a very hilly country, and descended into the region of the Saar and the Moselle, the heavens began to lower, as if they would render yet more sensible to us the condition of the more rugged western country. The valley of the Saar, where we first reached Bockenheim, a small place, and saw opposite to it Neusaarwerden, which is well built, with a pleasure-castle, is bordered on both sides by mountains which might be called melancholy, if at their foot an endless succession of meadows and fields, called the Huhnau, did not extend as far as Saaralbe, and beyond it, farther than the eye can reach. Great buildings, belonging to the former stables of the Duke of Lorraine, here attract the eye: they are at present used as a dairy, for which purpose, indeed, they are very well situated. We passed through Saargemünd to Saarbrück, and this little residence was a bright point in a land so rocky and woody. The town, small and hilly, but well adorned by the last prince, makes at once a pleasing impression, as the houses are all painted a grayish white, and the different elevation of them affords a variegated view. In the middle of a beautiful square, surrounded with handsome buildings, stands the Lutheran church, on a small scale, but in proportion with the whole. The front of the castle lies on the same level with the town; the back, on the contrary, on the declivity of a steep rock. This has not only been worked out terrace-fashion, to afford easy access to the valley, but an oblong garden-plot has also been obtained below, by turning off the stream on one side, and cutting away the rock on the other, after which this whole space was lastly filled up with earth and planted. The time of this undertaking fell in the epoch when they used to consult the architects about laying out gardens, just as at present they call in the aid of the landscape-painter's eye. The whole arrangement of the castle, the costly and the agreeable, the rich and the ornamental, betokened a life-enjoying owner, such as the deceased prince had been : the present sovereign was not at home. President von Günderode received us in the most obliging manner, and entertained us for three days better than we had a right to expect. I made use of the various acquaintance which we formed, to instruct myself in many respects. The life of the late prince, rich in pleasure, gave material enough for conversation, as well as the various expedients which he hit upon to make use of the advantages supplied by the nature of his land. Here I was now properly initiated into the interest for mountain countries, and the love for those economical and technical investigations which have busied me a great part of my life was first awakened within me. We heard of the rich coal-pits at Dutweil, of the iron and alum works, and even of a burning mountain; and we prepared ourselves to see these wonders close.

We now rode through woody mountains, which

must seem wild and dreary to him who comes out of a magnificent, fertile land, and which can attract us only by the internal contents of its bosom. We were made acquainted with one simple and one complicated piece of machinery, within a short distance of each other; namely, a scythe-smithy and a wire-drawing factory. If one is pleased at the first because it supplies the place of common hands, one cannot sufficiently admire the other; for it works in a higher organic sense, from which understanding and consciousness are scarcely to be separated. In the alum-works we made accurate inquiries about the production and purifying of this so necessary material; and when we saw great heaps of a white, greasy, loose, earthy matter, and asked the use of it, the labourers answered, smiling, that it was the scum thrown up in boiling the alum, and that Herr Stauf had it collected, as he hoped perchance to turn it to some profit. " Is Herr Stauf alive yet ? " exclaimed my companion in surprise. They answered in the affirmative, and assured us, that, according to the plan of our journey, we should not pass far from his lonely dwelling.

Our road now led up along the channels by which the alum-water is conducted down, and the principal horizontal works (*Stollen*), which they call the " *Landgrube,*" and from which the famous Dutweil coals are procured. These, when they are dry, have the blue colour of darkly tarnished steel; and the most beautiful succession of rainbow-tints plays over the surface with every movement. The deep abysses of the coal-levels, however, attracted us so much the less as their contents lay richly poured out around us. We now reached the open mine, in which the roasted alum-scales are steeped in lye; and, soon after, a strange occurrence surprised us, although we had been prepared. We entered into a chasm, and found ourselves in the region of the Burning Mountain. A strong smell of sulphur surrounded us; one side of the cavity was almost red-hot, covered with reddish stone burnt white; thick fumes arose from the crevices, and we felt the heat of the ground through our strong boot-soles. An event so accidental — for it is not known how this place became ignited — affords a great advantage for the manufacture of alum; since the alum-scales, of which the surface of the mountain consists, lie there perfectly roasted, and may be steeped in a short time and very well. The whole chasm has arisen by the calcined scales being gradually removed and used up. We clambered up out of this depth, and were on the top of the mountain. A pleasant beech-grove encircled the spot, which followed up to the chasm, and extended itself on both sides of it. Many trees were already dried up : some were withering near others, which, as yet quite fresh, felt no forebodings of that fierce heat which was approaching and threatening their roots also.

Upon this space different openings were steaming, others had already done smoking; and this fire had thus smouldered for ten years already through old broken-up pits and horizontal shafts, with which the mountain is undermined. It may, too, have penetrated to the clefts through new coal-beds : for, some hundred paces farther into the wood, they had contemplated following up manifest indications of an abundance of coal; but they had not excavated far before a strong smoke burst out against the labourers, and dispersed them. The opening was filled up again, yet we found the place still smoking as we went on our way past it to the residence of our hermit-like chemist. This is situated amid mountains and woods; the valleys there take very various and pleasing windings; the soil round about is black and of the coal kind, and strata of it frequently come in sight. A coal philosopher — *philosophus ver ignem*, as they said formerly — could scarcely have settled himself more suitably.

We approached a small house, not inconvenient for a dwelling, and found Herr Stauf, who immediately recognised my friend, and received him with lamentations about the new government. Indeed, we could see, from what he said, that the alum-works, as well as many other well-meant establishments, on account of external and perhaps internal circumstances also, did not pay their expenses, with much else of the sort. He belonged to the chemists of that time, who, with a hearty feeling for all that could be done with the products of nature, took delight in abstruse investigations of trifles and secondary matters, and, with their insufficient knowledge, were not dexterous enough to do that from which properly economical and mercantile profit is to be derived. Thus the use to which he hoped to turn that scum lay very far in the distance: thus he had nothing to show but a cake of sal-ammoniac, with which the Burning Mountain had supplied him.

Ready and glad to communicate his complaints to some human ear, the lean, decrepit little man, with a shoe on one foot and a slipper on the other, and with stockings hanging down and repeatedly pulled up in vain, dragged himself up the mountain to where the resin-house stands, which he himself had erected, and now, with great grief, sees falling to ruins. Here was found a connected row of furnaces, where coal was to be cleansed of sulphur, and made fit for use in iron-works; but at the same time they wished also to turn the oil and resin to account, — nay, they would not even lose the soot: and thus all failed together, on account of the many ends in view. During the life-time of the former prince, the business had been carried on in the spirit of an amateur, and in hope: now they asked for the immediate use, which was not to be shown.

After we had left our adept to his solitude, we has-tened — for it was now late — to the glass-house in

Friedrichsthal, where we became acquainted, on our way, with one of the most important and most wonderful operations of human ingenuity.

Nevertheless, some pleasant adventures, and a surprising firework at nightfall, not far from Neukirch, interested us young fellows almost more than these important experiences. For as a few nights before, on the banks of the Saar, shining clouds of glowworms hovered around us, betwixt rock and thicket; so now the spark-spitting forges played their sprightly firework toward us. We passed, in the depth of night, the smelting-houses situated in the bottom of the valley, and were delighted with the strange half-gloom of these dens of plank, which are but dimly lighted by a little opening in the glowing furnace. The noise of the water, and of the bellows driven by it; the fearful whizzing and shrieking of the blast of air, which, raging into the smelted ore, stuns the hearing and confuses the senses, — drove us away, at last, to turn into Neukirch, which is built up against the mountain.

But, notwithstanding all the variety and fatigue of the day, I could find no rest here. I left my friend to a happy sleep, and sought the hunting-seat, which lay still farther up. It looks out far over mountain and wood, the outlines of which were only to be recognised against the clear night sky, but the sides and depths of which were impenetrable to my sight. This well-preserved building stood as empty as it was lonely: no castellan, no huntsman, was to be found. I sat before the great glass doors upon the steps which run around the whole terrace. Here, surrounded by mountains, over a forest-grown, dark soil, which seemed yet darker in contrast with the clear horizon of a summer night, with the glowing, starry vault above me, I sat for a long time by myself on the deserted spot, and thought I never had felt such a solitude. How sweetly, then, was I surprised by the distant sound of a couple of

French horns, which at once, like the fragrance of balsam, enlivened the peaceful atmosphere. Then there awakened within me the image of a lovely being, which had retired into the background before the motley objects of these travelling days, but which now unveiled itself more and more, and drove me from the spot back to my quarters, where I made preparations to set off as early as possible.

The return was not used like the journey out. Thus we hurried through Zwey-brücken (Deux-Ponts), which, as a beautiful and notable residence, might well have deserved our attention. We cast a glance at the great, simple castle, on the extensive esplanades, regularly planted with linden-trees, and very well adapted for the training of race-horses; and on the large stables, and the citizens' houses which the prince had built to be raffled for. All this, as well as the costume and manners of the inhabitants, especially of the matrons and maids, had reference to a distant connection, and made plainly visible the relation with Paris, from which, for a long time, nothing transrhenane had been able to withdraw itself. We visited also the ducal wine-cellars, situated before the city, which are extensive, and furnished with large, well-made tuns. We went on farther, and at last found the country like that in the neighbourhood of Saarbrück. Between wild and savage mountains are a few villages: one here gets rid of the habit of looking about for corn. We mounted up, by the side of the Hornbach, to Bitsch, which lies on the important spot where the waters divide, and fall, a part into the Saar, a part into the Rhine. The latter were soon to draw us after them. Yet we could not refuse our attention to the little city of Bitsch, which very picturesquely winds around the mountain; nor to the fortress, which lies above. This is partly built on rocks, and partly hewn out of them. The subterraneous chambers are particularly worthy of

remark: here is not only space sufficient for the abode
of a number of men and cattle, but one even lights upon
large vaults for the drilling of troops, a mill, a chapel,
and whatever else could be required underground, provided the surface were in a state of disturbance.

We now followed the rapidly descending brooks
through the Bärenthal. The thick forests on both the
heights remain unused by the hand of man. Here trunks
of trees lie on each other rotting by thousands, and
young scions sprout up without number from their
half-mouldered progenitors. Here, in conversation with
some companions travelling on foot, the name Von
Dieterich again struck our ears, which we had often
heard honourably mentioned already in these woody
regions. The activity and cleverness of this man, his
wealth, and the use and applications of it, all seemed
in proportion. He could with justice take delight in
the acquisitions which he increased, and enjoy the
profits he secured. The more I saw of the world, the
more pleasure I took, not only in the universally
famous names, but in those also, especially, which
were mentioned in particular regions with reverence
and love; and thus I easily learned here, by a few
questions, that Von Dieterich, earlier than others, had
known how to make successful use of the mountain
treasures, iron, coal, and wood, and had worked his way
to an ever-growing opulence.

Niederbrunn, where we now arrived, was a new
proof of this. He had purchased this little place from
the Count of Leiningen and other part-owners, to erect
important iron-works in the place.

Here in these baths, already founded by the Romans,
floated around me with the spirit of antiquity, venerable relics of which, in fragments of bas-reliefs and
inscriptions, capitals and shafts, shone out strangely
toward me, from farmhouses, amidst household lumber
and furniture.

As we were ascending the adjacent Wasenburg also, I paid my respects to a well-preserved inscription, which discharged a thankful vow to Mercury, and is situated upon the great mass of rock which forms the base of the hill on one side.   The fortress itself lies on the last mountain, looking from Bitsch toward Germany.   It is the ruin of a German castle built upon Roman remains.   From the tower the whole of Alsace was once more surveyed, and the conspicious minster-spire pointed out the situation of Strasburg.   First of all, however, the great forest of Hagenau extended itself : and the towers of this town peered plainly from behind.   I was attracted thither.   We rode through Reichshof, where Von Dieterich built an imposing castle : and after we had contemplated from the hills near Niedermoder the pleasing course of the little river Moder, by the forest of Hagenau, I left my friend on a ridiculous coal-mine visitation, which, at Dutweil, might have been a somewhat more serious business; and I then rode through Hagenau, on the direct road — already indicated by my affection — to my beloved Sesenheim.

For all these views of a wild mountain region, and then, again, of a cheerful, fruitful, joyous land, could not rivet my mind's eye, which was directed to an amiable, attractive object.   This time, also, the way thither seemed to me more charming than its opposite, as it brought me again into the neighbourhood of a lady to whom I was heartily devoted, and who deserved as much respect as love.   But, before I lead my friends to her rural abode, let me be permitted to mention a circumstance which contributed very much to enliven and heighten my affection, and the satisfaction it afforded me.

How far I must have been behindhand in modern literature, may be gathered from the mode of life which I led at Frankfort, and from the studies to which I had devoted myself; nor could my residence in Strasburg have furthered me in this respect. Now Herder came, and brought besides his great knowledge many other aids, and the later publications besides. Among these he announced to us "The Vicar of Wakefield" as an excellent work, with the German translation of which he said he would make us acquainted by reading it aloud to us himself.

His method of reading was quite peculiar: whoever has heard him preach will be able to form a notion of it. He delivered everything, this romance included, in a serious and simple style, perfectly removed from all dramatically imitative representation: he even avoided that variety which is not only permitted, but even required, in an epical delivery, — a slight change of tone when different persons speak, by which what every one says is brought into relief, and the actor is distinguished from the narrator. Without being monotonous, Herder let everything go on in the same tone, just as if nothing was present before him, but all was merely historical; as if the shadows of this poetic creation did not act livingly before him, but only glided gently by. Yet this manner of delivery from his mouth had an infinite charm; for as he felt all most deeply, and knew how to estimate the variety of such a work, so the whole merit of a production appeared purely and the more clearly, as one was not disturbed by details sharply spoken out, nor interrupted in the feeling which the whole was meant to produce.

A Protestant country clergyman is, perhaps, the most beautiful subject for a modern idyl: he appears, like Melchizedek, as priest and king in one person. To the most innocent situation which can be imagined on earth, to that of a husbandman, he is, for the most part, united by similarity of occupation, as well as by equality in family relationships: he is a father, a master of a family, an agriculturist, and thus perfectly a member of the community. On this pure, beautiful earthly foundation, rests his higher calling; to him is it given to guide men through life, to take care of their spiritual education, to bless them at all the leading epochs of their existence, to instruct, to strengthen, to console them, and, if consolation is not sufficient for the present, to call up and guarantee the hope of a happier future. Imagine such a man, with pure human sentiments, strong enough not to deviate from them under any circumstances, and by this already elevated above the multitude, of whom one cannot expect purity and firmness; give him the learning necessary for his office, as well as a cheerful equable activity, which is even passionate as it neglects no moment to do good, — and you will have him well endowed. But at the same time add the necessary limitation, so that he must not only pause in a small circle, but may also perchance pass over to a smaller; grant him good nature, placability, resolution, and everything else praiseworthy that springs from a decided character, and over all this a cheerful spirit of compliance, and a smiling toleration of his own failings and those of others, — then you will have put together pretty well the image of our excellent Wakefield.

The delineation of this character on his course of life, through joys and sorrows, the ever-increasing interest of the story, by the combination of the entirely natural with the strange and the singular, make this novel one of the best which has ever been written ; besides this, it has the great advantage that it is quite moral, nay, in a pure sense, Christian — represents the reward of a good will and perseverance in the right, strengthens an unconditional confidence in God, and attests the final triumph of good over evil, and all this without a trace of cant or pedantry. The author was preserved from both by an elevation of mind that shows itself throughout in the form of irony, by which this little work must appear to us as wise as it is amiable. The author,

Doctor Goldsmith, has, without question, great insight
into the moral world, into its strength and its infirmi-
ties; but at the same time he can thankfully acknowledge that he is an Englishman, and reckon highly the
advantages which his country and his nation afford him.
The family, with the delineation of which he occupies
himself, stands upon one of the last steps of citizen comfort, and yet comes in contact with the highest; its narrow circle, which becomes still more contracted, touches
upon the great world through the natural and civil
course of things; this little skiff floats on the agitated
waves of English life, and in weal and woe has to expect injury or help from the vast fleet sailing around it.

I may suppose that my readers know this work, and
have it in recollection; whoever hears it named for the
first time here, as well as he who is induced to read it
again, will thank me. For the former, I would merely
make the cursory remark, that the vicar's wife is of
that good, busy sort, who allows herself and her own
to want for nothing, but who is also somewhat vain
of herself and her own. There are two daughters,
— Olivia, handsome, and more devoted to the external: and Sophia, charming and more given to the
internal: nor will I omit to mention an industrious
son, Moses, who is somewhat blunt, and emulous of his
father.

If Herder could be accused of any fault in his reading aloud, it was impatience; he did not wait until the
hearer had heard and comprehended a certain part of
the progress, so as to be able to feel and think correctly
about it: too hasty, he wanted to see effects at
once; and yet he was displeased even with this when
it manifested itself. He blamed the excess of feeling
which overflowed from me more and more at every
step. I felt like a man, like a young man: everything
was living, true, and present before me. He, considering only the intrinsic contents and form, saw clearly,

indeed, that I was overpowered by the subject-matter; and this he would not allow. Then Peglow's reflections, which were not of the most refined, were still worse received; but he was especially angry at our want of keenness in not seeing beforehand the contrasts of which the author often makes use, and in suffering ourselves to be moved and carried away by them without remarking the oft-returning artifice. He would not pardon us for not seeing at once, or at least suspecting at the very beginning, where Burchell is on the point of discovering himself by passing over in his narration from the third to the first person, that he himself is the lord of whom he is speaking; and when, finally, we rejoiced like children at the discovery and the transformation of the poor, needy wanderer into a rich, powerful lord, he immediately recalled the passage, which, according to the author's plan, we had overlooked, and read us a powerful lecture on our stupidity. It will be seen from this, that he regarded the work merely as a production of art, and required the same of us, who were yet wandering in that state where it is very allowable to let works of art affect us like productions of nature.

I was not at all perplexed by Herder's invectives; for young people have the happiness or unhappiness, that, when once anything has produced an effect on them, this effect must be wrought out within themselves, — from which much good, as well as much mischief, arises. The above work had left in me a great impression, for which I could not account; but, properly speaking, I felt in harmony with that ironical tone of mind which elevates itself above every object, above fortune and misfortune, good and evil, death and life, and thus attains to the possession of a truly poetical world. I could not, indeed, become conscious of this until later: it was enough that it gave me much to do at the moment; but I could by no means have expected to be so soon transposed from this fictitious world into a similar real one.

My fellow boarder, Weyland, who enlivened his quiet, laborious life by visiting from time to time his friends and relations in the country (for he was a native of Alsace), did me many services on my little excursions, by introducing me to different localities and families, sometimes in person, sometimes by recommendations. He had often spoken to me about a country clergyman who lived near Drusenheim, six leagues from Strasburg, in possession of a good benefice, with an intelligent wife and a pair of amiable daughters. The hospitality and agreeableness of this family were always highly extolled. It scarcely needed so much to draw thither a young knight who had already accustomed himself to spend all his leisure days and hours on horseback and in the open air. We decided, therefore, upon this trip; and my friend had to promise, that, on introducing me, he would say neither good nor ill of me, but would treat me with general indifference, and would allow me to make my appearance clad, if not meanly, yet somewhat poorly and negligently. He consented to this, and promised himself some sport from it.

It is a pardonable whim in men of consequence, to place their exterior advantages in concealment now and then, so as to allow their own internal human nature to operate with the greater purity. For this reason the incognito of princes, and the adventures resulting therefrom, are always highly pleasing: these appear disguised divinities, who can reckon at double its value all the good offices shown to them as individuals, and are in such a position that they can either make light of the disagreeable or avoid it. That Jupiter should be well pleased in his incognito with Philemon and Baucis, and Henry the Fourth with his peasants after a hunting party, is quite comformable to nature, and we like it well; but that a young man, without importance or name, should take it into his head to derive some pleasure from an incognito, might be construed by many as an unpardonable piece of arrogance. Yet since the question here is not of such views and actions, so far as they are praiseworthy or blamable, but so far as they can manifest themselves and actually occur, we will on this occasion, for the sake of our own amusement, pardon the youngster his self-conceit; and the more so, as I must here allege, that, from youth upwards, a love for disguising myself had been excited in me even by my stern father.

This time, too, partly by some cast-off clothes of my own, partly by some borrowed garments and by the manner of combing my hair, I had, if not disfigured myself, yet at least rigged myself out so oddly, that my friend could not help laughing on the way, especially as I knew how to imitate perfectly the bearing and gestures of such figures when they sit on horseback, and which are called " Latin riders." The fine road, the most splendid weather, and the neighbourhood of the Rhine, put us in the best humour. At Drusenheim we stopped a moment, he to make himself spruce, and I to rehearse my part, out of which I was afraid I should now and then fall. The country here has the characteristics of all the open, level Alsace. We rode on a pleasant foot-path over the meadows, soon reached Sesenheim, left our horses at the tavern, and walked leisurely toward the parsonage. " Do not be put out," said Weyland, showing me the house from a distance, " because it looks like an old miserable farmhouse : it is so much younger inside." We stepped into the courtyard : the whole pleased me well; for it had exactly that which is called picturesque, and which had so magically interested me in Dutch art. The effect which time produces on all human work was strongly perceptible. House, barn, and stable were just at that point of dilapidation where, indecisive and doubtful between preserving and rebuilding, one often neglects the one without being able to accomplish the other.

As in the village, so in the courtyard, all was quiet and deserted. We found the father, a little man, wrapped up within himself, but friendly notwithstanding, quite alone, for the family were in the fields. He bade us welcome, and offered us some refreshment, which we declined. My friend hurried away to look after the ladies, and I remained alone with our host. " You are perhaps surprised," said he, " to find me so miserably quartered in a wealthy village, and with a lucrative benefice; but," he continued, " this proceeds from irresolution. Long since, it has been promised me by the parish, and even by those in higher places, that the house shall be rebuilt; many plans have been already drawn, examined, and altered, none of them altogether rejected, and none carried into execution. This has lasted so many years, that I scarcely know how to command my impatience." I made him an answer such as I thought likely to cherish his hopes, and to encourage him to pursue the affair more vigorously. Upon this he proceeded to describe familiarly the personages on whom such matters depended; and, although he was no great delineator of character, I could nevertheless easily comprehend how the whole business must have been delayed. The confidential tone of the man was something peculiar: he talked to me as if he had known me for ten years, while there was nothing in his look for which I could have suspected that he was directing any attention to me. At last my friend came in with the mother. She seemed to look at me with quite different eyes. Her countenance was regular, and the expression of it intelligent: she must have been beautiful in her youth. Her figure was tall and spare, but not more so than became her years; and, when seen from behind, she had quite a youthful and pleasing appearance. The elder daughter then came bouncing in briskly: she inquired after Frederica, just as both the others had also done. The father assured them that he had not seen her since all three had gone out together. The daughter again went out at the door to look for her sister; the mother brought us some refreshment; and Weyland, with the old couple, continued the conversation, which referred to nothing but known persons and circumstances, — as, indeed, it is usually the case when acquaintances meet after some length of time, that they make inquiries, and mutually give each other information about the members of a large circle. I listened, and now learned how much I had to promise myself from this circle.

The elder daughter again came hastily back into the room, uneasy at not having found her sister. They were anxious about her, and blamed her for this or that bad habit; only the father said, very composedly, " Let her alone: she will come back ! " At this instant she really entered the door, and then truly a most charming star arose in this rural heaven. Both daughters still wore nothing but German, as they used to call it; and this almost obsolete national costume became Frederica particularly well. A short, white, full skirt, with a furbelow, not so long but that the neatest little feet were visible up to the ankle; a tight white bodice and a black taffeta apron, — thus she stood on the boundary between country girl and city girl. Slender and light, she tripped along as if she had nothing to carry; and her neck seemed almost too delicate for the large fair braids on her elegant little head. From cheerful blue eyes she looked very plainly round, and her pretty turned-up nose peered as freely into the air as if there could be no care in the world; her straw hat hung on her arm; and thus, at the first glance, I had the delight of seeing her, and knowing her at once in all her grace and loveliness.

I now began to act my part with moderation, half ashamed to play a joke on such good people, whom I had time enough to observe; for the girls continued the previous conversation, and that with passion and some display of temper. All the neighbours and connections were again brought forward; and there seemed, to my imagination, such a swarm of uncles and aunts, relations, cousins, comers, goers, gossips, and guests, that I thought myself lodged in the liveliest world possible. All the members of the family had exchanged some words with me, the mother looked at me every time she came in or went out, but Frederica first entered into conversation with me; and, as I took up and glanced through some music that was lying around, she asked me if I played also. When I answered in the affirmative, she requested me to perform something; but the father would not allow this, for he maintained that it was proper to serve the guest first with some piece of music or a song.

She played several things with some readiness, in the style which one usually hears in the country, and on a harpsichord, too, that the schoolmaster should have tuned long since, if he had only had time. She was now also to sing a song, a certain tender-melancholy affair; but she did not succeed in it. She rose and said, smiling, or rather with that touch of serene joy which ever reposed on her countenance, " If I sing badly, I cannot lay the blame on the harpsichord or the schoolmaster : but let us go out of doors; then you shall hear my Alsatian and Swiss songs, — they sound much better."

During supper, a notion which had already struck me occupied me to such a degree, that I became meditative and silent; although the liveliness of the elder sister, and the gracefulness of the younger, shook me often enough out of my contemplations. My astonishment at finding myself so actually in the Wakefield family was beyond all expression. The father, indeed, could not be compared to that excellent man; but where will you find his like? On the other hand, all the dignity which is peculiar to that husband here appeared in the wife. One could not see her without at the same time reverencing and fearing her. In her were remarked the fruits of a good education: her demeanour was quiet, easy, cheerful, and inviting.

If the elder daughter had not the celebrated beauty of Olivia, yet she was well made, lively, and rather impetuous: she everywhere showed herself active, and lent a helping hand to her mother in all things. To put Frederica in the place of Primrose's Sophia was not difficult; for little is said of the latter, it is only taken for granted that she is amiable: and this girl was amiable indeed. Now, as the same occupation and the same situation, wherever they may occur, produce similar, if not the same, effects; so here too many things were talked about, many things happened, which had already taken place in the Wakefield family. But when at last a younger son, long announced and impatiently expected by the father, rushed into the room, and boldly sat himself down by us, taking but little notice of the guests, I could scarcely help exclaiming, "Moses, are you here, too!"

The conversation carried on at table extended my insight into this country and family circle; since the discourse was about various droll incidents which had happened now here, now there. Frederica, who sat by me, thence took occasion to describe to me different localities which it was worth while to visit. As one little story always calls forth another, I was so much the better able to join in the conversation, and to relate similar incidents: and as, besides this, a good country wine was by no means spared, I stood in danger of

slipping out of my character; for which reason my
more prudent friend took advantage of the beautiful
moonlight, and proposed a walk, which was approved
at once. He gave his arm to the elder, I to the
younger; and thus we went through the wide field,
paying more attention to the heavens above us than
to the earth, which lost itself in extension around us.
There was, however, nothing of moonshine in Frederica's discourse: by the clearness with which she
spoke she turned night into day, and there was nothing in it which would have indicated or excited any
feeling, except that her expressions related more than
hitherto to me, since she represented to me her own
situation, as well as the neighbourhood and her acquaintances, just as far as I should be acquainted with
them; for she hoped, she added, I would make no ex-
ception, and would visit them again, as all strangers
had willingly done who had once stopped with them.

It was very pleasant to me to listen silently to the
description which she gave of the little world in which
she moved, and of the persons whom she particularly
valued. She thereby imparted to me a clear, and, at
the same time, such an amiable, idea of her situation
that it had a very strange effect on me; for I felt at
once a deep regret that I had not lived with her
sooner, and at the same time a truly painful envious
feeling toward all who had hitherto had the good
fortune to surround her. I at once watched closely,
as if I had a right to do so, all her descriptions of men,
whether they appeared under the names of neighbours,
cousins, or gossips, and my conjectures inclined now
this way, now that; but how could I have discovered
anything in my complete ignorance of all the circumstances? She at last became more and more talkative,
and I more and more silent. It was so pleasant to
listen to her; and as I heard only her voice, while the
form of her countenance, as well as the rest of the

world, floated dimly in the twilight, it seemed to me as if I could see into her heart, which I could not but find very pure, since it unbosomed itself to me in such unembarrassed loquacity.

When my companion retired with me into the guest-chamber, which had been prepared for us, he at once, with self-complacency, broke out into pleasant jesting, and took great credit to himself for having surprised me so much with the resemblance to the Primrose family. I chimed in with him by showing myself thankful. "Truly," cried he, "the story is quite complete. This family may very well be compared to that, and the gentleman in disguise here may assume the honour of passing for Mr. Burchell; moreover, since scoundrels are not so necessary in common life as in novels, I will for this time undertake the rôle of the nephew, and behave myself better than he did." However, I immediately changed this conversation, pleasant as it might be to me, and asked him, before all things, on his conscience, if he had not really betrayed me. He answered "No!" and I could believe him. They had rather inquired, said he, after the merry table-companion who boarded at the same house with him in Strasburg, and of whom they had been told all sorts of preposterous stuff. I now went to other questions: Had she ever been in love? Was she now in love? Was she engaged? He replied to all in the negative. "In truth," replied I, "such natural cheerfulness is inconceivable to me. Had she loved and lost, and again recovered herself, or had she been betrothed,— in both these cases I could account for it."

Thus we chatted together far into the night, and I was awake again at the dawn. My desire to see her once more seemed unconquerable; but, while I dressed myself, I was horrified at the accursed wardrobe I had so wantonly selected. The further I advanced in putting on my clothes, the meaner I seemed in my own eyes; for everything had been calculated for just this effect. My hair I might perchance have set to rights; but when at last I forced myself into the borrowed, worn-out gray coat, and the short sleeves gave me the most absurd appearance, I fell the more decidedly into despair, as I could see myself only piecemeal in a little looking-glass, since one part always looked more ridiculous than the other.

During this toilet my friend awoke, and with the satisfaction of a good conscience, and in the feeling of pleasurable hope for the day, looked out at me from the quilted silk coverlet. I had for a long time envied him for his fine clothes, as they hung over the chair; and, had he been of my size, I would have carried them off before his eyes, changed my dress outside, and, hurrying into the garden, left my accursed husk for him: he would have had good humour enough to put himself into my clothes, and the tale would have found a merry ending early in the morning. But that was not now to be thought of, — no more was any other feasible accommodation. To appear again before Frederica in the figure in which my friend could give me out as a laborious and accomplished but poor student of theology, — before Frederica, who the evening before had spoken so friendly to my disguised self, — that was altogether impossible. There I stood, vexed and thoughtful, and summoned all my power of invention; but it deserted me! But now when he, comfortably stretched out, after fixing his eyes upon me for awhile, all at once burst out into a laugh, and exclaimed, "No! it is true, you do look most cursedly!" I replied impetuously, "And I know what I will do. Good-by, and make my excuses!" "Are you mad?" cried he, springing out of bed, and trying to detain me. But I was already out of the door, down the stairs, out of the house and yard, off to the tavern: in an instant my horse was saddled; and I hurried away in mad vexation, galloping toward Drusenheim, then through that place, and still farther on.

Now, thinking myself in safety, I rode more slowly, and now first felt how infinitely against my will I was going away. But I resigned myself to my fate, made present to my mind the promenade of yesterday evening with the greatest calmness, and cherished the secret hope of seeing her soon again. But this quiet feeling soon changed again to impatience; and I now determined to ride rapidly into the city, change my dress, take a good, fresh horse, since then, as my passion made me believe, I could at all events return before dinner, or, as was more probable, for dessert, or toward evening, and beg my forgiveness.

I was just about to put spurs to my horse to execute this plan, when another, and, as seemed to me, very happy thought, passed through my mind. In the tavern at Drusenheim, the day before, I had noticed a son of the landlord very nicely dressed, who, early this morning, being busied about his rural arrangements, had saluted me from his courtyard. He was of my figure, and had for the moment reminded me of myself. No sooner thought than done! My horse was hardly turned round, when I found myself in Drusenheim: I brought him into the stable, and in a few words made the fellow my proposal, namely, that he should lend me his clothes, as I had something merry on foot at Sesenheim. I had no need to talk long: he agreed to the proposition with joy, and praised me for wishing to make some sport for the *Mamsells;* they were, he said, such capital people, especially Mamselle Reikchen;[1] and the parents, too, liked to see everything go on merrily and pleasantly. He looked at me attentively; and as from my appearance he might have taken me for a poor starveling, he said,

[1] Abbreviation for Frederica. — TRANS.

" If you wish to insinuate yourself, this is the right way." In the meanwhile we had already proceeded far in our toilet: and, properly speaking, he should not have trusted me with his holiday clothes on the strength of mine; but he was honest-hearted, and, moreover, had my horse in his stable. I soon stood there smart enough, gave myself a consequential air, and my friend seemed to regard his counterpart with complacency. " Topp,[1] Mr. Brother ! " said he, giving me his hand, which I grasped heartily : " don't come too near my girl; she might make a mistake ! "

My hair, which had now its full growth again, I could part at the top, much like his: and, as I looked at him repeatedly, I found it comical moderately to imitate his thicker eyebrows with a burnt cork, and bring mine nearer together in the middle; so that, with my enigmatical intentions, I might make myself an external riddle likewise. " Now, have you not," said I, as he handed me his beribboned hat, " something or other to be done at the parsonage, that I might announce myself there in a natural manner ? " " Very well," replied he; " but then, you must wait two hours yet. There is a woman confined at our house: I will offer to take the cake to the parson's wife [2] and you may carry it over. Pride must pay its penalty, and so must a joke." I resolved to wait; but these two hours were infinitely long, and I was dying with impatience when the third hour passed before the cake came out of the oven. At last I got it quite hot, and hastened away with my credentials in the most beautiful sunshine, accompanied for a distance by my counterpart, who promised to come after me in the evening and bring me my clothes. This, however, I

---

[1] The exclamation used on striking a bargain. It is, we believe, employed by some trades in England. — TRANS.

[2] The general custom of the country villages in Protestant Germany on such interesting occasions. — *American Note.*

briskly declined, and stipulated that I should deliver up to him his own.

I had not skipped far with my present, which I carried in a neat tied-up napkin, when, in the distance, I saw my friend coming toward me with the two ladies. My heart was uneasy, which was certainly unsuitable underneath this jacket. I stood still, took breath, and tried to consider how I should begin : and now only I noticed that the nature of the ground was very much in my favour; for they were walking on the other side of the brook, which, together with the strips of meadow through which it ran, kept the two foot-paths pretty far apart. When they were just opposite to me, Frederica, who had already perceived me long before, cried, " George, what are you bringing there ? " I was clever enough to cover my face with my hat, which I took off, while I held up the loaded napkin high in the air. " A christening-cake ! " cried she at that: "how is your sister ? " " Well," [1] said I ; for I tried to talk in a strange dialect, if not exactly in the Alsatian. " Carry it to the house," said the elder, " and, if you do not find my mother, give it to the maid ; but wait for us, we shall soon be back, — do you hear ? " I hastened along my path in the joyous feeling of the best hope, that, as the beginning was so lucky, all would go off well ; and I had soon reached the parsonage. I found nobody, either in the house or in the kitchen ; I did not wish to disturb the old gentleman, whom I might suppose busy in the study ; I therefore sat down on the bench before the door, with the cake beside me, and pressed my hat upon my face.

I cannot easily recall a more pleasant sensation. To sit again on this threshold, across which, a short time before, I had blundered out in despair ; to have seen her already again ; to have already heard again her dear voice, so soon after my chagrin had pictured

[1] In the original his answer is "Guet," for "Gut." — Trans.

to me a long separation; every moment to be expecting herself and a discovery, at which my heart throbbed, and yet, in this ambiguous case, a discovery without shame; for at the very beginning it was a merrier prank than any of those they had laughed at so much yesterday. Love and necessity are the best masters: they both acted together here, and their pupil was not unworthy of them.

But the maid came stepping out of the barn. "Now, did the cakes turn out well?" cried she to me: "how is your sister?" "All right," said I, and pointed to the cake without looking up. She took up the napkin, and muttered, "Now what's the matter with you to day again? Has Barbchen [1] been looking again at somebody else? Don't let us suffer for that! You will make a happy couple if you carry on so!" As she spoke pretty loud, the pastor came to the window, and asked what was the matter. She showed him to me: I stood up, and turned myself toward him, but still kept the hat over my face. When he had said something kind and bid me to stay, I went toward the garden, and was just going in, when the pastor's wife, who was entering the courtyard gate, called to me. As the sun was shining right in my face, I once more availed myself of the advantage my hat afforded me, and greeted her by scraping a leg; but she went into the house after she had bidden me not to go away without eating something. I now walked up and down in the garden: everything had hitherto had the best success, yet I breathed hard when I reflected that the young people now would soon return. But the mother unexpectedly stepped up to me, and was just going to ask me a question, when she looked me in the face, so that I could not conceal myself any longer, and the words stuck in her throat. "I am looking for George," said she, after a pause, "and whom do I find? Is it you,

[1] Diminutive of Barbara. — TRANS.

sir? How many forms have you, then?" "In earnest only one," replied I: "in sport as many as you like." "Which sport I will not spoil," smiled she: "go out behind the garden into the meadow until it strikes twelve, then come back; and I shall already have contrived the joke." I did so; but when I was beyond the hedges of the village gardens and was going along the meadows, toward me some country people came by the foot-path, and put me in some embarrassment. I therefore turned aside into a little wood, which crowned an elevation quite near, in order to conceal myself there till the appointed time. Yet what a strange feeling came over me when I entered it; for there appeared before me a neat place, with benches, from every one of which was a pretty view of the country. Here was the village and the steeple, here Drusenheim, and behind it the woody islands of the Rhine: in the opposite direction was the Vosgian mountain range, and at last the minster of Strasburg. These different heaven-bright pictures were set in bushy frames, so that one could see nothing more joyous and pleasing. I sat down upon one of the benches, and noticed on the largest tree an oblong little board with the inscription, "Frederica's Repose." It never occurred to me that I might have come to disturb this repose; for a budding passion has this beauty about it, that, as it is unconscious of its origin, neither can it have any thought of an end, nor, while it feels itself glad and cheerful, have any presentiment that it may also create mischief.

I had scarcely had time to look about me, and was losing myself in sweet reveries, when I heard somebody coming: it was Frederica herself. "George, what are you doing here?" she cried from a distance. "Not George!" cried I, running toward her, "but one who craves your forgiveness a thousand times." She looked at me with astonishment, but soon collected

herself, and said, after fetching her breath more deeply,
"You abominable man, how you frightened me!"
"The first disguise has led me into the second!" exclaimed I : "the former would have been unpardonable
if I had only known in any degree to whom I was
going; but this one you will surely forgive, for it is
the shape of persons whom you treat so kindly." Her
pale cheeks had coloured up with the most beautiful
rose-red. "You shall not be worse off than George, at
any rate! But let us sit down. I confess the fright
has gone into my limbs." I sat down beside her, exceedingly agitated. "We know everything already, up
to this morning, from your friend," said she, "now do
you tell me the rest." I did not let her say that
twice, but described to her my horror at my yesterday's figure, and my rushing out of the house, so
comically, that she laughed heartily and graciously:
then I went on to what followed, with all modesty,
indeed, yet passionately enough, so that it might have
passed for a declaration of love in historical form. At
last I solemnised my pleasure at finding her again, by
a kiss upon her hand, which she suffered to remain in
mine. Whereas she had taken upon herself the expense of the conversation during our moonlight walk,
of the night before, I now, on my part, richly repaid
the debt. The pleasure of seeing her again, and being
able to say to her everything that I had yesterday kept
back, was so great, that, in my eloquence, I did not
remark how meditative and silent she was. Once
more she deeply drew breath, and I over and over
again begged her forgiveness for the fright I had
caused her. How long we may have sat I know not,
but at once we heard some one call. It was her
sister's voice. "That will be a pretty story," said the
dear girl, restored to her perfect cheerfulness: "she is
coming hither on my side," she added, bending so as
half to conceal me; "turn away, so that you may not

be recognised at once." The sister entered the place, but not alone, — Weyland was with her; and both, when they saw us, stood still, as if petrified.

If we should all at once see a flame burst out violently from a quiet roof, or should meet a monster whose deformity was at the same time revolting and fearful, we should not be struck with such a fierce horror as that which seizes us when, unexpectedly, we see with our own eyes what we have believed morally impossible. "What is this?" cried the elder, with the rapidity of one who is frightened; "what is this? you with George, hand-in-hand! How am I to understand this?" "Dear sister," replied Frederica, very doubtfully, "the poor fellow. He is begging something of me: he has something to beg of you too, but you must forgive him beforehand." "I do not understand, I do not comprehend," said her sister, shaking her head, and looking at Weyland, who, in his quiet way, stood by in perfect tranquillity, and contemplated the scene without any kind of expression. Frederica arose and drew me after her. "No hesitating!" cried she: "let pardon be begged and granted!" "Well, then," said I, stepping pretty near the elder, "I have need of pardon." She drew back, gave a loud shriek, and was covered with blushes: she then threw herself down on the grass, laughed immoderately, and seemed as if she would never have done. Weyland smiled as if pleased, and cried, "You are a rare youth!" Then he shook my hand in his. He was not usually liberal with his caresses, but his shake of the hand had something hearty and enlivening about it; yet he was sparing of this also.

After having somewhat recovered and collected ourselves, we set out on our return to the village. On the way I learned how this singular meeting had been occasioned. Frederica had at last parted from the promenaders to rest herself in her little nook for a moment before dinner; and, when the other two came back to the house, the mother had sent them to call Frederica with as great haste as possible, because dinner was ready.

The elder sister manifested the most extravagant delight; and, when she learned that the mother had already discovered the secret, she exclaimed, " Now we have still to deceive my father, my brother, the servant-man, and the maid." When we were at the garden-hedge, Frederica insisted upon going first into the house with my friend. The maid was busy in the kitchen-garden; and Olivia (so let the elder sister be named here) called out to her, " Stop! I have something to tell you!" She left me standing by the hedge, and went up to the maid. I saw that they were speaking very earnestly. Olivia represented to her that George had quarrelled with Barbara, and seemed desirous of marrying her. The lass was not displeased at this: I was now called, and was to confirm what had been said. The pretty, stout girl cast down her eyes, and remained so until I stood quite near before her. But when, all at once, she perceived the strange face, she, too, gave a loud scream, and ran away. Olivia bade me run after her and hold her fast, so that she should not get into the house and make a noise; while she herself wished to go and see how it was with her father. On the way Olivia met the servant-boy, who was in love with the maid: I had in the meantime hurried after the maid, and held her fast. " Only think! what good luck!" cried Olivia: " it's all over with Barbara, and George marries Liese." " That I have thought for a long while," said the good fellow, and remained standing in an ill humour.

I had given the maid to understand that all we had to do was to deceive the father. We went up to the lad, who turned away and tried to withdraw: but Liese brought him back; and he, too, when he was undeceived, made the most extraordinary gestures. We went together to the house. The table was covered, and the father was already in the room. Olivia, who kept me behind her, stepped to the threshold, and said, " Father, have you any objection to George dining with us to-day ? but you must let him keep his hat on." " With all my heart ! " said the old man, " but why such an unusual thing ? Has he hurt himself ? " She led me forward as I stood with my hat on. " No," said she, leading me into the room : " but he has a bird-cage under it ; and the birds might fly out and make a terrible fuss, for there are nothing but wild ones." The father was pleased with the joke, without precisely knowing what it meant. At this instant she took off my hat, made a scrape, and required me to do the same. The old man looked at me and recognised me, but was not put out of his priestly self-possession. " Ay, ay, Mr. Candidate ! " exclaimed he, raising a threatening finger at me ; " you have changed saddles very quickly : and in the night I have lost an assistant, who yesterday promised me so faithfully that he would often mount my pulpit on week days." He then laughed heartily, bade me welcome, and we sat down to table. Moses came in much later ; for, as the youngest spoiled child, he had accustomed himself not to hear the dinner-bell. Besides, he took very little notice of the company, scarcely even when he contradicted them. In order to be more sure of him, they had placed me, not between the sisters, but at the end of the table, where George often used to sit. As he came in at the door behind me, he slapped me smartly on the shoulder, and said, " Good dinner to you, George ! " " Many thanks, squire," replied I. The strange voice and the strange face startled him. " What say you ? " cried Olivia : " does he not look very like his brother ? " " Yes, from behind," replied Moses, who managed to recover his composure immediately, " like all folks." He did not look at me again, and merely busied himself with zealously devouring the dishes, to make up for lost time. Then, too, he thought proper to rise on occasion and find something to do in the yard and the garden. At the dessert the real George came in, and made the whole scene still more lively. They began to banter him for his jealousy, and would not praise him for getting rid of a rival in me: but he was modest and clever enough, and, in a half-confused manner, mixed up himself, his sweetheart, his counterpart, and the *Mamsells* with each other, to such a degree, that at last nobody could tell about whom he was talking; and they were but too glad to let him consume in peace a glass of wine and a bit of his own cake.

After dinner there was some talk about going to walk; which, however, did not suit me very well in my peasant's clothes. But the ladies, early on that day already, when they learned who had run away in such a desperate hurry, had remembered that a fine hunting-coat (*Pekesche*) of a cousin of theirs, in which, when there, he used to go sporting, was hanging in the clothes-press. I, however, declined it, outwardly with all sorts of jokes, but inwardly with a feeling of vanity, not wishing, as the cousin, to disturb the good impression I had made as the peasant. The father had gone to take his afternoon nap: the mother, as always, was busy about her housewifery. But my friend proposed that I should tell them some story, to which I immediately agreed. We went into a spacious arbour, and I gave them a tale which I have since written out under the title of "The New Melusina."[1] It bears about the same relation to "The New Paris" as the youth bears to the boy; and I would insert it here, were I not afraid of injuring, by odd plays of fancy, the rural quality and simplicity which here agreeably

[1] This is introduced in "Wilhelm Meister's Wanderjahre." — TRANS.

surround us. In short, I succeeded in gaining the reward of the inventors and narrators of such productions: namely, in awakening curiosity, in fixing the attention, in provoking overhasty solutions of impenetrable riddles, in deceiving expectations, in confusing by the more wonderful which came into the place of the wonderful, in arousing sympathy and fear, in causing anxiety, in moving, and, at last, by the change of what was apparently earnest into an ingenious and cheerful jest, in satisfying the mind, and in leaving the imagination materials for new images, and the understanding materials for further reflection.

Should any one hereafter read this tale in print, and doubt whether it could have produced such an effect, let him remember, that, properly speaking, man is only called upon to act in the present. Writing is an abuse of language: reading silently to one's self is a sorry substitute for speech. Man effects all he can upon man by his personality, youth is most powerful upon youth, and hence also arise the purest influences. It is these which enliven the world, and allow it neither morally nor physically to perish. I had inherited from my father a certain didactic loquacity; from my mother the faculty of representing, clearly and forcibly, everything that the imagination can produce or grasp, of giving a freshness to known stories, of inventing and relating others, — nay, of inventing in the course of narration. By my paternal endowment I was for the most part annoying to the company; for who likes to listen to the opinions and sentiments of another, especially a youth, whose judgment, from defective experience, always seems insufficient? My mother, on the contrary, had thoroughly qualified me for social conversation. The emptiest tale has in itself a high charm for the imagination, and the smallest quantity of solid matter is thankfully received by the understanding.

By such recitals, which cost me nothing, I made
myself beloved by children, excited and delighted
youth, and drew upon myself the attention of older
persons. But in society, such as it commonly is, I
was soon obliged to stop these exercises; and I have
thereby lost but too much of the enjoyment of life and
of free mental advancement. Nevertheless, both these
parental gifts accompanied me throughout my whole
life, united with a third; namely, the necessity of
expressing myself figuratively and by comparisons. In
consideration of these peculiarities, which the acute
and ingenious Doctor Gall discovered in me according
to his theory, he assured me that I was, properly
speaking, born for a popular orator. At this disclosure
I was not a little alarmed; for if it were well founded,
whatever else I might have undertaken would have
proved a failure, from the fact that among my nation
there was nothing to harangue about.

Part Three

Es ist dafür gesorgt, dass die Bäume nicht in den Himmel wachsen.
Care is taken that the trees don't grow into the sky. — PROVERB

ELEVENTH BOOK.

AFTER I had, in that bower of Sesenheim, finished my tale, in which the ordinary and the impossible so agreeably alternated, I perceived that my hearers, who had already shown peculiar sympathy, were now enchanted in the highest degree by my singular narrative. They pressed me urgently to write down the tale, that they might often repeat it by reading it among themselves, and to others. I promised this the more willingly, as I thus hoped to gain a pretext for repeating my visit, and for an opportunity of forming a closer connection. The party separated for a moment; and all were inclined to feel, that, after a day spent in so lively a manner, the evening might fall rather flat. From this anxiety I was freed by my friend, who asked permission to take leave at once, in the name of us both, because, as an industrious academical citizen, regular in his studies, he wished to pass the night at Drusenheim, and to be early in the morning at Strasburg.

We both reached our right-quarters in silence, — I, because I felt a grapple on my heart, which drew me back; he, because he had something else on his mind, which he told me as soon as we had arrived. "It is strange," he began, "that you should just hit upon this tale. Did not you remark that it made quite a peculiar impression?" "Nay," answered I, "how could I help observing that the elder one laughed more than was consistent at certain passages, that the younger one shook her head, that all of you looked significantly at each other, and that you yourself were nearly put out of countenance ?   I do not deny that I almost felt embarrassed myself ; for it struck me that it was perhaps improper to tell the dear girls a parcel of stuff of which they had better been ignorant, and to give them such a bad opinion of the male sex as they must naturally have formed from the character of the hero."   "You have not hit it at all," said he; "and, indeed, how should you ?   These dear girls are not so unacquainted with such matters as you imagine, for the great society around them gives occasion for many reflections ; and there happens to be, on the other side of the Rhine, exactly such a married pair as you describe,— allowing a little for fancy and exaggeration, — the husband just as tall, sturdy, and heavy ; the wife so pretty and dainty, that he could easily hold her in his hand.   Their mutual position in other respects, their history altogether, so exactly accords with your tale, that the girls seriously asked me whether you knew the persons, and described them in jest.   I assured them that you did not, and you will do well to let the tale remain unwritten.   With the assistance of delays and pretexts, we may soon find an excuse."

I was much astonished, for I had thought of no couple on this or the other side of the Rhine ; nay, I could not have stated how I came by the notion.   In thought I liked to sport with such pleasantries, without any particular reference ; and I believed that, if I narrated them, it would be the same with others.

When I returned to my occupations in the city, I felt them more than usually wearisome ; for a man born to activity forms plans too extensive for his capacity, and overburdens himself with labour.   This goes on very well till some physical or moral impediment comes in the way, and clearly shows the disproportion of the powers to the undertaking.

I pursued jurisprudence with as much diligence as

was required to take my degree with some credit. Medicine charmed me, because it showed nature, if it did not unfold it on every side; and to this I was attached by intercourse and habit. To society I was obliged to devote some time and attention; for in many families I had fallen in for much, both of love and honour. All this might have been carried on, had not that which Herder had inculcated pressed upon me with an infinite weight. He had torn down the curtain which concealed from me the poverty of German literature; he had ruthlessly destroyed so many of my prejudices; in the sky of my fatherland there were few stars of importance left when he had treated all the rest as so many transient candle-snuffs; nay, my own hopes and fancies respecting myself he had so spoiled, that I began to doubt my own capabilities. At the same time, however, he dragged me on to the noble broad way which he himself was inclined to tread, drew my attention to his favourite authors, at the head of whom stood Swift and Hamann, and shook me up with more force than he had bound me down. To this manifold confusion was now added an incipient passion, which, while it threatened to absorb me, might indeed draw me from other relations, but could scarcely elevate me above them. Then came besides a bodily ailing, which made me feel after dinner as if my throat was closed up, and of which I did not easily get rid, till afterward, when I abstained from a certain red wine, which I generally and very willingly drank in the boarding-house. This intolerable inconvenience had quitted me at Sesenheim, so that I felt double pleasure in being there; but when I came back to my town-diet it returned, to my great annoyance. All this made me thoughtful and morose, and my outward appearance probably corresponded with my inward feelings.

In a worse humour than ever, because the malady

was violent after dinner, I attended the clinical lecture. The great care and cheerfulness with which our respected instructor led us from bed to bed; the minute observation of important symptoms; the judgment of the cause of complaint in general; the fine Hippocratic mode of proceeding, by which, without theory, and out of an individual experience, the forms of knowledge revealed themselves; the addresses with which he usually crowned his lectures, — all this attracted me toward him, and made a strange department, into which I only looked as through a crevice, so much the more agreeable and fascinating. My disgust at the invalids gradually decreased, as I learned to change their various states into distinct conceptions, by which recovery and the restoration of the human form and nature appeared possible. He probably had his eye particularly upon me, as a singular young man, and pardoned the strange anomaly which took me to his lectures. On this occasion he did not conclude his lecture, as usual, with a doctrine which might have reference to an illness that had been observed, but said cheerfully, " Gentlemen, there are some holidays before us : make use of them to enliven your spirits. Studies must not only be pursued with seriousness and diligence, but also with cheerfulness and freedom of mind. Give movement to your bodies, and traverse the beautiful country on horseback and on foot. He who is at home will take delight in that to which he has been accustomed; while for the stranger there will be new impressions, and pleasant reminiscences in future."

There were only two of us to whom this admonition could be directed. May the recipe have been as obvious to the other as it was to me ! I thought I heard a voice from heaven, and made all the haste I could to order a horse and dress myself out neatly. I sent for Weyland, but he was not to be found. This did not delay my resolution; but the preparations unfortunately went on slowly, and I could not depart so soon as I had hoped. Fast as I rode, I was overtaken by the night. The way was not to be mistaken, and the moon shed her light on my impassioned project. The night was windy and awful; and I dashed on, that I might not have to wait till morning before I could see her.

It was already late when I put up my horse at Sesenheim. The landlord, in answer to my question, whether there was still light in the parsonage, assured me that the ladies had only just gone home: he thought he had heard they were still expecting a stranger. This did not please me, as I wished to have been the only one. I hastened, that, late as I was, I might at least appear the first. I found the two sisters sitting at the door. They did not seem much astonished; but I was, when Frederica whispered into Olivia's ear, loud enough for me to hear, " Did I not say so? Here he is!" They conducted me into a room, where I found a little collation set out. The mother greeted me as an old acquaintance: and the elder sister, when she saw me in the light, broke out into loud laughter, for she had little command over herself.

After this first and somewhat odd reception, the conversation became at once free and cheerful; and a circumstance, which had remained concealed from me this evening, I learned on the following day. Frederica had predicted that I should come; and who does not feel some satisfaction at the fulfilment of a foreboding, even if it be a mournful one? All presentiments, when confirmed by the event, give man a higher opinion of himself, whether it be that he thinks himself in possession of so fine a susceptibility as to feel a relation in the distance, or acute enough to perceive necessary but still uncertain associations. Even Olivia's laugh remained no secret: she confessed that it seemed very comical to see me dressed and decked out on this occasion. Frederica, on the other hand, found it advantageous not to explain such a phenomenon as vanity, but rather to discover in it a wish to please her.

Early in the morning Frederica asked me to take a walk. Her mother and sister were occupied in preparing everything for the reception of several guests. By the side of this beloved girl I enjoyed the noble Sunday morning in the country, as the inestimable Hebel has depicted it. She described to me the party which was expected, and asked me to remain by her, that all the pleasure might, if possible, be common to us both, and be enjoyed in a certain order. " Generally," she said, " people amuse themselves alone. Sport and play is very lightly tasted; so that at last nothing is left but cards for one part, and the excitement of dancing for the other."

We therefore sketched our plan as to what should be done after dinner, taught each other some new social games, and were united and happy, when the bell summoned us to church, where, by her side, I found a somewhat dry sermon of her father's not too long.

The presence of the beloved one always shortens time, but this hour passed amid peculiar reflections. I repeated to myself the good qualities which she had just unfolded so freely before me, — her circumspect cheerfulness, her *naïveté* combined with self-consciousness, her hilarity with foresight, — qualities which seem incompatible, but which nevertheless were found together in her, and gave a pleasing character to her outward appearance. But now I had to make more serious reflections upon myself, which were somewhat prejudicial to a free state of cheerfulness.

Since that impassioned girl had cursed and sanctified my lips (for every consecration involves both), I had, superstitiously enough, taken care not to kiss any girl, because I feared that I might injure her in some unheard-of spiritual manner. I therefore subdued every desire by which a youth feels impelled to win from a charming girl this favour, which says much or little. But even in the most decorous company a heavy trial awaited me. Those little games, as they are called, which are more or less ingenious, and by which a joyous young circle is collected and combined, depend in a great measure upon forfeits, in the calling in of which kisses have no small value. I had resolved, once for all, not to kiss; and, as every want or impediment stimulates us to an activity to which we should otherwise not feel inclined, I exerted all the talent and humour I possessed to help myself through, and thus to win rather than lose, before the company and for the company. When a verse was desired for the redemption of a forfeit, the demand was usually directed to me. Now, I was always prepared, and on such occasions contrived to bring out something in praise of the hostess, or of some lady who had conducted herself most agreeably toward me. If it happened that a kiss was imposed upon me at all events, I endeavoured to escape by some turn which was considered satisfactory: and, as I had time to reflect on the matter beforehand, I was never in want of various elegant excuses; although those made on the spur of the moment were always most successful.

When we reached home, the guests, who had arrived from several quarters, were buzzing merrily one with another, until Frederica collected them together, and invited and conducted them to a walk to that charming spot. There they found an abundant collation, and wished to fill up with social games the period before dinner. Here, by agreement with Frederica, though she did not know my secret, I contrived to get up and go through games without forfeits, and redemptions of forfeits without kissing.

My skill and readiness were so much the more necessary, as the company, which was otherwise quite strange to me, seemed to have suspected some connection between me and the dear girl, and roguishly took the greatest pains to force upon me that which I secretly endeavoured to avoid. For in such circles, if people perceive a growing inclination between two young persons, they try to make them confused, or to bring them closer together; just as afterward, when once a passion has been declared, they take trouble on purpose to part them again. Thus, to the man of society, it is totally indifferent whether he confers a benefit or an injury, provided he be amused.

That morning I could observe, with more attention, the whole character of Frederica; so that, for the whole time, she always remained to me the same. The friendly greetings of the peasants, which were especially addressed to her, gave me to understand that she was beneficent to them, and created in them an agreeable feeling. The elder sister remained at home with her mother. Nothing that demanded bodily exertion was required of Frederica; but she was spared, they said, on account of her chest.

There are women who especially please us in a room, others who look better in the open air. Frederica belonged to the latter. Her whole nature, her form, never appeared more charming than when she moved along an elevated footpath. The grace of her deportment seemed to vie with the flowery earth, and the indestructible cheerfulness of her countenance with the blue sky. This refreshing atmosphere which surrounded her she carried home; and it might soon be perceived that she understood how to reconcile difficulties, and to obliterate with ease the impression made by little unpleasant contingencies.

The purest joy we can feel with respect to a beloved person is, to find that she pleases others. Frederica's conduct in society was beneficent to all. In walks, she floated about, an animating spirit, and knew how to supply the gaps which might arise here and there. The lightness of her movements we have already commended, and she was most graceful when she ran. As the deer seems just to fulfil its destination when it lightly flies over the sprouting corn, so did her peculiar nature seem most plainly to express itself when she ran with light steps over mead and furrow, to fetch something which had been forgotten, to seek something which had been lost, to summon a distant couple, or to order something necessary. On these occasions she was never out of breath, and always kept her equilibrium. Hence the great anxiety of her parents with respect to her chest must to many have appeared excessive.

Her father, who often accompanied us through meadows and fields, was not always provided with a suitable companion. On his account I joined him; and he did not fail to touch once more upon his favourite theme, and circumstantially to tell me about the proposed building of the parsonage. He particularly regretted that he could not again get the carefully finished sketches, so as to meditate upon them, and to consider this or that improvement. I observed, that the loss might be easily supplied, and offered to prepare a ground-plan, upon which, after all, everything chiefly depended. With this he was highly pleased, and settled that we should have the assistance of the schoolmaster, to stir up whom he at once hurried off, that the yard and foot-measure might be ready early on the morrow.

When he had gone, Frederica said, " You are right to humour my dear father on his weak side, and not, like others, who get weary of this subject, to avoid him, or to break it off. I must, indeed, confess to you that the rest of us do not desire this building: it would

be too expensive for the congregation and for us also.
A new house, new furniture! Our guests would not
feel more comfortable with us, now they are once accustomed to the old building. Here we can treat them
liberally: there we should find ourselves straitened
in a wider sphere. Thus the matter stands; but do
not you fail to be agreeable. I thank you for it from
my heart."

Another lady who joined us asked about some
novels, — whether Frederica had read them. She answered in the negative, for she had read but little
altogether. She had grown up in a cheerful, decorous
enjoyment of life, and was cultivated accordingly. I
had "The Vicar of Wakefield" on the tip of my
tongue, but did not venture to propose it, the similarity of the situations being too striking and too important. "I am very fond of reading novels," she said:
"one finds in them such nice people, whom one would
like to resemble."

The measurement of the house took place the following day. It was a somewhat slow proceeding, as I
was as little accustomed to such arts as the schoolmaster. At last a tolerable project came to my aid.
The good father told me his views, and was not displeased when I asked permission to prepare the plan
more conveniently in the town. Frederica dismissed
me with joy: she was convinced of my affection, and
I of hers: and the six leagues no longer appeared a
distance. It was so easy to travel to Drusenheim in
the diligence, and by this vehicle, as well as by mes-
sengers, ordinary and extraordinary, to keep up a connection; George being entrusted with the despatches.

When I had arrived in the town, I occupied myself
in the earliest hours (for there was no notion of a long
sleep) with the plan, which I drew as neatly as possible. In the meantime I had sent Frederica some
books, accompanied by a few kind words. I received

an answer at once, and was charmed with her light, pretty, hearty hand. Contents and style were natural, good, amiable, as if they came from within; and thus the pleasing impression she had made upon me was ever kept up and renewed. I but too readily recalled to myself the endowments of her beautiful nature, and nurtured the hope that I should see her soon, and for a longer time.

There was now no more any need of an address from our good instructor. He had by those words, spoken at the right time, so completely cured me, that I had no particular inclination to see him and his patients again. The correspondence with Frederica became more animated. She invited me to a festival, to which also some friends from the other side of the Rhine would come. I was to make arrangements for a longer time. This I did by packing a stout portmanteau upon the diligence, and in a few hours I was in her presence. I found a large, merry party, took the father aside, and handed him the plan, at which he testified great delight. I talked over with him what I had thought while completing it. He was quite beside himself with joy, and especially praised the neatness of the drawing. This I had practised from my youth upwards, and had on this occasion taken especial pains, with the finest paper. But this pleasure was very soon marred for our good host, when, against my counsel, and in the joy of his heart, he laid the sketch before the company. Far from uttering the desired sympathy, some thought nothing at all of this precious work; others, who thought they knew something of the matter, made it still worse, blaming the sketch as not artistical, and, when the old man looked off for a moment, handled the clean sheets as if they were only so many rough draughts; while one, with the hard strokes of a lead-pencil, marked his plans of improvement on the fine paper in such a manner that a restoration of the primitive purity was not to be thought of.

I was scarcely able to console the extremely irritated man, whose pleasures had been so outrageously destroyed, much as I assured him that I myself looked upon them only as sketches, which we would talk over, and on which we would construct new drawings. In spite of all this he went off in a very ill humour; and Frederica thanked me for my attention to her father, as well as for my patience during the unmannerly conduct of the other guests.

But I could feel no pain nor ill humour in her presence. The party consisted of young and tolerably noisy friends, whom, nevertheless, an old gentleman tried to outdo, proposing even odder stuff than they practised. Already, at breakfast, the wine had not been spared. At a very well-furnished dinner-table there was no want of any enjoyment; and the feast was relished the more by everybody, after the violent bodily exercise during the somewhat warm. weather; and if the official gentleman went a little too far in the good things, the young people were not left much behind him.

I was happy beyond all bounds at the side of Frederica, — talkative, merry, ingenious, forward, and yet kept in moderation by feeling, esteem, and attachment. She, in a similar position, was open, cheerful, sympathising, and communicative. We all appeared to live for the company, and yet lived only for each other.

After the meal they sought the shade ; social games were begun, and the turn came to forfeits. On redeeming the forfeits, everything of every kind was carried to excess : the gestures which were commanded, the acts which were to be done, the problems which were to be solved, all showed a mad joy which knew no limits. I myself heightened these wild jokes by many a comical prank, and Frederica shone by many a droll thought ; she appeared to me more charming than ever, all hypochondriacal superstitious fancies had vanished: and, when the opportunity offered of heartily kissing one whom I loved so tenderly, I did not miss it, still less did I deny myself a repetition of this pleasure.

The company's hope of having some music was at last satisfied: it was heard, and all hastened to the dance. *Allemandes*, waltzing and turning, were beginning, middle and end. All had given up to this national dance, — even I did honour enough to my private dancing-mistress; and Frederica, who danced as she walked, sprang, and ran, was delighted to find in me a very expert partner. We generally kept together, but were soon obliged to leave off; and she was advised on all sides not to go on any farther in this wild manner. We consoled ourselves by a solitary walk, hand in hand, and, when we had reached that quiet spot, by the warmest embrace, and the most faithful assurance that we loved each other heartily.

Older persons, who had risen with us from the game, took us with them. At supper people did not return to their sober senses either. Dancing went on far into the night, and there was as little want of healths and other incitements to drinking as at noon.

I had scarcely for a few hours slept very profoundly, when I was awakened by a heat and tumult in my blood. It is at such times and in such situations that care and repentance usually attack a man, who is stretched out defenceless. My imagination at once presented to me the liveliest forms: I saw Lucinda, how, after the most ardent kiss, she passionately receded from me, and, with glowing cheek and sparkling eyes, uttered that curse, by which she intended to menace her sister only, but by which she also unconsciously menaced innocent persons, who were unknown to her. I saw Frederica standing opposite to her, paralysed at the sight, pale, and feeling the consequences of the curse, of which she knew nothing. I found myself between them, as little able to ward off the spiritual effects of the adventure as to avoid the evil-boding kiss. The delicate health of Frederica seemed to hasten the threatened calamity; and now her love to me wore a most unhappy aspect, and I wished myself at the other side of the world.

But something still more painful to me, which lay in the background, I will not conceal. A certain conceit kept that superstition alive in me; my lips, whether consecrated or cursed, appeared to me more important than usual; and with no little complacency was I aware of my self-denying conduct, in renouncing many an innocent pleasure, partly to preserve my magical advantage, partly to avoid injuring a harmless being by giving it up.

But now all was lost and irrevocable: I had returned into a mere common position; and I thought that I had harmed, irretrievably injured, the dearest of beings. Thus, far from my being freed from the curse, it was flung back from my lips into my own heart.

All this together raged in my blood, already excited by love and passion, wine and dancing, confused my thoughts and tortured my feelings, so that, especially as contrasted with the joys of the day before, I was in a state of despair which seemed unbounded. Fortunately daylight peered in upon me through a chink in the shutter; and the sun, vanquishing all the powers of night, set me again upon my feet: I was soon in the open air, and refreshed, if not restored.

Superstition, like many other fancies, very easily loses in power, when, instead of flattering our vanity, it stands in its way, and would fain produce an evil hour to this delicate being. We then see well enough that we can get rid of it when we choose: we renounce it the more easily, as all of which we deprive ourselves turns to our own advantage. The sight of Frederica, the feeling of her love, the cheerfulness of everything around me, all reproved me, that, in the midst of the happiest days, I could harbour such dismal night-birds in my bosom. The confiding conduct of the dear girl, which became more and more intimate, made me thoroughly rejoiced ; and I felt truly happy when, at parting, she openly gave a kiss to me, as well as the other friends and relations.

In the city many occupations and dissipations awaited me, from the midst of which I collected myself for the sake of my beloved, by means of a correspondence, which we regularly established. Even in her letters she always remained the same : whether she related anything new, or alluded to well-known occurrences, lightly described or cursorily reflected, it was always as if, even with her pen, she appeared going, coming, running, bounding with a step as light as it was sure. I also liked very much to write to her, for the act of rendering present her good qualities increased my affection even during absence ; so that this intercourse was little inferior to a personal one, — nay, afterward became pleasanter and dearer to me.

For that superstition had been forced to give way altogether. It was indeed based upon the impressions of earlier years ; but the spirit of the day, the liveliness of youth, the intercourse with cold, sensible men, all was unfavourable to it, so that it would not have been easy to find among all who surrounded me a single person to whom a confession of my whims would not have been perfectly ridiculous. But the worst of it was, that the fancy, while it fled, left behind it a real contemplation of that state in which young people are placed, whose early affections can promise themselves no lasting result. So little was I assisted in getting free from error, that understanding and reflection used me still worse in this instance. My passion increased the more I learned to know the virtue of the excellent girl; and the time approached when I was to lose, perhaps for ever, so much that was dear and good.

We had quietly and pleasantly passed a long time together, when friend Weyland had the waggery to bring with him to Sesenheim "The Vicar of Wakefield," and, when they were talking of reading aloud, to hand it over to me unexpectedly, as if nothing further was to be said. I managed to collect myself, and read with as much cheerfulness and freedom as I could. Even the faces of my hearers at once brightened, and it did not seem unpleasant to them to be again forced to a comparison. If they had found comical counterparts to Raymond and Melusina, they here saw themselves in a glass which by no means gave a distorted likeness. They did not openly confess, but they did not deny, that they were moving among persons akin, both by mind and feeling.

All men of a good disposition feel, with increasing cultivation, that they have a double part to play in the world, — a real one and an ideal one; and in this feeling is the ground of everything noble to be sought. The real part which has been assigned to us we experience but too plainly; with respect to the second, we seldom come to a clear understanding about it. Man may seek his higher destination on earth or in heaven, in the present or in the future: he yet remains on this account exposed to an eternal wavering, to an influence from without which ever disturbs him, until he once for all makes a resolution to declare that that is right which is suitable to himself.

Among the most venial attempts to acquire something higher, to place one's self on an equality with something higher, may be classed the youthful impulse to compare one's self with the characters in novels. This is highly innocent, and, whatever may be urged against it, the very reverse of mischievous. It amuses at times when we should necessarily die of *ennui*, or grasp at the reaction of passion.

How often is repeated the litany about the mischief of novels! and yet what misfortune is it if a pretty girl or a handsome young man put themselves in the place of a person who fares better or worse than themselves? Is the citizen life worth so much? or do the necessities of the day so completely absorb the man, that he must refuse every beautiful demand which is made upon him?

The historico-poetical Christian names which have intruded into the German church in the place of the sacred names, not unfrequently to the annoyance of the officiating clergyman, are without doubt to be regarded as small ramifications of the romantico-poetical pictures. This very impulse to honour one's child by a well-sounding name — even if the name has nothing further behind it — is praiseworthy; and this connection of an imaginary world with the real one diffuses an agreeable lustre over the whole life of the person. A beautiful child, whom with satisfaction we call "Bertha," we should think we offended if we were to call it "Urselblandine." With a cultivated man, not to say a lover, such a name would certainly falter on the lips. The cold world, which judges only from one side, is not to be blamed if it sets down as ridiculous and objectionable all that comes forward as imaginary; but the thinking connoisseur of mankind must know how to estimate it according to its worth.

For the position of the loving couple on the fair Rhinebank, this comparison, to which a wag had compelled them, produced the most agreeable results. We do not meditate on ourselves when we look in a mirror; but we feel that we exist, and allow ourselves to pass. Thus is it also with those moral imitations, in which we recognise our manners and inclinations, our habits and peculiarities, as in a silhouette, and strive to grasp it and embrace it with brotherly affection.

The habit of being together became more and more confirmed, and nothing else was known but that I belonged to this circle. The affair was allowed to take its course without the question being directly asked as to what was to be the result. And what parents are there who do not find themselves compelled to let daughters and sons continue for awhile in such a wavering condition, until accidentally something is confirmed for life, better than it could have been produced by a long-arranged plan.

It was thought that perfect confidence could be placed, both in Frederica's sentiments and in my rectitude, of which, on account of my forbearance, even from innocent caresses, a favourable opinion had been entertained. We were left unobserved, as was generally the custom, there and then ; and it depended on ourselves to go over the country, with a larger or smaller party, and to visit the friends in the neighbourhood. On both sides of the Rhine, in Hagenau, Fort Louis, Philippsburg, the Ortenau, I found dispersed those persons whom I had seen united at Sesenheim, every one by himself, a friendly, hospitable host, throwing open kitchen and cellar just as willingly as gardens and vineyards, — nay, the whole spot. The islands on the Rhine were often a goal for our water-expeditions. There, without pity, we put the cool inhabitants of the clear Rhine into the kettle, on the spit, into the boiling fat, and would here, perhaps more than was reasonable, have settled ourselves in the snug fishermen's huts, if the abominable Rhine-gnats (*Rhein-schnaken*) had not, after some hours, driven us away. At this intolerable interruption of one of our most charming parties of pleasure, when everything else was prosperous, when the affection of the lovers seemed to increase with the good success of the enterprise, and we had nevertheless come home too soon, unsuitably and inopportunely, I actually, in the presence of the good reverend father, broke out into blasphemous expressions, and assured him that these gnats alone were sufficient to take from me the thought that a good and wise Deity had created the world. The pious old gentleman, by way of reply, solemnly called me to order, and explained to me that these gnats and other vermin had not arisen until after the fall of our first parents, or that, if there were any of them in paradise, they had only pleasantly hummed there, and had not stung. Although I felt calmed at once, — for an angry man may easily be appeased if we can succeed in making him smile, — I nevertheless asserted that there was no need of the angel with the burning sword to drive the guilty pair out of the garden; my host, I said, must rather allow me to think that this was effected by means of great gnats on the Tigris and the Euphrates. And thus I again made him laugh; for the old man understood a joke, or at any rate let one pass.

However, the enjoyment of the daytime and season in this noble country was more serious and more elevating to the heart. One had only to resign one's self to the present, to enjoy the clearness of the pure sky, the brilliancy of the rich earth, the mild evenings, the warm nights, by the side of a beloved one, or in her vicinity. For months together we were favoured with pure ethereal mornings, when the sky, having watered the earth with superfluous dew, displayed all its magnificence; and, that this spectacle might not become too simple, clouds after clouds piled themselves over the distant mountains, now in this spot, now in that. They stood for days, nay, for weeks, without obscuring the pure sky; and even the transient storms refreshed the country, and gave lustre to the green, which again glistened in the sunshine before it could become dry. The double rainbow, the two-coloured

borders of a dark gray and nearly black streak in the
sky, were nobler, more highly coloured, more decided,
but also more transient, than I had ever observed.
In the midst of these objects, the desire of poetising,
which I had not felt for a long time, again came
forward. For Frederica I composed many songs to
well-known melodies. They would have made a pretty
little book: a few of them still remain, and will easily
be found among my others.

Since, on account of my strange studies and other
circumstances, I was often compelled to return to the
town, there arose for our affection a new life, which
preserved us from all that unpleasantness which usually
attaches itself as an annoying consequence to such
little love affairs. Though far from me, she yet laboured
for me, and thought of some new amusement against
I should return; though far from her, I employed
myself for her, that by some new gift or new notion I
myself might be again new to her. Painted ribbons
had then just come into fashion: I painted at once for
her a few pieces, and sent them on with a little poem,
as on this occasion I was forced to stop away longer
than I had anticipated. That I might fulfil and even
go beyond my promise of getting for her father a new
and elaborated plan, I persuaded a young adept in
architecture to work instead of myself. He took as
much pleasure in the task as he had kindness for me,
and was still further animated by the hope of a good
reception in so agreeable a family. He finished the
ground-plan, sketch, and section of the house; courtyard and garden were not forgotten; and a detailed
but very moderate estimate was added, to show the
possibility of carrying out an extensive project.

These testimonials of our friendly endeavours obtained for us the kindest reception: and, since the
good father saw that we had the best will to serve
him, he came forward with one wish more; it was the

wish to see his pretty but one-coloured chair adorned
with flowers and other ornaments. We showed ourselves accommodating. Colours, pencils, and other
requisites were fetched from the tradesmen and apothe-
caries of the nearest towns. But, that we might not
be wanting in a "Wakefield" mistake, we did not
remark, until all had been most industriously and
variously painted, that we had taken the wrong varnish,
which would not dry: neither sunshine nor draught,
neither fair nor wet weather, were of any avail. In
the meanwhile we were obliged to make use of an
old lumber-room, and nothing was left us but to rub
out the ornaments with more assiduity than we had
painted them. The unpleasantness of this work was
still increased when the girls entreated us, for Heaven's
sake, to proceed slowly and cautiously, for the sake of
sparing the ground; which, however, after this operation, was not again to be restored to its former brilliancy.

By such little disagreeable contingencies which happened at intervals, we were, however, just as little
interrupted in our cheerful life as Doctor Primrose and
his amiable family; for many an unexpected pleasure
befell both ourselves and our friends and neighbours.
Weddings and christenings, the erection of a building,
an inheritance, a prize in the lottery, were reciprocally
announced and enjoyed. We shared all joy together,
like a common property, and wished to heighten it by
mind and love. It was not the first nor the last time
that I found myself in families and social circles at
the very moment of their highest bloom; and, if I may
flatter myself that I contributed something toward the
lustre of such epochs, I must, on the other hand, be
reproached with the fact, that on this very account
such times passed the more quickly and vanished the
sooner.

But now our love was to undergo a singular trial.

I will call it a trial (*Prüfung*), although this is not the right word. The country family with which I was intimate was related to some families in the city of good note and respectability, and comfortably off as to circumstances. The young townspeople were often at Sesenheim. The older persons, the mothers and aunts, being less movable, heard so much of the life there, of the increasing charms of the daughters, and even of my influence, that they first wished to become acquainted with me, and after I had often visited them, and had been well received by them, desired also to see us once altogether, especially as they thought they owed the Sesenheim folks a friendly reception in return.

There was much discussion on all sides. The mother could scarcely leave her household affairs; Olivia had a horror of the town, for which she was not fitted; and Frederica had no inclination for it: and thus the affair was put off, until it was at last brought to a decision by the fact that it happened to be impossible for me to come into the country; for it was better to see each other in the city, and under some restraint, than not to see each other at all. And thus I now found my fair friends, whom I had been only accustomed to see in a rural scene, and whose image had only appeared to me hitherto before a background of waving boughs, flowing brooks, nodding field-flowers, and a horizon open for miles, — I now saw them, I say, for the first time, in town-rooms, which were indeed spacious but yet narrow, if we take into consideration the carpets, glasses, clocks, and porcelain figures.

The relation of a lover to the beloved object is so decided, that the surrounding objects are of little significance: the heart, nevertheless, desires that these shall be the suitable, natural, and customary objects. With my lively feeling for everything present, I could not at once adapt myself to the contradiction of the moment. The respectable and calmly noble demeanour of the mother was perfectly adapted to the circle: she was not different from the other ladies. Olivia, on the other hand, showed herself as impatient as a fish out of water. As she had formerly called to me in the gardens, or beckoned me aside in the fields, if she had anything particular to say to me, she also did the same here, when she drew me into the recess of a window. This she did awkwardly and with embarrassment, because she felt that it was not becoming, and did it notwithstanding. She had the most unimportant things in the world to say to me, — nothing but what I knew already; for instance, that she wished herself by the Rhine, over the Rhine, or even in Turkey. Frederica, on the contrary, was highly remarkable in this situation. Properly speaking, she also did not suit it either; but it bore witness to her character, that, instead of finding herself adapted to this condition, she unconsciously moulded the condition according to herself. She acted here as she had acted with the society in the country. She knew how to animate every moment. Without creating any disturbance, she put all in motion, and exactly by this pacified society, which really is only disturbed by *ennui*. She thus completely fulfilled the desire of her town aunts, who wished for once, on their sofas, to be witnesses of those rural games and amusements. If this was done to satisfaction, so also were the wardrobe, the ornaments and whatever besides distinguished the town nieces, who were dressed in the French fashion, considered and admired without envy. With me, also, Frederica had no difficulty; since she treated me the same as ever. She seemed to give me no other preference than that of communicating her desires and wishes to me rather than to another, and thus recognising me as her servant.

To this service she confidently laid claim on one of the following days, when she privately told me that the ladies wished to hear me read. The daughters of the house had spoken much on this subject, for at Sesenheim I had read what and when I was desired. I was ready at once, but craved quiet and attention for several hours. This was conceded; and one evening I read through the whole of "Hamlet" without interruption, entering into the sense of the piece as well as I was able, and expressing myself with liveliness and passion, as is possible in youth. I earned great applause. Frederica drew her breath deeply from time to time, and a transient red had passed over her cheeks. These two symptoms of a tender heart internally moved, while cheerfulness and calmness were externally apparent, were not unknown to me, and were indeed the only reward which I had striven to obtain. She joyfully collected the thanks of the party for having caused me to read, and in her graceful manner did not deny herself the little pride at having shone in me and through me.

This town visit was not to have lasted long, but the departure was delayed. Frederica did her part for the social amusement, and I was not wanting: but the abundant sources which yield so much in the country now dried up in their turn; and the situation was the most painful, as the elder sister gradually lost all self-control. The two sisters were the only persons in the society who dressed themselves in the German fashion. Frederica had never thought of herself in any other way, and believed herself so right everywhere, that she made no comparisons with any one else; but Olivia found it quite insupportable to move about in a society of genteel appearance attired so like a maid-servant. In the country she scarcely remarked the town costume of others, and did not desire it; but in the town she could not endure the country style. All this, together

with the different lot of town ladies, and the thousand
trifles of a series of circumstances totally opposed to
her own notions, so worked for some days in her
impassioned bosom, that I was forced to apply all my
flattering attention to appease her, according to the
wish of Frederica. I feared an impassioned scene. I
looked forward to the moment when she would throw
herself at my feet, and implore me by all that was
sacred to rescue her from this situation. She was good
to a heavenly degree if she could conduct herself in
her own way; but such a restraint at once made her
uncomfortable, and could at last drive her even to
despair. I now sought to hasten that which was
desired by the mother and Olivia, and not repugnant
to Frederica. I did not refrain from praising her as a
contrast to her sister; I told her what pleasure it gave
me to find her unaltered, and, even under the present
circumstances, just as free as the bird among the
branches. She was courteous enough to reply that I
was there, and that she wished to go neither in nor out
when I was with her.

At last I saw them take their departure, and it
seemed as though a load had fallen from my heart;
for my own feelings had shared the condition of Frederica and Olivia: I was not passionately tormented
like the latter, but I felt by no means as comfortable
as the former.

Since I had properly gone to Strasburg to take my
degree, it may be rightly reckoned among the irregu-
larities of my life, that I treated this material business
as a mere collateral affair. All anxiety as to my examination I had put aside in a very easy fashion; but I
had now to think of the disputation,[1] for on my departure from Frankfort I had promised my father, and
resolved within myself, to write one. It is the fault of

[1] A polemic dissertation written on taking a university degree.
— TRANS.

those who can do many things, nay, much, that they trust everything to themselves; and youth must indeed be in this position, if anything is to be made of it. A survey of the science of jurisprudence and all its framework I had pretty well acquired; single subjects of law sufficiently interested me; and, as I had the good Leyser for my model, I thought I should get tolerably through with my own little common sense. Great movements were showing themselves in jurisprudence; judgments were to be more according to equity; all rights by usage were daily seen to be compromised; and, in the criminal department especially, a great change was impending. As for myself, I felt well enough that I lacked an infinite deal to fill up the legal commonplace which I had proposed. The proper knowledge was wanting, and no inner tendency urged me to such subjects. Neither was there any impulse from without, — nay, quite another faculty [1] had completely carried me away. In general, if I was to take any interest in a thing, it was necessary for me to gain something from it, to perceive in it something that appeared fertile to me, and gave me prospects. Thus I had once more noted down some materials, had afterward made collections, had taken my books of extracts in hand, had considered the point which I wished to maintain, the scheme according to which I wished to arrange the single elements; but I was sharp enough soon to perceive that I could not get on, and that, to treat a special matter, a special and long-pursuing industry was requisite, — nay, that such a special task cannot be successfully accomplished unless, upon the whole, one is at any rate an old hand, if not a master.

The friends to whom I communicated my embarrassment thought me ridiculous, because one can dispute upon theses us well as, nay, even better than, upon a treatise; and in Strasburg this was not uncommon. I

[1] Medicine. — TRANS.

was by no means averse to such an expedient; but my father, to whom I wrote on the subject, desired a regular work, which, as he thought, I could very well prepare, if I only chose so to do and allowed myself proper time. I was now compelled to take up some general topic, and to choose something which I should have at my fingers' ends. Ecclesiastical history was almost better known to me than the history of the world; and that conflict in which the Church — the publicly recognised worship of God — finds itself, and always will find itself, in two different directions, had always highly interested me. For now it is in an eternal conflict with the state, over which it will exalt itself; now with the individuals, all of whom it will gather to itself. The state, on its side, will not yield the superior authority to the Church; and the individuals oppose its restraints. The state desires everything for public, universal ends; the individual for ends belonging to the home, heart, and feelings. From my childhood upwards I had been a witness of such movements, when the clergy now offended their authorities, now their congregations. I had therefore established the principle in my young mind, that the state — the legislator — had the right to determine a worship, according to which the clergy should teach and conduct themselves, and the laity, on the other hand, should direct themselves publicly and externally; while there should be no question about any one's thoughts, feelings, or notions. Thus I thought I had at once got rid of all collisions. I therefore chose for my disputation the first half of this theme; namely, that the legislator was not only authorised, but bound, to establish a certain worship, from which neither the clergy nor the laity might free themselves. I carried out this theme partly historically, partly argumentatively, showing that all public religions had been introduced by leaders of armies, kings, and powerful men; that this had even been the case with Christianity. The example of Protestantism lay quite close at hand. I went to work at this task with so much the more boldness, as I really only wrote it to satisfy my father, and desired and hoped nothing more ardently than that it might not pass the censorship. I had imbibed from Behrisch an unconquerable dislike to see anything of mine in print; and my intercourse with Herder had discovered to me but too plainly my own insufficiency, — nay, a certain mistrust in myself had through this means been perfectly matured. As I drew this work almost entirely out of myself, and wrote and spoke Latin with fluency, the time which I expended on the treatise passed very agreeably. The matter had at least some foundation; the style, naturally speaking, was not bad; the whole was pretty well rounded off. As soon as I had finished it, I went through it with a good Latin scholar, who, although he could not, on the whole, improve my style, yet easily removed all striking defects; so that something was produced that was fit to be shown. A fair copy was at once sent to my father, who disapproved of one thing, namely, that none of the subjects previously taken in hand had been worked out; but nevertheless, as a thorough Protestant, he was well pleased with the boldness of the plan. My singularities were tolerated, my exertions were praised, and he promised himself an important effect from the publication of the work.

I now handed over my papers to the faculty, who fortunately behaved in a manner as prudent as it was polite. The dean, a lively, clever man, began with many laudations of my work, then went on to what was doubtful, which he contrived gradually to change into something dangerous, and concluded by saying that it might not be advisable to publish this work as an academical dissertation. The aspirant had shown himself to the faculty as a thinking young man, of whom they might hope the best: they would willingly, not to delay the affair, allow me to dispute on theses. I could afterward publish my treatise, either in its present condition or more elaborated, in Latin, or in another language. This would everywhere be easy to me as a private man and a Protestant, and I should have the pleasure of an applause more pure and more general. I scarcely concealed from the good man what a stone his discourse rolled from my heart: at every new argument which he advanced, that he might not trouble me nor make me angry by his refusal, my mind grew more and more easy, and so did his own at last, when, quite unexpectedly, I offered no resistance to his reasons, but, on the contrary, found them extremely obvious, and promised to conduct myself according to his counsel and guidance. I therefore sat down again with my repetent. Theses were chosen and printed: and the disputation, with the opposition of my fellow boarders, went off with great merriment, and even with facility; for my old habit of turning over the *Corpus Juris* was very serviceable to me, and I could pass for a well-instructed man. A good feast, according to custom, concluded the solemnity.

My father, however, was very dissatisfied that the little work had not been regularly printed as a disputation; because he had hoped that I should gain honour by it on my entrance into Frankfort. He therefore wished to publish it specially; but I represented to him that the subject, which was only sketched, could be more completely carried out at some future time. He put up the manuscript carefully for this purpose, and many years afterward I saw it among his papers.

I took my degree on the 6th August, 1771; and on the following day Schöpflin died, in the seventy-fifth year of his age. Even without closer contact, he had had an important influence upon me; for eminent contemporaries may be compared to the greater stars, toward which, so long as they merely stand above the horizon, our eye is turned, and feels strengthened and cultivated, if it is only allowed to take such perfections into itself. Bountiful Nature had given Schöpflin an advantageous exterior, a slender form, kindly eyes, a ready mouth, and a thoroughly agreeable presence. Neither had she been sparing in gifts of mind to her favourite; and his good fortune was the result of innate and carefully cultivated merits, without any troublesome exertion. He was one of those happy men who are inclined to unite the past and the present, and understand how to connect historical knowledge with the interests of life. Born in the Baden territory, educated at Basle and Strasburg, he quite properly belonged to the paradisiacal valley of the Rhine, as an extensive and well-situated fatherland. His mind being directed to historical and antiquarian objects, he readily seized upon them with a felicitous power of representation, and retained them by the most convenient memory. Desirous as he was, of both learning and teaching, he pursued a course of study and of life which equally advanced. He soon emerges, and rises above the rest, without any kind of interruption; diffuses himself with ease through the literary and citizen world, for historical knowledge passes everywhere, and affability attaches itself everywhere. He travels through Germany, Holland, France, Italy; he comes in contact with all the learned men of his time; he amuses princes; and it is only when, by his lively loquacity, the hours of the table or of audience are lengthened that he is tedious to the people at court. On the other hand, he acquires the confidence of the statesmen, solves for them the most profound legal questions, and thus finds everywhere a field for his talent. In many places they attempt to retain him, but he remains faithful to Strasburg and the French court. His immovable German honesty is recognised even there: he is even protected against the powerful Prætor Klinglin, who is secretly his enemy. Sociable and talkative by nature, he extends his intercourse with the world, as well as his knowledge and occupations ; and we should hardly be able to understand whence he got all his time, did we not know that a dislike to women accompanied him through his whole life, and that thus he gained many days and hours which are happily thrown away by those who are well disposed toward the ladies.

For the rest, he belongs, as an author, to the ordinary sort of character, and, as an orator, to the multitude. His programme, his speeches, and addresses are devoted to the particular day — to the approaching solemnity; nay, his great work, " Alsatia Illustrata," belongs to life, as he recalls the past, freshens up faded forms, reanimates the hewn and the formed stone, and brings obliterated broken inscriptions for a second time before the eyes and mind of his reader. In such a manner his activity fills all Alsatia and the neighbouring country; in Baden and the Palatinate he preserves to an extreme old age an uninterrupted influence; at Mannheim he founds the Academy of Sciences, and remains president of it till his death.

I never approached this eminent man, excepting on one night, when we gave him a torch-serenade. Our pitch-torches more filled with smoke than lighted the courtyard of the old chapter-house, which was overarched by linden-trees. When the noise of the music had ended, he came forward, and stepped into the midst of us, — and here also was in his right place. The slender, well-grown, cheerful old man stood with his light, free manners, venerably before us, and held us worthy the honour of a well-considered address, which he delivered to us in an amiable paternal manner, without a trace of restraint or pedantry, so that we really thought ourselves something for the moment; for, indeed, he treated us like the kings and princes whom he had been so often called upon to address in public. We testified our satisfaction aloud; trumpets and drums repeatedly sounded; and the dear, hopeful academical plebs then found its way home with hearty satisfaction.

His scholars and companions in study, Koch and Oberlin, were men in close connection with me. My taste for antiquarian remains was passionate. They often let me into the museum, which contained, in many ways, the vouchers to his great work on Alsace. Even this work I had not known intimately until after that journey, when I had found antiquities on the spot; and now, being perfectly advanced, I could, on longer or shorter expeditions, render present to myself the valley of the Rhine as a Roman possession, and finish colouring many a dream of times past.

Scarcely had I made some progress in this, when Oberlin directed me to the monuments of the Middle Ages, and made me acquainted with the ruins and remains, the seals and documents, which those times have left behind them, — nay, sought to inspire me with an inclination for what we called the Minnesingers and heroic poets. To this good man, as well as to Herr Koch, I have been greatly indebted; and, if things had gone according to their wish, I should have had to thank them for the happiness of my life. The matter stood thus: —

Schöpflin, who for his whole lifetime had moved in the higher sphere of political law, and well knew the great influence which such and kindred studies are likely to procure for a sound head, in courts and cabinets, felt an insuperable, nay, unjust, aversion from the situation of a civilian, and had inspired his scholars with the like sentiments. The above-mentioned two men, friends of Salzmann, had taken notice of me in a most friendly manner. My impassioned grasping at external objects, the manner in which I continued to bring forward their advantages, and to communicate to them a particular interest, they prized higher than I did myself. My slight, and, I may say, my scanty, occupation with the civil law had not remained unobserved by them; they were well enough acquainted with me to know how easily I was to be influenced: I had made no secret of my liking for an academical life; and they therefore thought to gain me over to history, political law, and rhetoric, at first for a time, but afterward more decidedly. Strasburg itself offered advantages enough. The prospect of the German Chancery at Versailles, the precedent of Schöpflin, whose merits, indeed, seemed to me unattainable, were to incite to emulation, if not to imitation; and perhaps a similar talent was thus to be cultivated, which might be both profitable to him who could boast of it, and useful to others who might choose to employ it on their own account. These, my patrons, and Salzmann with them, set a great value on my memory, and my capacity for apprehending the sense of languages, and chiefly by these sought to further their views and plans.

I now intend to describe at length, how all this came to nothing, and how it happened that I again passed over from the French to the German side. Let me be allowed, as heretofore, to make some general reflections, by way of transition.

There are few biographies which can represent a pure, quiet, steady progress of the individual. Our life, as well as that whole in which we are contained, is, in an incomprehensible manner, composed of freedom and necessity. That which we would do is a prediction of what we shall do, under all circumstances. But these circumstances lay hold on us in their own fashion. The *what* lies in us, the *how* seldom depends on us, after the *wherefore* we dare not ask, and on this account we are rightly referred to the *quia*.

The French tongue I had liked from my youth upwards: I had become acquainted with the language
through a bustling life, and with a bustling life through
the language. It had become my own, like a second
mother-tongue, without grammar and instruction — by
mere intercourse and practice. I now wished to use it
with still greater fluency, and gave Strasburg the preference, as a second university residence, to other high
schools; but, alas! it was just there that I had to experience the very reverse of my hopes, and to be turned
rather from than to this language and these manners.

The French, who generally aim at good behaviour,
are indulgent toward foreigners who begin to speak
their language: they will not laugh any one out
of countenance at a mistake, or blame him in direct
terms. However, since they cannot endure sins committed against their language, they have a manner
of repeating, and, as it were, courteously confirming,
what has been said with another term, at the same
time making use of the expression which should properly have been employed, thus leading the intelligent
and the attentive to what is right and proper.

Now, although, if one is in earnest, — if one has self-
denial enough to profess one's self a pupil, one gains a
great deal, and is much advanced by this plan, — one
nevertheless always feels in some degree humiliated,
and, since one talks for the sake of the subject matter,
also, often too much interrupted, or even distracted,
so that one impatiently lets the conversation drop.
This happened with me more than with others; as I
always thought that I had to say something interesting,
and, on the other hand, to hear something important,
and did not wish to be always brought back merely to
the expression, — a case which often occurred with me,
as my French was just as motley as that of any other
foreigner. I had observed the accent and idiom of
footmen, valets, guards, young and old actors, theat-

rical lovers, peasants, and heroes: and this Babylonish idiom was rendered still more confused by another odd ingredient; as I liked to hear the French reformed clergy, and visited their churches the more willingly, as a Sunday walk to Bockenheim was on this account not only permitted but ordered. But even this was not enough: for as, in my youthful years, I had always been chiefly directed to the German of the sixteenth century, I soon included the French also of that noble epoch among the objects of my inclination. Montaigne, Amyot, Rabelais, Marot, were my friends, and excited in me sympathy and delight. Now, all these different elements moved in my discourse chaotically one with another, so that for the hearer the meaning was lost in the oddity of the expression; nay, an educated Frenchman could no more courteously correct me, but had to censure me and tutor me in plain terms. I therefore fared here once more as I had fared at Leipzig, except that on this occasion I could not appeal to the right of my native place to speak idiomatically, as well as other provinces, but, being on a foreign ground and soil, was forced to adapt myself to traditional laws.

Perhaps we might even have resigned ourselves to this, if an evil genius had not whispered into our ears that all endeavours by a foreigner to speak French would remain unsuccessful; for a practised ear can perfectly well detect a German, Italian, or Englishman under a French mask. One is tolerated, but never received into the bosom of the only church of language.

Only a few exceptions were granted. They named to us a Herr von Grimm; but even Schöpflin, it seemed, did not reach the summit. They allowed that he had early seen the necessity of expressing himself in French to perfection; they approved of his inclination to converse with every one, and especially to entertain the great and persons of rank; they praised him, that, living in the place where he was, he had made the language of the country his own, and had endeavoured as much as possible to render himself a Frenchman of society and orator. But what does he gain by the denial of his mother-tongue, and his efforts of speaking a foreign language? He cannot make it right with anybody. In society they consider him vain; as if any one would or could converse with others without some feeling for self and self-complacency! Then, the refined connoisseurs of the world and of language assert that there is in him more of dissertation and dialogue than of conversation, properly so called. The former was generally recognised as the original and fundamental sin of the Germans, the latter as the cardinal virtue of the French. As a public orator he fares no better. If he prints a well-elaborated address to the king or the princes, the Jesuits, who are ill disposed to him as a Protestant, lay wait for him, and show that his terms of expression are "not French."

Instead of consoling ourselves with this, and bearing as green wood that which had been laid upon the dry, we were annoyed at such pedantic injustice. We despair, and, by this striking example, become the more convinced that it is a vain endeavour to try to satisfy the French by the matter itself, as they are too closely bound to the external conditions under which everything is to appear. We therefore embrace the opposite resolution of getting rid of the French language altogether, and of directing ourselves more than ever, with might and earnestness, to our own mother-tongue.

And for this we found opportunity and sympathy in actual life. Alsace had not been connected with France so long that an affectionate adherence to the old constitution, manners, language, and costume did not still exist with old and young. If the conquered party loses half his existence by compulsion, he looks upon it as disgraceful voluntarily to part with the other half. He therefore holds fast to all that can recall to him the good old time, and foster in him the hope that a better epoch will return. Very many inhabitants of Strasburg formed little circles, separate, indeed, but nevertheless united in spirit, which were always increased and recruited by the numerous subjects of German princes who held considerable lands under French sovereignty; since fathers and sons, either for the sake of study or business, resided for a longer or shorter time at Strasburg.

At our table nothing but German was spoken. Salzmann expressed himself in French with much fluency and elegance, but, with respect to his endeavours and acts, was a perfect German. Lerse might have been set up as a pattern of a German youth. Meyer, of Lindau, liked to get on with good German too well to shine in good French; and if, among the rest, many were inclined to the Gallic speech and manners, they yet, while they were with us, allowed the general tone to prevail with them.

From the language we turned to political affairs. We had not, indeed, much to say in praise of our own imperial constitution. We granted that it consisted of mere legal contradictions, but exalted ourselves so much the more above the present French constitution, which lost itself in mere lawless abuses; while the government only showed its energy in the wrong place, and was forced to admit that a complete change in affairs was already publicly prophesied with black forebodings.

If, on the other hand, we looked toward the north, we were shone upon by Frederick, the polar-star, who seemed to turn about himself Germany, Europe, — nay, the whole world. His preponderance in everything was most strongly manifested when the Prussian exercise and even the Prussian stick was introduced into the French army. As for the rest, we forgave him his predilection for a foreign language; since we felt satisfaction that his French poets, philosophers, and *littérateurs* continued to annoy him, and often declared that he was to be considered and treated only as an intruder.

But what, more than all, forcibly alienated us from the French, was the unpolite opinion, repeatedly maintained, that the Germans in general, as well as the king, who was striving after French cultivation, were deficient in taste. With regard to this kind of talk, which followed every judgment like a burden, we endeavoured to solace ourselves with contempt: but we could so much the less come to a clear understanding about it, as we were assured that Menage had already said, that the French writers possessed everything but taste; and had also learned, from the then living Paris, that all the authors were wanting in taste, and that Voltaire himself could not escape this severest of reproaches. Having been before and often directed to nature, we would allow of nothing but truth and uprightness of feeling, and the quick, blunt expression of it.

> " Friendship, love, and brotherhood,
> Are they not self-understood ? "

was the watchword and cry of battle, by which the members of our little academical horde used to know and enliven each other. This maxim lay at the foundation of all our social banquets, on the occasions of which we did not fail to pay many an evening visit to Cousin Michel,[1] in his well-known " Germanhood."

If, in what has hitherto been described, only external

---

[1] " Michel " is exactly to the Germans what " John Bull " is to the English. — TRANS.

contingent causes and personal peculiarities are found, the French literature had in itself certain qualities which were rather repulsive than attractive to an aspiring youth. It was advanced in years and genteel; and by neither of these qualities can youth, which looks about for enjoyment of life and for freedom, be delighted.

Since the sixteenth century, the course of French literature had never been seen to be completely interrupted, — nay, the internal and religious disturbances, as well as the external wars, had accelerated its progress; but, as we heard generally maintained, it was a hundred years ago that it had existed in its full bloom. Through favourable circumstances, they said, an abundant harvest had at once ripened, and had been happily gathered in; so that the great talents of the eighteenth century had to be moderately contented with mere gleanings.

Meanwhile, however, much had become antiquated, — first of all comedy, which had to be freshened up to adapt itself less perfectly, indeed, but still with new interest, to actual life and manners. Of the tragedies, many had vanished from the stage; and Voltaire did not let slip the important opportunity which offered of editing Corneille's works, that he might show how defective his predecessor had been, whom, according to the general voice, he had not equalled.

And even this very Voltaire, the wonder of his time, had grown old, like the literature which for nearly a century he had animated and governed. By his side still existed and vegetated many *littérateurs*, in a more or less active and happy old age, who one by one disappeared. The influence of society upon authors increased more and more; for the best society, consisting of persons of birth, rank, and property, chose for one of their chief recreations literature, which thus

became quite social and genteel. Persons of rank and
littérateurs mutually cultivated and necessarily per-
verted each other, for the genteel has always something excluding in its nature; and excluding also was
the French criticism, being negative, detracting and
faultfinding. The higher class made use of such
judgments against the authors: the authors, with
somewhat less decorum, proceeded in the same manner against each other, — nay, against their patrons.
If the public was not to be awed, they endeavoured
to take it by surprise, or gain it by humility; and
thus — apart from the movements which shook Church
and state to their inmost core — there arose such a
literary ferment, that Voltaire himself stood in need
of his full activity, and his whole preponderance, to
keep himself above the torrent of general disesteem.
Already he was openly called an old, capricious child;
his endeavours, carried on indefatigably, were regarded
as the vain efforts of a decrepit age; certain principles
on which he had stood during his whole life, and to
the spread of which he had devoted his days, were
no more held in esteem and honour; nay, his Deity,
by acknowledging whom he continued to declare himself free from atheism, was not conceded him; and
thus he himself, the grandsire and patriarch, was
forced, like his youngest competitor, to watch the
present moment, to catch at new power, to do his
friends too much good and his enemies too much
harm, and, under the appearance of a passionate striving for the love of truth, to act deceitfully and falsely.
Was it worth the trouble to have led such a great,
active life, if it were to end in greater dependence than
it had begun? How insupportable such a position
was, did not escape his high mind, his delicate sensibility. He often relieved himself by leaps and thrusts,
gave the reins to his humour, and carried a few of his
sword-cuts too far, at which friends and enemies, for

the most part, showed themselves indignant; for everyone thought he could play the superior to him, though no one could equal him. A public which only hears the judgment of old men becomes overwise too soon, and nothing is more unsatisfactory than a mature judgment adopted by an immature mind.

To us youths, before whom, with our German love of truth and nature, honesty toward both ourselves and others hovered as the best guide, both in life and learning, the factious dishonesty of Voltaire and the perversion of so many worthy subjects became more and more annoying; and we daily strengthened ourselves in our aversion from him. He could never cease degrading religion and the sacred books, for the sake of injuring priestcraft,[1] as they called it, and had thus produced in me many an unpleasant sensation. But when I now learned, that, to weaken the tradition of a deluge, he had denied all petrified shells, and only admitted them as *lusus naturæ,* he entirely lost my confidence; for my own eyes had, on the Baschberg, plainly enough shown me that I stood on the bottom of an old dried-up sea, among the *exuviæ* of its original inhabitants. These mountains had certainly been once covered by waves, whether before or during the deluge did not concern me: it was enough that the valley of the Rhine had been a monstrous lake, a bay extending beyond the reach of the eyesight; out of this I was not to be talked. I thought much more of advancing in the knowledge of lands and mountains, let what would be the result.

French literature, then, had grown old and genteel in itself, and through Voltaire. Let us devote some further consideration to this remarkable man.

---

[1] "Um den so genannten Pfaffen zu schaden." As we have not the word for a priest which exactly expresses the contempt involved in " Pfaffe," the word "priest*craft* " has been introduced. — TRANS.

From his youth upwards, Voltaire's wishes and endeavours had been directed to an active and social life, to politics, to gain on a large scale, to a connection with the heads of the earth, and a profitable use of this connection, that he himself might be one of the heads of the earth also. No one has easily made himself so dependent for the sake of being independent. He even succeeded in subjugating minds: the nation became his own. In vain did his opponents unfold their moderate talents and their monstrous hate: nothing succeeded in injuring him. The court he could never reconcile to himself; but, by way of compensation, foreign kings were his tributaries; Catharine, and Frederick the Great, Gustavus of Sweden, Christian of Denmark, Peniotowsky of Poland, Henry of Prussia, Charles of Brunswick, acknowledged themselves his vassals; even popes thought they must coax him by some acts of indulgence. That Joseph the Second had kept aloof from him did not at all redound to the honour of this prince; for it would have done no harm to him and his undertakings, if, with such a fine intellect and with such noble views, he had been somewhat more practically clever,[1] and a better appreciator of the mind.

What I have stated here in a compressed form, and in some connection, sounded at that time as a cry of the moment, as a perpetual discord, unconnected and uninstructive in our ears. Nothing was heard but the praise of those who had gone before. Something good and new was required, but the newest was never liked. Scarcely had a patriot exhibited on the long inanimate stage national-French, heart-inspiring subjects, scarcely had the " Siege of Calais " gained enthusiastic applause, than the piece, together with all its national comrades, was considered empty, and in every sense objectionable.

---

[1] " Practically clever " is put as a kind of equivalent for the difficult word " geist reich." — TRANS.

The delineations of manners by Destouches, which had so often delighted me when a boy, were called weak; the name of this honest man had passed away: and how many authors could I not point out, for the sake of whom I had to endure the reproach, that I judged like a provincial, if I showed any sympathy for such men and their works, in opposition to any one who was carried along by the newest literary torrent!

Thus, to our other German comrades, we became more and more annoying. According to our view, according to the peculiarity of our own nature, we had to retain the impressions of objects, to consume them but slowly, and, if it was to be so, to let them go as late as possible. We were convinced, that by faithful observation, by continued occupation, something might be gained from all things, and that by persevering zeal we must at last arrive at a point where the ground of the judgment may be expressed at the same time with the judgment itself. Neither did we fail to perceive that the great and noble French world offered us many an advantage and much profit, for Rousseau had really touched our sympathies. But, if we considered his life and his fate, he was nevertheless compelled to find the great reward for all he did in this, — that he could live unacknowledged and forgotten at Paris.

Whenever we heard the encyclopedists mentioned, or opened a volume of their monstrous work, we felt as if we were going between the innumerable moving spools and looms in a great factory, where, what with the mere creaking and rattling; what with all the mechanism, embarrassing both eyes and senses; what with the mere incomprehensibility of an arrangement, the parts of which work into each other in the most manifold way; what with the contemplation of all that is necessary to prepare a piece of cloth, — we feel disgusted with the very coat which we wear upon our backs.

Diderot was sufficiently akin to us; as, indeed, in everything, for which the French blame him, he is a true German. But even his point of view was too high, his circle of vision was too extended, for us to range ourselves with him, and place ourselves at his side. Nevertheless, his children of nature, whom he continued to bring forward and dignify with great rhetorical art, pleased us very much; his brave poachers and smugglers enchanted us; and this rabble afterward throve but too well upon the German Parnassus. It was he also, who, like Rousseau, diffused a disgust of social life, — a quiet introduction to those monstrous changes of the world in which everything permanent appeared to sink.

However, we ought now to put aside these considerations, and to remark what influence these two men have had upon art. Even here they pointed, even from here they urged us, toward nature.

The highest problem of any art is, to produce by semblance the illusion of some higher reality. But it is a false endeavour to realise the appearance until at last only something commonly real remains.

As an ideal locality, the stage, by the application of the laws of perspective to *coulisses* ranged one behind the other, had attained the greatest advantage; and this very gain they now wished wantonly to abandon, by shutting up the sides of the theatre, and forming real room-walls. With such an arrangement of the stage, the piece itself, the actors' mode of playing, in a word, everything, was to coincide; and thus an entirely new theatre was to arise.

The French actors had, in comedy, attained the summit of the true in art. Their residence at Paris; their observations of the externals of the court; the connection of the actors and actresses with the highest classes, by means of love-affairs, — all contributed to transplant to the stage the greatest realness and seemliness of social life; and on this point the friends of nature found but little to blame. However, they thought they made a great advance, if they chose for their pieces earnest and tragical subjects, in which the citizen-life should not be wanting, used prose for the higher mode of expression, and thus banished unnatural verse, together with unnatural declamation and gesticulation.

It is extremely remarkable, and has not been generally noticed, that, at this time, even the old, severe, rhythmical, artistical tragedy was threatened with a revolution, which could only be averted by great talents and the power of tradition.

In opposition to the actor Lecain, who acted his heroes with especial theatrical decorum, with deliberation, elevation, and force, and kept himself aloof from the natural and ordinary, came forward a man named Aufresne, who declared war against everything unnatural, and in his tragic acting sought to express the highest truth. This method might not have accorded with that of the other Parisian actors. He stood alone, while they kept together; and, adhering to his views obstinately enough, he chose to leave Paris rather than alter them, and came through Strasburg. There we saw him play the part of Augustus in " Cinna," that of Mithridates, and others of the sort, with the truest and most natural dignity. He appeared as a tall, handsome man, more slender than strong, not, properly speaking, with an imposing, but nevertheless with a noble, pleasing demeanour. His acting was well considered and quiet, without being cold, and forcible enough where force was required. He was a very well practised actor, and one of the few who know how to turn the artificial completely into nature, and nature completely into the artificial. It is really those few whose good qualities, being misunderstood, always originate the doctrine of false " naturalness."

And thus will I also make mention of a work, which is indeed small, but which made an epoch in a remarkable manner, — I mean Rousseau's "Pygmalion." A great deal could be said upon it; for this strange production floats between nature and art, with the full endeavour of resolving the latter into the former. We see an artist who has produced what is most perfect, and yet does not find any satisfaction in having, according to art, represented his idea externally to himself, and given to it a higher life; no, it must also be drawn down to him into the earthly life. He will destroy the highest that mind and deed have produced, by the commonest act of sensuality.

All this and much else, right and foolish, true and half-true, operating upon us as it did, still more perplexed our notions: we were driven astray through many byways and roundabout ways; and thus on many sides was prepared that German literary revolution, of which we were witnesses, and to which, consciously or unconsciously, willingly or unwillingly, we unceasingly contributed.

We had neither impulse nor tendency to be illumined and advanced in a philosophical manner: on religious subjects we thought we had sufficiently enlightened ourselves, and therefore the violent contest of the French philosophers with the priesthood was tolerably indifferent to us. Prohibited books, condemned to the flames, which then made a great noise, produced no effect upon us. I mention as an instance, to serve for all, the "Système de la Nature," which we took in hand out of curiosity. We did not understand how such a book could be dangerous. It appeared to us so dark, so Cimmerian, so deathlike, that we found it a trouble to endure its presence, and shuddered at it as at a spectre. The author fancies he gives his book a peculiar recommendation, when he declares in his preface, that as a decrepit old man, just sinking into the grave, he wishes to announce the truth to his contemporaries and to posterity.

We laughed at him; for we thought we had observed, that by old people nothing in the world that is lovable and good is, in fact, appreciated. " Old churches have dark windows: to know how cherries and berries taste, we must ask children and sparrows." These were our gibes and maxims; and thus that book, as the very quintessence of senility, appeared to us as unsavoury, nay, absurd. " All was to be of necessity," so said the book, " and therefore there was no God." But might not there be a God by necessity too? asked we. We indeed confessed, at the same time, that we could not withdraw ourselves from the necessities of day and night, the seasons, the influence of climate, physical and animal condition: we nevertheless felt within us something that appeared like perfect freedom of will, and again something which endeavoured to counterbalance this freedom.

The hope of becoming more and more rational, of making ourselves more and more independent of external things, nay, of ourselves, we could not give up. The word freedom sounds so beautiful, that we cannot do without it, even though it should designate an error.

Not one of us had read the book through, for we found ourselves deceived in the expectations with which we had opened it. A system of nature was announced; and therefore we hoped to learn really something of nature, — our idol. Physics and chemistry, descriptions of heaven and earth, natural history and anatomy, with much else, had now for years, and up to the last day, constantly directed us to the great, adorned world; and we would willingly have heard both particulars and generals about suns and stars, planets and moons, mountains, valleys, rivers and seas, with all that live and move in them. That, in the

course of this, much must occur which would appear
to the common man as injurious, to the clergy as dangerous, and to the state as inadmissible, we had no
doubt; and we hoped that the little book had not un-
worthily stood the fiery ordeal. But how hollow and
empty did we feel in this melancholy, atheistical half-
night, in which earth vanished with all its images,
heaven with all its stars. There was to be a matter
in motion from all eternity; and by this motion, right
and left and in every direction, without anything further, it was to produce the infinite phenomena of existence. Even all this we should have allowed to pass, if
the author, out of his moved matter, had really built up
the world before our eyes. But he seemed to know as
little about nature as we did; for, having set up some
general ideas, he quits them at once, for the sake of
changing that which appears as higher than nature,
or as a higher nature within nature, into material,
heavy nature, which is moved, indeed, but without
direction or form — and thus he fancies he has gained
a great deal.

If, after all, this book had done us some harm, it
was this, — that we took a hearty dislike to all philosophy, and especially metaphysics, and remained in that
dislike; while, on the other hand, we threw ourselves
into living knowledge, experience, action, and poetising,
with all the more liveliness and passion.

Thus, on the very borders of France, we had at once
got rid and clear of everything French about us. The
French way of life we found too defined and genteel,
their poetry cold, their criticism annihilating, their
philosophy abstruse, and yet insufficient; so that we
were on the point of resigning ourselves to rude
nature, at least by way of experiment, if another
influence had not for a long time prepared us for
higher and freer views of the world, and intellectual
enjoyments as true as they were poetical, and swayed

us, first moderately and secretly, but afterward with more and more openness and force.

I need hardly say that Shakespeare is meant; and, having once said this, no more need be added. Shakespeare has been recognised by the Germans, more by them than by other nations, perhaps even more than by his own. We have richly bestowed on him all that justice, fairness, and forbearance which we refused to ourselves. Eminent men have occupied themselves in showing his talents in the most favourable light; and I have always readily subscribed to what has been said to his honour, in his favour, or even by way of excuse for him. The influence this extraordinary mind had upon me has been already shown; an attempt has been made with respect to his works, which has received approbation; and therefore this general statement may suffice for the present, until I am in a position to communicate to such friends as like to hear me, a gleaning of reflections on his great deserts, such as I was tempted to insert in this very place.

At present I will only show more clearly the manner in which I became acquainted with him. It happened pretty soon at Leipzig, through Dodd's "Beauties of Shakespeare." Whatever may be said against such collections, which give authors in a fragmentary form, they nevertheless produce many good effects. We are not always so collected and so ready that we can take in a whole work according to its merits. Do we not, in a book, mark passages which have an immediate reference to ourselves? Young people especially, who are wanting in a thorough cultivation, are laudably excited by brilliant passages; and thus I myself remember, as one of the most beautiful epochs of my life, that which is characterised by the above-mentioned work. Those noble peculiarities, those great sayings, those happy descriptions, those humourous traits, all struck me singly and powerfully.

Wieland's translation now made its appearance. It was devoured, communicated, and recommended to friends and acquaintances. We Germans had the advantage, that many important works of foreign nations were first brought over to us in an easy and cheerful fashion. Shakespeare, translated in prose, first by Wieland, afterward by Eschenburg, was able, as a kind of reading universally intelligible, and suitable to any reader, to diffuse itself speedily, and to produce a great effect. I value both rhythm and rhyme, whereby poetry first becomes poetry; but that which is really, deeply, and fundamentally effective, that which is really permanent and furthering, is that which remains of the poet when he is translated into prose. Then remains the pure, perfect substance, of which, when absent, a dazzling exterior often contrives to make a false show, and which, when present, such an exterior contrives to conceal. I therefore consider prose translations more advantageous than poetical, for the beginning of youthful culture; for it may be remarked, that boys, to whom everything must serve as a jest, delight themselves with the sound of words and the fall of syllables, and, by a sort of parodistical wantonness, destroy the deep contents of the noblest work. Hence I would have it considered whether a prose translation of Homer should not be undertaken next; though this, indeed, must be worthy of the degree at which German literature stands at present. I leave this, and what has been already said, to the consideration of our worthy pedagogues, to whom an extensive experience on this matter is most at command. I will only, in favour of my proposition, mention Luther's translation of the Bible; for the circumstance that this excellent man handed down a work, composed in the most different styles, and gave us its poetical, historical, commanding, didactic tone in our mother-tongue, as if all were cast in one mould, has done more to advance religion than if he had attempted to imitate, in detail, the peculiarities of the original. In vain has been the subsequent endeavour to make Job, the Psalms, and the other lyrical books, capable of affording enjoyment in their poetical form. For the multitude, upon whom the effect is to be produced, a plain translation always remains the best. Those critical translations, which vie with the original, really only seem to amuse the learned among themselves.

And thus in our Strasburg society did Shakespeare, translated and in the original, by fragments and as a whole, by passages and by extracts, influence us in such a manner, that, as there are men well versed in the Bible (*Bibelfest*), so did we gradually make ourselves thoroughly acquainted with Shakespeare, imitated in our conversations those virtues and defects of his time with which he had made us so well acquainted, took the greatest delight in his "quibbles," [1] and, by translating them, nay, with original recklessness, tried to rival him. To this, the fact that I had seized upon him, above all, with great enthusiasm, did not a little contribute. A happy confession that something higher hovered over me was infectious for my friends, who all resigned themselves to this mode of thought. We did not deny the possibility of knowing such merits more closely, of comprehending them, of judging them with penetration; but this we reserved for later epochs. At present we only wished to sympathise gladly, and to imitate with spirit; and, while we had so much enjoyment, we did not wish to inquire and haggle about the man who afforded it, but unconditionally to revere him.

If any one would learn immediately what was thought, talked about, and discussed in this lively society, let him read Herder's essay on Shakespeare,

[1] This English word is used in the original. — Trans.

in the part of his works upon the German manner and art (" Ueber deutsche Art und Kunst "), and also Lenz's remarks on the theatre (" Anmerkungen übers Theater "), to which a translation of " Love's Labour's Lost " was added.[1] Herder penetrates into the deepest interior of Shakespeare's nature, and exhibits it nobly : Lenz conducts himself more like an iconoclast against the traditions of the theatre, and will have everything everywhere treated in Shakespeare's manner. Since I have had occasion to mention this clever and eccentric man here, this is the place to say something about him by way of experiment. I did not become acquainted with him till toward the end of my residence at Strasburg. We saw each other seldom, — his company was not mine ; but we sought an opportunity of meeting, and willingly communicated with each other, because, as contemporary youths, we harboured similar views. He had a small but neat figure ; a charming little head, to the elegant form of which his delicate but somewhat flat features perfectly corresponded ; blue eyes, blond hair, — in short, a person such as I have from time to time met among Northern youths ; a soft, and, as it were, cautious step ; a pleasant but not quite flowing speech ; and a conduct which, fluctuating between reserve and shyness, well became a young man. Small poems, especially his own, he read very well aloud. For his turn of mind I only know the English word " whimsical," which, as the dictionary shows, comprises very many singularities under one notion. No one, perhaps, was more capable than he to feel and imitate the extravagances and excrescences of Shakespeare's genius. To this the translation above mentioned bears witness. He treated his author with great freedom, was not in the least close and faithful ;

---

[1] A complete edition of Lenz's works was published by Tieck in 1828. In that will be found the essay and play in question, to the last of which he gives the name Amor vincit omnia. — TRANS.

but he knew how to put on the armour, or rather the motley jacket, of his predecessor so very well, to adapt himself with such humour to his gestures, that he was certain to obtain applause from those who were interested in such matters.

The absurdities of the clowns especially constituted our whole happiness; and we praised Lenz as a favoured man, when he succeeded in rendering as follows the epitaph on the deer shot by the princess:

"Die schöne Princessin schoss und traf
Eines jungen Hirschleins Leben;
Es fiel dahin in schweren Schlaf
Und wird ein Brätlein geben.
Der Jagdhund boll! Ein L zu Hirsch
So wird es denn ein Hirschel;
Doch setzt ein römisch L zu Hirsch
So macht es funfzig Hirschel.
Ich mache hundert Hirsche draus
Schreib Hirschell mit zwei LLen." [1]

The tendency toward the absurd, which is displayed freely and unrestrictedly in youth, but afterward recedes more into the background, without being on that account utterly lost, was in full bloom among us; and we sought, even by original jests, to celebrate our great master. We were very proud when we could lay before the company something of the kind, which was

[1] The lines in Shakespeare, which the above are intended to imitate, are the following:

"The praiseful princess pierced and pricked a pretty pleasing pricket;
Some say a sore; but not a sore, till now made sore with shooting.
The dogs did yell; put l to sore, then sorel jumps from thicket;
Or pricket, sore, or else sorel; the people fall a-hooting.
If sore be sore, then l to sore makes fifty sores; O sore l!
Of one sore I a hundred make, by adding but one more l."

Lenz's words, which cannot be rendered intelligibly into English, furnish an instance of Goethe's meaning, when he commends Lenz as happily catching the spirit of the original, without the slightest pretence to accuracy. — TRANS.

in any degree approved, as, for instance, the following on a riding-master, who had been hurt on a wild horse.

> " A rider in this house you'll find.
> A master too is he:
> The two into a nosegay bind,
> 'Twill riding-master be.
> If master of the ride, I wis,
> Full well he bears the name:
> But if the ride the master is,
> On him and his be shame." [1]

About such things serious discussions were held as to whether they were worthy of the clown or not, whether they flowed from the genuine pure fool's spring, and whether sense and understanding had at all mingled in an unfitting and inadmissible manner. Altogether our singular views were diffused with the greater ardour, and more persons were in a position to sympathise with them, as Lessing, in whom great confidence was placed, had, properly speaking, given the first signal in his " Dramaturgie."

In a society so attuned and excited I managed to take many a pleasant excursion into Upper Alsace, whence, however, on this very account, I brought back no particular instruction. The number of little verses which flowed from us on that occasion, and which might serve to adorn a lively description of a journey, are lost. In the crossway of Molsheim Abbey we admired the painted windows: in the fertile spot between Colmar and Schlettstadt resounded some comic

---

[1] The above doggerel is pretty faithful, but it is as well to give the original.

> " Ein Ritter wohnt in diesem Haus ;
> Ein Meister auch daneben ;
> Macht man davon einen Blumenstrauss
> So wird's einen Rittmeister geben.
> Ist er nun Meister von dem Ritt
> Führt er mit Recht den Namen ;
> Doch nimmt der Ritt den Meister mit,
> Weh ihm und seinem Samen." — TRANS.

hymns to Ceres; the consumption of so many fruits being circumstantially set forth and extolled, and the important question as to the free or restricted trade in them being very merrily taken up. At Ensisheim we saw the monstrous aerolite hanging up in the church, and, in accordance with the scepticism of the time, ridiculed the credulity of man, never suspecting that such air-born beings, if they were not to fall into our cornfields, were at any rate to be preserved in our cabinets.

Of a pilgrimage to the Ottilienberg, accomplished with a hundred, nay, a thousand, of the faithful, I still love to think. Here, where the foundation wall of a Roman castle still remained, a count's beautiful daughter, of a pious disposition, was said to have dwelt among ruins and stony crevices. Near the chapel where the wanderers edify themselves, her well is shown; and much that is beautiful is narrated. The image which I formed of her, and her name, made a deep impression upon me. I carried both about with me for a long time, until at last I endowed with them one of my later, but not less beloved, daughters,[1] who was so favourably received by pure and pious hearts.

On this eminence also is repeated to the eye the majestic Alsace, always the same, and always new. Just as in an amphitheatre, let one take one's place where he will, he surveys the whole people, but sees his neighbours most plainly; so it is here with bushes, rocks, hills, woods, fields, meadows, and districts near and in the distance. They wished to show us even Basle in the horizon; that we saw it, I will not swear: but the remote blue of the Swiss mountains even here exercised its rights over us, by summoning us to itself, and, since we could not follow the impulse, by leaving a painful feeling.

[1] By this *daughter* he means Ottilie in the "Elective Affinities." — TRANS.

To such distractions and cheerful recreations I abandoned myself the more readily, and even with a degree of intoxication, because my passionate connection with Frederica now began to trouble me. Such a youthful affection cherished at random may be compared to a bombshell thrown at night, which rises with a soft, brilliant track, mingles with the stars, nay, for a moment, seems to pause among them, then, in descending, describes the same path in the reverse direction, and at last brings destruction to the place where it has terminated its course. Frederica always remained equal to herself: she seemed not to think, nor to wish to think, that the connection would so soon terminate. Olivia, on the contrary, who indeed also missed me with regret, but nevertheless did not lose so much as the other, had more foresight, or was more open. She often spoke to me about my probable departure, and sought to console herself, both on her own and her sister's account. A girl who renounces a man to whom she has not denied her affections is far from being in that painful situation in which a youth finds himself who has gone so far in his declarations to a lady. He always plays a pitiful part; since a certain survey of his situation is expected of him as a growing man, and a decided levity does not suit him. The reasons of a girl who draws back always seem sufficient, those of a man — never.

But how should a flattering passion allow us to foresee whither it may lead us? For, even when we have quite sensibly renounced it, we cannot get rid of it: we take pleasure in the charming habit, even if this is to be in an altered manner. Thus it was with me. Although the presence of Frederica pained me, I knew of nothing more pleasant than to think of her while absent, and to converse with her. I went to see her less frequently, but our correspondence became so much the more animated. She knew how to bring before me her situation with cheerfulness, her feelings with grace; and I called her merits to mind with fervour and with passion. Absence made me free, and my whole affection first truly bloomed by this communication in the distance. At such moments I could quite blind myself as to the future, and was sufficiently distracted by the progress of time and of pressing business. I had hitherto made it possible to do the most various things by always taking a lively interest in what was present, and belonged to the immediate moment; but, toward the end, all became too much crowded together, as is always the case when one is to free one's self from a place.

One more event, which happened in an interval, took up the last days. I happened to be in respectable company at a country-house, whence there was a noble view of the front of the minster, and the tower which rises over it. "It is a pity," said some one, "that the whole was not finished, and that we have only one tower." "It is just as unpleasant to me," answered I, "to see this one tower not quite completed, for the four volutes leave off much too bluntly: there should have been upon them four light spires, with a higher one in the middle where the clumsy cross is standing."

When I had expressed this strong opinion with my accustomed animation, a little lively man addressed me, and asked, "Who told you so?" "The tower itself," I replied: "I have observed it so long and so attentively, and have shown it so much affection, that it at last resolved to make me this open confession." "It has not misinformed you," answered he: "I am the best judge of that, for I am the person officially placed over the public edifices. We still have among our archives the original sketches, which say the same thing, and which I can show to you." On account of my speedy departure I pressed him to show me this kindness as speedily as possible. He let me see the precious rolls: I soon, with the help of oiled paper, drew the spires, which were wanting in the building as executed, and regretted that I had not been sooner informed of this treasure. But this was always to be the case with me, that, by looking at things and considering them, I should first attain a conception, which perhaps would not have been so striking and so fruitful if it had been given ready made.

Amid all this pressure and confusion I could not forego seeing Frederica once more. Those were painful days, the memory of which has not remained with me. When I reached her my hand from my horse, the tears stood in her eyes; and I felt very uneasy. I now rode along the foot-path toward Drusenheim, and here one of the most singular forebodings took possession of me. I saw, not with the eyes of the body, but with those of the mind, my own figure coming toward me, on horseback, and on the same road, attired in a dress which I had never worn, — it was pike-gray (*hecht-grau*), with somewhat of gold. As soon as I shook myself out of this dream, the figure had entirely disappeared. It is strange, however, that, eight years afterward, I found myself on the very road, to pay one more visit to Frederica, in the dress of which I had dreamed, and which I wore, not from choice, but by accident. However it may be with matters of this kind generally, this strange illusion in some measure calmed me at the moment of parting. The pain of quitting for ever noble Alsace, with all I had gained in it, was softened; and, having at last escaped the excitement of a farewell, I, on a peaceful and quiet journey, pretty well regained my self-possession.

Arrived at Mannheim, I hastened with great eagerness to see the hall of antiquities, of which a great boast was made. Even at Leipzig, on the occasion of Winckelmann's and Lessing's writings, I had heard much said of those important works of art, but so much the less had I seen them : for except Laocoon, the father, and the Faun with the crotola, there were no casts in the academy ; and whatever Oeser chose to say to us on the subject of those works was enigmatical enough. How can a conception of the end of art be given to beginners?

Director Verschaffel's reception was kind. I was conducted to the saloon by one of his associates, who, after he had opened it for me, left me to my own inclinations and reflections. Here I now stood, open to the most wonderful impressions, in a spacious, four-cornered, and, with its extraordinary height, almost cubical, saloon, in a space well lighted from above by the windows under the cornice ; with the noblest statues of antiquity, not only ranged along the walls, but also set up one with another over the whole area, — a forest of statues, through which one was forced to wind ; a great, ideal, popular assembly, through which one was forced to press. All these noble figures could, by opening and closing the curtains, be placed in the most advantageous light ; and, besides this, they were movable on their pedestals, and could be turned about at pleasure.

After I had for a time sustained the first impression of this irresistible mass, I turned to those figures which attracted me the most ; and who can deny that the Apollo Belvidere, with his well-proportioned colossal stature, his slender build, his free movement, his conquering glance, carried off the victory over our feelings in preference to all the others? I then turned to Laocoon, whom I here saw for the first time in connection with his sons. I brought to mind, as well as possible, the discussions and contests which had been held concerning him, and tried to get a point of view of my own ; but I was now drawn this way, now that. The dying gladiator long held me fast ; but the group of Castor and Pollux, that precious though problematical relic, I had especially to thank for my happiest moments. I did not know how impossible it was at once to account to one's self for a sight affording enjoyment. I forced myself to reflect; and, little as I succeeded in attaining any sort of clearness, I felt that every individual figure from this great assembled mass was comprehensible, that every object was natural and significant in itself.

Nevertheless my chief attention was directed to Laocoon; and I decided for myself the famous question, why he did not shriek, by declaring to myself that he could not shriek. All the actions and movements of the three figures proceeded, according to my view, from the first conception of the group. The whole position — as forcible as artistical — of the chief body was composed with reference to two impulses, — the struggle against the snakes, and the flight from the momentary bite. To soften this pain, the abdomen must be drawn in, and shrieking rendered impossible. Thus I also decided that the younger son was not bitten, and in other respects sought to elicit the artistical merits of this group. I wrote a letter on the subject to Oeser, who, however, did not show any special esteem for my interpretation, but only replied to my good will with general terms of encouragement. I was, however, fortunate enough to retain that thought, and to allow it to repose in me for several years, until it was at last annexed to the whole body of my experiences and convictions, in which sense I afterward gave it in editing my " Propylæa."

After a zealous contemplation of so many sublime plastic works, I was not to want a foretaste of antique architecture. I found the cast of a capital of the Rotunda, and do not deny, that at the sight of those acanthus leaves, as huge as they were elegant, my faith in the Northern architecture began somewhat to waver.

This early sight, although so great and so effective

throughout my whole life, was nevertheless attended with but small results in the time immediately following. I could have wished much rather to begin a book, instead of ending one, with describing it; for no sooner was the door of the noble saloon closed behind me than I wished to recover myself again, — nay, I endeavoured to remove those forms, as being burdensome, from my memory: and it was only by a long, circuitous route that I was brought back into this sphere. However, the quiet fruitfulness of such impressions as are received with enjoyment, and without dissecting judgment, is quite invaluable. Youth is capable of this highest happiness, if it will not be critical, but allows the excellent and the good to act upon it without investigation and discrimination.

TWELFTH BOOK.

THE wanderer had now at last reached home, — more healthy and cheerful than on the first occasion, but still in his whole being there appeared something overstrained, which did not fully indicate mental health. At the very first I put my mother into such a position, that, between my father's sincere spirit of order and my own various eccentricities, she was forced to occupy herself with bringing passing events into a certain medium. At Mayence a boy playing the harp had so well pleased me, that, as the fair was close at hand, I invited him to Frankfort, and promised to give him lodging and to encourage him. In this occurrence appeared once more that peculiarity which has cost me so much in my lifetime; namely, that I liked to see younger people gather around me, and attach themselves to me, by which, indeed, I am at last encumbered with their fate. One unpleasant experience after another could not reclaim me from this innate impulse, which, even at present, and in spite of the clearest conviction, threatens from time to time to lead me astray. My mother, being more clear-sighted than I, plainly foresaw how strange it would seem to my father, if a musical fair-vagabond went from such a respectable house to taverns and drinking-houses to earn his bread. Hence she found him with board and lodging in the neighbourhood. I recommended him to my friends, and thus the lad did not fare badly. After several years I saw him again, when he had grown taller and more clumsy, without having ad-

vanced much in his art. The good lady, well contented
with this first attempt at squaring and hushing up,
did not think that this art would immediately become
completely necessary to her. My father, leading a
contented life amid his old tastes and occupations, was
comfortable, like one, who, in spite of all hinderances
and delays, carries out his plans. I had now gained
my degree, and the first step to the further graduating
course of citizen-life was taken. My "Disputation"
had obtained his applause: a further examination of it,
and many a preparation for a future edition, gave him
occupation. During my residence in Alsace, I had
written many little poems, essays, notes on travel, and
several loose sheets. He found amusement in bringing
these under heads, in arranging them, and in devising
their completion, and was delighted with the expectation that my hitherto insuperable dislike to see any of
these things printed would soon cease. My sister had
collected around her a circle of intelligent and amiable
women. Without being domineering, she domineered
over all, as her good understanding could overlook
much, and her good will could often accommodate
matters; moreover, she was in the position of playing
the confidant rather than the rival. Of my older
friends and companions, I found in Horn the unalter-
ably true friend and cheerful associate. I also became
intimate with Riese, who did not fail to practise and
try my acuteness by opposing, with a persevering contradiction, doubt and negation to a dogmatic enthusiasm
into which I too readily fell. Others by degrees entered into this circle, whom I shall afterward mention;
but, among the persons who rendered my new residence in my native city pleasant and profitable, the
brothers Schlosser certainly stood at the head. The
elder, Hieronymus, a profound and elegant jurist, enjoyed universal confidence as counsellor. His favourite
abode was amongst his books and papers, in rooms

where the greatest order prevailed: there I have never found him otherwise than cheerful and sympathising. In a more numerous society, too, he showed himself agreeable and entertaining; for his mind, by extensive reading, was adorned with all the beauty of antiquity. He did not, on occasion, disdain to increase the social pleasures by agreeable Latin poems; and I still possess several sportive distiches which he wrote under some portraits drawn by me of strange and generally known Frankfort caricatures. Often I consulted with him as to the course of life and business I was now commencing; and, if an hundredfold inclinations and passions had not torn me from this path, he would have been my surest guide.

Nearer to me, in point of age, was his brother George, who had again returned from Treptow, from the service of the Duke Eugene of Würtemberg. While he had advanced in knowledge of the world and in practical talent, he had not remained behindhand in a survey of German and foreign literature. He liked, as before, to write in all languages, but did not further excite me in this respect, as I devoted myself exclusively to German, and only cultivated other languages so far as to enable me, in some measure, to read the best authors in the original. His honesty showed itself the same as ever; nay, his acquaintance with the world may have occasioned him to adhere with more severity and even obstinacy to his well-meaning views.

Through these two friends, I very soon became acquainted with Merck, to whom I had not been unfavourably announced by Herder, from Strasburg. This strange man, who had the greatest influence on my life, was a native of Darmstadt. Of his early education I can say but little. After finishing his studies, he conducted a young man to Switzerland, where he remained for some time, and came back married. When I made his acquaintance, he was military paymaster at Darmstadt. Born with mind and understanding, he had acquired much elegant knowledge, especially in modern literature, and had paid attention to all times and places in the history of the world and of man. He had the talent of judging with certainty and acuteness. He was prized as a thorough, resolute man of business, and a ready accountant. With ease he gained an entrance everywhere, as a very pleasant companion for those to whom he had not rendered himself formidable by sarcasms. His figure was long and lean; a sharp, prominent nose was remarkable; light blue, perhaps gray, eyes gave something tiger-like to his glance, which wandered attentively here and there. Lavater's "Physiognomy" has preserved his profile for us. In his character there was a wonderful contradiction. By nature a good, noble, upright man, he had embittered himself against the world, and allowed this morbid whim to sway him to such a degree, that he felt an irresistible inclination to be wilfully a rogue, or even a villain. Sensible, quiet, kind at one moment, he would the next, — just as a snail puts out his horns, — take it into his head to do something which might hurt, wound, or even injure, another. Yet, as one readily associates with something dangerous when one believes one's self safe from it, I felt so much the greater inclination to live with him, and to enjoy his good qualities, since a confident feeling allowed me to suspect that he would not turn his bad side toward me. While now, by this morally restless mind, by this necessity of treating men in a malignant and spiteful way, he on one side destroyed social life, another disquiet, which also he very carefully fostered within himself, opposed his internal comfort; namely, he felt a certain *dilettantish* impulse to production, in which he indulged the more readily, as he expressed himself easily and happily in prose and verse, and might well venture to play a part among the *beaux-esprits* of the time. I myself still possess poetical epistles full of uncommon boldness, force, and Swift-like gall, which are highly remarkable from their original views of persons and things, but are at the same time written with such wounding power, that I could not publish them, even at present, but must either destroy them, or preserve them for posterity as striking documents of the secret discord in our literature. However, the fact, that in all his labours he went to work negatively and destructively, was unpleasant to himself; and he often declared that he envied me that innocent love of setting forth a subject which arose from the pleasure I took, both in the original and the imitation.

For the rest, his literary *dilettantism* would have been rather useful than injurious to him, if he had not felt an irresistible impulse to enter also into the technical and mercantile department. For when he once began to curse his faculties, and was beside himself that he could not, with sufficient genius, satisfy his claims to a practical talent, he gave up now plastic art, now poetry, and thought of mercantile and manufacturing undertakings, which were to bring in money while they afforded him amusement.

In Darmstadt there was, besides, a society of very cultivated men. Privy Councillor von Hesse, Minister of the Landgrave, Professor Petersen, Rector Wenck, and others, were the naturalised persons whose worth attracted by turns many neighbours from other parts, and many travellers through the city. The wife of the privy councillor and her sister, Demoiselle Flachsland, were ladies of uncommon merit and talents; the latter, who was betrothed to Herder, being doubly interesting from her own qualities, and her attachment to so excellent a man.

How much I was animated and advanced by this circle is not to be expressed. They liked to hear me read to them my works, either completed or begun:

they encouraged me, when I openly and circumstantially told what I was then planning, and blamed me when on every new occasion I laid aside what I had already commenced. " Faust " had already advanced; " Götz von Berlichingen " was gradually building itself up in my mind; the studies of the fifteenth and sixteenth centuries occupied me; and the minster had left in me a very serious impression, which could well stand as a background to such poetical inventions.

What I had thought and imagined with respect to that style of architecture, I wrote in a connected form. The first point on which I insisted was, that it should be called German, and not Gothic; that it should be considered not foreign, but native. The second point was, that it could not be compared with the architecture of the Greeks and Romans, because it sprang from quite another principle. If these, living under a more favourable sky, allowed their roof to rest upon columns, a wall, broken through, arose of its own accord. We, however, who must always protect ourselves against the weather, and everywhere surround ourselves with walls, have to revere the genius who discovered the means of endowing massive walls with variety, of apparently breaking them through, and of thus occupying the eye in a worthy and pleasing manner on the broad surface. The same principle applied to the steeples, which are not, like cupolas, to form a heaven within, but to strive toward heaven without, and to announce to the countries far around the existence of the sanctuary which lies at their base. The interior of these venerable piles I only ventured to touch by poetical contemplation and a pious tone.

If I had been pleased to write down these views, the value of which I will not deny, clearly and distinctly, in an intelligible style, the paper, " On German Architecture, *I : M :* Ervini a Steinbach," would then, when I published it, have produced more effect, and would sooner have drawn the attention of the native friends of art. But, misled by the example of Herder and Hamann, I obscured these very simple thoughts and observations by a dusty cloud of words and phrases, and, both for myself and others, darkened the light which had arisen within me. However, the paper was well received, and reprinted in Herder's work on German manner and art.

Whereas, partly from inclination, partly with poetical and other views, I very readily occupied myself with the antiquities of my country, and sought to render them present to my mind, I was from time to time distracted from this subject by Biblical studies and religious sympathies; since Luther's life and deeds, which shine forth so magnificently in the sixteenth century, always necessarily brought me back to the Holy Scriptures, and to the observation of religious feelings and opinions. To look upon the Bible as a work of compilation, which had gradually arisen, and had been elaborated at different times, was flattering to my little self-conceit, since this view was then by no means predominant, — much less was it received in the circle in which I lived. With respect to the chief sense, I adhered to Luther's expression: in matters of detail, I went to Schmidt's literal translation, and sought to use my little Hebrew as well as possible. That there are contradictions in the Bible, no one will now deny. These they tried to reconcile by laying down the plainest passage as a foundation, and endeavouring to assimilate to that those that were contradictory and less clear. I, on the contrary, wished to find out, by examination, what passage best expressed the sense of the matter. To this I adhered, and rejected the rest as interpolated.

For a fundamental opinion had already confirmed itself in me, without my being able to say whether it had been imparted to me, or had been excited in me, or had arisen from my own reflection. It was this: that in anything which is handed down to us, especially in writing, the real point is the ground, the interior, the sense, the tendency of the work; that here lies the original, the divine, the effective, the intact, the indestructible; and that no time, no external operation or condition, can in any degree affect this internal primeval nature, at least no more than the sickness of the body affects a well-cultivated soul. Thus, according to my view, the language, the dialect, the peculiarity, the style, and finally the writing, were to be regarded as the body of every work of mind; this body, although nearly enough akin to the internal, was yet exposed to deterioration and corruption; as, indeed, altogether no tradition can be given quite pure, according to its nature; nor indeed, if one were given pure, could it be perfectly intelligible at every following period, — the former on account of the insufficiency of the organs through which the tradition is made; the latter on account of the difference of time and place, but especially the diversity of human capacities and modes of thought; for which reason the interpreters themselves never agree.

Hence it is everybody's duty to inquire into what is internal and peculiar in a book which particularly interests us, and at the same time, above all things, to weigh in what relation it stands to our own inner nature, and how far, by that vitality, our own is excited and rendered fruitful. On the other hand, everything external that is ineffective with respect to ourselves, or is subject to a doubt, is to be consigned over to criticism, which, even if it should be able to dislocate and dismember the whole, would never succeed in depriving us of the only ground to which we hold fast, nor even in perplexing us for a moment with respect to our once-formed confidence.

This conviction, sprung from faith and sight, which

in all cases that we recognise as the most important, is applicable and strengthening, lies at the fountain of the moral as well as the literary edifice of my life, and is to be regarded as a well-invested and richly productive capital; although in particular cases we may be seduced into making an erroneous application. By this notion, the Bible first became really accessible to me. I had, as is the case in the religious instruction of Protestants, run through it several times, — nay, had made myself acquainted with it, by way of leaps from beginning to end and back again. The blunt naturalness of the Old Testament, and the tender *naïveté* of the New, had attracted me in particular instances: as a whole, indeed, it never properly appealed to me; but now the diverse characters of the different books no more perplexed me; I knew how to represent to myself their significance faithfully and in proper order, and had too much feeling for the book to be ever able to do without it. By this very side of feeling I was protected against all scoffing, because I saw its dishonesty at once. I not only detested it, but could even fall in a rage about it; and I still perfectly remember, that, in my childishly fanatical zeal, I should have completely throttled Voltaire, on account of his "Saul," if I could only have got at him. On the other hand, every kind of honest investigation pleased me greatly: the revelations as to the locality, and costume of the East, which diffused more and more light, I received with joy, and continued to exercise all my acuteness on such valuable traditions.

It is known, that, at an earlier period, I tried to initiate myself into the situation of the world, as described to us by the first book of Moses. As I now thought to proceed stepwise, and in proper order, I seized, after a long interruption, on the second book. But what a difference! Just as the fulness of childhood had vanished from my life, so did I find the second book separated from the first by a monstrous chasm. The utter forgetfulness of a bygone time is already expressed in the few important words, " Now there arose a new king over Egypt, which knew not Joseph." But the people also, innumerable as the stars of heaven, had almost forgotten the ancestor to whom, under the starry heaven, Jehovah had made the very promise which was now fulfilled. I worked through the five books with unspeakable trouble and insufficient means and powers, and in doing this fell upon the strangest notions. I thought I had discovered that it was not our Ten Commandments which stood upon the tables; that the Israelites did not wander through the desert for forty years, but only for a short time; and thus I fancied that I could give entirely new revelations as to the character of Moses.

Even the New Testament was not safe from my inquiries; with my passion for dissection, I did not spare it: but, with love and affection, I chimed in with that wholesome word, " The evangelists may contradict each other, provided only the gospel does not contradict itself." In this region also, I thought I should make all sorts of discoveries. That gift of tongues imparted at Pentecost with lustre and clearness, I interpreted for myself in a somewhat abstruse manner, not adapted to procure many adherents.

Into one of the chief Lutheran doctrines, which has been still more sharpened by the Hernhutters, — namely, that of regarding the sinful principle as predominant in man, — I endeavoured to accommodate myself, but without remarkable success. Nevertheless, I had made the terminology of this doctrine tolerably my own, and made use of it in a letter, which, in the character of country pastor, I was pleased to send to a new brother in office. However, the chief theme in the paper was that watchword of the time, called "Toleration," which prevailed among the better order of brains and minds.

Such things, which were produced by degrees, I had printed at my own cost in the following year, to try myself with the public; made presents of them, or sent them to Eichenberg's shop, in order to get rid of them as fast as possible without deriving any profit myself. Here and there a review mentions them, now favourably, now unfavourably; but they soon passed away. My father kept them carefully in his archives, otherwise I should not have possessed a copy of them. I shall add these, as well as some things of the kind which I have found, to the new edition of my works.

Since I had really been seduced into the sybilline style of such papers, as well as into the publication of them, by Hamann, this seems to me a proper place to make mention of this worthy and influential man, who was then as great a mystery to us as he has always remained to his native country. His " Socratic Memorabilia" was more especially liked by those persons who could not adapt themselves to the dazzling spirit of the time. It was suspected that he was a profound, well-grounded man, who, accurately acquainted with the public world and with literature, allowed of something mysterious and unfathomable, and expressed himself on this subject in a manner quite his own. By those who then ruled the literature of the day, he was indeed considered an abstruse mystic; but an aspiring youth suffered themselves to be attracted by him. Even the " Quiet-in-the-lands," as they were called, — half in jest, half in earnest, — those pious souls, who, without professing themselves members of any society, formed an invisible church, — turned their attention to him; while to my friend Fräulein von Klettenberg, and no less to her friend Moser, the "Magus from the North" was a welcome apparition. People ·put themselves the more in connection with him, when they had learned that he was tormented by narrow domestic circumstances, but nevertheless understood how to maintain this beautiful and lofty mode of thought. With the great influence of President von Moser, it would have been easy to provide a tolerable and convenient existence for such a frugal man. The matter was set on foot; nay, so good an understanding and mutual approval was attained, that Hamann undertook the long journey from Königsberg to Darmstadt. But, as the president happened to be absent, that odd man, no one knows on what account, returned at once; though a friendly correspondence was kept up. I still possess two letters from the Köngisberger to his patron, which bear testimony to the wondrous greatness and sincerity of their author.

But so good an understanding was not to last long. These pious men had thought the other one pious in their own fashion: they had treated him with reverence as the "Magus of the North," and thought that he would continue to exhibit himself with a reverend demeanour. But already in the "Clouds," an after-piece of "Socratic Memorabilia," he had given some offence; and when he now published the "Crusades of a Philologist," — on the title-page of which was to be seen, not only the goat-profile of a horned Pan, but also, on one of the first pages, a large cock, cut in wood, and setting time to some young cockerels, who stood before him with notes in their claws, made an exceedingly ridiculous appearance, by which certain church music, of which the author did not approve, was to be made a laughing-stock, — there rose among well minded and sensitive people a dissatisfaction, which was exhibited to the author, who, not being edified by it, shunned a closer connection. Our interest in this man was, however, always kept alive by Herder, who, remaining in correspondence with us and his betrothed, communicated to us at once all that proceeded from that extraordinary man. To these belonged his critiques and notices, inserted in the *Königsberg Zeitung*, all of which bore a very singular character. I possess an almost complete collection of his works, and a very important essay on Herder's prize paper concerning the origin of language, in which, in the most peculiar manner, he throws flashes of light upon this specimen of Herder.

I do not give up the hope of superintending myself, or at least furthering, an edition of Hamann's works; and then, when these documents are again before the public, it will be time to speak more closely of the author, his nature and character. In the meantime, however, I will here adduce something concerning him, especially as eminent men are still living who felt a great regard for him, and whose assent or correction will be very welcome to me. The principle to which all Hamann's expressions may be referred is this: " All that man undertakes to perform, whether by deed, by word, or otherwise, must proceed from all his powers united: everything isolated is worthless." A noble maxim, but hard to follow. To life and art it may indeed be applied: but in every communication by words, that is not exactly poetic, there is, on the contrary, a grand difficulty; for a word must sever itself, isolate itself, in order to say or signify anything. Man, while he speaks, must, for the moment, become one-sided: there is no communication, no instruction, without severing. Now, since Hamann, once for all, opposed this separation, and because he felt, imagined, and thought in unity, chose to speak in unity likewise, and to require the same of others, he came into opposition with his own style, and with all that others produced. To produce the impossible, he therefore grasps at every element: the deepest and most mystical contemplations in which nature and mind meet each other, — illuminating flashes of the understanding which beam forth from such a contact, significant images which float in these regions, forcible aphorisms from sacred and profane writers, with whatever else of a humourous kind could be added, — all this forms the wondrous aggregate of his style and his communications. Now, although one cannot join him in his depths, cannot wander with him on his heights, cannot master the forms which float before him, cannot from an infinitely extended literature exactly find out the sense of a passage which is only hinted at, we find, that, the more we study him, the more dim and dark it becomes; and this darkness always increases with years, because his allusions were directed to certain definite peculiarities which prevailed for the moment in life and in literature. In my collection there are some of his printed sheets, where he has cited with his own hand, in the margin, the passages to which his hints refer. If one opens them, there is again a sort of equivocal double light, which appears to us highly agreeable: only one must completely renounce what is ordinarily called understanding. Such leaves merit to be called sybilline, for this reason: that one cannot consider them in and for themselves, but must wait for an opportunity to seek refuge with their oracles. Every time that one opens them, one fancies one has found something new; because the sense which abides in every passage touches and excites us in a curious manner.

I never saw him, nor did I hold any immediate communication with him by correspondence. It seems to me that he was extremely clear in the relations of life and friendship, and that he had a correct feeling for the positions of persons among each other, and with reference to himself. Whatever letters of his I saw were excellent, and much plainer than his works, because here the reference to time, circumstances, and personal affairs was more clearly prominent. I thought, however, that I could discern this much generally, that he, feeling the superiority of his mental gifts, in the most naïve manner, always considered himself somewhat wiser and more shrewd than his correspondents, whom he treated rather ironically than heartily. If this held good only of single cases, it applied to the majority, as far as my own observation went, and was the cause that I never felt a desire to approach him.

On the other hand, a kindly literary communication between Herder and us was maintained with great vivacity; though it was a pity that he could not keep himself quiet. But Herder never left off his teasing and scolding; and much was not required to irritate Merck, who also contrived to excite me to impatience. Because Herder, among all authors and men, seemed to respect Swift most, he was among us called the "Dean;" and this gave further occasion to all sorts of perplexities and annoyances.

Nevertheless, we were highly pleased when we learned that he was to have an appointment at Bückeburg, which would bring him double honour; for his new patron had the highest fame as a clear-headed and brave, though eccentric, man. Thomas Abbt had been known and celebrated in this service: his country still mourned his death, and was pleased with the monument which his patron had erected for him. Now Herder, in the place of the untimely deceased, was to fulfil all those hopes which his predecessor had so worthily excited.

The epoch in which this happened gave a double brilliancy and value to such an appointment; for several German princes already followed the example of the Count of Lippe, inasmuch as they took into their service, not merely learned men, and men of business, properly so called, but also persons of mind and promise. Thus, it was said, Klopstock had been invited by the Margrave Charles of Baden, not for real business, but that by his presence he might impart a grace and be useful to the higher society. As now the regard felt for this excellent prince, who paid attention to all that was useful and beautiful, increased in consequence; so also was the veneration for Klopstock not a little heightened. Everything that emanated from him was held dear and valuable, and we carefully wrote down his odes and elegies as we could get them. We were therefore highly delighted when the great Landgravine Caroline of Hesse-Darmstadt made a collection of them; and we obtained possession of one of the few copies, which enabled us to complete our own manuscript collection. Hence those first readings have long been most in favour with us, — nay, we have often refreshèd and delighted ourselves with poems which the author afterward rejected. So true it is, that the life which presses forth out of a "fine soul" works with the greater freedom the less it appears to be drawn by criticism into the department of art.

Klopstock, by his character and conduct, had managed to attain regard and dignity, both for himself and for other men of talent; now they were also, if possible, to be indebted to him for the security and improvement of their domestic condition. For the book trade, in the previous period, had more to do with important scientific books, belonging to the different faculties — with stock works, for which a moderate remuneration was paid. But the production of poetical works was looked upon as something sacred, and in this case the acceptance or increase of any remuneration would have been regarded almost as simony. Authors and publishers stood in the strangest reciprocal position. Both appeared, accordingly as it was taken, as patrons and clients. The authors, who, irrespectively of their talent, were generally respected and revered by the public as highly moral men, had a mental rank, and felt themselves rewarded by the success of their labours: the publishers were well satisfied with the second place, and enjoyed a considerable profit. But now opulence again set the rich bookseller above the poor poet, and thus everything stood in the most beautiful equilibrium. Magnanimity and gratitude were not unfrequent on either side. Breitkopf and Gottsched lived, all their lives, as inmates of the same house. Stinginess and meanness, especially that of piracy, were not yet in vogue.

Nevertheless, a general commotion had arisen among the German authors. They compared their own very moderate, if not poor, condition, with the wealth of the eminent booksellers: they considered how great was the fame of a Gellert, of a Rabener, and in what narrow domestic circumstances a universally esteemed German poet must struggle on, if he did not render life easy by some other calling. Even the mediocre and lesser minds felt a strong desire to see their situation improved, — to make themselves free of the publishers.

Now Klopstock came forward, and offered his " Republic of Letters " (" Gelehrten-Republik ") for subscription. Although the latter cantos of " The Messiah," partly on account of their subject, partly on account of the treatment, could not produce the same effect as the earlier ones, which, themselves pure and innocent, came into a pure and innocent time, the same respect was always maintained for the poet, who, by the publication of his odes, had drawn to himself the hearts, minds, and feelings of many persons. Many well-thinking men, among whom were several of great influence, offered to secure payment beforehand. This was fixed at a *louis d'or*, the object being, it was said, not so much to pay for the book, as on this occasion to reward the author for his services to his country. Now every one pressed forward : even youths and young girls, who had not much to expend, opened their saving-boxes; men and women, the higher and the middle classes, contributed to this holy offering; and perhaps a thousand subscribers, all paying in advance, were collected. Expectation was raised to the highest pitch, and confidence was as great as possible.

After this, the work, on its appearance, was to experience the strangest result in the world: it was, indeed, of important value, but by no means universally interesting. Klopstock's thoughts on poetry and literature were set forth in the form of an old German druidical republic: his maxims on the true and false were expressed in pithy, laconic aphorisms, in which, however, much that was instructive was sacrificed to the singularity of form. For authors and *littérateurs*, the book was and is invaluable; but it was only in this circle that it could be useful and effective. Whoever had himself been thinking followed the thinker; he who knew how to seek and prize what was genuine, found himself instructed by the profound, honest man; but the amateur, the general reader, was not enlightened, — to him the book remained sealed; and yet it had been placed in all hands; and, while every one expected a perfectly serviceable work, most of them obtained one from which they could not get the smallest taste. The astonishment was general; but the esteem for the man was so great, that no grumbling, scarcely a murmur, arose. The young and beautiful part of the world got over their loss, and now freely gave away the copies they had so dearly purchased. I received several from kind female friends, but none of them have remained with me.

This undertaking, which was successful to the author, but a failure to the public, had the ill consequence, that there was now no further thought about subscriptions and prepayments; nevertheless, the wish had been too generally diffused for the attempt not to be renewed. The Dessau publishing-house now offered to do this on a large scale. Learned men and publishers were here, by a close compact, to enjoy, both in a certain proportion, the hoped-for advantage. The necessity, so long painfully felt, again awakened a great confidence; but this could not last long : and, after a brief endeavour, the parties separated, with a loss on both sides.

However, a speedy communication among the friends of literature was already introduced. The *Musenal-manache* [1] united all the young poets with each other : the journals united the poet with other authors. The pleasure I found in production was boundless; to what I had produced I remained indifferent; only when, in social circles, I made it present to myself and others, my affection for it was renewed. Moreover, many persons took an interest in both my larger and smaller works, because I urgently pressed every one who felt in any degree inclined and adapted to production, to produce something independently, after his own fashion, and was, in turn, challenged by all to new poetising and writing. These mutual impulses, which were carried even to an extreme, gave every one a happy influence in his own fashion : and from this whirling and working, this living and letting-live, this taking and giving, which was carried on by so many youths, from their own free hearts, without any theoretical guiding-star, according to the innate character of each, and without any special design, arose that famed, extolled, and decried epoch in literature, when a mass of young, genial men, with all that audacity and assumption such as are peculiar to their own period of youth, produced, by the application of their powers, much that was good, and, by the abuse of these, much ill-feeling and mischief; and it is, indeed, the action and reaction which proceeded from this source, that form the chief theme of this volume.

[1] Annual publications devoted to poetry only. — TRANS.

In what can young people take the highest interest, how are they to excite interest among those of their own age, if they are not animated by love, and if affairs of the heart, of whatever kind they may be, are not living within them? I had in secret to complain of a love I had lost : this made me mild and tolerant, and more agreeable to society than in those brilliant times when nothing reminded me of a want or a fault, and I went storming along completely without restraint.

Frederica's answer to my farewell letter rent my heart. It was the same hand, the same tone of thought, the same feeling, which had formed itself for me and by me. I now, for the first time, felt the loss which she suffered, and saw no means to supply it, or even to alleviate it. She was completely present to me; I always felt that she was wanting to me; and, what was worst of all, I could not forgive myself for my own misfortune. Gretchen had been taken away from me; Annette had left me; now, for the first time, I was guilty. I had wounded the most lovely heart to its very depths; and the period of a gloomy repentance, with the absence of a refreshing love, to which I had grown accustomed, was most agonising, nay, insupportable. But man wishes to live, and hence I took an honest interest in others : I sought to disentangle their embarrassments, and to unite what was about to part, that they might not have the same lot as myself. They were hence accustomed to call me the " confidant," and, on account of wandering about the district, the " wanderer." For producing that peace of mind, which I felt beneath the open sky, in the valleys, on the heights, in the fields and in the woods, the situation of Frankfort was serviceable, as it lay in the middle between Darmstadt and Hamborg, two pleasant places, which are on good terms with each other, through the relationship of both courts. I accustomed myself to live on the road, and, like a

messenger, to wander about between the mountains
and the flat country. Often I went alone, or in company, through my native city, as if it did not at all
concern me, dined at one of the great inns in the High
Street, and, after dinner, went farther on my way.
More than ever was I directed to the open world and
to free nature. On my way I sang to myself strange
hymns and dithyrambics, of which one, entitled " The
Wanderer's Storm-song " ("Wanderer's Sturmlied "),
still remains. This half-nonsense I sang aloud, in an
impassioned manner, when I found myself in a terrific
storm, which I was obliged to meet.

My heart was untouched and unoccupied : I consci-
entiously avoided all closer connection with women ;
and thus it remained concealed from me, that, inatten-
tive and unconscious as I was, an amiable spirit was
secretly hovering around me. It was not until many
years afterward, nay, until after her death, that I
learned of her secret, heavenly love, in a manner that
necessarily overwhelmed me. But I was innocent, and
could purely and honestly pity an innocent being ; nay,
I could do this the more, as the discovery occurred at
an epoch when, completely without passion, I had the
happiness of living for myself and my own intellectual inclinations.

At the time when I was pained by my grief at
Frederica's situation, I again, after my old fashion,
sought aid from poetry. I again continued the poetical
confession which I had commenced, that, by this self-
tormenting penance, I might be worthy of an internal
absolution. The two Marias in " Götz von Berlichingen " and " Clavigo," and the two bad characters who
act the parts of their lovers, may have been the results
of such penitent reflections.

But as in youth one soon gets over injuries and
diseases, because a healthy system of organic life can
supplant a sick one, and allow it time to grow healthy

again, corporeal exercises, on many a favourable opportunity, came forward with very advantageous effect;
and I was excited in many ways to man myself afresh,
and to seek new pleasures of life and enjoyments.
Riding gradually took the place of those sauntering,
melancholy, toilsome, and, at the same time, tedious
and aimless rambles on foot: one reached one's end
more quickly, merrily, and commodiously. The young
people again introduced fencing; but in particular, on
the setting in of winter, a new world was revealed
to us, since I at once determined to skate, — an exercise which I had never attempted, — and, in a short
time, by practice, reflection, and perseverance, brought
it as far as was necessary to enjoy with others a gay,
animated course on the ice, without wishing to distinguish myself.

For this new joyous activity we were also indebted
to Klopstock, — to his enthusiasm for this happy
species of motion, which private accounts confirmed,
while his odes gave an undeniable evidence of it. I
still exactly remember, that on a cheerful, frosty morning, I sprang out of bed, and uttered aloud these
passages:

> " Already, glad with feeling of health,
> Far down along the shore, I have whitened
> The covering crystal.

> " How softly winter's growing day
> Lights up the lake, while glittering frost
> Night has upon it spread like stars."

My hesitating and wavering resolution was fixed at
once, and I flew straight to the place where so old a
beginner might with some degree of propriety make
his first trial. And, indeed, this manifestation of our
strength well deserved to be commended by Klopstock;
for it is an exercise which brings us into contact with
the freshest childhood, summons the youth to the full

enjoyment of his suppleness, and is fitted to keep off a stagnant old age. We were immoderately addicted to this pleasure. To pass thus a splendid Sunday on the ice did not satisfy us: we continued our movement late into the night. For as other exertions fatigue the body, so does this give it a constantly new power. The full moon rising from the clouds, over the wide nocturnal meadows, which were frozen into fields of ice; the night-breeze, which rustled toward us on our course; the solemn thunder of the ice, which sank as the water decreased; the strange echo of our own movements, — rendered the scenes of Ossian just present to our minds. Now this friend, now that, uttered an ode of Klopstock's in a declamatory recitative; and, if we found ourselves together at dawn, the unfeigned praise of the author of our joys broke forth:

" And should he not be immortal,
  Who such health and pleasures for us did find,
  As the horse, though bold in his course, never gave,
  And as even the ball is without? "

Such gratitude is earned by a man who knows how to honour and worthily extend an earthly act by spiritual incitement.

And thus, as children of talent, whose mental gifts have, at an early period, been cultivated to an extraordinary degree, return, if they can, to the simplest sports of youth, did we, too, often forget our calling to more serious things. Nevertheless, this very motion, so often carried on in solitude, — this agreeable soaring in undetermined space, — again excited many of my internal wants, which had, for a time, lain dormant; and I have been indebted to such hours for a more speedy elaboration of older plans.

The darker ages of German history had always occupied my desire for knowledge and my imagination. The thought of dramatising " Götz von Berlichingen," with all the circumstances of his time, was one which I much liked and valued. I industriously read the chief authors: to Datt's work, "De Pace Publica," I devoted all my attention; I had sedulously studied it through, and rendered those singular details as visible to me as possible. These endeavours, which were directed to moral and poetical ends, I could also use in another direction; and I was now to visit Wetzlar. I had sufficient historical preparation; for the Imperial Chamber had arisen in consequence of the public tranquillity, and its history could serve as an important clew through the confused events of Germany. Indeed, the constitution of the courts and armies gives the most accurate insight into the constitution of every empire. Even the finances, the influence of which are considered so important, come much less under consideration; for, if the whole is deficient, it is only necessary to take from the individual what he has laboriously scraped together: and thus the state is always sufficiently rich.

What occurred to me at Wetzlar is of no great importance; but it may inspire a greater interest, if the reader will not disdain a cursory history of the Imperial Chamber, in order to render present to his mind the unfavourable moment at which I arrived there.

The lords of the earth are such, principally because they can assemble around them, in war, the bravest and most resolute, and, in peace, the wisest and most just. Even to the state of a German emperor belonged a court of this kind, which always accompanied him in his expeditions through the empire. But neither this precaution, nor the Suabian law, which prevailed in the South of Germany, nor the Saxon law, which prevailed in the North, — neither the judges appointed to maintain them, nor the decisions of the peers of the contending parties, — neither the umpires recognised by agreement, nor friendly compacts instituted by the clergy, — nothing, in short, could quiet that excited chivalric spirit of feuds which had been roused, fostered, and made a custom among the Germans, by internal discord, by foreign campaigns, by the crusades especially, and even by judicial usages. To the emperor as well as to the powerful estates, these squabbles were extremely annoying; while through them, the less powerful became troublesome to each other, and, if they combined, to the great also. All outward strength was paralysed, while internal order was destroyed; and, besides this, a great part of the country was still encumbered with the *Vehmgericht*, of the horrors of which a notion may be formed, if we think that it degenerated into a secret police, which at last even fell into the hands of private persons.

Many attempts to steer against these evils had been made in vain, until at last the estates urgently proposed a court formed from among themselves. This proposal, well-meant as it might have been, nevertheless indicated an extension of the privileges of the estates, and a limitation of the imperial power. Under Frederick III. the matter is delayed: his son Maximilian, being pressed from without, complies. He appoints the chief judge, the estates send the assistants. There were to be four and twenty of them, but at first twelve are thought sufficient.

A universal fault, of which men are guilty in their undertakings, was the first and perpetual fundamental defect of the Imperial Chamber: insufficient means were applied to a great end. The number of the assessors was too small. How was the difficult and extensive problem to be solved by them? But who could urge an efficient arrangement? The emperor could not favour an institution which seemed to work more against him than for him: far more reason had he to complete the formation of his own court, — his own council. If, on the other hand, we regard the interest of the estates, all that they could properly have to do with was the stoppage of bloodshed. Whether the wound was healed, did not so much concern them; and now there was to be, besides, a new expense. It may not have been quite plainly seen, that, by this institution, every prince increased his retinue, for a decided end indeed, — but who readily gives money for what is necessary? Every one would be satisfied if he could have what is useful "for God's sake."

At first the assistants were to live by fees; then followed a moderate grant from the estates: both were scanty. But, to meet the great and striking exigency, willing, clever, and industrious men were found; and the court was established. Whether it was perceived that the question here was concerning only the alleviation and not the cure of the evil, or whether, as in similar cases, the flattering hope was entertained that much was to be done with little, is not to be decided. It is enough that the court served rather as a pretext to punish the originators of mischief, than completely to prevent wrong. But it has scarcely met, than a power grows out of itself: it feels the eminence on which it is placed; it recognises its own great political importance. It now endeavours, by a striking activity, to acquire for itself a more decided respect: they briskly get through what can and must be rapidly despatched, what can be decided at the moment, or what can otherwise be easily judged; and thus, throughout the empire, they appear effective and dignified. On the other hand, matters of weightier import, the lawsuits properly so called, remained behindhand; and this was no misfortune. The only concern of the state is, that possession shall be certain and secure: whether it is also legal, is of less consequence. Hence, from the monstrous and ever-swelling number of delayed suits, no mischief arose to the empire. Against people who employed force, provision was already made, and with such matters could be settled: but those, on the other hand, who legally disputed about possession, lived, enjoyed, or starved, as they could; they died, were ruined, or made it up; but all this was the good or evil of individual families, — the empire was gradually tranquillised. For the Imperial Chamber was endowed with a legal club-law against the disobedient: had it been able to hurl the bolt of excommunication, this would have been more effective.

But now, what with the number of assessors, which was sometimes increased, sometimes diminished; what with the many interruptions; what with the removal of the court from one place to another, — these arrears, these records, necessarily increased to an infinite extent. Now, in the distress of war, a part of the archives was sent for safety from Spire to Aschaffenburg; a part to Worms; the third fell into the hands of the French, who thought they had gained the state-archives, but would afterward have been glad to get rid of such a chaos of paper, if any one would but have furnished the carriages.

During the negotiations for the peace of Westphalia, the chosen men, who were assembled, plainly saw what sort of a lever was required to move from its place a load like that of Sisyphus. Fifty assessors were now to be appointed, but the number was never made up; the half of it was again made to suffice, because the expense appeared too great; but, if the parties interested had all seen their advantage in the matter, the whole might well have been afforded. To pay five and twenty assessors, about one hundred thousand florins (*gulden*) were required, and how easily could double that amount have been raised in Germany! The proposition to endow the Imperial Chamber with confiscated church property could not pass, for how could the two religious parties agree to such a sacrifice? The Catholics were not willing to lose any more; and the Protestants wished to employ what they had gained, each for his own private ends. The division of the empire into two religious parties had here, in several respects, the worst influence. The interest which the estates took in this their court diminished more and more; the more powerful wished to free themselves from the confederation; licenses exempting their possessor from being prosecuted before any higher tribunal were sought with more and more eagerness; the greater kept back with their payments; while the lesser, who, moreover, believed themselves wronged in the estimates, delayed as long as they could.

How difficult was it, therefore, to raise the supplies necessary for payment. Hence arose a new occupation, a new loss of time for the Chamber: previously the so-called annual "visitations" had taken care of this matter. Princes in person, or their councillors, went only for months or weeks to the place of the court, examined the state of the treasury, investigated the arrears, and undertook to get them in. At the same time, if anything was about to create an impediment in the course of law or the court, or any abuse to creep in, they were authorised to provide a remedy. The faults of the institution they were to discover and remove, but it was not till afterward that the investigation and punishment of the personal crimes of its members became a part of their duty. But because parties engaged in litigation always like to extend their hopes a moment longer, and on this account always seek and appeal to higher authorities, so did these "visitators" become a court of revision, from which at first, in determined manifest cases, persons hoped to find restitution, but at last, in all cases, delay and perpetuation of the controversy, to which the appeal to the imperial diet, and the endeavour of the two religious parties, if not to outweigh each other, at any rate to preserve an equilibrium, contributed their part.

But if one considers what this court might have been without such obstacles, without such disturbing and destructive conditions, one cannot imagine it remarkable and important enough. Had it been supplied at the beginning with a sufficient number of persons, had a sufficient support been secured to them, the monstrous influence which this body might have attained, considering the aptness of the Germans, would have been immeasurable. The honourable title of "Amphictyons," which was only bestowed on them oratorically, they would actually have deserved, — nay, they might have elevated themselves into an intermediate power, while revered by the head and the members.

But, far removed from such great effects, the court, excepting for a short time under Charles V. and before the Thirty Years' War, dragged itself miserably along. One often cannot understand how men could be found for such a thankless and melancholy employment. But what a man does every day he puts up with, if he has any talent for it, even if he does not exactly see that anything will come of it. The German, especially, is of this persevering turn of mind; and thus for three hundred years the worthiest men have employed themselves on these labours and objects. A characteristic gallery of such figures would even now excite interest and inspire courage.

For it is just in such anarchical times that the able man takes the strongest position, and he who desires what is good finds himself right in his place. Thus, for instance, the *Directorium* of Fürstenberg was still held in blessed memory; and with the death of this excellent man begins the epoch of many pernicious abuses.

But all these defects, whether later or earlier, arose from one only original source, — the small number of persons. It was decreed that the assistants were to act in a fixed order, and according to a determined arrangement. Every one could know when the turn would come to him, and which of the cases belonging to him it would affect: he could work up to this point, — he could prepare himself. But now the innumerable arrears had heaped themselves up; and they were forced to resolve to select the more important cases, and to deal with them out of order. But, with a pressure of important affairs, the decision as to which matter has the more weight is difficult; and selection leaves room for favour. Now another critical case occurred. The referent tormented both himself and the court with a difficult, involved affair; and at last no one was found willing to take up the judgment. The parties had come to an agreement, had separated, had died, had changed their minds. Hence they resolved to take in hand only the cases of which they were reminded. They wished to be convinced of the continued persistency of the parties, and hence was given an introduction to the greatest defects: for he who commends his affairs must commend them to somebody; and to whom can one commend them better than to him who has them already in his hands? To keep this one regularly secret was impossible; for how could he remain concealed with so many subordinates, all acquainted with the matter? If acceleration is requested, favour may well be requested likewise; for the very fact that people urge their cause shows that they consider it just. This will, perhaps, not be done in a direct manner: certainly it will be first done through subordinates; these must be gained over, and thus an introduction is given to all sorts of intrigues and briberies.

The Emperor Joseph, following his own impulse, and in imitation of Frederick, first directed his attention to arms and the administration of justice. He cast his eyes upon the Imperial Chamber: traditional wrongs, introduced abuses, had not remained unknown to him. Even here something was to be stirred up, shaken, and done. Without inquiring whether it was his imperial right, without foreseeing the possibility of a happy result, he proposed a revival of the "visitation," and hastened its opening. For one hundred and sixty years no regular "visitation" had taken place: a monstrous chaos of papers lay swelled up and increased every year, since the seventeen assessors were not even able to despatch the current business. Twenty thousand cases had been heaped up: sixty could be settled every year, and double that number was brought forward. Besides, it was not a small number of revisions that awaited the "visitators:" they were estimated at fifty thousand. Many other abuses, in addition to this, hindered the course of justice; but the most critical matter of all was the personal delinquency of some assessors, which appeared in the background.

When I was about to go to Wetzlar, the "visitation" had been already for some years in operation, the parties accused had been suspended from office, the investigation had been carried a long way; and, because the masters and commissioners of German political law could not let pass this opportunity of exhibiting their sagacity and devoting it to the common weal, several profound, well-designed works appeared, from which every one who possessed only some preparatory knowledge could derive solid instruction. When, on this occasion, they went back into the constitution of the empire and the books written upon it, it was striking to me how the monstrous condition of this thoroughly diseased body, which was kept alive by a miracle alone, was the very thing that most suited the learned. For the venerable German industry, which was more directed to the collection and development of details than to results, found here an inexhaustible impulse to new employment; and whether the empire was opposed to the emperor, the lesser to the greater estates, or the Catholics to the Protestants, there was necessarily always, according to the diversity of interest, a diversity of opinion, and always an occasion for new contests and controversies.

Since I had rendered all these older and newer circumstances as present to my mind as possible, it was impossible for me to promise myself much pleasure from my abode at Wetzlar. The prospect of finding in a city, which was indeed well situated, but small and ill built, a double world, — first the domestic, old traditional world, then a foreign new one, authorised to scrutinise the other with severity, — a judging and a judged tribunal; many an inhabitant in fear and anxiety, lest he might also be drawn into the impending investigation; persons of consideration, long held in respect, convicted of the most scandalous misdeeds, and marked out for disgraceful punishment, — all this together made the most dismal picture, and could not lure me to go deeper into a business, which, involved in itself, seemed so much perplexed by wrong.

That, excepting the German civil and public law, I should find nothing remarkable in the scientific way, that I should be without all poetical communication, I thought I could foresee, when, after some delay, the desire of altering my situation more than impulse to knowledge led me to this spot. But how surprised I was, when, instead of a crabbed society, a third academical life sprang toward me. At a large *table-d'hôte* I found a number of young, lively people, nearly all subordinates to the commission : they gave me a friendly reception; and the very first day it remained no secret to me, that they had cheered their moon-meetings by a romantic fiction. With much wit and cheerfulness they represented a table of knights. At the top sat the grand master, by his side the chancellor, then the most important officers of the state;

now followed the knights, according to their seniority. Strangers, on the other hand, who visited, were forced to be content with the lowest places; and to these the conversation was almost unintelligible, because the language of the society, in addition to the chivalric expressions, was enriched with many allusions. To every one a name with an epithet was assigned. Me they called "Götz von Berlichingen the honest." The former I earned by the attention to the gallant German patriarch, the latter by my upright affection and devotion for the eminent men with whom I became acquainted. To the Count von Kielmannsegg I was much indebted during this residence. He was the most serious of all, highly clever, and to be relied on. There was Von Goué, a man hard to be deciphered and described, a blunt, kind, quietly reserved Hanoverian figure. He was not wanting in talent of various kinds. It was conjectured concerning him that he was a natural son: he loved, besides, a certain mysterious deportment, and concealed his most peculiar wishes and plans under various eccentricities; as indeed he was, properly speaking, the very soul of the odd confederation of knights, without having striven to attain the post of grand master. On the contrary, when, just at this time, the head of the knighthood departed, he caused another to be elected, and through him exercised his influence. Thus he managed so to direct several little trifles, that they appeared of importance, and could be carried out in mythical forms. But with all this no serious purpose could be remarked in him: he was only concerned to get rid of the tedium which he and his colleagues, during their protracted occupation, necessarily felt, and to fill up the empty space, if only with cobwebs. For the rest, this mythical caricature was carried on with great external seriousness; and no one found it ridiculous if a certain mill was treated as a castle, and the miller as lord of the fortress, if "The Four Sons of

Haimon" was declared a canonical book, and, on the occasion of ceremonies, extracts from it were read with veneration. The dubbing of knights took place with traditional symbols, borrowed from several orders of knighthood. A chief motive for jest was the fact, that what was manifest was treated as a secret: the affair was carried on publicly, and yet nothing was to be said about it. The list of the whole body of knights was printed with as much importance as a calendar of the imperial diet: and if families ventured to scoff at this, and to declare the whole matter absurd and ridiculous, they were punished by an intrigue being carried on until a solemn husband or near relation was induced to join the company and to be dubbed a knight; for then there was a splendid burst of malicious joy at the annoyance of the connections.

Into this chivalric state of existence another strange order had insinuated itself, which was to be philosophical and mystical, and had no name of its own. The first degree was called the " Transition," the second the " Transition's transition," the third the " Transition's transition to the transition," and the fourth the " Transition's transition to the transition's transition." To interpret the high sense of this series of degrees was now the duty of the initiated; and this was done according to the standard of a little printed book, in which these strange words were explained, or rather amplified, in a manner still more strange. Occupation with these things was the most desirable pastime. The folly of Behrisch and the perversity of Lenz seemed here to have united : I only repeat, that not a trace of purpose was to be found behind these veils.

Although I very readily took part in such fooleries, had first brought into order the extracts from " The Four Sons of Haimon," made proposals how they should be read on feasts and solemn occasions, and even understood how to deliver them myself with great emphasis, I had, nevertheless, grown weary of such things before; and therefore, as I missed my Frankfort and Darmstadt circles, I was highly pleased to have found Gotter, who attached himself to me with honest affection, and to whom I showed in return a hearty good will. His turn of mind was delicate, clear, and cheerful; his talents were practised and well regulated; he aimed at French elegance, and was pleased with that part of English literature which is occupied with moral and agreeable subjects. We passed together many pleasant hours, in which we communicated to each other our knowledge, plans, and inclinations. He excited me to many little works, especially as, being in connection with the people of Göttingen, he desired some of my poems for Boie's " Almanach."

I thus came into contact with those, who, young and full of talent, held themselves together, and afterward effected so much and in such various ways. The two Counts Stolberg, Bürger, Voss, Hölty, and others were assembled in faith and spirit around Klopstock, whose influence extended in every direction. In such a poetical circle, which became more and more extended, was developed, at the same time with such manifold poetical merits, another turn of mind, to which I can give no exactly proper name. It might be called the need of independence, which always arises in time of peace, and exactly when, properly speaking, one is not dependent. In war we bear the rude force as well as we can; we feel ourselves physically and economically, but not morally, wounded; the constraint shames no one, and it is no disgraceful service to serve the time; we accustom ourselves to suffer from foes and friends; we have wishes, but no particular views. In peace, on the contrary, man's love of freedom becomes more and more prominent; and the more free one is, the more free one wishes to be. We will not tolerate anything over us; we will not be restrained, no one shall be restrained; and this tender, nay, morbid, feeling, appears in noble souls under the form of justice. This spirit and feeling then showed itself everywhere: and, just because few were oppressed, it was wished to free even these from temporary oppression; and thus arose a certain moral feud, a mixture of individuals with the government, which, with laudable beginnings, led to inevitably unfortunate results.

Voltaire, by the protection which he had bestowed on the family of Calas, had excited great attention and made himself respected. In Germany the attempt of Lavater against the *Landvogt* (sheriff of the province) had been almost more striking and important. The æsthetical feeling, united with youthful courage, strove forward; and as, shortly before, persons had studied to obtain offices, they now began to act as overlookers of those in office: and the time was near when the dramatist and novelist loved best to seek their villains among ministers and official persons. Hence arose a world, half real, half imaginary, of action and reaction, in which we afterward lived to see the most violent imputations and instigations, in which the writers of periodical publications and journals with a sort of passion indulged under the garb of justice, went to work the more irresistibly, as they made the public believe that it was itself the true tribunal, — a foolish notion, as no public has an executive power, and in dismembered Germany public opinion neither benefited nor injured any one.

Among us young people, there was indeed nothing to be traced which could have been culpable; but a certain similar notion, composed of poetry, morality, and a noble striving, and which was harmless but yet fruitless, had taken possession of us.

By his "Hermann's-Schlacht,"[1] and the dedication

---

[1] The fight of Hermann, the "Arminius" of Tacitus, against the Romans.— TRANS.

of it to Joseph the Second, Klopstock had produced a wonderful excitement. The Germans who freed themselves from Roman oppression were nobly and powerfully represented, and this picture was well suited to awaken the self-feeling of a nation. But because in peace patriotism really consists only in this, that every one sweeps his own door, minds his own business, and learns his own lesson, that it may go well with his house; so did the feeling for fatherland, excited by Klopstock, find no object on which it could exercise itself. Frederick had saved the honour of one part of the Germans against a united world; and every member of the nation, by applause and reverence of this great prince, was allowed to share in his victory: but what was to come of this excited warlike spirit of defiance? what direction should it take, and what effect produce? At first it was merely a poetical form; and the songs, which have since been criticised, and deemed so ridiculous, were accumulated through this impulse, — this incitement. There were no external enemies to fight, so people made tyrants for themselves; and for this purpose princes and their servants were obliged to bestow their figures, first only in general outline, but gradually with particulars. Here it was that poetry attached itself with vehemence to that interference with the administration of justice which is blamed above; and it is remarkable to see poems of that time written in a spirit by which everything of a higher order, whether monarchical or aristocratic, is abolished.

For my own part, I continued to make poetry the expression of my own whims and feelings. Little poems like the "Wanderer" belong to this time: they were inserted in the "Göttingen Musenalmanach." But, from whatever of the above-mentioned mania had worked itself into me, I shortly endeavoured to free myself in "Götz von Berlichingen;" since I described how in disordered times this brave, well-thinking man resolves to take the place of the law and the executive power, but is in despair when, to the supreme authority, which he recognises and reveres, he appears in an equivocal light, and even rebellious.

By Klopstock's odes, it was not so much the Northern mythology as the nomenclature of the divinities that had been introduced into German poetry; and, although I gladly made use of everything else that was offered me, I could not bring myself to use this, for the following causes: I had long become acquainted with the fables of the Edda, from the preface to Mallet's "Danish History," and had at once made myself master of them. They belonged to those tales, which, when asked by a company, I liked best to relate. Herder put Resenius into my hands, and made me better acquainted with the heroic *sagas*. But all these things, worthy as I held them, I could not bring within the circle of my own poetic faculty. Nobly as they excited my imagination, they nevertheless were inaccessible to the perception of the senses; while the mythology of the Greeks, changed by the greatest artists in the world into visible, easily imagined forms, still existed before our own eyes in abundance. Gods in general I did not allow often to appear; because, at all events, they had their abode out of the Nature which I understood how to imitate. Now, what could have induced me to substitute Woden for Jupiter, and Thor for Mars, and instead of the Southern, accurately described figures, to introduce forms of mist, nay, mere verbal sounds, into my poems? On the one side, they were related to the equally formless heroes of Ossian, only they were ruder and more gigantic: on the other, I brought them into contact with the cheerful tale; for the humouristic vein which runs through the whole Northern myths was to me highly pleasing and remarkable. It appeared to me the only one which jests with itself throughout, — wondrous giants, magicians, and monsters opposed to an odd dynasty of gods, and only occupied in leading astray and deriding the highest persons during their government; while they threaten them, besides, with disgraceful and inevitable destruction.

I felt a similar if not an equal interest for the Indian fables, with which I first became acquainted through Dapper's "Travels," and likewise added with great pleasure to my store of tales. In subsequent repetitions I succeeded especially with the Altar of Ram: and, notwithstanding the great number of persons in this tale, the ape Hannemann remained the favourite of my public. But even these unformed and over-formed monsters could not satisfy me in a true poetic sense: they lay too far from the truth, toward which my mind unceasingly strove.

But against all these goblins, so repulsive to art, my feeling for the beautiful was to be protected by the noblest power. Always fortunate is that epoch in a literature when the great works of the past rise up again as if thawed, and come into notice; because they then produce a perfectly fresh effect. Even the Homeric light rose again quite new to us, and indeed quite in the spirit of the time, which highly favoured such an appearance; for the constant reference to nature had at last the effect, that we learned to regard even the works of the ancients from this side. What several travellers had done for explanation of the Holy Scriptures, others had done for Homer. By Guys the matter was introduced: Wood gave it an impulse. A Göttingen review of the original work, which was at first very rare, made us acquainted with the design, and taught us how far it had been carried out. We now no longer saw in those poems a strained and inflated heroism, but the reflected truth of a primeval present, and sought to bring this as closely to us as possible. At the same time we could not give our assent when it was maintained, that, in order rightly to understand the Homeric natures, one must make one's self acquainted with the wild races and their manners, as described by the travellers in new worlds; for it cannot be denied that both Europeans and Asiatics are represented in the Homeric poems as at a higher grade of culture, — perhaps higher than the time of the Trojan war could have enjoyed. But that maxim was nevertheless in harmony with the prevailing confession of nature, and so far we let it pass.

Amidst all these occupations, which were related to the knowledge of mankind in the higher sense, as well as most nearly and dearly to poetry, I was nevertheless forced every day to experience that I was residing in Wetzlar. The conversation on the situation of the business of the " Visitation," and its ever-increasing obstacles, the discovery of new offences, was heard every hour. Here was the holy Roman Empire once more assembled, not for mere outward forms, but for an occupation which penetrated to the very depths. But even here that half-empty banqueting-hall on the coronation-day occurred to me, where the bidden guests remained without, because they were too proud. Here, indeed, they had come; but even worse symptoms were to be seen. The want of coherence in the whole, the mutual opposition of the parts, were continually apparent; and it remained no secret that princes had confidentially communicated to each other this notion, that they must see whether, on this occasion, something could not be gained from the supreme authority.

What a bad impression the petty detail of all the anecdotes of neglects and delays, of injustices and corruptions, must make upon a young man who desired what was good, and with this view cultivated his mind, every honest person will feel. Under such circumstances, where was a reverence for the law and the judge to

arise ? Even if the greatest confidence had been placed
in the effects of the " Visitation," — if it could have
been believed that it would fully accomplish its high
purpose, — still no satisfaction was to be found here
for a joyous, inwardly striving youth. The formalities
of the proceeding all tended toward delay : if any one
desired to do anything, and be of any importance, he
was obliged to serve the party in the wrong, — always
the accused, — and to be skilled in the fencing art of
twisting and evading.

Since, amid this distraction, I could not succeed in
any æsthetic labours, I again and again lost myself in
æsthetic speculations ; as indeed all theorising indicates
a defect or stagnation of productive power. As previously with Merck, so now sometimes with Gotter, I
endeavoured to find out the maxims according to which
one might go to work in production. But neither with
me nor with them would it succeed. Merck was a
skeptic and eclectic ; Gotter adhered to such examples
as pleased him most. The Sulzer theory was published more for the amateur than the artist. In this
sphere moral effects are required above all things :
and here at once arises a dissension between the class
that produces and that which uses ; for a good work
of art can, and will indeed, have moral consequences,
but to require moral ends of the artist is to destroy
his profession.

What the ancients had said on these important subjects I had read industriously for some years, by skips
at least, if not in regular order. Aristotle, Cicero,
Quintilian, Longinus, — none were unconsidered ; but
this did not help me in the least, for all these men pre-
supposed an experience which I lacked. They led me
into a world infinitely rich in works of art : they unfolded the merits of excellent poets and orators, of most
of whom the names alone are left us, and convinced
me but too well that a great abundance of objects

must lie before us ere we can think upon them; that one must first accomplish something one's self, nay, fail in something, to learn to know one's own capacities, and those of others. My acquaintance with so much that was good in those old times, was only according to school and book, and by no means vital; since, even with the most celebrated orators, it was striking that they had altogether formed themselves in life, and that one could never speak of the peculiarities of their character as artists, without at the same time mentioning the personal peculiarities of their disposition. With the poets this seemed less to be the case; and thus the result of all my thoughts and endeavours was the old resolution to investigate inner and outer nature, and to allow her to rule herself in loving imitation.

For these operations, which rested in me neither day nor night, lay before me two great, nay, monstrous, materials, the wealth of which I had only to prize, in order to produce something of importance. There was the older epoch, into which falls the life of Götz von Berlichingen; and the modern one, the unhappy bloom of which is depicted in "Werther." Of the historical preparation to that first work I have already spoken: the ethical occasions of the second shall now be introduced.

The resolution to preserve my internal nature according to its peculiarities, and to let external nature influence me according to its qualities, impelled me to the strange element in which "Werther" is designed and written. I endeavoured to free myself inwardly from all that was foreign to me; to regard the external with love; and to allow all beings, from man downwards, as low as they were comprehensible, to act upon me, each after its own kind. Thus arose a wonderful affinity with the single objects of nature, and a hearty concord, a harmony with the whole; so that every change, whether of place and region, or of the times of the day and year, or whatever else could happen, affected me in the deepest manner. The glance of the painter became associated with that of the poet: the beautiful rural landscape, animated by the pleasant river, increased my love of solitude, and favoured my silent observations as they extended on all sides.

But since I had left the family circle in Sesenheim, and again my family circle at Frankfort and Darmstadt, a vacuum had remained in my bosom which I was not able to fill up: I therefore found myself in a situation where the inclinations, if they appear in any degree veiled, gradually steal upon us, and can render abortive all our good resolutions.

And now, when the author has attained this step of his undertaking, he for the first time feels light-hearted in his labour; since from henceforward this book first becomes what it properly ought to be. It has not been announced as an independent work: it is much more designed to fill up the gaps of an author's life, to complete much that is fragmentary, and to preserve the memory of lost and forgotten ventures. But what is already done neither should nor can be repeated; and the poet would now vainly call upon those darkened powers of the soul, vainly ask of them to render present again those charming circumstances which rendered the period in Lahnthal so agreeable to him. Fortunately the genius had already provided for that, and had impelled him, in the vigorous period of youth, to hold fast, describe, and, with sufficient boldness and at the favourable hour, publicly to exhibit, that which had immediately gone by. That the little book "Werther" is here meant, requires no further indication; but something is to be gradually revealed, both of the persons introduced in it and the views which it exhibits.

Among the young men, who, attached to the embassy, had to prepare themselves for their future career of office, was one whom we were accustomed to call only the "Bridegroom." He distinguished himself by a calm, agreeable deportment, clearness of views, definiteness both in speaking and in acting. His cheerful activity, his persevering industry, so much recommended him to his superiors, that an appointment at an early period was promised him. Being justified by this, he ventured to betroth himself to a lady, who fully corresponded to his tone of mind and his wishes. After the death of her mother, she had shown herself extremely active as the head of a numerous young family, and had alone sustained her father in his widowhood; so that a future husband might hope the same for himself and his posterity, and expect a decided domestic felicity. Every one confessed, without having these selfish ends immediately in view, that she was a desirable lady. She belonged to those, who, if they do not inspire ardent passion, are nevertheless formed to create a general feeling of pleasure. A figure lightly built and neatly formed; a pure, healthy temperament, with a glad activity of life resulting from it; an unembarrassed management of the necessities of the day, — all these were given her together. I always felt happy in the contemplation of such qualities, and I readily associated myself to those who possessed them; and, if I did not always find opportunity to render them real service, I rather shared with them than with others the enjoyment of those innocent pleasures which youth can always find at hand, and seize without any great cost or effort. Moreover, since it is now settled that ladies decorate themselves only for each other, and are unwearied among each other to heighten the effect of their adornments, those were always the most agreeable to me, who, with simple purity, give their friend, their bridegroom, the silent assurance that all is really done for him alone, and that a whole life could be so carried on without much circumstance and outlay.

Such persons are not too much occupied with themselves: they have time to consider the external world, and patience enough to direct themselves according to it, and to adapt themselves to it; they become shrewd and sensible without exertion, and require but few books for their cultivation. Such was the bride.[1] The bridegroom, with his thoroughly upright and confiding turn of mind, soon made many whom he esteemed acquainted with her, and, as he had to pass the greatest part of his day in a zealous attention to business, was pleased when his betrothed, after the domestic toils were ended, amused herself otherwise, and took social recreation in walks and rural parties with friends of both sexes. Lottie — for so we shall call her — was unpretending in two senses: first, by her nature, which was rather directed to a general kindly feeling than to particular inclinations; and then, she had set her mind upon a man, who, being worthy of her, declared himself ready to attach his fate to hers for life. The most cheerful atmosphere seemed to surround her; nay, if it be a pleasing sight to see parents bestow an uninterrupted care upon their children, there is something still more beautiful when brothers and sisters do the same for each other. In the former case we think we can perceive more of natural impulse and social tradition; in the latter, more of choice and of a free exercise of feeling.

The newcomer, perfectly free from all ties, and careless in the presence of a girl, who, already engaged to another, could not interpret the most obliging services as acts of courtship, and could take the more pleasure in them accordingly, quietly went his way, but was soon so drawn in and riveted, that he no longer knew himself. Indolent and dreamy, because nothing present satisfied him, he found what he had lacked in a

---

[1] Persons betrothed are in German called " bride " and " bridegroom." — TRANS.

female friend, who, while she lived for the whole year, seemed only to live for the moment. She liked him much as her companion; he soon could not bear her absence, as she formed for him the connecting link with the every-day world; and, during extensive household occupations, they were inseparable companions in the fields and in the meadows, in the vegetable-ground and in the garden. If business permitted, the bridegroom was also of the party: they had all three accustomed themselves to each other without intention, and did not know how they had become so mutually indispensable. During the splendid summer they lived through a real German idyl, to which the fertile land gave the form, and a pure affection the poetry. Wandering through ripe cornfields, they took delight in the dewy morning; the song of the lark, the cry of the quail, were pleasant tones; sultry hours followed, monstrous storms came on, — they grew more and more attached to each other, and by this continuous love many a little domestic annoyance was easily extinguished. And thus one ordinary day followed another, and all seemed to be holidays, — the whole calender should have been printed red. He will understand me who recollects what was predicted by the happily unhappy friend of "The New Heloise:" "And, sitting at the feet of his beloved, he will break hemp; and he will wish to break hemp to-day, to-morrow, and the day after, — nay, for his whole life."

I can say but little, though just as much as may be necessary, respecting a young man whose name was afterward but too often mentioned. This was Jerusalem, the son of the freely and tenderly thinking theologian. He also had an appointment with an embassy; his form was pleasing, of a middle height, and well built; his face was rather round than long; his features were soft and calm; and he had the other appurtenances of a handsome blond youth, with blue eyes, rather attractive than speaking. His dress was that introduced in Lower Germany in imitation of the English, — a blue frock, waistcoat and breeches of yellow leather, and boots with brown tops. The author never visited him, nor saw him at his own residence, but often met him among his friends. The expressions of this young man were moderate but kindly. He took interest in productions of the most different kinds, and especially loved those designs and sketches in which the tranquil character of solitary spots is caught. On such occasions he showed Gesner's etchings, and encouraged the amateurs to study them. In all that mummery and knighthood he took no part, but lived for himself and his own sentiments. It was said he had a decided passion for the wife of one of his friends. In public they were never seen together. In general very little could be said of him, except that he occupied himself with English literature. As the son of an opulent man, he had no occasion, either painfully to devote himself to business, or to make pressing applications for an early appointment.

Those etchings by Gesner increased the pleasure and interest in rural objects; and a little poem, which we passionately received into our circle, allowed us from henceforward to think of nothing else. Goldsmith's "Deserted Village" necessarily delighted every one at that stage of culture in that sphere of thought. Not as living and active, but as a departed, vanished existence was described, all that one so readily looked upon, that one loved, prized, sought passionately in the present to take part in it with the cheerfulness of youth. High days and holidays in the country, church consecrations and fairs, the solemn assemblage of the elders under the village linden-tree, supplanted in its turn by the lively delight of youth in dancing, while the more educated classes show their sympathy. How seemly did these pleasures appear, moderated as they were by

an excellent country pastor, who understood how to
smooth down and remove all that went too far, — that
gave occasion to quarrel and dispute. Here, again, we
found an honest Wakefield, in his well-known circle,
yet no longer in his living bodily form, but as a shadow
recalled by the soft, mournful tones of the elegiac poet.
The very thought of this picture is one of the happiest
possible, when once the design is formed to evoke once
more an innocent past with a graceful melancholy.
And in this kindly endeavour, how well has the Englishman succeeded in every sense of the word! I
shared the enthusiasm for this charming poem with
Gotter, who was more felicitous than myself with the
translation undertaken by us both; for I had too painfully tried to imitate in our language the delicate significance of the original, and thus had well agreed with
single passages, but not with the whole.

If, as they say, the greatest happiness rests on a sense
of longing (*sehnsucht*), and if the genuine longing can
only be directed to something unattainable, everything
had fallen together to render the youth whom we now
accompany on his wanderings the happiest of mortals.
An affection for one betrothed to another; the effort
to acquire the masterpieces of foreign literature for our
own; the endeavour to imitate natural objects, not
only with words, but also with style and pencil, without any proper technical knowledge, — each of these
particulars would singly have sufficed to melt the heart
and oppress the bosom. But that the sweetly suffering youth might be torn out of this state, and that
new circumstances might be prepared for new disquiet,
the following events occurred:

Höpfner, professor of law, was at Giessen. He was
acknowledged and highly esteemed by Merck and
Schlosser as clever in his office, and as a thinking and
excellent man. I had long ago desired his acquaintance; and now, when these two friends thought to pay

him a visit, to negotiate about some literary matters, it was agreed that I should likewise go to Giessen on this opportunity. Because, however, — as generally happens with the wilfulness of glad and peaceful times, — we could not easily do anything in the direct way, but, like genuine children, sought to get a jest, even out of what was necessary, I was now, as an unknown person, to appear in a strange form, and once more satisfy my desire to appear disguised. One bright morning before sunrise, I went from Wetzlar along the Lahn, up the charming valley: such ramblings again constituted my greatest felicity. I invented, connected, elaborated, and was quietly happy and cheerful with myself: I set right what the ever-contradictory world had clumsily and confusedly forced upon me. Arrived at the end of my journey, I looked out for Höpfner's residence, and knocked at his study. When he had cried out, "Come in!" I modestly appeared before him as a student who was going home from the universities, and wished on his way to become acquainted with the most worthy men. For his questions as to my more intimate circumstances, I was prepared; I made up a plausible, prosaic tale, with which he seemed satisfied: and, as I gave myself out for a jurist, I did not come off badly; for I well knew his merits in this department, and also that he was occupied with natural law. Conversation, however, sometimes came to a standstill; and it seemed as if he were looking for a *Stammbuch*,[1] or for me to take my leave. Nevertheless, I managed to delay my departure, as I expected with certainty the arrival of Schlosser, whose punctuality was well known to me. He actually came, and, after a side glance, took little notice of me. Höpfner, however, drew me into conversation, and showed himself throughout as a humane and kindly man. I at last took my leave, and

---

[1] *Stammbuch* is a sort of album for autographs and short contributions. – TRANS.

hastened to the inn, where I exchanged a few hurried words with Merck, and awaited further proceedings.

The friends had resolved to ask Höpfner to dinner, and also that Christian Heinrich Schmid who had played a part, though a very subordinate one, in German literature. For him the affair was really designed, and he was to be punished in a mirthful manner. When the guests had assembled in the dining-room, I asked, through the waiter, whether the gentlemen would allow me to dine with them. Schlosser, whom a certain earnestness well became, opposed this proposition, because they did not wish their conversation interrupted by a third party. But on the pressing demand of the waiter and the advocacy of Höpfner, who assured the other that I was a very tolerable person, I was admitted, and, at the commencement of the meal, behaved as if modest and abashed. Schlosser and Merck put no restraint upon themselves, and went on about many subjects as freely as if no stranger were present. I now showed myself somewhat bolder, and did not allow myself to be disturbed when Schlosser threw out at me much that was in earnest, and Merck something sarcastic; but I directed against Schmid all my darts, which fell sharply and surely on the uncovered places, which I well knew.

I had been moderate over my pint of table-wine; but the gentlemen ordered better wine to be brought, and did not fail to give me some. After many affairs of the day had been talked over, conversation went into general matters; and the question was discussed, which will be repeated as long as there are authors in the world, — the question, namely, whether literature was rising, or declining; progressing, or retrograding? This question, about which old and young, those commencing and those retiring, seldom agree, was discussed with cheerfulness, though without any exact design of coming decidedly to terms about it. At last I took up the discourse, and said, "The different literatures, as it seems to me, have seasons, which, alternating with each other, as in nature, bring forth certain phenomena, and assert themselves in due order. Hence I do not believe that any epoch of a literature can be praised or blamed on the whole: especially it displeases me when certain talents, which are brought out by their time, are raised and vaunted so highly, while others are censured and depreciated. The throat of the nightingale is excited by the spring, but at the same time also that of the cuckoo. The butterflies, which are so agreeable to the eye, and the gnats, which are so painful to the feelings, are called into being by the same heat of the sun. If this were duly considered, we should not hear the same complaints renewed every ten years; and the vain trouble which is taken to root out this or that offensive thing would not so often be wasted." The party looked at me, wondering whence I had got so much wisdom and tolerance. I, however, continued quite calmly to compare literary phenomena with natural productions, and (I know not how) came to the molluscæ, of which I contrived to set forth all sorts of strange things. I said that there were creatures to whom a sort of body, nay, a certain figure, could not be denied; but that, since they had no bones, one never knew how to set about rightly with them, and they were nothing better than living slime; nevertheless, the sea must have such inhabitants. Since I carried the simile beyond its due limits to designate Schmid, who was present, and that class of characterless *littérateurs*, I was reminded that a simile carried too far at last becomes nothing. "Well, then, I will return to the earth," I replied, "and speak of the ivy. As these creatures have no bones, so this has no trunk; but, wherever it attaches itself, it likes to play the chief part. It belongs to old walls, in which there is nothing more to destroy; but from new buildings it is properly removed. It sucks up the goodness of the trees, and is most insupportable to me when it clambers up a post, and assures me that this is a living trunk, because it has covered it with leaves."

Notwithstanding my being again reproached with the obscurity and inapplicability of similes, I became more and more excited against all parasitical creatures, and, as far as my knowledge of nature then extended, managed the affair pretty well. I at last sang a *vivat* to all independent men, a *pereat* to those who forced themselves upon them, seized Höpfner's hand after dinner, shook it violently, declared him to be the best man in the world, and finally embraced both him and the others right heartily. My excellent new friend thought he was really dreaming, until Schlosser and Merck at last solved the riddle ; and the discovered joke diffused a general hilarity, which was shared by Schmid himself, who was appeased by an acknowledgment of his real merits, and the interest we took in his tastes.

This ingenious introduction could not do otherwise than animate and favour the literary congress, which was, indeed, chiefly kept in view. Merck, active now in æsthetics, now in literature, now in commerce, had stimulated the well-thinking, well-informed Schlosser, whose knowledge extended to so many branches, to edit the Frankfort *Gelehrte Anzeige* ("Learned Advertiser") for that year. They had associated to themselves Höpfner, and other university men in Giessen, a meritorious schoolman, Rector Wenck in Darmstadt, and many other good men. Every one of them possessed enough historical and theoretical knowledge in his department, and the feeling of the times allowed these men to work in one spirit. The human and cosmopolitan is encouraged: really good men justly celebrated are protected against obtrusion of every kind : their defence is undertaken against enemies, and especially against scholars who use what has been taught them to the detriment of their instructors. Nearly the most interesting articles are the critiques on other periodical publications, the *Berlin Library* (" Bibliothek "), the *German Mercury*, where the cleverness in so many departments, the judgment as well as the fairness of the papers, is rightly admired.

As for myself, they saw well enough that I was deficient in everything that belongs to a critic, properly so called. My historical knowledge was unconnected: the histories of the world, science, and literature had only attracted me by epochs, the objects themselves only partially and in masses. My capacity of giving life to things, and rendering them present to me out of their real connection, put me in the position that I could be perfectly at home in a certain century or in a department of science, without being in any degree instructed as to what preceded or what followed. Thus a certain theoretico-practical sense had been awakened in me, by which I could give account of things, rather as they should be than as they were, without any proper philosophical connection, but by way of leaps. To this was added a very easy power of apprehension, and a friendly reception of the opinions of others, if they did not stand in direct opposition to my own convictions.

That literary union was also favoured by an animated correspondence, and by frequent personal communication, which was possible from the vicinity of the places. He who had first read a book was to give an account of it ; often another reviewer of the same book was found ; the affair was talked over, connected with kindred subjects ; and, if at last a certain result had been obtained, one of them took the office of editing. Thus many reviews are as clever as they are spirited, as pleasant as they are satisfactory. I often had the task of introducing the matter : my friends also permitted me to jest in their works, and to appear independently with objects to which I felt myself equal, and in which I especially took interest. In vain should I endeavour, either by description or reflection, to recall the proper spirit and sense of those days, if the two years of the above-mentioned periodical did not furnish me with the most decisive documents. Extracts from passages, in which I again recognise myself, may appear in future in their proper place, together with similar essays.

During this lively interchange of knowledge, opinions, and convictions, I very soon became better acquainted with Höpfner, and became very fond of him. As soon as we were alone, I spoke with him about subjects connected with his department, which was to be my department also, and found a very naturally connected explanation and instruction. I was not then as yet plainly conscious that I could learn something from books and conversation, but not from continuous professional lectures. A book allowed me to pause at a passage, and even to look back, which is impossible with oral delivery and a teacher. Often, at the beginning of the lecture, some thought in which I indulged laid hold of me; and thus I lost what followed, and altogether got out of the connection. Thus it had happened to me with respect to the lectures on jurisprudence: and on this account I could take many opportunities of talking with Höpfner, who entered very readily into my doubts and scruples, and filled up many gaps; so that the wish arose in me to remain with him at Giessen, and derive instruction from him, without removing myself too far from Wetzlar inclinations. Against this wish of mine my two friends had laboured, first unconsciously, but afterward consciously; for both were in a hurry, not only to leave the place themselves, but had also an interest to remove me from the spot.

Schlosser disclosed to me that he had formed, first a

friendly, then a closer, connection with my sister, and that he was looking about for an early appointment, that he might be united to her. This explanation surprised me to some degree, although I ought to have found it out long ago in my sister's letters; but we easily pass over that which may hurt the good opinion which we entertain of ourselves: and I now remarked for the first time, that I was really jealous about my sister, — a feeling which I concealed from myself the less, as, since my return from Strasburg, our connection had been much more intimate. How much time we had expended in communicating each little affair of the heart, love-matters, and other matters, which had occurred in the interval! In the field of imagination, too, had there not been revealed to me a new world, into which I sought to conduct her also? My own little productions, and a far-extended world-poetry, was gradually to be made known to her. Thus I made for her *impromptu* translations of those passages of Homer in which she could take the greatest interest. Clarke's literal translation I read off in German, as well as I could: my version generally found its way into metrical turns and terminations; and the liveliness with which I had apprehended the images, the force with which I expressed them, removed all the obstacles of a cramped order of words: what I gave with mind, she followed with mind also. We passed many hours of the day in this fashion: while, if her company met, the Wolf Fenris and the Ape Hannemann were unanimously called for; and how often have I not been obliged to repeat circumstantially how Thor and his comrades were deluded by the magical giants! Hence, from these fictions, such a pleasant impression has remained with me, that they belong to the most valuable things which my imagination can recall. Into the connection with the Darmstadt people I had drawn my sister also; and now my wanderings and occasional absence necessarily bound us closer together, as I discoursed with her by letter respecting everything that occurred to me, communicated to her every little poem, if even only a note of admiration, and let her first see all the letters which I received, and all the answers which I wrote. All these lively impulses had been stopped since my departure from Frankfort; my residence at Wetzlar was not fertile enough for such a correspondence; and, moreover, my attachment to Charlotte may have infringed upon my attentions to my sister; she certainly felt that she was alone, perhaps neglected, and therefore the more readily gave a hearing to the honest wooing of an honourable man, who, serious and reserved, estimable, and worthy of confidence, had passionately bestowed on her his affections, with which he was otherwise very niggardly. I had to give in and let my friend be happy; though I did not fail in secret to say confidently to myself, that, if the brother had not been absent, the friend would not have fared so well.

My friend and apparent brother-in-law was now very anxious that I should return home, because, by my mediation, a freer intercourse was possible, of which the feelings of this man, so unexpectedly attacked by a tender passion, seemed to stand extremely in need. Therefore, on his speedy departure, he elicited from me the promise that I would immediately follow him.

Of Merck, whose time was free, I hoped that he would delay his sojourn in Giessen, that I might be able to pass some hours of the day with my good Höpfner, while my friend employed his time on the Frankfort *Gelehrte Anzeige;* but he was not to be moved; and as my brother-in-law was driven from the university by love, he was driven by hate. For as there are innate antipathies, — just as certain men cannot endure cats, while this or that is repugnant to the soul

of others, — so was Merck a deadly enemy to all the
academical citizens (the students), who indeed at that
time, at Giessen, took delight in the greatest rudeness.
For me they were well enough; I could have used them
as masks for one of my carnival plays: but with him the
sight of them by day, and their noise by night, destroyed every sort of good humour. He had spent the
best days of his youth in French Switzerland, and had
afterward enjoyed the pleasant intercourse of people
of the court, world, and business, and of cultivated
littérateurs: several military persons, in whom a desire
for mental culture had been awakened, sought his
society; and thus he had passed his life in a very cultivated circle. That the students' disorderly conduct
vexed him, was therefore not to be wondered at; but
his aversion to them was really more passionate than
became a sound man, although he often made me
laugh by his witty descriptions of their monstrous
appearance and behaviour. Höpfner's invitations and
my persuasions were of no avail: I was obliged to
depart with him as soon as possible for Wetzlar.

I could scarcely wait any time, till I had introduced
him to Charlotte; but his presence in this circle did
me no good: for as Mephistopheles, let him go where
he will, hardly brings a blessing with him; so did he,
by his indifference toward that beloved person, cause
me no joy, even if he did not make me waver. This I
might have foreseen, if I had recollected that it was
exactly those slender, delicate persons who diffuse a
lively cheerfulness around them, without making further pretensions, who did not remarkably please him.
He very quickly preferred the Juno-form of one of her
friends; and, since he lacked time to form a close connection, he bitterly blamed me for not exerting myself
to gain this magnificent figure, especially as she was
free and without any tie. He thought that I did not
understand my own advantage, and that he here —

very unwillingly — perceived my especial taste for wasting my time.

If it is dangerous to make a friend acquainted with the perfections of one's beloved, because he also may find her charming and desirable, no less is the reverse danger, that he may perplex us by his dissent. This, indeed, was not the case here, for I had too deeply impressed upon myself the picture of her amiability for it to be so easily obliterated; but his presence and his persuasions nevertheless hastened my resolution to leave the place. He represented to me a journey on the Rhine, which he was going to take with his wife and son, in the most glowing colours, and excited in me the desire to see at last, with my eyes, those objects of which I had often heard with envy. Now, when he had departed, I separated myself from Charlotte with a purer conscience, indeed, than from Frederica, but still not without pain. This connection also had, by habit and indulgence, grown more passionate than right on my side : while, on the other hand, she and her bridegroom kept themselves with cheerfulness in a measure which could not be more beautiful and amiable; and the security which resulted just from this caused me to forget every danger. I could not, however, conceal from myself that this adventure must come to a speedy end; for the union of the young man with the amiable girl depended on a promotion which was immediately to be expected: and as man, if he is in any degree resolute, even dares to make a virtue of necessity; so did I embrace the determination voluntarily to depart before being driven away by what might be insupportable to me.

THIRTEENTH BOOK.

It had been agreed with Merck, that in the fine season we should meet at Coblentz at Frau von Laroche's. I sent to Frankfort my baggage, and whatever I might want on my way down the Lahn, by an opportunity which offered, and now wandered down that beautiful river, so lovely in its windings, so various in its shores, free as to my resolution, but oppressed as to my feelings, — in a condition when the presence of silently living nature is so beneficial to us. My eye, accustomed to discern those beauties of a landscape that suited the painter, and were above him, rioted in the contemplation of near and distant objects, of bushy rocks, of sunny heights, of damp valleys, of enthroned castles, and of the blue range of mountains inviting us from the distance.

I wandered on the right bank of the river, which at some depth and distance below me, and partly concealed by a rich bush of willows, glided along in the sunlight. Then again arose in me the old wish, worthily to imitate such objects. By chance I had a handsome pocket-knife in my left hand; and at the moment, from the depth of my soul, arose, as it were, an absolute command, according to which, without delay, I was to fling this knife into the river. If I saw it fall, my wish to become an artist would be fulfilled; but if the sinking of the knife was concealed by the overhanging bush of willows, I was to abandon the wish and the endeavour. This whim had no sooner arisen in me than it was executed. For without regarding the usefulness of the knife, which comprised many instruments in itself, I cast it with the left hand, as I held it, violently toward the river. But here I had to experience that deceptive ambiguity of oracles, of which, in antiquity, such bitter complaints were made. The sinking of the knife into the water was concealed from me by the extreme twigs of the willows; but the water, which rose from the fall, sprang up like a strong fountain, and was perfectly visible. I did not interpret this phenomenon in my favour; and the doubt which it excited in me was afterward the cause that I pursued these exercises more interruptedly and more negligently, and gave occasion for the import of the oracle to fulfil itself. For the moment, at least, the external world was spoiled for me: I abandoned myself to my imaginations and feelings, and left the well-situated castles and districts of Weilburg, Limburg, Diez, and Nassau, one by one, behind me, generally walking alone, but often for a short time associating myself with another.

After thus pleasantly wandering for some days, I arrived at Ems, where I several times enjoyed the soft bath, and then went down the river in a boat. Then the old Rhine opened itself upon me; the beautiful situation of Oberlahnstein delighted me; but noble and majestic above all appeared to me the castle Ehrenbreitstein, which stood perfectly armed in its power and strength. In most lovely contrast lay at its feet the well-built little place called Thal, where I could easily find my way to the residence of Privy Councillor von Laroche. Announced by Merck, I was very kindly received by this noble family, and soon considered as a member of it. My literary and sentimental tendencies bound me to the mother, a cheerful feeling for the world bound me to the father, and my youth bound me to the daughters.

The house, quite at the end of the valley, and little

elevated above the river, had a free prospect down the stream. The rooms were high and spacious; and the walls, like a gallery, were hung with pictures, placed close together. Every window on every side formed a frame to a natural picture, which came out very vividly by the light of a mild sun. I thought I had never seen such cheerful mornings and such splendid evenings.

I was not long the only guest in the house. As a member of the congress which was held here, — partly with an artistic view, partly as a matter of feeling, — Leuchsenring, who came up from Düsseldorf, was likewise appointed. This man, possessing a fine knowledge of modern literature, had, on different travels, but especially during a residence in Switzerland, made many acquaintances, and, as he was pleasant and insinuating, had gained much favour. He carried with him several boxes, which contained the confidential correspondence with many friends; for there was altogether such a general openness among people, that one could not speak or write to a single individual, without considering it directed to many. One explored one's own heart and that of others; and with the indifference of the government toward such a communication, the great rapidity of the Taxisch [1] post, the security of the seal, and the reasonableness of the postage, this moral and literary intercourse soon spread itself around.

Such correspondences, especially with important persons, were carefully collected; and extracts from them were often read at friendly meetings. Thus, as political discourses had little interest, one became pretty well acquainted with the extent of the moral world.

---

[1] The post, managed by the Princes of Thurn and Taxis, in different parts of Germany. An ancestor of this house first directed the post system in Tyrol, in 1450 ; and Alexander Ferdinand von Thurn received, in 1744, the office of Imperial Postmaster-General, as a fief of the empire. — TRANS.

Leuchsenring's boxes contained many treasures in this sense. The letters of one Julie Bondelli were very much esteemed : she was famed as a lady of sense and merit, and a friend of Rousseau. Whoever had stood in any relation to this extraordinary man, took part in the glory which emanated from him; and in his name a silent community had been disseminated far and wide.

I liked to be present at these readings; as I was thus transported into an unknown world, and learned to know the real truth of many an event that had just passed. All, indeed, was not valuable ; and Herr von Laroche, a cheerful man of the world and of business, who, although a Catholic, had already in his writings made free with the monks and priesthood, thought that he here saw a fraternity where many a worthless individual supported himself by a connection with persons of importance, by which, in the end, he, but not they, were admired. Generally this excellent man withdrew from the company when the boxes were opened. Even if he did listen to some letters now and then, a waggish remark was to be expected. Among other things, he once said, that by this correspondence he was still more convinced of what he had always believed, namely, that ladies might spare their sealing-wax ; as they need only fasten their letters with pins, and might be assured that they would reach their address unopened. In the same way he was accustomed to jest with everything that lay out of the sphere of life and activity, and in this followed the disposition of his lord and master, Count Stadion, minister to the Elector of Mayence, who certainly was not fitted to counterbalance the worldliness and coldness of the boy by a reverence for everything like mysterious foreboding.

An anecdote respecting the great practical sense of the count may here find a place. When he took a liking to the orphan Laroche, and chose him for a pupil, he at once required from the boy the services of a secretary. He gave him letters to answer, despatches to prepare, which he was then obliged to copy fair, oftener to write in cipher, to seal, and to direct. This lasted for many years. When the boy had grown up into a youth, and really did that which he had hitherto only supposed he was doing, the count took him to a large writing-table, in which all his letters and packets lay unbroken, having been preserved as exercises of the former time.

Another exercise which the count required of his pupil will not find such universal applause. Laroche had been obliged to practise himself in imitating, as accurately as possible, the handwriting of his lord and master, that he might thus relieve him from the trouble of writing himself. Not only in business, but also in love-affairs, the young man had to take the place of his preceptor. The count was passionately attached to a lady of rank and talent. If he stopped in her society till late at night, his secretary was, in the meanwhile, sitting at home, and hammering out the most ardent love-letters : the count chose one of these, and sent it that very night to his beloved, who was thus necessarily convinced of the inextinguishable fire of her passionate adorer. Such early experiences were scarcely fitted to give the youth the most exalted notion of written communications about love.

An irreconcilable hatred of the priesthood had established itself in this man, who served two spiritual electors, and had probably sprung from the contemplation of the rude, tasteless, mind-destroying foolery which the monks in Germany were accustomed to carry on in many parts, and thus hindered and destroyed every sort of cultivation. His letters on Monasticism caused great attention : they were received with great applause by all Protestants and many Catholics.

If Herr von Laroche opposed everything that can be called sensibility, and even decidedly avoided the very appearance of it, he nevertheless did not conceal a tender paternal affection for his eldest daughter, who, indeed, was nothing else but amiable. She was rather short than tall of stature, and delicately built: her figure was free and graceful, her eyes very black, while nothing could be conceived purer and more blooming than her complexion. She also loved her father, and inclined to his sentiments. Being an active man of business, most of his time was consumed in works belonging to his calling; and, as the guests who stopped at his house were really attracted by his wife and not by him, society afforded him but little pleasure. At table he was cheerful and entertaining, and at least endeavoured to keep his board free from the spice of sensibility.

Whoever knows the views and mode of thought of Frau von Laroche, — and, by a long life and many writings, she has become honourably known to every German, — may perhaps suspect that a domestic incongruity must have arisen here. Nothing of the kind. She was the most wonderful woman, and I know no other to compare to her. Slenderly and delicately built, rather tall than short, she had, even to her more advanced years, managed to preserve a certain elegance, both of form and of conduct, which pleasantly fluctuated between the conduct of a noble lady and that of one of the citizen class. Her dress had been the same for several years. A neat little cap with wings very well became her small head and delicate face, and her brown or gray clothing gave repose and dignity to her presence. She spoke well, and always knew how to give importance to what she said by an expression of feeling. Her conduct was perfectly the same toward everybody. But, with all this, the greatest peculiarity of her character is not yet expressed: it is difficult to designate it. She seemed to take interest in everything, but really nothing acted upon her. She was gentle toward every one, and could endure everything without suffering: the jests of her husband, the tenderness of her friends, the sweetness of her children, — to all this she replied in the same manner; and thus she always remained herself, without being affected in the world by good and evil, or in literature by excellence and weakness. To this disposition she owes that independence which she maintains even to an advanced age, through many sad, nay, sorrowful, events. But, not to be unjust, I must state that her sons, then children of dazzling beauty, often elicited from her an expression different from that which served her for daily use.

Thus I lived for a time in a wonderfully pleasant society, until Merck came with his family. Here arose at once new affinities; for while the two ladies approached each other, Merck had come into closer contact with Herr von Laroche as a connoisseur of the world and of business, as a well-informed and travelled man. The boy associated himself with the boys; and the daughters, of whom the eldest soon particularly attracted me, fell to my share. It is a very pleasant sensation when a new passion begins to stir in us, before the old one is quite extinct. Thus, when the sun is setting, one often likes to see the moon rise on the opposite side, and takes delight in the double lustre of the two heavenly luminaries.

There was now no lack of rich entertainment, either in or out of the house. We wandered about the spot, and ascended Ehrenbreitstein on this side of the river, and the Carthaus on the other. The city, the Moselle bridge, the ferry which took us over the Rhine, all gave us the most varied delight. The new castle was not yet built: we were taken to the place where it was to stand, and allowed to see the preparatory sketches.

Nevertheless, amid those cheerful circumstances was internally developed that element of unsociableness, which, both in cultivated and uncultivated circles, ordinarily shows its malign effects. Merck, at once cold and restless, had not long listened to that correspondence before he uttered aloud many waggish notions concerning the things which were the subjects of discourse, as well as the persons and their circumstances; while he revealed to me in secret the oddest things, which really were concealed under them. Political secrets were never touched on, nor, indeed, anything that could have had a definite connection: he only made me attentive to persons, who, without remarkable talents, contrive, by a certain tact, to obtain personal influence, and, by an acquaintance with many, try to make something out of themselves; and from this time forwards I had opportunity to observe several men of the sort. Since such persons usually change their place, and as travellers come, now here, now there, they have the advantage of novelty, which should neither be envied nor spoiled; for this is a mere customary matter, which every traveller has often experienced to his benefit, and every resident to his detriment.

Be that as it may, it is enough, that, from that time forward, we cherished an uneasy, nay, envious, attention to people of the sort, who went about on their own account, cast anchor in every city, and sought to gain an influence, at least, in some families. I have represented a tender and soft specimen of these guild brethren in "Pater Brey;" another, of more aptness and bluntness, in a carnival play to be hereafter published, which bears the title, "Satyros, or the Deified Wood-devil." This I have done, if not with fairness, at least with good humour.

However, the strange elements of our little society still worked quite tolerably one upon another : we were partly united by our own manner and style of breeding, and partly restrained by the peculiar conduct of our hostess, who, being but lightly touched by that which passed around her, always resigned herself to certain ideal notions, and, while she understood how to utter them in a friendly and benevolent way, contrived to soften everything sharp that might arise, in the company, and to smooth down all that was uneven.

Merck had sounded a retreat just at the right time, so that the party separated on the best of terms. I went with him and his in a yacht, which was returning up the Rhine toward Mayence ; and, although this vessel went very slowly of itself, we nevertheless besought the captain not to hurry himself. Thus we enjoyed at leisure the infinitely various objects, which, in the most splendid weather, seem to increase in beauty every hour, and, both in greatness and agreeableness, ever to change anew ; and I only wish, that while I utter the names, Rheinfels and St. Goar, Bacharach, Bingen, Ellfeld, and Biberich, every one of my readers may be able to recall these spots to memory.

We had sketched industriously, and had thus, at least, gained a deeper impression of the thousand-fold changes of those splendid shores. At the same time, by being so much longer together, by a familiar communication on so many sorts of things, our connection became so much the more intimate, that Merck gained a great influence over me ; and I, as a good companion, became indispensable to him for a comfortable existence. My eye, sharpened by nature, again turned to the contemplation of art, for which the beautiful Frankfort collections afforded me the best opportunity, both in paintings and engravings ; and I have been much indebted to the kindness of MM. Ettling and Ehrenreich, but especially to the excellent Nothnagel. To see nature in art became with me a passion, which, in its highest moments, must have appeared to others, passionate amateurs as they might be, almost like madness; and how could such an inclination be better fostered than by a constant observation of the excellent works of the Netherlanders? That I might make myself practically acquainted with these things, Nothnagel gave me a little room, where I found everything that was requisite for oil painting, and painted after nature some simple subjects of still life, one of which, a tortoise-shell knife-handle, inlaid with silver, so astonished my master who had last visited me an hour before, that he maintained one of his subordinate artists must have been with me during the time.

Had I patiently gone on practising on such objects, catching their light, and the peculiarities of their surface, I might have formed a sort of practical skill, and made a way for something higher. I was, however, prevented by the fault of all *dilettantes*, — that of beginning with what is most difficult, and ever wishing to perform the impossible; and I soon involved myself in greater undertakings, in which I stuck fast, both because they were beyond my technical capabilities, and because I could not always maintain pure and operative that loving attention and patient industry by which even the beginner accomplishes something.

At the same time, I was once more carried into a higher sphere, by finding an opportunity of purchasing some fine plaster casts of antique heads. The Italians, who visit the fairs, often brought with them good specimens of the kind, and sold them cheap, after they had taken moulds of them. In this manner I set up for myself a little museum; as I gradually brought together the heads of the Laocoon, his sons, and Niobe's daughters. I also bought miniature copies of the most important works of antiquity from the estate of a deceased friend of art, and thus sought once more to revive. as much as possible, the great impression which I had received at Mannheim.

While I was endeavouring to cultivate, foster, and maintain all the talent, taste, or other inclination that might live within me, I applied a good part of the day, according to my father's wish, in the duties of an advocate, for the practice of which I chanced to find the best opportunity. After the death of my grandfather, my uncle Textor had come into the council, and consigned to me the little offices to which I was equal; while the brothers Schlosser did the same. I made myself acquainted with the documents: my father also read them with much pleasure; as, by means of his son, he again saw himself in an activity of which he had been long deprived. We talked the matters over, and with great facility: I then made the necessary statements. We had at hand an excellent copyist, on whom one could rely for all legal formalities; and this occupation was the more agreeable to me, as it brought me closer to my father, who, being perfectly satisfied with my conduct in this respect, readily looked with an eye of indulgence on all my other pursuits, in the ardent expectation that I should now soon gather in a harvest of fame as an author.

Since, in every epoch, all things are connected together, because the ruling views and opinions are ramified in the most various manner; so in the science of law those maxims were gradually pursued, according to which religion and morals were treated. Among the attorneys, as the younger people, and then among the judges, as the elder, a spirit of humanity was diffused: and all vied with each other in being as humane as possible, even in legal affairs. Prisons were improved, crimes excused, punishments lightened, legitimations rendered easy, separations and unequal marriages encouraged; and one of our eminent lawyers gained for himself the highest fame, when he contrived, by hard fighting, to gain for the son of an executioner an entrance into the college of surgeons. In vain did guilds and corporations oppose: one dam after another was broken through. The toleration of the religious parties toward each other was not merely taught, but practised; and the civil constitution was threatened with a still greater influence, when the effort was made to recommend to that good-humoured age, with understanding, acuteness, and power, toleration toward the Jews. Those new subjects for legal treatment, which lay without the law and tradition, and only laid claim to a fair examination, to a kindly sympathy, required, at the same time, a more natural and animated style. Here for us, the youngest, was opened a cheerful field, in which we bustled about with delight; and I still recollect that an imperial councillor's agent, in a case of the sort, sent me a very polite letter of commendation. The French *plaidoyés* served us for patterns and for stimulants.

We were thus on the way to become better orators than jurists, a fact to which George Schlosser once called my attention, blaming me while doing so. I told him that I had read to my clients a controversy, written with much energy, in their favour, at which they had shown the greatest satisfaction. To this he replied, " In this case you have proved more an author than an advocate. We must never ask how such a paper may please the client, but how it may please the judge."

As the occupations to which one devotes his day are never so serious and pressing that he cannot find time enough in the evening to go to the play; so it was with me, who, in the want of a really good stage, did not cease thinking of the German theatre, in order to discover how one might coöperate upon it with any degree of activity. Its condition in the second half of the last century is sufficiently known, and every one who wishes to be instructed about it finds assistance at hand everywhere. On this account I only intend to insert here a few general remarks.

The success of the stage rested more upon the personality of the actors than upon the value of the pieces. This was especially the case with pieces half or wholly extemporised, when everything depended on the humour and talent of the comic actors. The matter of such plays must be taken from the common-est life, in conformity with the people before whom they are acted. From this immediate application arises the greatest applause, which these plays have always gained. They were always at home in South Germany, where they are retained to the present day; and the change of persons alone renders it necessary to give, from time to time, some change to the character of the farcical masks. However, the German theatre, in conformity with the serious character of the nation, soon took a turn toward the moral, which was still more accelerated by an external cause. For the question arose, among strict Christians, whether the theatre belonged to those sinful things which are to be shunned at all events, or to those indifferent things which may turn out good for the good, and bad for the bad. Some zealots denied the latter, and held fast the opinion that no clergyman should ever enter the theatre. Now, the opposite opinion could not be maintained with energy, unless the theatre was de-clared to be not only harmless, but even useful. To be useful, it must be moral; and in this direction it developed itself in North Germany the more as, by a sort of half-taste, the comic character[1] was banished, and, although intelligent persons took his part, was forced to retire, having already gone from the coarse-ness of the German *Hanswurst* (jack-pudding) into

[1] " Die lustige person." That is to say, the permanent buffoon, like " Kasperle " in the German puppet-shows, or " Sganarelle " in Molière's broad comedies. — TRANS.

the neatness and delicacy of the Italian and French harlequins. Even Scapin and Crispin gradually vanished : the latter I saw played for the last time by Koch in his old age.

Richardson's novels had already made the middle classes attentive to a more delicate morality. The severe and inevitable consequences of a feminine *faux pas* were analysed in a frightful manner in " Clarissa." Lessing's " Miss Sara Sampson " treated the same theme, whilst " The Merchant of London " exhibited a misguided youth in the most terrible situation. The French dramas had the same end, but proceeded more moderately, and contrived to please by some accommodation at the end. Diderot's " Père de Famille," " The Honorable Criminal," " The Vinegar Dealer," " The Philosopher without Knowing It," " Eugenia," and other works of the sort, suited that honest feeling of citizen and family which began more and more to prevail. With us, " The Grateful Son," " The Deserter from Parental Love," and all of their kin, went the same way. " The Minister," " Clementini," and other pieces by Gehler, " The German Father of a Family," by Gemming, all brought agreeably to view the worth of the middle and even of the lower class, and delighted the great public. Eckhof, by his noble personality, which gave to the actor's profession a dignity in which it had hitherto been deficient, elevated to an uncommon degree the leading characters in such pieces; since, as an honest man, the expression of honesty succeeded with him to perfection.

While now the German theatre was completely inclining to effeminacy, Schröder arose as both author and actor, and, prompted by the connection between Hamburg and England, adapted some English comedies. The material of these he could only use in the most general way, since the originals are for the most part formless; and, if they begin well and according to

a certain plan, they wander from the mark at last.
The sole concern of their authors seems to be the
introduction of the oddest scenes; and whoever is
accustomed to a sustained work of art, at last unwillingly finds himself driven into the boundless.
Besides this, a wild, immoral, vulgarly dissolute tone
so decidedly pervades the whole, to an intolerable
degree, that it must have been difficult to deprive the
plan and the characters of all their bad manners.
They are a coarse, and, at the same time, dangerous,
food, which can only be enjoyed and digested by a
large and half-corrupted populace at a certain time.
Schröder did more for these things than is usually
known: he thoroughly altered them, assimilated them
to the German mind, and softened them as much as
possible. But still a bitter kernel always remains in
them; because the joke often depends on the ill-usage
of persons, whether they deserve it or not. In these
performances, which were also widely spread upon our
stage, lay a secret counterpoise to that too delicate
morality; and the action of both kinds of drama
against each other fortunately prevented the monotony
into which people would otherwise have fallen.

The Germans, kind and magnanimous by nature,
like to see no one ill-treated. But as no man, of
however good a disposition, is safe having something
put upon him contrary to his inclination, and as, moreover, comedy in general, if it is to please, always pre-
supposes or awakens something of malice in the
spectator; so, by a natural path, did people come to
a conduct which hitherto had been deemed unnatural:
this consisted in lowering the higher classes, and more
or less attacking them. Satire, whether in prose or
verse, had always avoided touching the court and
nobility. Rabener refrained from all jokes in that
direction, and remained in a lower circle. Zachariä
occupies himself much with country noblemen, comi-

cally sets forth their tastes and peculiarities; but this is done without contempt. Thümmel's "Wilhelmine," an ingenious little composition, as pleasant as it is bold, gained great applause, perhaps because the author, himself a nobleman and courtier, treated his own class unsparingly. But the boldest step was taken by Lessing, in his "Emilia Galotti," where the passions and intrigues of the higher classes are delineated in a bitter and cutting manner. All these things perfectly corresponded to the excited spirit of the time; and men of less mind and talent thought they might do the same, or even more: as indeed Grossmann, in six unsavoury dishes, served up to the malicious public all the tidbits of his vulgar kitchen. An honest man, Hofrath Reinhardt, was the majordomo at this unpleasant board, to the comfort and edification of all the guests. From this time forward the theatrical villains were always chosen from the higher ranks; and a person had to be a gentleman of the bedchamber, or at least a private secretary, to be worthy of such a distinction. But for the most godless examples, the highest offices and places in the court and civil list were chosen, in which high society, even the justiciaries, found their place as villains of the first water.

But, as I must fear already that I have been carried beyond the time which is now the subject in hand, I return to what concerns me, in order to mention the impulse which I felt to occupy myself in my leisure hours with the theatrical plans which I had once devised.

By my lasting interest in Shakespeare's works, I had so expanded my mind, that the narrow compass of the stage, and the short time allotted to a representation, seemed to me by no means sufficient to bring forward something important. The life of the gallant Götz von Berlichingen, written by himself, impelled me into the historic mode of treatment; and

my imagination so much extended itself, that my
dramatic form also went beyond all theatrical bounds,
and sought more and more to approach the living
events. I had, as I proceeded, talked circumstantially
on this subject with my sister, who was interested,
heart and soul, in such things, and renewed this conversation so often, without going to any work, that
she at last, growing impatient, and at the same time
wishing me well, urgently entreated me not to be
always casting my words into the air, but, once for
all, to set down upon paper that which must have
been so present to my mind. Determined by this
impulse, I began one morning to write, without having
made any previous sketch or plan. I wrote the first
scenes, and in the evening they were read aloud to
Cornelia. She gave them much applause, but only
conditionally, since she doubted that I should go on
so; nay, she even expressed a decided unbelief in my
perseverance. This only incited me the more: I
wrote on the next day, and also the third. Hope increased with the daily communications, and from step
to step everything gained more life; while the matter,
moreover, had become thoroughly my own. Thus I
kept, without interruption, to my work, which I pursued straight on, looking neither backward nor forward, neither to the right nor to the left; and in about
six weeks I had the pleasure to see the manuscript
stitched. I communicated it to Merck, who spoke
sensibly and kindly about it. I sent it to Herder,
who, on the contrary, expressed himself unkindly and
severely, and did not fail, in some lampoons written
for the occasion, to give me nicknames on account of
it. I did not allow myself to be perplexed by this,
but took a clear view of my object. The die was now
cast; and the only question was, how to play the
game best. I plainly saw that even here no one
would advise me; and, as after some time I could

regard my work as if it had proceeded from another hand, I indeed perceived, that, in my attempt to renounce unity of time and place, I had also infringed upon that higher unity which is so much the more required. Since, without plan or sketch, I had merely abandoned myself to my imagination and to an internal impulse, I had not deviated much at the beginning, and the first acts could fairly pass for what they were intended to be. In the following acts, however, and especially toward the end, I was unconsciously carried along by a wonderful passion. While trying to describe Adelheid as amiable, I had fallen in love with her myself, — my pen was involuntarily devoted to her alone, — the interest in her fate gained the preponderance; and as, apart from this consideration, Götz, toward the end, is without activity, and afterward only returns to an unlucky participation in the "Bauernkrieg,"[1] nothing was more natural than that a charming woman should supplant him in the mind of the author, who, casting off the fetters of art, thought to try himself in a new field. This defect, or rather this culpable superfluity, I soon perceived; since the nature of my poetry always impelled me to unity. I now, instead of the biography of Götz and German antiquities, kept my own work in mind, and sought to give it more and more historical and national substance, and to cancel that which was fabulous or merely proceeded from passion. In this I indeed sacrificed much, as the inclination of the man had to yield to the conviction of the artist. Thus, for instance, I had pleased myself highly by making Adelheid enter in a terrific nocturnal gypsy-scene, and perform wonders by her beautiful presence. A nearer examination banished her; and the love-affair between Franz and his noble, gracious lady, which was very circumstantially carried on in the fourth and

[1] The peasant war, answering to the *Jaquerie* in France. — TRANS.

fifth acts, was much condensed, and could only be suffered to appear in its chief points.

Therefore, without altering anything in the first manuscript, which I still actually possess in its original shape, I determined to rewrite the whole, and did this with such activity, that in a few weeks an entirely new-made piece lay before me. I went to work upon this all the quicker, the less my intention was ever to have the second poem printed; as I looked upon this likewise as a mere preparatory exercise, which in future I should again lay at the foundation of a new treatment, to be accomplished with greater industry and deliberation.

When I began to lay before Merck many proposals as to the way in which I should set about this task, he laughed at me, and asked what was the meaning of this perpetual writing and rewriting? The thing, he said, by this means, becomes only different, and seldom better: one must see what effect one thing produces, and then again try something new. "Be in time at the hedge, if you would dry your linen!"[1] he exclaimed, in the words of the proverb: hesitation and delay only make uncertain men. On the other hand, I replied to him, that it would be unpleasant to me to offer to a bookseller a work on which I had bestowed so much affection, and perhaps to receive a refusal as an answer; for how would they judge of a young, nameless, and also audacious author? As my dread of the press gradually vanished, I had wished to see printed my comedy "Die Mitschuldigen," upon which I set some value; but I found no publisher inclined in my favour.

Here the technically mercantile taste of my friend was at once excited. By means of the *Frankfort Zeitung* (Gazette), he had already formed a connection with learned men and booksellers; and therefore

---

[1] *Anglicé :* Make hay while the sun shines. — TRANS.

he thought that we ought to publish at our own expense this singular and certainly striking work, and that we should derive a larger profit from it. Like many others, he used often to reckon up for the booksellers their profit, which with many works was certainly great, especially if one left out of the account how much was lost by other writings and commercial affairs. In short, it was settled that I should procure the paper, and that he should take care of the printing. Thus we went heartily to work, and I was not displeased gradually to see my wild dramatic sketch in clean proof-sheets: it looked really neater than I myself expected. We completed the work, and it was sent off in many parcels. Before long a great commotion arose everywhere: the attention which it created became universal. But because, with our limited means, the copies could not be sent quickly enough to all parts, a pirated edition suddenly made its appearance. As, moreover, there could be no immediate return, especially in ready money, for the copies sent out, so was I, as a young man in a family whose treasury could not be in an abundant condition, at the very time when much attention, nay, much applause, was bestowed upon me, extremely perplexed as to how I should pay for the paper by means of which I had made the world acquainted with my talent. On the other hand, Merck, who knew better how to help himself, entertained the best hopes that all would soon come right again; but I never perceived that to be the case.

Through the little pamphlets which I had published anonymously, I had, at my own expense, become acquainted with the critics and the public; and I was thus pretty well prepared for praise and blame, especially as for many years I had constantly followed up the subject, and had observed how those authors were treated to whom I had devoted particular attention.

Here, even in my uncertainty, I could plainly perceive how much that was unfounded, one-sided, and arbitrary, was recklessly uttered. Now the same thing befell me; and, if I had not had some basis of my own, how much would the contradictions of cultivated men have perplexed me! Thus, for instance, there was in *The German Mercury* a diffuse, well-meant criticism, composed by some man of limited mind. Where he found fault, I could not agree with him, — still less when he stated how the affair could have been done otherwise. It was therefore highly gratifying to me, when immediately afterward I found a pleasant explanation by Wieland, who in general opposed the critic, and took my part against him. However,. the former review was printed likewise: I saw an example of the dull state of mind among well-informed and cultivated men. How, then, would it look with the great public?

The pleasure of talking over such things with Merck, and thus gaining light upon them, was of short duration; for the intelligent Landgravine of Hesse-Darmstadt took him with her train on her journey to Petersburg. The detailed letters which he wrote to me gave me a farther insight into the world, which I could the more make my own as the descriptions were made by a well-known and friendly hand. But nevertheless I remained very solitary for a long time, and was deprived just at this important epoch of his enlightening sympathy, of which I then stood in so much need.

For as one may happen to form the resolution, of becoming a soldier, and of going to the wars, and courageously determines to bear danger and difficulties, as well as to endure wounds and pains, and even death, but at the same time never calls to mind the particular cases in which those generally anticipated evils may surprise us in an extremely unpleasant

manner; so it is with every one who ventures into
the world, especially an author: and so it was with
me. As the great part of mankind is more excited
by a subject than by the treatment of it, so it was
to the subject that the sympathy of young men for
my pieces was generally owing. They thought they
could see in them a banner under the guidance of
which all that is wild and unpolished in youth might
find a vent; and those of the very best brains, who
had previously harboured a similar crotchet, were thus
carried away. I still possess a letter — I know not
to whom — from the excellent, and, in many respects,
unique, Bürger, which may serve as an important
voucher of the effect and excitement which was then
produced by that phenomenon. On the other side,
some men blamed me for painting the club-law in
too favourable colours, and even attributed to me the
intention of bringing those disorderly times back again.
Others took me for a profoundly learned man, and
wished me to publish a new edition, with notes, of
the original narrative of the good Götz, — a task to
which I felt by no means adapted, although I allowed
my name to be put on the title to the new impression.
Because I had understood how to gather the flowers
of a great existence, they took me for a careful
gardener. However, this learning and profound knowledge of mine were much doubted by others. A respectable man of business quite unexpectedly pays me
a visit. I considered myself highly honoured by this,
especially when he opened his discourse with the
praise of my "Götz von Berlichingen," and my good
insight into German history; but I was nevertheless
astonished when I perceived that he had really come
for the sole purpose of informing me that Götz von
Berlichingen was not a brother-in-law to Franz von
Sichingen, and that therefore, by this poetical matrimonial alliance, I have committed a great historical

error. In excuse I pleaded the fact, that Götz himself calls him so, but was met by the reply, that this is a form of expression which only denotes a nearer and more friendly connection, just as in modern times we call postilions "brothers-in-law,"[1] without being bound to them by any family tie. I thanked him as well as I could for this information, and only regretted that the evil was now not to be remedied. This was regretted by him also; while he exhorted me in the kindest manner to a further study of the German history and constitution, and offered me his library, of which I afterwards made a good use.

A droll event of the sort which occurred to me, was the visit of a bookseller, who, with cheerful openness, requested a dozen of such pieces, and promised to pay well for them. That we made ourselves very merry about this may be imagined: and yet, in fact, he was not so very far wrong; for I was already greatly occupied in moving backwards and forwards from this turning-point in German history, and in working up the chief events in a similar spirit,—a laudable design, which, like many others, was frustrated by the rushing flight of time.

That play, however, had not solely occupied the author; but while it was devised, written, rewritten, printed, and circulated, other images and plans were moving in his mind. Those which could be treated dramatically had the advantage of being oftenest thought over and brought near to execution; but at the same time was developed a transition to another form, which is not usually classed with those of the drama, but yet has a great affinity with them. This transition was chiefly brought about by a peculiarity of the author, which fashioned soliloquy into dialogue.

Accustomed to pass his time most pleasantly in

[1] It is a German peculiarity to apply the word "Schwager" (brother-in-law) to a postilion. — TRANS.

society, he changed even solitary thought into social
converse, and this in the following manner: He had
the habit, when he was alone, of calling before his
mind any person of his acquaintance. This person he
entreated to sit down, walked up and down by him,
remained standing before him, and discoursed with
him on the subject he had in his mind. To this the
person answered as occasion required, or by the ordinary gestures signified his assent or dissent, — in which
every man has something peculiar to himself. The
speaker then continued to carry out further that which
seemed to please the guest, or to qualify and define
more nearly that of which he disapproved, and, finally,
was polite enough to give up his notion. The oddest
part of the affair was, that he never selected persons of
his intimate acquaintance, but those whom he saw but
seldom, nay, several who lived at a distance in the
world, and with whom he had had a transient connection. They were, however, chiefly persons who, more
of a receptive than communicative nature, are ready
with a pure feeling to take interest in the things which
fall within their sphere; though he often summoned
contradicting spirits to these dialectic exercises. Persons of both sexes, of every age and rank, accommodated themselves to these discussions, and showed
themselves obliging and agreeable; since he only conversed on subjects which were clear to them, and
which they liked. Nevertheless, it would have appeared extremely strange to many of them, could they
have learned how often they were summoned to these
ideal conversations; since many of them would scarcely
have come to a real one.

How nearly such a mental dialogue is akin to a
written correspondence is plain enough: only in the
latter one sees returned the confidence one has bestowed; while, in the former, one creates for one's self
a confidence which is new, ever-changing, and unre-

turned. When, therefore, he had to describe that disgust which men, without being driven by necessity, feel for life, the author necessarily hit at once upon the plan of giving his sentiments in letters: for all gloominess is a birth, a pupil, of solitude; whoever resigns himself to it flies all opposition, and what is more opposed to him than a cheerful society? The enjoyment in life felt by others is to him a painful reproach; and thus, by that which should charm him out of himself, he is directed back to his inmost soul. If he at all expresses an opinion on this matter, it will be by letters; for no one feels immediately opposed to a written effusion, whether it be joyful or gloomy: while an answer containing opposite reasons gives the lonely one an opportunity to confirm himself in his whims, — an occasion to grow still more obdurate. The letters of Werther, which are written in this spirit, have so various a charm, precisely because their different contents were first talked over with several individuals in such ideal dialogues; while it was afterward in the composition itself that they appeared to be directed to one friend and sympathiser. To say more on the treatment of a little book which has formed the subject of so much discussion would hardly be advisable; but, with respect to the contents, something may yet be added.

That disgust with life has its physical and its moral causes: the former we will leave to the investigation of the physician, the latter to that of the moralist, and, in a matter so often elaborated, only consider the chief point, where the phenomenon most plainly expresses itself. All comfort in life is based upon a regular recurrence of external things. The change of day and night, of the seasons, of flowers and fruits, and whatever else meets us from epoch to epoch, so that we can and should enjoy it, — these are the proper springs of earthly life. The more open we are to these enjoyments, the happier do we feel ourselves; but if the changes in these phenomena roll up and down before us without our taking interest in them, if we are insensible to such beautiful offers, then comes on the greatest evil, the heaviest disease: we regard life as a disgusting burden. It is said of an Englishman, that he hanged himself that he might no longer dress and undress himself every day. I knew a worthy gardener, the superintendent of the laying out of a large park, who once cried out with vexation, "Shall I always see these clouds moving from east to west?" The story is told of one of our most excellent men, that he saw with vexation the returning green of spring, and wished that, by way of change, it might once appear red. These are properly the symptoms of a weariness of life, which does not unfrequently result in suicide, and which in thinking men, absorbed in themselves, was more frequent than can be imagined.

Nothing occasions this weariness more than the return of love. The first love, it is rightly said, is the only one; for in the second, and by the second, the highest sense of love is already lost. The conception of the eternal and infinite, which elevates and supports it, is destroyed; and it appears transient like everything else that recurs. The separation of the sensual from the moral, which, in the complicated, cultivated world sunders the feelings of love and desire, produces here also an exaggeration which can lead to no good.

Moreover, a young man soon perceives in others, if not in himself, that moral epochs change as well as the seasons of the year. The graciousness of the great, the favour of the strong, the encouragement of the active, the attachment of the multitude, the love of individuals, — all this changes up and down; and we can no more hold it fast than the sun, moon, and stars. And yet these things are not mere natural events; they escape us either by our own or by another's fault; but change they do, and we are never sure of them.

But that which most pains a sensitive youth is the unceasing return of our faults; for how late do we learn to see, that, while we cultivate our virtues, we rear our faults at the same time! The former depend upon the latter as upon their root, and the latter send forth secret ramifications as strong and as various as those which the former send forth in open light. Because, now, we generally practise our virtues with will and consciousness, but are unconsciously surprised by our faults, the former seldom procure us any pleasure, while the latter constantly bring trouble and pain. Here lies the most difficult point in self-knowledge, that which makes it almost impossible. If we conceive, in addition to all this, young, boiling blood, an imagination easily to be paralysed by single objects, and, moreover, the uncertain movements of the day, we shall not find unnatural an impatient striving to free one's self from such a strait.

However, such gloomy contemplations, which lead him who has resigned himself to them into the infinite, could not have developed themselves so decidedly in the minds of the German youths, had not an outward occasion excited and furthered them in this dismal business. This was caused by English literature, especially the poetical part, the great beauties of which are accompanied by an earnest melancholy, which it communicates to every one who occupies himself with it. The intellectual Briton, from his youth upwards, sees himself surrounded by a significant world, which stimulates all his powers: he perceives, sooner or later, that he must collect all his understanding to come to terms with it. How many of their poets have in their youth led a loose and riotous life, and soon found themselves justified in complaining of the vanity of earthly things! How many of them have tried their fortune in worldly occupations, have taken parts, principal or subordinate, in parliament, at court, in the ministry, in situations with the embassy, shown their active coöperation in the internal troubles and changes of state and government, and, if not in themselves, at any rate in their friends and patrons, more frequently made sad than pleasant experiences! How many have been banished, imprisoned, or robbed of their property!

Even the circumstance of being the spectator of such great events calls man to seriousness; and whither can seriousness lead farther than to a contemplation of the transient nature and worthlessness of all earthly things? The German also is serious; and thus English poetry was extremely suitable to him, and, because it proceeded from a higher state of things, even imposing. One finds in it throughout a great, apt understanding, well practised in the world; a deep, tender heart; an excellent will; an impassioned action, — the very noblest qualities which can be praised in an intellectual and cultivated man; but all this put together still makes no poet. True poetry announces itself thus, that, as a worldly gospel, it can by internal cheerfulness and external comfort free us from the earthly burdens which press upon us. Like an air-balloon, it lifts us, together with the ballast which is attached to us, into higher regions, and lets the confused labyrinths of the earth lie developed before us as in a bird's-eye view. The most lively, as well as the most serious, works, have the same aim of moderating both pleasure and pain by a felicitous intellectual form. Let us only in this spirit consider the majority of the English poems, chiefly morally didactic, and on the average they will only show us a gloomy weariness of life. Not only Young's "Night Thoughts," where this theme is preëminently worked out, but even the other contemplative poems stray, before one is aware of it, into this dismal region, where the understanding is presented with a problem which it cannot solve; since even religion, much as it can always construct for itself, leaves it in the lurch. Whole volumes might be compiled, which could serve as a commentary to this frightful text:

" Then old age and experience, hand in hand,
Lead him to death, and make him understand,
After a search so painful and so long,
That all his life he has been in the wrong."

What further makes the English poets thorough misanthropes, and diffuses over their writings the unpleasant feeling of repugnance against everything, is the fact, that the whole of them, on account of the various divisions of their commonwealth, must devote themselves for the best part, if not for the whole, of their lives to one party or another. Now, because a writer of the sort cannot praise and extol those of the party to which he belongs, nor the cause to which he adheres, since, if he did, he would only excite envy and hostility, he exercises his talent in speaking as badly as possible of those on the opposite side, and in sharpening, nay, poisoning, the satirical weapons as much as he can. When this is done by both parties, the world which lies between is destroyed and wholly annihilated; so that, in a great mass of sensibly acting people, one can discover, to use the mildest terms, nothing but folly and madness. Even their tender poems are occupied with mournful subjects. Here a deserted girl is dying; there a faithful lover is drowned, or is devoured by a shark before, by his hurried swimming, he reaches his beloved; and if a poet like Gray lies down in a churchyard, and again begins those well-known melodies, he, too, may gather around him a number of friends to melancholy. Milton's " Allegro" has first to scare away gloom in vehement verses, before he can attain a very moderate pleasure; and even the cheerful Goldsmith loses himself in elegiac feelings, when his "Deserted Village," as charmingly, as sadly, exhibits to us a lost paradise which his "Traveller" seeks over the whole earth.

I do not doubt that lively works, cheerful poems, can be brought forward and opposed to what I have said ; but the greatest number, and the best of them, certainly belong to the older epoch: and the newer works, which may be set down in the class, are likewise of a satirical tendency, are bitter, and treat women especially with contempt.

In short, those serious poems, undermining human nature, which, in general terms, have been mentioned above, were the favourites which we sought out before all others, one seeking, according to his disposition, the lighter elegiac melancholy, another the heavy, oppressive despair, which gives up everything. Strangely enough, our father and instructor, Shakespeare, who so well knew how to diffuse a pure cheerfulness, strengthened our feeling of dissatisfaction. Hamlet and his soliloquies were spectres which haunted all the young minds. The chief passages every one knew by heart and loved to recite; and everybody fancied he had a right to be just as melancholy as the Prince of Denmark, though he had seen no ghost, and had no royal father to avenge.

But that to all this melancholy a perfectly suitable locality might not be wanting, Ossian had charmed us even to the "Ultima Thule," where on a gray, boundless heath, wandering among prominent moss-covered gravestones, we saw the grass around us moved by an awful wind, and a heavily clouded sky above us. It was not till moonlight that the Caledonian night became day: departed heroes, faded maidens, floated around us, until at last we really thought we saw the spirit of Loda in his fearful form.

In such an element, with such surrounding influences, with tastes and studies of this kind, tortured by unsatisfied passions, by no means excited from without to important actions, with the sole prospect that we must adhere to a dull, spiritless citizen life, we became — in gloomy wantonness — attached to the thought, that we could at all events quit life at pleasure, if it no longer suited us, and thus miserably enough helped ourselves through the disgusts and weariness of the days. This feeling was so general, that "Werther" produced its great effect precisely because it struck a chord everywhere, and openly and intelligently exhibited the internal nature of a morbid youthful delusion. How accurately the English were acquainted with this sort of wretchedness is shown by the few significant lines, written before the appearance of "Werther:"

> "To griefs congenial prone,
> More wounds than nature gave he knew;
> While misery's form his fancy drew
> In dark ideal hues and horrors not its own."

Suicide is an event of human nature, which, whatever may be said and done with respect to it, demands the sympathy of every man, and in every epoch must be discussed anew. Montesquieu grants his heroes and great men the right of killing themselves as they think fit, since he says that it must be free to every one to close the fifth act of his tragedy as he pleases. But the persons here alluded to are not such as have led an active and important life, who have sacrificed their days for a great empire, or for the cause of freedom, and whom one cannot blame if they think to follow in another world the idea which inspires them, as soon as it has vanished from the earth. We are here dealing with those whose life is embittered by a want of action, in the midst of the most peaceful circumstances in the world, through exaggerated demands upon themselves. Having myself been in this predicament, and having known best the pain I then suffered, and the exertion it cost me to free myself, I will not conceal the reflections I made with much deliberation on the various kinds of death one might choose.

There is something so unnatural in a man tearing himself away from himself, not only injuring, but destroying, himself, that he mostly seizes upon mechanical means to carry his design into execution. When Ajax falls upon his sword, it is the weight of his body which does him the last service. When the warrior binds his shield-bearer not to let him fall into the hands of the enemy, it is still an external force which he secures, only a moral instead of a physical one. Women seek in water a cooling for their despair, and the extremely mechanical means of fire-arms ensure a rapid act with the very least exertion. Hanging, one does not like to mention, because it is an ignoble death. In England it is more likely to occur; because there, from youth upwards, one sees so many hanged, without the punishment being precisely dishonourable. By poison, by opening the veins, the only intention is to depart slowly from life; and that most refined, rapid, and painless death by an adder, was worthy of a queen who had passed her life in pleasure and brilliancy. But all these are external aids, enemies with which man forms an alliance against himself.

When I considered all these means, and looked about further in history, I found among all those who killed themselves no one who did this deed with such greatness and freedom of mind as the emperor Otho. He, having the worst of it as a general, but being by no means reduced to extremities, resolves to quit the world for the benefit of the empire, which in some measure already belongs to him, and for the sake of sparing so many thousands. He has a cheerful supper with his friends, and the next morning it is found that he has plunged a sharp dagger into his heart. This deed alone seemed to me worthy of imitation; and I was convinced, that whoever could not act in this like Otho, had no right to go voluntarily out of the world. By these convictions I freed myself, not so much from the danger as from the whim of suicide, which in those splendid times of peace, and with an indolent youth, had managed to creep in. Among a considerable collection of weapons, I possessed a handsome, well-polished dagger. This I laid every night by my bed; and, before I extinguished the candle, I tried whether I could succeed in plunging the sharp point a couple of inches deep into my heart. Since I never could succeed in this, I at last laughed myself out of the notion, threw off all hypochondriacal fancies, and resolved to live. But, to be able to do this with cheerfulness, I was obliged to solve a poetical problem, by which all that I had felt, thought, and fancied upon this important point should be reduced to words. For this purpose I collected the elements which had been at work in me for a few years, I rendered present to my mind the cases which had most afflicted and tormented me, but nothing would come to a definite form: I lacked an event, a fable, in which they could be overlooked.

All at once I heard the news of Jerusalem's death, and, immediately after the general report, the most accurate and circumstantial description of the occurrence; and at this moment the plan of "Werther" was formed, and the whole shot together from all sides, and became a solid mass, just as water in a vessel, which stands upon the point of freezing, is converted into hard ice by the most gentle shake. To hold fast this singular prize, to render present to myself, and to carry out in all its parts, a work of such important and various contents, was the more material to me, as I

had again fallen into a painful situation, which left me
even less hope than those which had preceded it, and
foreboded only sadness, if not vexation.

It is always a misfortune to step into new relations
to which one has not been inured: we are often against
our will lured into a false sympathy, the incomplete-
ness [1] of such positions troubles us; and yet we see no
means, either of completing them or of removing them.

Frau von Laroche had married her eldest daughter
at Frankfort, and often came to visit her, but could not
reconcile herself to the position which she herself had
chosen. Instead of feeling comfortable, or endeavouring to make any alteration, she indulged in lamentations, so that one was really forced to think that her
daughter was unhappy; although as she wanted nothing, and her husband denied her nothing, one could not
well see in what her unhappiness properly consisted.
In the meantime I was well received in the house, and
came into contact with the whole circle, which consisted of persons who had partly contributed to the
marriage, partly wished for it a happy result. The
Dean of St. Leonhard, Dumeitz, conceived a confidence,
nay, a friendship, for me. He was the first Catholic
clergyman with whom I had come into close contact,
and who, because he was a clear-sighted man, gave
me beautiful and sufficient explanations of the faith,
usages, and external and internal relations of the
oldest church. The figure of a well-formed though not
young lady, named Serviéres, I still accurately remember. I likewise came into contact with the Alessina-
Schweizer, and other families, forming a connection
with the sons, which long continued in the most
friendly manner, and all at once found myself domesti-
cated in a strange circle, in the occupations, pleasures,
and even religious exercises of which I was induced,

---

[1] "Halbheit," "Halfness" — if there were such a word —
would be the proper expression.— TRANS.

nay, compelled, to take part. My former relation to
the young wife, which was, properly speaking, only
that of a brother to a sister, was continued after marriage; my age was suitable to her own; I was the
only one in the whole circle in whom she heard an
echo of those intellectual tones to which she had been
accustomed from her youth. We lived on together in
a childish confidence; and, although there was nothing
impassioned in our intercourse, it was tormenting
enough, because she could not become reconciled to
her new circumstances, and, although blessed with the
goods of fortune, had to act as the mother of several
stepchildren, being moreover transplanted from the
cheerful vale of Ehrenbreitstein and a joyous state
of youth into a gloomily situated mercantile house.
Amid so many new family connections was I hemmed
in, without any real participation or coöperation. If
they were satisfied with each other, all seemed to go
on as a matter of course; but most of the parties concerned turned to me in cases of vexation, which by
my lively sympathy I generally rendered worse rather
than better. In a short time this situation became
quite insupportable to me: all the disgust at life which
usually springs from such half-connections seemed to
burden me with double and threefold weight, and
a new strong resolution was necessary to free myself
from it.

Jerusalem's death, which was occasioned by his
unhappy attachment to the wife of his friend, shook
me out of the dream; and because I not only visibly
contemplated that which had occurred to him and me,
but something similar, which befell me at the moment,
also stirred me to passionate emotion, I could not
do otherwise than breathe into that production, which
I had just undertaken, all that warmth which leaves
no distinction between the poetical and the actual. I
had completely isolated myself, nay, prohibited the

visits of my friends; and internally also I put everything aside that did not immediately belong to the subject. On the other hand, I embraced everything that had any relation to my design, and repeated to myself my nearest life, of the contents of which I had as yet made no practical use. Under such circumstances, after such long and so many preparations in secret, I wrote " Werther " in four weeks, without any scheme of the whole, or treatment of any part, being previously put on paper.

The manuscript, which was now finished, lay before me as a rough draught, with few corrections and alterations. It was stitched at once, for the binding is to a written work of about the same use as the frame is to a picture: one can much better see whether there is really anything in it. Since I had written thus much almost unconsciously, like a somnambulist, I was myself astonished, now I went through it, that I might alter and improve it in some respects. But in the expectation, that after some time, when I had seen it at a certain distance, much would occur to me that would turn to the advantage of the work, I gave it to my younger friends to read, upon whom it produced an effect so much the greater, as, contrary to my usual custom, I had told no one of it, nor discovered my design beforehand. Yet here again it was the subject-matter which really produced the effect, and in this respect they were in a frame of mind precisely the reverse of my own; for by this composition, more than by any other, I had freed myself from that stormy element, upon which, through my own fault and that of others, through a mode of life both accidental and chosen, through design and thoughtless precipitation, through obstinacy and pliability, I had been driven about in the most violent manner. I felt, as if after a general confession, once more happy and free, and justified in beginning a new life.

The old nostrum had been of excellent service to me on this occasion. But, while I felt relieved and enlightened by having turned reality into poetry, my friends were led astray by my work; for they thought that poetry ought to be turned into reality, that such a moral was to be imitated, and that, at any rate one ought to shoot one's self. What had first happened here among a few, afterward took place among the larger public; and this little book, which had been so beneficial to me, was decried as extremely injurious.

But all the evils and misfortunes which it may have produced were nearly prevented by an accident, since even after its production it ran the risk of being destroyed. The matter stood thus: Merck had lately returned from Petersburg; I had spoken to him but little, because he was always occupied, and only told him, in the most general terms, of that "Werther" which lay next my heart. He once called upon me; and, as he did not seem very talkative, I asked him to listen to me. He seated himself on the sofa; and I began to read the tale, letter by letter. After I had gone on thus for awhile, without luring from him any sign of admiration, I adopted a more pathetic strain; but what were my feelings, when, at a pause which I made, he struck me down in the most frightful manner, with, "Well, that's very pretty," and withdrew without adding anything more. I was quite beside myself; for as I took great pleasure in my works, but at first passed no judgment on them, I here firmly believed that I had made a mistake in subject, tone, and style, — all of which were doubtful, — and had produced something quite inadmissible. Had a fire been at hand, I should at once have thrown in the work; but I again plucked up courage, and passed many painful days, until he at last assured me, in confidence, that at that moment he had been in the most frightful situation in which a man can be placed. On this account, he said, he had neither seen nor heard anything, and did not even know what the manuscript was about. In the meantime the matter had been set right, as far as was possible: and Merck, in the times of his energy, was just the man to accommodate himself to anything monstrous; his humour returned, only it had grown still more bitter than before. He blamed my design of rewriting " Werther," with the same expressions which he had used on a former occasion, and desired to see it printed just as it was. A fair copy was made, which did not remain long in my hands; for, on the very day on which my sister was married to George Schlosser, a letter from Weygand of Leipzig chanced to arrive, in which he asked me for a manuscript: such a coincidence I looked upon as a favourable omen. I sent off " Werther," and was very well satisfied, when the remuneration I received for it was not entirely swallowed up by the debts which I had been forced to contract on account of " Götz von Berlichingen."

The effect of this little book was great, nay, immense, and chiefly because it exactly hit the temper of the times. For as it requires but a little match to blow up an immense mine, so the explosion which followed my publication was mighty, from the circumstance that the youthful world had already undermined itself; and the shock was great, because all extravagant demands, unsatisfied passions, and imaginary wrongs were suddenly brought to an eruption. It cannot be expected of the public that it should receive an intellectual work intellectually. In fact, it was only the subject, the material part, that was considered, as I had already found to be the case among my own friends; while at the same time arose that old prejudice, associated with the dignity of a printed book, — that it ought to have a moral aim. But a true picture of life has none. It neither approves nor censures, but develops sentiments and actions in their consequences, and thereby enlightens and instructs.

Of the reviews I took little notice. The matter was settled, as far as I was concerned; and the good folks might now try what they could make of it. Yet my friends did not fail to collect these things, and, as they were already initiated into my views, to make merry with them. The "Joys of Young Werther," with which Nicolai came forth, gave us occasion for many a jest. This otherwise excellent, meritorious, and well-informed man, had already begun to depreciate and oppose everything that did not accord with his own way of thinking, which, as he was of a very narrow mind, he held to be the only correct way. Against me, too, he must needs try his strength; and his pamphlet was soon in our hands. The very delicate vignette, by Chodowiecki, gave me much delight: as at that time I admired this artist extravagantly. The jumbling medley itself was cut out of that rough household stuff which the human understanding, in its homely limits, takes especial pains to make sufficiently coarse. Without perceiving that there was nothing here to qualify, that Werther's youthful bloom, from the very first, appears gnawed by the deadly worm, Nicolai allows my treatment to pass current up to the two hundred and fourteenth page; and then, when the desolate mortal is preparing for the fatal step, the acute pyschological physician contrives to palm upon his patient a pistol, loaded with chickens' blood, from which a filthy spectacle, but happily no mischief, arises. Charlotte becomes the wife of Werther, and the whole affair ends to the satisfaction of everybody.

So much I can recall to memory, for the book never came before my eyes again. I had cut out the vignette, and placed it among my most favourite engravings. I then, by way of quiet, innocent revenge, composed a little burlesque poem, "Nicolai at the

Grave of Werther," which, however, cannot be communicated. On this occasion, too, the pleasure of
giving everything a dramatic shape was again predominant. I wrote a prose dialogue between Charlotte
and Werther, which was tolerably comical: Werther
bitterly complains that his deliverance by chickens'
blood has turned out so badly. His life is saved, it is
true; but he has shot his eyes out. He is now in
despair at being her husband, without being able to see
her; for the complete view of her person would to him
be much dearer than all those pretty details of which
he could assure himself by the touch. Charlotte, as
may be imagined, has no great catch in a blind husband; and thus occasion is given to abuse Nicolai
pretty roundly for interfering unasked in other people's
affairs. The whole was written in a good-natured
spirit, and painted, with prophetic forebodings, that
unhappy, conceited humour of Nicolai's, which led him
to meddle with things beyond his compass, which gave
great annoyance both to himself and others, and by
which, eventually, in spite of his undoubted merits, he
entirely destroyed his literary reputation. The original
of this *jeu d'esprit* was never copied, and has been lost
sight of for years. I had a special predilection for the
little production. The pure, ardent attachment of the
two young persons was rather heightened than diminished by the comico-tragic situation into which they
were thus transposed. The greatest tenderness prevailed throughout; and even my adversary was not
treated ill-naturedly, but only humourously. I did
not, however, let the book itself speak quite so politely:
in imitation of an old rhyme it expressed itself thus:

> "By that conceited man — by *him*
> I'm dangerous proclaimed;
> The wight uncouth, who cannot **swim**,
> By him the water's blamed.

> That Berlin pack, priest-ridden lot —
> Their ban I am not heeding;
> And he who understands me not
> Ought to improve in reading."

Being prepared for all that might be alleged against Werther, I found those attacks, numerous as they were, by no means annoying; but I had no anticipation of the intolerable torment provided for me by sympathisers and well-wishers. These, instead of saying anything civil to me about my book just as it was, wished to know, one and all, what was really true in it; at which I grew very angry, and often expressed myself with great discourtesy. To answer this question, I should have been obliged to pull to pieces and destroy the form of a work on which I had so long pondered, with the view of giving a poetical unity to its many elements; and in this operation, if the essential parts were not destroyed, they would, at least, have been scattered and dispersed. However, upon a closer consideration of the matter, I could not take the public inquisitiveness in ill part. Jerusalem's fate had excited great attention. An educated, amiable, blameless young man, the son of one of the first theologians and authors, healthy and opulent, had at once, without any known cause, destroyed himself. Every one asked how this was possible: and, when they heard of an unfortunate love-affair, the whole youth were excited; and, as soon as it transpired that some little annoyances had occurred to him in the higher circles, the middle classes also became excited; indeed, every one was anxious to learn further particulars. Now, there appeared in "Werther" an exact delineation, as it was thought, of the life and character of that young man. The locality and person tallied; and the narrative was so very natural, that they considered themselves fully informed and satisfied. But on the other hand, on closer examination, there was so much that did not fit, that there arose, for those who sought the truth, an unmanageable business, because a critical investigation must necessarily produce a hundred doubts. The real groundwork of the affair was, however, not to be fathomed; for all that I had interwoven of my own life and suffering could not be deciphered, because, as an unobserved young man, I had secretly, though not silently, pursued my course.

While engaged in my work, I was fully aware how highly that artist was favoured who had an opportunity of composing a Venus from the study of a variety of beauties. Accordingly I took leave to model my Charlotte according to the shape and qualities of several pretty girls, although the chief characteristics were taken from the one I loved best. The inquisitive public could therefore discover similarities in various women, and even to the ladies themselves it was not quite indifferent to be taken for the right one. But these several Charlottes caused me infinite trouble, because every one who only looked at me seemed determined to know where the proper one really resided. I endeavoured to save myself, like Nathan [1] with the three rings, by an expedient, which, though it might suit higher beings, would not satisfy either the believing or the reading public. I hoped, after a time, to be freed from such tormenting inquiries; but they pursued me through my whole life. I endeavoured, on my travels, to escape from them, by assuming an *incognito*; but even this remedy was, to my disappointment, unavailing: and thus the author of the little work, had he even done anything wrong and mischievous, was sufficiently, I may say disproportionately, punished by such unavoidable importunities.

Subjected to this kind of infliction, I was taught but too unequivocally, that authors and their public are

[1] " Nathan the Wise," in Lessing's play, founded on Boccaccio's tale of the rings. — TRANS.

separated by an immense gulf, of which, happily, neither of them has any conception. The uselessness, therefore, of all prefaces I had long ago seen; for the more pains a writer takes to render his views clear, the more occasion he gives for embarrassment. Besides, an author may preface as elaborately as he will, the public will always go on making precisely those demands which he has endeavoured to avoid. With a kindred peculiarity of readers, which (particularly with those who print their judgments) seems remarkably comical, I was likewise soon acquainted: for they cherish the delusion that an author, in producing anything, becomes their debtor; and he always falls short of what they wished and expected of him, although, before they had seen our work, they had not the least notion that anything of the kind existed, or was even possible. Independently of all this, it was now the greatest fortune, or misfortune, that every one wished to make the acquaintance of this strange young author, who had stepped forward so unexpectedly and so boldly. They desired to see him, to speak to him, and, even at a distance, to hear something from him: thus he had to encounter a very considerable crowd, sometimes pleasant, sometimes disagreeable, but always diverting him from his pursuits. For enough works already begun lay before him, — nay, and would have given him abundance of work for some years if he could have kept to them with his old fervour; but he was drawn forth from the quiet, the twilight, the obscurity, which alone can favour pure creation, into the noise of daylight, where one is lost in others, where one is led astray, alike by sympathy and by coldness, by praise and by blame, because outward contact never accords with the epoch of our inner culture, and therefore, as it cannot further us, must necessarily injure us.

Yet more than by all the diversions of the day, the author was kept from the elaboration and completion of greater works by the taste then prevalent in this society for *dramatising* everything of importance which occurred in actual life. What that technical expression (for such it was in our inventive society) really meant, shall here be explained. Excited by intellectual meetings on days of hilarity, we were accustomed, in short extemporary performances, to communicate, in fragments, all the materials we had collected toward the formation of larger compositions. One single simple incident, a pleasantly *naïve* or even silly word, a blunder, a paradox, a clever remark, personal singularities or habits, nay, a peculiar expression, and whatever else would occur in a gay and bustling life, took the form of a dialogue, a catechism, a passing scene, or a drama, — often in prose, but oftener in verse.

By this practice, carried on with genial passion, the really poetic mode of thought was established. We allowed objects, events, persons, to stand for themselves in all their bearings; our only endeavour being to comprehend them clearly and exhibit them vividly. Every expression of approbation or disapprobation was to pass in living forms before the eyes of the spectator. These productions might be called animated epigrams, which, though without edges or points, were richly furnished with marked and striking features. The "Jahrmarktsfest" ("Fair-festival") is an epigram of this kind, or rather a collection of such epigrams. All the characters there introduced are meant for actual living members of that society, or for persons at least connected and in some degree known to it; but the meaning of the riddle remained concealed to the greater part: all laughed, and few knew that their own marked peculiarities served as the jest. The prologue to "Bahrdt's Newest Revelations" may be looked upon as a document of another kind: the smallest pieces are among the miscellaneous poems, a great many have been destroyed or lost, and some that still exist do not admit of being published. Those which appeared in print only increased the excitement of the public, and curiosity about the author: those which were handed about in manuscript entertained the immediate circle, which was continually increasing. Doctor Bahrdt, then at Giessen, paid me a visit, apparently courteous and confiding : he joked about the prologue, and wished to be placed on a friendly footing. But we young people still continued to omit no opportunity at social festivals, of sporting, in a malicious vein, at the peculiarities which we had remarked in others, and successfully exhibited.

Although it was by no means displeasing to the young author to be stared at as a literary meteor, he nevertheless tried, with glad modesty, to testify his esteem for the most deserving men of his country, among whom, before all others, the admirable Justus Möser claims especial mention. The little essays on political subjects by this incomparable man had been printed some years before in the *Osnaburg Intelligenzblätter*, and made known to me through Herder, who overlooked nothing of worth that appeared in his time, especially if in print. Möser's daughter, Frau von Voigt, was occupied in collecting these scattered papers. We had scarcely patience to wait for their publication; and I placed myself in communication with her, to assure her, with sincere interest, that the essays, which, both in matter and form, had been addressed only to a limited circle, would be useful and beneficial everywhere. She and her father received these assurances from a stranger, not altogether unknown, in the kindest manner; since an anxiety which they had felt was thus preliminarily removed.

What is in the highest degree remarkable and commendable in these little essays, all of which, being composed in one spirit, form together a perfect whole, is the very intimate knowledge they display of the

whole civil state of man. We see a system resting
upon the past, and still in vigorous existence. On the
one hand, there is a firm adherence to tradition; on
the other, movement and change which cannot be prevented. Here alarm is felt at a useful novelty; there
pleasure in what is new, although it be useless, or even
injurious. With what freedom from prejudice the
author explains the relative position of different ranks,
and the connection in which cities, towns, and villages
mutually stand! We learn their prerogatives, together
with the legal grounds of them: we are told where the
main capital of the state is invested, and what interest
it yields. We see property and its advantages on the
one hand; on the other, taxes and disadvantages of various kinds; and then the numerous branches of industry;
and in all this past and present times are contrasted.

Osnaburg, as a member of the Hanseatic League, we
are told, had in the earlier periods an extensive and
active commerce. According to the circumstances of
those times, it had a remarkable and fine situation: it
could receive the produce of the country, and was not
too far removed from the sea to transport it in its own
ships. But now, in later times, it lies deep in the
interior, and is gradually removed and shut out from
the sea-trade. How this has occurred, is explained in
all its bearings. The conflict between England and the
coasts, and of the havens with the interior, is mentioned; here are set forth the great advantages of those
who live on the seaside, and deliberate plans are proposed for enabling the inhabitants of the interior to
obtain similar advantages. We then learn a great deal
about trades and handicrafts, and how these have been
outstripped by manufactures, and undermined by shop-
keeping: decline is pointed out as the result of various
causes, and this result, in its turn, as the cause of a
further decline, in an endless circle, which it is difficult to unravel; yet it is so clearly set forth by the

vigilant citizen, that one fancies one can see the way to escape from it. The author throughout displays the clearest insight into the most minute circumstances. His proposals, his counsel — nothing is drawn from the air, and yet they are often impracticable, on which account he calls his collection " patriotic fancies ; " although everything in it is based on the actual and the possible.

But as everything in public life is influenced by domestic condition, this especially engages his attention. As objects, both of his serious and sportive reflections, we find the changes in manners and customs, dress, diet, domestic life, and education. It would be necessary to indicate everything which exists in the civil and social world, to exhaust the list of subjects which he discusses. And his treatment of them is admirable. A thorough man of business discourses with the people in weekly papers, respecting whatever a wise and beneficent government undertakes or carries out, that he may bring it to their comprehension in its true light. This is by no means done in a learned manner, but in those varied forms which may be called poetic, and which, in the best sense of the word, must certainly be considered rhetorical. He rises at all times above his subject, and understands how to give a cheerful view of the most serious subjects; now half-concealed behind this or that mask, now speaking in his own person, always complete and exhausting his subject, at the same time always in good humour; more or less ironical, thoroughly to the purpose, honest, well-meaning, sometimes rough and vehement; — and all this so well regulated, that the spirit, understanding, facility, skill, taste, and character of the author cannot but be admired. In the choice of subjects of general utility, deep insight, enlarged views, happy treatment, profound yet cheerful humour, I know no one to whom I can compare him but Franklin.

Such a man had an imposing effect upon us, and the greatest influence on a youthful generation, which demanded something sound, and stood ready to appreciate it. We thought we could adapt ourselves to the form of his exposition; but who could hope to make himself master of so rich an entertainment, and to handle the most unmanageable subjects with so much ease?

But this is our fairest and sweetest illusion, — which we must not forego, however much pain it may cause us through life, — that we would, where possible, appropriate to ourselves, nay, even reproduce and exhibit as our own, that which we prize and honour in others.

FOURTEENTH BOOK.

WITH the movement which was spreading among the public, now arose another of greater importance perhaps to the author, as it took place in his immediate circle.

His early friends, who had read in manuscript those poetical compositions which were now creating so much sensation, and therefore regarded them almost as their own, gloried in a success which they had boldly enough predicted. This number was augmented by new adherents, especially by such as felt conscious of a creative power in themselves, or were desirous of calling one forth and cultivating it.

Among the former, Lenz was the most active; and he deported himself strangely enough. I have already sketched the outward appearance of this remarkable mortal, and have touched affectionately on his talent for humour. I will now speak of his character, in its results rather than descriptively; because it would be impossible to follow him through the mazy course of his life, and to transfer to these pages a full exhibition of his peculiarities.

Generally known is that self-torture, which, in the lack of all outward grievances, had now become fashionable and which disturbed the very best minds. That which gives but a transient pain to ordinary men, who never meditate on that which they seek to banish from their minds, was, by the better order, acutely observed, regarded, and recorded in books, letters, and diaries. But now men united the strictest moral requisitions on themselves and others with an excessive negligence in action; and vague notions arising from this half-self-knowledge misled them into the strangest habits and out-of-the-way practices. But this painful work of self-contemplation was justified by the rising empirical psychology, which, while it was not exactly willing to pronounce everything that produces inward disquiet to be wicked and objectionable, still could not give it an unconditional approval; and thus was originated an eternal and inappeasable contest. In carrying on and sustaining this conflict, Lenz surpassed all the other idlers and dabblers who were occupied in mining into their own souls; and thus he suffered from the universal tendency of the times, which was said to have been let loose by Werther: but a personal peculiarity distinguished him from all the rest. While they were undeniably frank and honest creatures, he had a decided inclination to intrigue, and, indeed, to intrigue for its own sake, without having in view any special object, — any reasonable, attainable, personal object. On the contrary, it was always his custom to propose to himself something whimsical, which served, for that very reason, to keep him constantly occupied. In this way all his life long his imagination made him act a false part; his love, as well as his hate, was imaginary; he dealt with his thoughts and feelings in a wilful manner, so as always to have something to do. He endeavoured to give reality to his sympathies and antipathies by the most perverse means, and always himself destroyed his own work. Thus he never benefited any one he loved, and never injured any one he hated. In general he seemed to sin only to punish himself, and to intrigue for no purpose but to graft a new fable upon an old one.

His talent, in which tenderness, facility, and subtlety rivalled each other, proceeded from a real depth, — from an inexhaustible creative power, — but was thoroughly morbid with all its beauty. Such qualities are precisely the most difficult to judge. It is impossible to overlook great features in his works: a lovely tenderness steals along through pieces of caricature so odd and so silly that they can hardly be pardoned, even in a humour so thorough and unassuming, and such a genuine comic talent. His days were made up of mere nothings, to which his nimble fancy could ever give a meaning; and he was the better able to squander hours away, since, with a happy memory, the time which he did employ in reading was always fruitful, and enriched his original mode of thought with various materials.

He had been sent to Strasburg with some Livonian gentlemen, and a more unfortunate choice of a Mentor could not have been made. The elder baron went back for a time to his native country, and left behind him a lady to whom he was tenderly attached. In order to keep at a distance the second brother, who was playing court to the same lady, as well as other lovers, and to preserve the precious heart for his absent friend, Lenz determined either to feign that he had fallen in love with the beauty, or, if you please, actually to do so. He carried through this plan with the most obstinate adherence to the ideal he had formed of her, without being aware that he, as well as the others, only served her for jest and pastime. So much the better for him! For him, too, it was nothing but a game, which could only be kept up by her meeting him in the same spirit, now attracting him, now repelling him, now encouraging him, and now slighting him. We may be sure, that, if he had become aware of the way the affair sometimes went on, he would, with great delight, have congratulated himself on the discovery.

As for the rest, he, like his pupils, lived mostly with officers of the garrison; and thus the strange notions he afterward brought out in his comedy "Die Soldaten"

("The Soldiers") probably originated. At any rate, this early acquaintance with military men had on him the peculiar effect, that he forthwith fancied himself a great judge of military matters. And yet from time to time he really studied the subject in detail with such effect, that some years afterward he prepared a long memorial to the French minister of war, from which he promised himself the best results. The faults of the department were tolerably well pointed out; but, on the other hand, the remedies were ridiculous and impracticable. However, he cherished a conviction that he should by this means gain great influence at court, and was anything but grateful to those of his friends who, partly by reasoning, and partly by active opposition, compelled him to suppress, and afterward to burn, this fantastic work, after it had been fair-copied, put under cover with a letter, and formally addressed.

First of all by word of mouth, and afterward by letter, he had confided to me all the mazes of his tortuous movements with regard to the lady above mentioned. The poetry which he could infuse into the commonest incidents often astonished me; so that I urged him to employ his talents in turning the essence of this long-winded adventure to account, and to make a little romance out of it. But that was not in his line: he could only succeed when he poured himself out for ever upon details, and span an endless thread without any purpose. Perhaps it will be possible, at a future time, to deduce from these premises some account of his life up to the time that he became a lunatic. At present I confine myself to what is immediately connected with the subject in hand.

Hardly had "Götz von Berlichingen" appeared, when Lenz sent me a prolix essay written on small draught-paper, such as he commonly used, without leaving the least margin, either at the top, the bottom, or the sides.

It was entitled, " Ueber unsere Ehe " (" On our Marriage "), and, were it still in existence, might enlighten us much more now than it then did me, when I was as yet in the dark as to him and his character. The leading purpose of this long manuscript was, to compare my talent with his own ; now he seemed to make himself inferior to me, now to represent himself as my equal ; but it was all done with such humourous and neat turns of expression, that I gladly received the view he intended to convey, and all the more so as I did, in fact, rate very high the gifts he possessed, and was always urging him to concentrate himself out of his aimless rambling, and to use his natural capacities with some artistical control. I replied in the most friendly way to this confidential communication ; and, as he had encouraged the greatest intimacy between us (as the whimsical title indicates), from that time forward I made known to him everything I had either finished or designed. In return he successively sent me his manuscripts: " Der Hofmeister " (" Private Tutor "), " Der Neue Menoza " (" The New Menoza "), " Die Soldaten " (" The Soldiers "), the imitations of Plautus, and the translation from the English which I have before spoken of as forming the supplement to his remarks on the theatre.

While reading the latter, I was somewhat struck to find him in a laconic preface speaking in such a way as to convey the idea that this essay, which contained a vehement attack upon the regular theatre, had, many years before, been read to a society of the friends of literature at a time, in short, when " Götz " was not yet written. That there should have been among Lenz's acquaintances at Strasburg a literary circle of which I was ignorant seemed somewhat problematical : however, I let it pass, and soon procured publishers for this and his other writings, without having the least suspicion that he had selected me as the chief

been compelled to cast away, he had never possessed: relations of society from which they would have to emancipate themselves had never fettered him. Thus might he be regarded as one of the purest disciples of that gospel of nature; and, in view of his own persevering efforts and his conduct as a man and son, he might well exclaim, "All is good as it comes from the hands of nature!" But the conclusion, "All is corrupted in the hands of man!" was also forced upon him by adverse experience. It was not with himself that he had to struggle, but beyond and out of himself with the conventional world, from whose fetters the Citizen of Geneva designed to set us free. And as from the circumstances of his youth the struggle he had to undergo had often been difficult and painful, he had been driven back upon himself too violently to attain a thoroughly serene and joyous development. On the contrary, as he had had to force his way against an opposing world, a trait of bitterness had crept into his character, which he afterward in some degree fed and cherished, but for the most part strove against and conquered.

His works, as far as I am able to recall them, bespeak a strong understanding, an upright mind, an active imagination, a ready perception of the varieties of human nature, and a characteristic imitation of generic differences. His girls and boys are open and amiable, his youths ardent, his men plain and intelligent, the personages whom he paints in an unfavourable light are not overdrawn; he is not wanting in cheerfulness and good humour, in wit and happy notions; allegories and symbols are at his command; he can entertain and please us; and the enjoyment would be still purer if he did not here and there mar, both for himself and us, his gay, pointed jesting by a touch of bitterness. Yet this it is which makes him what he is. The modes of living and of writing become as varied as they are, from the fact that every one wavers theoretically between knowledge and error, and practically between creation and 'destruction.

Klinger should be classed with those who have formed themselves for the world, out of themselves, out of their own souls and understandings. Because this takes place in and among a greater mass, and because among themselves they use, with power and effect, an intelligible language flowing out of universal nature and popular peculiarities, such men always cherish a warm hostility to all forms of the schools, especially if these forms, separated from their living origin, have degenerated into phrases, and have thus lost altogether their first fresh significance. Such men almost invariably declare war against new opinions, views, and systems, as well as against new events and rising men of importance who announce or produce great changes. They are, however, not so much to blame on this account: their opposition is not unnatural when they see all that which they are indebted to for their own existence and culture menaced with ruin and in great danger.

In an energetic character, this adherence to its own views becomes the more worthy of respect when it has been maintained throughout a life in the world and in affairs, and when a mode of dealing with current events, which to many might seem rough and arbitrary, being employed at the right time, has led surely to the desired end. This was the case with Klinger: without pliability (which was never the virtue of the born citizen of the empire [1]) he had nevertheless risen, steadily and honourably, to posts of great importance, had managed to maintain his position, and, as he advanced in the approbation and favour of his highest patrons, never forgot his old friends, or the path he had left behind. Indeed, through all degrees

[1] That is to say, a native of one of the imperial cities.

of absence and separation, he laboured pertinaciously
to preserve the most complete constancy of remembrance; and it certainly deserves to be remarked, that
in his coat of arms, though adorned by the badges of
several orders, he, like another Willigis, did not disdain to perpetuate the tokens of his early life.

It was not long before I formed a connection with
Lavater. Passages of my "Letter of a Pastor to his Colleagues" had greatly struck him, for much of it agreed
perfectly with his own views. With his never-tiring
activity, our correspondence soon became lively. At
the time it commenced, he was making preparations
for his larger work on Physiognomy, the introduction
to which had already been laid before the public. He
called on all the world to send him drawings and
outlines, and especially representations of Christ; and,
although I could do as good as nothing in this way,
he nevertheless insisted on my sending him a sketch
of the Saviour such as I imagined him to look. Such
demands for the impossible gave occasion for jests of
many kinds, for I had no other way of defending myself against his peculiarities but by bringing forward
my own.

The number of those who had no faith in Physiognomy, or, at least, regarded it as uncertain and deceit-
ful, was very great; and several who had a liking for
Lavater felt a desire to try him, and, if possible, to
play him a trick. He had ordered of a painter in
Frankfort, who was not without talent, the profiles of
several well-known persons. Lavater's agent ventured
upon the jest of sending Bahrdt's portrait as mine,
which soon brought back a merry but thundering epistle,
full of all kinds of expletives, and asseverations that
this was not my picture, — together with everything
that on such an occasion Lavater would naturally have
to say in confirmation of the doctrine of Physiognomy.
My true likeness, which was sent afterward, he allowed

to pass more readily; but even here the opposition into which he fell, both with painters and with individuals, showed itself at once. The former could never work for him faithfully and sufficiently; the latter, whatever excellences they might have, came always too far short of the idea which he entertained of humanity and of men to prevent his being somewhat repelled by the special characteristics which constitute the personality of the individual.

The conception of Humanity which had been formed in himself and in his own humanity, was so completely akin to the living image of Christ which he cherished within him, that it was impossible for him to understand how a man could live and breathe without at the same time being a Christian. My own relation to the Christian religion lay merely in my sense and feeling, and I had not the slightest notion of that physical affinity to which Lavater inclined. I was, therefore, vexed by the importunity with which a man so full of mind and heart attacked me, as well as Mendelssohn and others, maintaining that every one must either become a Christian with him, a Christian of his sort, or else that one must bring him over to one's own way of thinking, and convince him of precisely that in which one had found peace. This demand, so directly opposed to that liberal spirit of the world to which I was more and more tending, did not have the best effect upon me. All unsuccessful attempts at conversion leave him who has been selected for a proselyte stubborn and obdurate; and this was especially the case with me when Lavater at last came out with the hard dilemma, — "Either Christian or Atheist!" Upon this I declared, that, if he would not leave me my own Christianity as I had hitherto cherished it, I could readily decide for Atheism, particularly as I saw that nobody knew precisely what either meant.

This correspondence, vehement as it was, did not

disturb the good terms we were on. Lavater had an incredible patience, pertinacity, and endurance; he was confident in his theory; and, with his determined plan to propagate his convictions in the world, he was willing by waiting and mildness to effect what he could not accomplish by force. In short, he belonged to the few fortunate men whose outward vocation perfectly harmonises with the inner one, and whose earliest culture, coinciding in all points with their subsequent pursuits, gives a natural development to their faculties. Born with the most delicate moral susceptibilities, he had chosen for himself the clerical profession. He received the necessary instruction, and displayed various talents, but without inclining to that degree of culture which is called learned. He also, though born so long before, had, like ourselves, been caught by the spirit of Freedom and Nature which belonged to the time, and which whispered flatteringly in every ear, " You have materials and solid power enough within yourself, without much outward aid : all depends upon your developing them properly." The obligation of a clergyman to work upon men morally in the ordinary sense, and religiously in the higher sense, fully coincided with his mental tendencies. His marked impulse, even as a youth, was to impart to others, and to excite in them, his own just and pious sentiments; and his favourite occupation was the observation of himself and of his fellow men. The former was facilitated, if not forced upon him, by an internal sensitiveness; the latter by a keen glance, which could quickly read the outward expression. Still, he was not born for contemplation : properly speaking, the gift of conveying his ideas to others was not his. But he felt rather, with all his powers, impelled to activity, to action; and I have never known any one who was more unceasingly active than Lavater. But because our inward moral nature is incorporated in outward conditions, whether we belong to a family, a class, a guild, a city, or a state, he was obliged, in his desire to influence others, to come into contact with all these external things, and to set them in motion. Hence arose many a collision, many an entanglement, especially as the commonwealth of which he was by birth a member, enjoyed, under the most precise and accurately defined limits, an admirable hereditary freedom. The republican from his boyhood is accustomed himself to think and to converse on public affairs. In the first bloom of his life the youth sees the period approaching when, as a member of a free corporation, he will have to give or to withhold his vote. If he wishes to form a just and independent judgment, he must, before all things, convince himself of the worth of his fellow citizens; he must learn to know them; he must inquire into their sentiments and their capacities; and thus, in aiming to read others, he becomes intimate with his own bosom.

Under such circumstances Lavater was trained early; and this business of life seems to have occupied him more than the study of languages, and that analytic criticism which is not only allied to that study, but is its foundation as well as its aim. In later years, when his attainments and his views had reached a boundless comprehensiveness, he frequently said, both in jest and in earnest, that he was not a learned man. It is precisely to this want of deep and solid learning that we must ascribe the fact that he adhered to the letter of the Bible, and even to the translation, and found in it nourishment, and assistance enough for all that he sought and designed.

Very soon, however, this circle of action in a corporation or guild, with its slow movement, became too narrow for the quick nature of its occupant. For a youth, to be upright is not difficult; and a pure conscience revolts at the wrong of which it is still innocent. The oppressions of a bailiff (*Landvogt*) lay plain before the eyes of the citizens, but it was by no means easy to bring him to justice. Lavater, having associated a friend with himself, anonymously threatened the guilty bailiff. The matter became notorious, and an investigation was rendered necessary. The criminal was punished, but the prompters of this act of justice were blamed if not abused. In a well-ordered state, even the right must not be brought about in a wrong way.

On a tour which Lavater now made through Germany, he came into contact with educated and right thinking men; but that served only to confirm his previous thoughts and convictions, and on his return home he worked from his own resources with greater freedom than ever. A noble and good man, he was conscious within himself of a lofty conception of humanity; and whatever inexperience contradicts such a conception, — all the undeniable defects which remove every one from perfection, — he reconciled by his idea of the Divinity which in the midst of ages came down into human nature in order completely to restore its earlier image.

So much by way of preface on the tendencies of this eminent man; and now, before all things, for a bright picture of our meeting and personal intercourse. Our correspondence had not long been carried on, when he announced to me and to others, that in a voyage up the Rhine, which he was about to undertake, he would soon visit Frankfort. Immediately there arose a great excitement in our world; all were curious to see so remarkable a person; many hoped to profit by him in the way of moral and religious culture; the skeptics prepared to distinguish themselves by grave objections; the conceited felt sure of entangling and confounding him by arguments in which they had strengthened themselves, — in short, there was everything, there was all the favour and disfavour, which await a distinguished man who intends to meddle with this motley world.

Our first meeting was hearty: we embraced each
other in the most friendly way, and I found him just
like what I had seen in many portraits of him. I
saw living and active before me an individual quite
unique, and distinguished in a way that no one had
seen before or will see again. Lavater, on the contrary, at the first moment, betrayed, by some peculiar
exclamations, that I was not what he had expected.
Hereupon I assured him, with the realism which had
been born in me, and which I had cultivated, that, as
it had pleased God and Nature to make me in that
fashion, we must rest content with it. The most important of the points on which in our letters we had
been far from agreeing, became at once subjects of conversation; but we had not time to discuss them
thoroughly, and something occurred to me that I had
never before experienced.

The rest of us, whenever we wish to speak of affairs
of the soul and of the heart, were wont to withdraw
from the crowd and even from all society, because in
the many modes of thinking, and the different degrees
of culture among men, it is difficult to be on an understanding, even with a few. But Lavater was of a
wholly different turn: he liked to extend his influence
as far as possible, and was not at ease except in a
crowd, for the instruction and entertainment of which
he possessed an especial talent, based on his great skill
in physiognomy. He had a wonderful facility of dis-
criminating persons and minds, by which he quickly
understood the mental state of all around him. Whenever, therefore, this judgment of men was met by a
sincere confession, a true-hearted inquiry, he was able,
from the abundance of his internal and external experience, to satisfy every one with an appropriate answer.
The deep tenderness of his look, the marked sweetness
of his lips, and even the honest Swiss dialect which
was heard through his High German, with many other

things that distinguished him, immediately placed all whom he addressed quite at their ease. Even the slight stoop in his carriage, together with his rather hollow chest, contributed not a little to balance in the eyes of the remainder of the company the weight of his commanding presence. Toward presumption and arrogance he knew how to demean himself with calmness and address; for, while seeming to yield, he would suddenly bring forward, like a diamond-shield, some grand view, of which his narrow-minded opponent would never have thought: and at the same time he would so agreeably moderate the light which flowed from it, that such men felt themselves instructed and convinced, — so long at least as they were in his presence. Perhaps with many the impression continued to operate long afterward, for even conceited men are also kindly: it is only necessary by gentle influences to soften the hard shell which encloses the fruitful kernel.

What caused him the greatest pain was the presence of persons whose outward ugliness must irrevocably stamp them decided enemies of his theory as to the significance of forms. They commonly employed a considerable amount of common sense, and other gifts and talents, in vehement hostility and paltry doubts, to weaken a doctrine which appeared offensive to their self-love; for it was not easy to find any one so magnanimous as Socrates, who interpreted his faun-like exterior in favour of an acquired morality. To Lavater the hardness, the obduracy, of such antagonists was horrible: and his opposition was not free from passion; just as the smelting-fire must attack the resisting ore as something troublesome and hostile.

In such a case a confidential conversation, such as might appeal to our own cases and experience, was not to be thought of: however, I was much instructed by observing the manner in which he treated men, — instructed, I say, not improved by it; for my position was wholly different from his. He that works morally loses none of his efforts, for there comes from them much more fruit than the parable of the Sower too modestly represents. But he whose labours are artistic fails utterly in every work that is not recognised as a work of art. From this it may be judged how impatient my dear sympathising readers were accustomed to make me, and for what reasons I had such a great dislike to come to an understanding with them. I now felt but too vividly the difference between the effectiveness of my labours and those of Lavater. His prevailed while he was present, mine when I was absent. Every one who at a distance was dissatisfied with him became his friend when they met; and every one, who, judging by my work, considered me amiable, found himself greatly deceived when he came in contact with a man of coldness and reserve.

Merck, who had just come over from Darmstadt, acted the part of Mephistopheles, especially ridiculing the importunities of the women. As some of these were closely examining the apartments which had been set apart for the prophet, and, above all, his bed-chamber, the wag said that "the pious souls wished to see where they had laid the Lord." Nevertheless he, as well as the others, was forced to let himself be exorcised. Lips, who accompanied Lavater, drew his profile as completely and successfully as he did those of other men, both important and unimportant, who were to be heaped together in the great work on Physiognomy.

For myself, Lavater's society was highly influential and instructive; for his pressing incitements to action set my calm, artistic, contemplative nature into motion, not indeed to any advantage at the moment, because the circumstances did but increase the distraction which had already laid hold of me. Still, so many things were talked about between us, as to give rise to the most earnest desire on my part to prolong the discussion. Accordingly I determined to accompany him if he went to Ems; so that, shut up in the carriage and separated from the world, we might freely go over those subjects which lay nearest to both our hearts.

Meanwhile the conversations between Lavater and Fräulein Von Klettenberg were to me exceedingly interesting and profitable. Here two decided Christians stood in contrast to each other, and it was quite plain how the same belief may take a different shape according to the sentiments of different persons. In those tolerant times it was often enough repeated, that every man had his own religion and his own mode of worship. Although I did not maintain this exactly, I could, in the present case, perceive that men and women need a different Saviour. Fräulein Von Klettenberg looked upon hers as upon a lover to whom one yields one's self without reserve, concentrating all joy and hope on him alone, and without doubt or hesitation confiding to him the destiny of life. Lavater, on the other hand, treated his as a friend, to be imitated lovingly and without envy, whose merits he recognised and valued highly, and whom, for that very reason, he strove to copy and even to equal. What a difference between these two tendencies, which in general exhibit the spiritual necessities of the two sexes! Hence we may perhaps explain the fact that men of more delicate feeling have so often turned to the Mother of God as a paragon of female beauty and virtue, and, like Sannazaro, have dedicated to her their lives and talents, occasionally condescending to play with the Divine Infant.

How my two friends stood with regard to each other, and how they felt toward each other, I gathered, not only from conversations at which I was present, but also from revelations which both made to me in private. I could not agree entirely with either; for my Christ had also taken a form of his own, in accordance

with my views. Because they would not allow mine
to pass at all, I teased them with all sorts of paradoxes
and exaggerations, and, when they got impatient, left
them with a jest.

The contest between knowledge and faith was not
yet the order of the day, but the two words and the
ideas connected with them occasionally came forward ;
and the true haters of the world maintained that one
was as little to be relied on as the other. Accordingly
I took pleasure in declaring in favour of both, though
without being able to gain the assent of my friends.
In Faith, I said, everything depends on the fact of believing : what is believed is perfectly indifferent. Faith
is a profound sense of security in regard to both the
present and the future ; and this assurance springs
from confidence in an immense, all-powerful, and inscrutable Being. The firmness of this confidence is the
one grand point ; but what we think of this Being depends on our other faculties, or even on circumstances,
and is wholly indifferent. Faith is a holy vessel into
which every one stands ready to pour his feelings, his
understanding, his imagination, as perfectly as he can.
With knowledge it is directly the opposite. There the
point is, not whether we know, but what we know, how
much we know, and how well we know it. Hence it
comes that men may dispute about knowledge, because
it can be corrected, widened, and contracted. Knowledge begins with the particular, is endless and formless,
can never be all comprehended, or at least but dreamily,
and thus remains exactly the opposite of Faith.

Half-truths of this kind, and the errors which arise
from them, may, when poetically exhibited, be exciting
and entertaining ; but in life they disturb and confuse
conversation. For that reason I was glad to leave
Lavater alone with all those who wished to be edified
through, and together with, him, a deprivation for
which I was, as I subsequently found, fully compensated

by the journey we made together to Ems. Beautiful summer weather attended us, and Lavater was gay and most amiable. For, though of a religious and moral turn, he was by no means narrow-minded, and was not unmoved when, by the events of life, those around him were excited to cheerfulness and gaiety. He was sympathising, spirited, witty, and liked the same qualities in others, provided that they were kept within the bounds which his delicate sense of propriety prescribed. If any one ventured farther, he used to clap him on the shoulder, and by a hearty " *Bisch guet !* " would call the rash man back to good manners. This journey afforded me instruction and inspiration of many kinds, which, however, contributed to a knowledge of his character rather than to the government and culture of my own. At Ems I saw him again at once surrounded by society of every sort ; and I went back to Frankfort, because my little affairs were in such a state that I could scarcely absent myself from them at all.

But I was not destined to be restored so speedily to repose. Basedow now came in to attract me, and touch me on another side. A more decided contrast could not be found than that between these two men. A single glance at Basedow showed the difference. Lavater's features lay open to the observer; but those of Basedow were crowded together, and, as it were, drawn inward. Lavater's eye, beneath a very wide eyelid, was clear, and expressive of piety : Basedow's was deep in his head, small, black, sharp, gleaming from under bristly brows ; while, on the contrary, Lavater's frontal bone was edged with two arches of the softest brown hair. Basedow's strong, rough voice, quick, sharp expressions, a kind of sarcastic laugh, a rapid change of subjects in conversation, with other peculiarities, were all the opposite of the qualities and manners by which Lavater had spoiled us. Basedow was also much sought after in Frankfort, and his great talents were admired; but he was not the man, either to edify souls or to lead them. His sole office was, to give a better cultivation to the wide field he had marked out for himself, so that Humanity might afterward take up its dwelling in it with greater ease and accordance with nature; but to this end he hastened even too directly.

I could not altogether acquiesce in his plans, or even get a clear understanding of his views. I was, of course, pleased with his desire of making all instruction living and natural: his wish, too, that the ancient languages should be practised on present objects, appeared to me laudable; and I gladly acknowledged all that in his project tended to the promotion of activity and a fresher view of the world. But I was displeased that the illustrations of his elementary work were even more distracting than its subjects: whereas, in the actual world, possible things alone stand together; and for that reason, in spite of all variety and apparent confusion, the world has still a regularity in all its parts. Basedow's elementary work, on the contrary, sunders it completely, inasmuch as things which in the world never are combined, are here put together on account of the association of ideas; and consequently the book is without even those palpable methodical advantages which we must acknowledge in the similar work of Amos Comenius.

But the conduct of Basedow was much more strange and difficult to comprehend than his doctrine. The purpose of his journey was, by personal influence, to interest the public in his philanthropic enterprise, and, indeed, to open, not only hearts, but purses. He had the power of speaking grandly and convincingly of his scheme, and every one willingly conceded what he asserted. But in a most inexplicable way he pained the feelings of the very men whose assistance he wished to gain; nay, he outraged them unnecessarily, through his inability to keep back his opinions and fancies on religious subjects. In this respect, too, Basedow appeared the very opposite of Lavater. While the latter received the Bible literally, and with its whole contents, as being word for word in force, and applicable, even at the present day, the former had the most unquiet itching to renovate everything, and to remodel both the doctrines and the ceremonies of the Church in conformity with some odd notions of his own. Most imprudently he showed no mercy to those conceptions which come not immediately from the Bible, but from its interpretation, — all those expressions, technical philosophical terms, or sensible figures, with which Councils and Fathers of the Church had tried to explain the inexpressible, or to confute heretics. In a harsh and unwarrantable way, and before all alike, he declared himself the sworn enemy of the Trinity, and would never desist from arguing against this universally admitted mystery. I, too, had to suffer a good deal from this kind of entertainment in private conversation, and was compelled again and again to listen to his tirades about the "Hypostasis" and "Ousia," as well as the "Prosopon." To meet them all, I had recourse to the weapons of paradox, and, soaring even above the flight of his opinions, ventured to oppose his rash assertions with something rasher of my own. This gave a new excitement to my mind; and as Basedow was much more extensively read, and had more skill in the fencing tricks of disputation than a follower of nature like myself, I had always to exert myself the more, the more important were the points which were discussed between us.

Such a splendid opportunity to exercise, if not to enlighten, my mind, I could not allow to pass away in a hurry. I prevailed on my father and friends to manage my most pressing affairs, and now set off again from Frankfort in the company of Basedow. But what a difference did I feel when I recalled the gentle spirit which breathed from Lavater! Pure himself, he created around him a pure circle. At his side one became like a maiden, for fear of presenting before him anything repulsive. Basedow, on the contrary, being altogether absorbed in himself, could not pay any attention to his external appearance. His ceaseless smoking of wretched tobacco was of itself extremely disagreeable, especially as his pipe was no sooner out, than he brought forth a dirtily prepared kind of tinder, which took fire quickly, but gave out a horrid stench, and every time poisoned the air insufferably with the first whiff. I called this preparation " The Basedovian Stench-tinder " (stink-schwamm), and declared that it ought to be introduced into Natural History under this name. This greatly amused him; and, to my disgust, he minutely explained the hated preparation, taking a malicious pleasure in my aversion from it. It was one of the deeply rooted, disagreeable peculiarities of this admirably gifted man, that he was fond of teasing, and would sting the most dispassionate persons. He could never see any one quiet, but would, in a hoarse voice, provoke him with mocking irony, or put him to confusion by an unexpected question, and laughed bitterly when he had gained his end; yet he was pleased when the object of his jests was quick enough to collect himself, and gave him a retort.

How much greater was now my longing for Lavater! He, too, seemed to be rejoiced when he saw me again, and confided to me much that he had learned, especially in reference to the various characters of his fellow guests, among whom he had already succeeded in making many friends and disciples. For my part I found here several old acquaintances; and in those whom I had not seen for many years, I began to notice what in youth long remains concealed from us, namely, that men grow old and women change. The company became more numerous every day. There was no end to the dancing; and as, in the two principal bath-houses, people came into pretty close contact, the familiarity led to many a practical joke. Once I disguised myself as a village clergyman, while an intimate friend took the character of his wife: by our excessive and troublesome politeness, we were tolerably amusing to the elegant society, and so put every one into good humour. Of serenades at evening, midnight, and morning, there was no lack; and we juniors enjoyed but little sleep.

To make up for these dissipations, I always passed a part of the night with Basedow. He never went to bed, but dictated without cessation. Occasionally he cast himself on the couch, and slumbered; while his amanuensis sat quietly, pen in hand, ready to continue his work when the half-awakened author should once again give free course to his thoughts. All this took place in a close, confined chamber, filled with the fumes of tobacco and the odious tinder. As often as I was disengaged from a dance, I hastened up to Basedow, who was ready at once to speak and dispute on any question; and when, after a time, I hurried again to the ballroom, before I had closed the door behind me he would resume the thread of his essay as composedly as if he had been engaged with nothing else.

We also made together many excursions into the neighbourhood, visiting the *châteaux*, especially those of noble ladies, who were everywhere more inclined than the men to receive anything laying claim to intellect or mind. At Nassau, at the house of Frau von Stein, a most estimable lady, who enjoyed universal respect, we found a large company. Frau von Laroche was likewise present, and there was no lack of young ladies and children. Here Lavater was doomed to be put to many a physiognomical temptation, which consisted mainly in our seeking to palm upon him the accidents of cultivation as original forms; but his eye was too sure to be deceived. I, too, was called on as much as ever to maintain the truth of the "Sorrows of Werther," and to name the residence of Charlotte, a desire which I declined to gratify, not in the politest manner. On the other hand, I collected the children around me in order to tell them very wonderful stories, all about well-known things, in which I had the great advantage, that no member of my circle of hearers could ask me with any importunity what part was truth and what fiction.

Basedow affirmed that the only thing necessary was a better education of youth, and to promote this end he called upon the higher and wealthy classes for considerable contributions. But hardly had his reasoning and his impassioned eloquence excited, not to say, won to his purpose, the sympathy of his auditors, when the evil anti-trinitarian spirit came upon him; so that, without the least sense of where he was, he broke forth into the strangest discourses, which in his own opinion were highly religious, but, according to the convictions of those around him, highly blasphemous. All sought a remedy for this evil: Lavater, by gentle seriousness; I, by jests, leading off from the subject; and the ladies by amusing walks; but harmony could not be restored. A Christian conversation, such as had been expected from the presence of Lavater; a discourse on education, such as had been anticipated from Basedow; and a sentimental one, for which it was thought I should be ready, — all were at once disturbed and destroyed. On our return home, Lavater reproached him; but I punished him in a humourous way. The weather was warm, and the tobacco-smoke had perhaps contributed to the dryness of Basedow's palate: he was dying for a glass of beer; and, seeing a tavern at a distance on the road, he eagerly ordered the coachman to stop there. But, just as he was driving up to the door, I called out to him loudly and imperiously, " Go on ! " Basedow, taken by surprise, could hardly get the contrary command out of his husky voice. I urged the coachman more vehemently, and he obeyed me. Basedow cursed me, and was ready to fall on me with his fists ; but I replied to him with the greatest composure, " Father, be quiet ! You ought to thank me. Luckily you didn't see the beer-sign ! It was two triangles put together across each other. Now, you commonly get mad about one triangle ; and, if you had set eyes on two, we should have had to get you a strait-jacket." This joke threw him into a fit of immoderate laughter, in the intervals of which he scolded and cursed me ; while Lavater exercised his patience on both the young fool and the old one.

When, in the middle of July, Lavater was preparing to depart, Basedow thought it advantageous to join him ; while I had become so accustomed to this rare society, that I could not bring myself to give it up. We had a delightful journey down the Lahn : it was refreshing alike to heart and senses. At the sight of an old ruined castle, I wrote the song " Hoch auf dem alten Thurme steht " (" High on the ancient Turret stands "), in Lips's album ; and, as it was well received, I wrote, after my evil habit, all kinds of doggerel rhymes and comicalities on the succeeding pages, in order to destroy the impression. I rejoiced to see the magnificent Rhine once more, and was delighted with the astonishment of those who had never before enjoyed this splendid spectacle. We landed at Coblentz : wherever we went, the crowd was very great ; and each of the three excited interest and curiosity. Basedow and I seemed to strive which could behave most outrageously. Lavater conducted himself rationally and with judgment, only he could not conceal his favourite opinions; and thus with the best designs he appeared very odd to all men of mediocrity.

I have preserved the memory of a strange dinner at a hotel in Coblentz, in some doggerel rhymes, which will, perhaps, stand with all their kindred in my New Edition. I sat between Lavater and Basedow; the former was instructing a country parson on the mysteries of the Revelation of St. John; and the latter was in vain endeavouring to prove, to an obstinate dancing-master, that baptism was an obsolete usage, not calculated for our times. As we were going on to Cologne, I wrote in an album, —

> As though to Emmaus, on their ride,
>   Storlike you might have seen them,
> A prophet sat on either side,
>   The worldly child between them.

Luckily this worldly child had also a side which was turned toward the heavenly, and which was now to be moved in a way wholly peculiar. While in Ems I had rejoiced to hear, that, in Cologne, we should find the brothers Jacobi, who with other eminent men had set out to meet and show attention to our two remarkable travellers. On my part, I hoped for forgiveness from them for sundry little improprieties which had originated in the great love of mischief that Herder's keen humour had excited in us. The letters and poems in which Gleim and George Jacobi publicly rejoiced in each other, had given us opportunity for all sorts of sport; and we had not reflected that there is just as much self-conceit in giving pain to others when they are comfortable, as in showing an excess of kindness to one's self or to one's friends. By this means, a certain dissension had arisen between the Upper and Lower Rhine, of so slight importance, however, that mediation was easy. For this the ladies were particularly well adapted. Sophia Laroche had already given us the best idea of the noble brothers. Mlle. Fahlmer, who had come to Frankfort from Düsseldorf, and who was intimate with their circle, by the great tenderness of her sympathies, and the uncommon cultivation of her mind, furnished an evidence of the worth of the society in which she had grown up. She gradually put us to shame by her patience with our harsh Upper-Saxon manner, and taught us forbearance by letting us feel that we ourselves stood in need of it. The true-heartedness of the younger sister of the Jacobis, the gaiety of the wife of Fritz Jacobi, turned our minds and eyes more and more to these regions. The latter was qualified to captivate me entirely; possessed of a correct feeling without a trace of sentimentality, and with a lively way of speaking, she was a fine Netherlands woman, who, without any expression of sensuality, by her robust nature called to mind the women of Rubens. Both these ladies, in longer and shorter visits at Frankfort, had formed the closest alliance with my sister, and had expanded and enlivened the severe, stiff, and somewhat loveless, nature of Cornelia. Thus Düsseldorf and Pempelfort had interested our minds and hearts, even in Frankfort.

Accordingly our first meeting in Cologne was at once frank and confidential, for the good opinion of the ladies had not been without its influence at home. I was not now treated, as hitherto on the journey, as merely the misty tail of the two great comets: all around paid me particular attention, and showed me abundant kindness, which they also seemed inclined to receive from me in return. I was weary of my previous follies and impertinences, behind which, in truth, I only hid my impatience, to find during the journey so little care taken to satisfy my heart and soul. Hence, what was within me burst out like a torrent; and this is perhaps the reason why I recollect so little of individual events. The thoughts we have had, the

pictures we have seen, can be again called up before
the mind and the imagination: but the heart is not so
complaisant; it will not repeat its agreeable emotions.
And least of all are we able to recall moments of enthusiasm: they come upon us unprepared, and we yield
to them unconsciously. For this reason, others, who
observe us at such moments, have a better and clearer
insight into what passes within us than we ourselves.

Religious conversations I had hitherto gently declined: to plain questions I had not unfrequently
replied with harshness, because they seemed to me
too narrow in comparison with what I sought. When
any one wished to force upon me his sentiments and
opinions of my compositions, but especially when I was
afflicted with the demands of common sense, and people
told me decidedly what I ought to have done or left
undone, I got out of all patience: and the conversation
broke off, or crumbled to pieces; so that no one went
away with a particularly good opinion of me. It would
have been much more natural to make myself gentle
and friendly, but my feelings would not be schooled.
They needed to be expanded by free good will, and to
be moved to a surrender by sincere sympathy. One
feeling which prevailed greatly with me, and could
never find an expression odd enough for itself, was a
sense of the past and present together in one, — a phenomenon which brought something spectral into the
present. It is expressed in many of my smaller and
larger works, and always has a beneficial influence in a
poem, though, whenever it began to mix itself up with
actual life, it must have appeared to every one strange,
inexplicable, perhaps gloomy.

Cologne was the place where antiquity had such an
incalculable effect upon me. The ruins of the cathe-
dral (for an unfinished work is like one destroyed)
called up the emotions to which I had been accustomed at Strasburg. Artistic considerations were out

of the question; too much and too little were given me; and there was no one who could help me out of the labyrinth of what had been performed and what proposed, of the fact and of the plan, of what had been built and what only designed, as our industrious, persevering friends nowadays are ready to do. In company with others I did indeed admire its wonderful chapels and columns; but when alone I always gloomily lost myself in this world-edifice, thus checked in its creation while far from complete. Here, too, was a great idea never realised! It would seem, indeed, as if the architecture were there only to convince us, that by many men, in a series of years, nothing can be accomplished, and that in art and in deeds only that is achieved which, like Minerva, springs full-grown and armed from the head of its inventor.

At these moments, which oppressed more than they cheered my heart, I little thought that the tenderest and fairest emotion was in store for me near at hand. I was persuaded to visit Jappach's house, and here all that I had been wont to form for myself in my mind came actually and sensibly before my eyes. This family had probably long ago become extinct; but on the ground floor, which opened upon a garden, we found everything unchanged. A pavement of brownish-red tiles, of a rhomboidal form, regularly laid; carved chairs with embroidered seats and high backs; flap-tables; metal chandeliers curiously inlaid, on heavy feet; an immense fireplace with its appropriate utensils; everything in harmony with those early times, and in the whole room nothing new, nothing belonging to the present but ourselves. But what more than all heightened and completed the emotions thus strangely excited was a large family picture over the fireplace. There sat the former wealthy inhabitant of this abode, surrounded by his wife and children, — there were they in all the freshness of life, and as if of yesterday, or rather of to-day; and yet all of them had passed away. These young, round-cheeked children had grown old; and, but for this clever likeness, not a trace of them would have remained. How I acted, how I demeaned myself, when overcome by these impressions, I cannot say. The lowest depths of my human affections and poetic sensibilities were laid bare in the boundless stirring of my heart: all that was good and loving in my soul seemed to open and break forth. In that moment, without further probation or debate, I gained for life the affection and confidence of those eminent men.

As a result of this union of soul and intellect, in which all that was living in each came forth upon his lips, I offered to recite my newest and most favourite ballads. "Der König von Thule" ("The King of Thule"), and "Es war ein Buhle frech genug" ("There was a barefaced lover who"[1]), had a good effect; and I brought them forth with more feeling, as my poems were still bound to my heart, and as they seldom passed my lips. For, in the presence of persons who I feared could not sympathise with my tender sensibility, I felt restrained; and frequently, in the midst of a recitation, I have become confused, and could not get right again. How often, for that reason, have I been accused of wilfulness, and of a strange, whimsical disposition!

Although poetic composition just then mainly occupied me, and exactly suited my temperament, I was still no stranger to reflection on all kinds of subjects; and Jacobi's tendency to the unfathomable, which was so original, and so much in accordance with his nature, was most welcome and agreeable to me. Here no

[1] The title of the poem is "Der untreue Knabe" ("The Faithless Boy"); and in the first line of it, as published in Göthe's collected works, "Knabe" will be found instead of "Buhle." — TRANS.

controversy arose, — neither a Christian one, as with Lavater, nor a didactic one, as with Basedow. The thoughts which Jacobi imparted to me flowed immediately from his heart. How profoundly was I moved when, in unlimited confidence, he revealed to me even the most hidden longings of his soul! From so amazing a combination of mental wants, passion, and ideas, I could only gather presentiments of what might, perhaps, afterward grow more clear to me. Happily, I had already prepared, if not fully cultivated, myself in this respect, having in some degree appropriated the thoughts and mind of an extraordinary man, though my study of him had been incomplete and hasty; but I was already conscious of important influences derived from this source. This mind, which had worked upon me thus decisively, and which was destined to affect so deeply my whole mode of thinking, was Spinoza. After looking through the world in vain, to find a means of development for my strange nature, I at last fell upon the "Ethics" of this philosopher. Of what I read out of the work, and of what I read into it, I can give no account. But I certainly found in it a sedative for my passions, and that a free, wide view over the sensible and moral world seemed to open before me. But what especially riveted me to him was the utter disinterestedness which shone forth in his every sentence. That wonderful sentiment, "He who truly loves God must not desire God to love him in return," together with all the preliminary propositions on which it rests, and all the consequences that follow from it, filled my whole mind. To be disinterested in everything, but most of all in love and friendship, was my highest desire, my maxim, my practice; so that that subsequent hasty saying of mine, "If I love thee, what is that to thee?" was spoken right out of my heart. Moreover, it must not be forgotten here that the closest unions are those of opposites. The all-composing calmness of Spinoza was in striking contrast with my all-disturbing activity; his mathematical method was the direct opposite of my poetic humour and my way of writing; and that very precision, which was thought ill-adapted to moral subjects, made me his enthusiastic disciple, his most decided worshipper. Mind and heart, understanding and sense, sought each other with an eager affinity, binding together the most different natures.

At this time, however, all within was fermenting and seething in the first action and reaction. Fritz Jacobi, the first whom I suffered to look into the chaos, and whose nature was also toiling in its own extreme depths, heartily received my confidence, responded to it, and endeavoured to lead me to his own opinions. He, too, felt an unspeakable mental want: he, too, did not wish to have it appeased by outward aid, but aimed at development and illumination from within. I could not comprehend what he communicated to me of the state of his mind, so much the less, indeed, because I could form no idea as to my own. Still, as he was far in advance of me in philosophical thought, and even in the study of Spinoza, he endeavoured to guide and enlighten my obscure efforts. Such a purely intellectual relationship was new to me, and excited a passionate longing for further communion. At night, after we had parted, and retired to our chambers, I often sought him again. With the moonlight trembling over the broad Rhine, we stood at the window, and revelled in that full interchange of ideas, which, in such splendid moments of confidence, swell forth so abundantly.

Still, of the unspeakable joy of those moments, I can now give no account. Much more distinct to my mind is an excursion to the hunting-seat of Bensberg, which, lying on the right shore of the Rhine, commanded the most splendid prospect. What delighted me beyond measure was the decorations of the walls by Weenix. They represented a large, open hall, surrounded by columns; at the foot of these, as if forming the plinth, lay all the animals that the chase can furnish, skilfully arranged; and over these again the eye ranged over a wide landscape. The wonderful artist had expended his whole skill in giving life to these lifeless creatures. In the delineation of their widely varying coats, the bristles, hair, or feathers, with the antlers and claws, he had equalled nature; while, in the effect produced, he had excelled her. When we had admired these works of art sufficiently as a whole, we were led to reflect on the handling by which such pictures, combining so much spirit and mechanical skill, were produced. We could not understand how they could be created by the hands of man, or by any of his instruments. The pencil was not sufficient: peculiar preparations must be supposed to make such variety possible. Whether we came close to them, or withdrew to a distance, our astonishment was equal: the cause was as wonderful as the effect.

Our further journey up the Rhine was cheerful and happy. The widening of the river invites the mind to expand itself likewise, and to look into the distance. We arrived at Düsseldorf, and thence came to Pempelfort, a most delightful and beautiful resting-place, where a spacious mansion, opening upon extensive and well-kept gardens, collected together a thoughtful and refined circle. The members of the family were numerous; and strangers, who found abundant enjoyment in so rich and agreeable a neighbourhood, were never wanting.

In the Düsseldorf gallery, my predilection for the Flemish school found ample nourishment. There were whole halls filled with these vigorous, sturdy pictures, brilliant with a fulness of nature; and, if my judgment was not enlarged, my store of knowledge was enriched, and my love for art confirmed.

The beautiful composure, contentment, and firmness, which marked the leading character of this family circle, quickly manifested themselves to the observant eye of the thoughtful guest, who could not fail to perceive that a wide sphere of influences had here its centre. The activity and opulence of the neighbouring cities and villages contributed not a little to enhance this feeling of inward satisfaction. We visited Elberfeld, and were delighted with the busy aspect of so many flourishing manufactories. Here we fell in again with our friend Jung, commonly known as Stilling, who had gone even to Coblentz to meet us, and who always had his faith in God and his truth toward men as his most precious attendants. Here we saw him in his own circle, and saw with pleasure the confidence reposed in him by his fellow citizens, who, though occupied with earthly gain, did not leave the heavenly treasures out of view. The sight of this industrious region was satisfactory, because its prosperity was the result of order and neatness. In the contemplation of these things we passed happy days.

When I returned to my friend Jacobi, I enjoyed the rapturous feeling springing from a union of the innermost soul. We were both inspired by the liveliest hope of an influence in common; and I urgently pressed him to make an exhibition, in some striking form or other, of all that was acting and moving within him. This was the means by which I had escaped from many perplexities, and I hoped that it would relieve him also. He did not object, but undertook the task with zeal; and how much that is good and beautiful and consolatory has he accomplished! And so, at last, we parted with the happy feeling of eternal union, and wholly without a presentiment that our labours would assume the opposite directions, which, in the course of life, they so markedly took.

Whatever else occurred to me on the return down the Rhine has altogether vanished from my memory, partly because the second impressions of natural objects are wont, in my mind, to be mingled with the first; and partly because, with my thoughts turned inwardly, I was endeavouring to arrange the varied experience I on myself had gained, and to work up what had affected me. Of one important result, as it impelled me to creative efforts which kept me occupied for a long time, I will now speak.

With my lawless disposition, with a life and action so aimless and purposeless, the observation could not long escape me, that Lavater and Basedow employed intellectual and even spiritual means for earthly ends. It soon struck me, who spent my talents and my days on no object whatever, that these two men, while endeavouring to preach their doctrines, to teach and to convince, had each, in his own way, certain views in the background, the advancement of which was to them of great consequence. Lavater went to work gently and prudently, Basedow vehemently, rudely, and even awkwardly; but both were so convinced of the excellence of their favourite schemes and undertakings, and their mode of prosecuting them, that so far all were compelled to look upon them as men of sincerity, and to love and to honour them as such. In praise of Lavater especially, it could be said that he actually had higher objects; and, if he acted according to the wisdom of this world, it was in the belief that the end would hallow the means. As I observed them both, nay, indeed frankly told them my opinions and heard theirs in return, the thought arose in me, that every highly gifted man is called upon to diffuse whatever there is of divine within him. In attempting this, however, he comes in contact with the rough world; and, in order to act upon it, he must put himself on the same level. Thus, in a great measure, he compromises his high advantages, and finally forfeits them altogether. The heavenly, the eternal, is buried in a body of earthly designs, and hurried with it to the fate of the transient. From this point of view I now regarded the career of these two men, and they seemed to me worthy, both of honour and of compassion; for I thought I could foresee that each would be compelled to sacrifice the higher to the lower. As I pursued all reflections of this kind to their farthest limits, and looked beyond the extent of my narrow experience for similar cases in history, the plan occurred to me of taking the life of Mahomet, whom I had never been able to think an impostor, for a dramatic exhibition of those courses which in actual life, I was strongly convinced, invariably lead to ruin much more than to good. I had shortly before read with great interest, and studied, the life of the Eastern Prophet, and was therefore tolerably prepared when the thought occurred to me. The sketch approached, on the whole, the regular form to which I was again inclining; although I still used in moderation the liberty gained for the stage, and arranged time and place according to my own pleasure. The piece began with Mahomet alone under the open sky, singing a hymn. In it he adores first of all the innumerable stars as so many gods; but as the friendly star, Gad (our Jupiter), rises, he offers to him, as the king of the stars, exclusive adoration. Not long after the moon ascends the horizon, and wins the eye and heart of the worshipper, who, presently refreshed and strengthened by the dawning sun, is called upon for new praises. But these changing phenomena, however delightful, are still unsatisfactory; and the mind feels that it must rise yet above itself. It mounts, therefore, to God, the Only, Eternal, Infinite, to whom all these splendid yet limited creatures owe their existence. I composed this hymn with great delight: it is now lost, but might easily be restored for the purpose of a cantata, and would commend itself to the r usical composer by the variety of its expression. It would, however, be necessary to imagine it sung, according to the original plan, by the conductor of a caravan with his family and tribe; and thus the alternation of the voices, and the strength of the chorus, would be provided for.

After Mahomet has thus converted himself, he imparts these feelings and sentiments to his friends. His wife and Ali become his disciples without reserve. In the second act he zealously attempts, supported by the still more ardent Ali, to propagate this faith in the tribe. Assent and opposition follow the variety of character. The contest begins, the strife becomes violent, and Mahomet is compelled to flee. In the third act he defeats his enemies, and, making his religion the public one, purifies the Kaaba from idols; but, as all this cannot be done by power, he is obliged to resort to cunning. What in his character is earthly increases and extends itself: the divine retires and is obscured. In the fourth act Mahomet pursues his conquests, his doctrine becomes a pretence rather than an end: all conceivable means must be employed, and barbarities become abundant. A woman, whose husband has been put to death by Mahomet's order, poisons him. In the fifth act he feels that he is poisoned. His great calmness, the return to himself and to a higher sense, make him worthy of admiration. He purifies his doctrine, establishes his kingdom, and dies.

Such was the sketch of a work which long occupied my mind, for usually I was obliged to have the materials in my head before I commenced the execution. I meant to represent the power which genius exercises over men by character and intellect, and what are its gains and losses in the process. Several of the songs, to be introduced in the drama, were composed beforehand : all that remains of them, however, is what stands among my poems under the title "Mahomet's Gesang" ("Mahomet's Song"). According to the plan, this was to be sung by Ali in honour of his master, at the highest point of his success, just before the changed aspect of affairs resulting from the poison. I recollect also the outlines of several scenes, which here to unfold would lead me too far.

FIFTEENTH BOOK.

FROM these manifold diversions, which, however, generally gave occasion for serious, and even religious, reflections, I always returned to my noble friend, Fräulein von Klettenberg, whose presence calmed, at least for a moment, my stormy and undirected impulses and passions, and to whom, next to my sister, I liked best to communicate designs like that I have just spoken of. I might, indeed, have perceived that her health was constantly failing : but I concealed it from myself ; and this I was the better able to do as her cheerfulness increased with her illness. She used to sit, neatly dressed, in her chair at the window, and kindly listened to the narratives of my little expeditions as well as to what I read aloud to her. Often, too, I made sketches, in order to make her understand the better the description of the places I had seen. One evening I had been recalling to my mind many different images, when, in the light of the setting sun, she and all around her appeared before me as if transfigured ; and I could not refrain from making a drawing of her, and of the surrounding objects in the chamber, as well as my poor skill permitted. In the hands of a skilful artist like Kersting it would have made a beautiful picture. I sent it to a fair friend at a distance, and added a song as commentary and supplement :

> In this magic glass reflected,
>   See a vision, mild and blessed :
> By the wing of God protected,
>   Is our suffering friend at rest.

Mark how her endeavours bore her
 From life's waves to realms above :
See thine image stand before her,
 And the God who died from love.

Feel what I, amid the floating
 Of that heavenly ether, knew,
When, the first impression noting,
 Hastily this sketch I drew.

Though in these stanzas, as had often happened before, I expressed myself as "a stranger and foreigner," in short, as a heathen, she did not take offence at it. On the contrary, she assured me, that in so doing I pleased her much more than when I attempted to employ the Christian terminology, which somehow I could never apply correctly. Indeed, it had become a standing custom with me, whenever I read to her missionary intelligence, which she was always fond of listening to, to take the part of the pagans against the missionaries, and to praise their old condition as preferable to their new one. Still, she was ever gentle and friendly, and seemed not to have the least fear about me or my salvation.

My gradual alienation from her creed arose from the fact that I had laid hold of it at first with too great zeal, with passionate love. Ever since I became more intimately acquainted with the Moravians, my inclination to this society, which had united under the victorious banners of Christ, had constantly increased. It is exactly in the moment of its earliest formation that a positive religion possesses its greatest attraction. On that account it is delightful to go back to the time of the apostles, where all stands forth as fresh and immediately spiritual. And thus it was that the Moravian doctrine acquired something of a magical charm by appearing to continue or rather to perpetuate the condition of those first times. It connected its origin with them; when it seemed to perish, it still wound its way through the world, although by unnoticed tendrils; at last one little germ took root beneath the protection of a pious and eminent man, and so from an unnoticed and apparently accidental beginning expanded once more over the wide world. In this society the most important point was, the inseparable combination of the religious and civil constitution by which the teacher was at the same time the ruler, and the father the judge. What was still more distinctive of their fraternity, was that the religious head, to whom unlimited faith was yielded in spiritual things, was also entrusted with the guidance of temporal affairs; and his counsels, whether for the government of the whole body, or for the guidance of the individuals, if confirmed by the issue of the *lot*, were implicitly followed. Its peace and harmony, to which at least outward appearances testified, was most alluring; while, on the other hand, the missionary vocation seemed to call forth and to give employment to all man's active powers. The excellent persons whose acquaintance I made at Marienborn, which I had visited in the company of Councillor Moritz, the agent of Count von Isenburg, had gained my unqualified esteem; and it only depended on themselves to make me their own. I studied their history and their doctrine, and the origin and growth of their society, so as to be able to give an account of it and to talk about it to all who might feel interested in it. Nevertheless, the conviction was soon forced upon me, that with the brethren I did not pass for a Christian any more than I did with Fräulein von Klettenberg. At first this disturbed me, but afterward my inclination to them became somewhat cooler. However, I could not for a long time discover the precise ground of difference, although it was obvious enough, until at last it was forced upon me more by accident than by reflection. What separated me from this brother-

hood, as well as from other good Christian souls,
was the very point on which the Church has more
than once fallen into dissension. On the one hand,
it was maintained, that, by the Fall, human nature
had been so corrupted to its innermost core, that
not the least good could be found in it, and that therefore man must renounce all trust in his own powers,
and look to grace and its operations for everything.
The other party, while it admitted the hereditary
imperfections of man, nevertheless, ascribed to nature
a certain germ of good within, which, animated by
divine grace, was capable of growing up to a joyous
tree of spiritual happiness. By this latter conviction
I was unconsciously penetrated to my inmost soul,
even while with tongue and pen I maintained the
opposite side. But I had hitherto gone on with such
ill-defined ideas, that I had never once clearly stated
the dilemma to myself. From this dream I was unexpectedly roused one day, when in a religious conversation, having distinctly advanced opinions to my mind
most innocent, I had in return to undergo a severe
lecture. The very thought of such a thing, it was
maintained, was genuine Pelagianism, a pernicious doctrine which was again appearing, to the great injury
of modern times. I was astonished and even terrified.
I went back to Church history, studied the doctrine
and fate of Pelagius more closely, and now saw clearly
how these two irreconcilable opinions had fluctuated in
favour through whole centuries, and had been embraced
and acknowledged by different men, according as they
were of a more active or of a more passive nature.

The course of past years had constantly led me
more and more to the exercise of my own powers. A
restless activity was at work within me, with the best
desire for moral development. The world without
demanded that this activity should be regulated and
employed for the advantage of others ; and this great

demand I felt called upon, in my own case, to meet. On all sides I had been directed to nature, and she had appeared to me in her whole magnificence: I had been acquainted with many good and true men, who were toiling to do their duty, and for the sake of duty; to renounce them, nay, to renounce myself, seemed impossible. The gulf which separated me from the doctrine of man's total depravity now became plain to me. Nothing, therefore, remained to me but to part from this society; and as my love of the Holy Scriptures, as well as of the founder of Christianity and its early professors, could not be taken from me, I formed a Christianity for my private use, and sought to establish and build it up by an attentive study of history, and a careful observation of those who were favourable to my opinion.

As everything which I once warmly embraced immediately put on a poetic form, I now took up the strange idea of treating epically the history of the Wandering Jew, which popular books had long since impressed upon my mind. My design was to bring out, in the course of the narrative, such prominent points of the history of religion and the Church as I should find convenient. I will now explain the way in which I treated this fable, and what meaning I gave to it.

In Jerusalem, according to the legend, there was a shoemaker of the name of Ahasuerus. For this character my Dresden shoemaker was to supply the main features. I had furnished him with the spirit and humour of a craftsman of the school of Hans Sachs, and ennobled him by an inclination to Christ. Accordingly as, in his open workshop, he liked to talk with the passers-by, jested with them, and, after the Socratic fashion, touched up every one in his own way, the neighbours, and others of the people, took pleasure in lingering at his booth: even Pharisees and Sadducees spoke to him, and the Saviour himself and his disciples would often stop at his door. The shoemaker, whose thoughts were directed solely toward the world, I painted as feeling, nevertheless, a special affection for our Lord, which, for the most part, evinced itself by a desire to bring this lofty being, whose mind he did not comprehend, over to his own way of thinking and acting. Accordingly, in a modest manner, he recommends Christ to abandon his contemplative life, and to leave off going about the country with such idlers, and drawing the people away from their labour into the wilderness. A multitude, he said, was always ready for excitement; and nothing good could come of it.

On the other hand, the Lord endeavoured, by parables, to instruct him in his higher views and aims; but these were all thrown away on his mere matter-of-fact intellect. Thus, as Christ becomes more and more an important character, and finally a public person, the friendly workman pronounces his opinion still more sharply and vehemently, maintaining that nothing but disorder and tumult could follow from such proceedings, and that Christ would be at last compelled to put himself at the head of a party, though that could not possibly be his design. Finally, when things had taken the course history narrates, and Christ had been seized and condemned, Ahasuerus gives full vent to his indignation, when Judas, who undesignedly had betrayed his Lord, in his despair enters the workshop, and with lamentations relates how his plans had been crossed. He had been, he said, as well as the shrewdest of the other disciples, firmly convinced that Christ would declare himself regent and head of the nation. His purpose was only, by this violence, to compel the Lord, whose hesitation had hitherto been invincible, to hasten the declaration. Accordingly he had incited the priesthood to an act which previously they had not had courage to do. The disciples, on their side, were not without arms; and probably all would have turned out well, if the Lord had not given himself up, and left them in the most forlorn state. Ahasuerus, whom this narrative in no ways tends to propitiate, only exasperates the agony of the poor ex-apostle, who rushes out, and goes and hangs himself.

As Jesus is led past the workshop of the shoemaker, on his way to execution, the well-known scene of the legend occurs. The sufferer faints under the burden of the cross, and Simon of Cyrene is compelled to carry it. Upon this Ahasuerus comes forward, and sustains the part of those harsh common-sense people, who, when they see a man involved in misfortune through his own fault, feel no pity, but, struck by an untimely sense of justice, make the matter worse by their reproaches. As he comes out, he repeats all his former warnings, changing them into vehement accusations, which his attachment to the sufferer seems to justify. The Saviour does not answer; but at the instant the loving Veronica covers his face with the napkin, on which, as she removes it and raises it aloft, Ahasuerus sees depicted the features of the Lord, not indeed as those of the sufferer of the moment, but as of one transfigured and radiant with celestial life. Amazed by this phenomenon, he turns away his eyes, and hears the words, "Over the earth shalt thou wander till thou shalt once more see me in this form." Overwhelmed at the sentence, it is not till after some time that the artisan comes to himself: he then finds that every one has gone to the place of execution, and that the streets of Jerusalem are empty. Disquiet and curiosity drive him forth, and he begins his wandering.

I shall, perhaps, speak elsewhere of all this, and of the incident by which the poem was ended, indeed, but not finished. The beginning, some detached passages, and the conclusion, were written. But I never completed the work. I lacked time for the studies

necessary to give it the finish and bearing that I
wished. The few sheets I did write were the more
willingly left to repose in obscurity, as a new and
necessary epoch was now formed in my mental character by the publication of "Werther."

The common fate of man, which all of us have to
bear, must fall most heavily on those whose intellectual powers expand very early. For a time we
may grow up under the protection of parents and
relatives; we may lean for awhile upon our brothers
and sisters and friends, be supported by acquaintances,
and made happy by those we love; but, in the end,
man is always driven back upon himself: and it seems
as if the Divinity had taken a position toward men so
as not always to respond to their reverence, trust, and
love, at least, not in the precise moment of need. Early
enough, and by many a hard lesson, had I learned, that,
at the most urgent crises, the call to us is, "Physician,
heal thyself;" and how frequently had I been compelled to sigh out in pain, "I tread the wine-press
alone!" So now, while I was looking about for the
means of establishing my independence, I felt that
the surest basis on which to build was my own creative talents. For many years I had never known it
to fail me for a moment. What, waking, I had seen
by day, often shaped itself into regular dreams at
night; and, when I opened my eyes, there appeared
to me either a wonderful new whole, or a part of one
already commenced. Usually, my time for writing
was the early morning: but in the evening too, or
even late at night, when wine and social intercourse had
raised my spirits, I was ready for any topic that might
be suggested; only let a subject of some character be
offered, and I was at once prepared and ready. While,
then, I reflected upon this natural gift, and found that
it belonged to me as my own, and could neither be
favoured nor hindered by any external matters, I

easily, in thought, built my whole existence upon it.
This conception soon assumed a distinct form : the old
mythological image of Prometheus occurred to me,
who, separated from the gods, peopled a world from
his own workshop. I clearly felt that a creation of
importance could be produced only when its author
isolated himself. My productions, which had met
with so much applause, were children of solitude:
and, since I had stood in a wider relation to the
world, I had not been wanting in the power or the
pleasure of invention; but the execution halted, because I had, neither in prose nor in verse, a style
properly my own, and consequently, with every new
work, had always to begin at the beginning and try
experiments. As in this I had to decline and even to
exclude the aid of men; so, after the fashion of Prometheus, I separated myself from the gods also, and
the more naturally, as, with my character, and mode
of thinking, one tendency always swallowed up and
repelled all others.

The fable of Prometheus became living in me. The
old Titan web I cut up according to my own measure-
ments, and, without further reflection, began to write a
piece in which was painted the difficulty Prometheus
was placed in, with respect to Jupiter and the later
gods, in consequence of his making men with his own
hand, giving them life by the aid of Minerva, and
founding a third dynasty. And, in fact, the reigning
gods had good cause to feel aggrieved ; since they might
now appear in the light of wrongful intruders between
the Titans and men. To this singular composition belongs, as a monologue, that poem, which has become
remarkable in German literature, by having called forth
a declaration from Lessing against Jacobi on certain
weighty matters of thought and feeling. It thus served
as the match to an explosion which revealed and brought
into discussion the most secret relations of men of

worth, — relations of which they, perhaps, were not themselves conscious, and which were slumbering in a society otherwise most enlightened. The schism was so violent, that, with the concurrence of further incidents, it caused us the loss of one of our most valuable men, namely, Mendelssohn.

Although philosophical and even religious considerations may be, and before now have been, attached to this subject, still it belongs peculiarly to poetry. The Titans are the foil of polytheism, as the devil may be considered the foil of monotheism; though, like the only God to whom he stands in contrast, he is not a poetic figure. The Satan of Milton, though boldly enough drawn, still remains in the disadvantageous light of a subordinate existence, attempting to destroy the splendid creation of a higher being: Prometheus, on the contrary, has this advantage, that, even in spite of superior beings, he is able to act and to create. It is also a beautiful thought, and well suited to poetry, to represent men as created, not by the Supreme Ruler of the world, but by an intermediate agent, who, however, as a descendant of the most ancient dynasty, is of worth and importance enough for such an office. Thus, and, indeed, under every aspect, the Grecian mythology is an inexhaustible mine of divine and human symbols.

Nevertheless, the Titanic, gigantic, heaven-storming character afforded no suitable material for my poetic art. It better suited me to represent that peaceful, plastic, and always patient, opposition, which, recognising the superior power, still presumes to claim equality. And yet the bolder members of the race, Tantalus, Ixion, Sisyphus, were also my saints. Admitted to the society of the gods, they would not deport themselves submissively enough, but, by their haughty bearing as guests, provoked the anger of their host and patron, and drew upon themselves a sorrowful banishment. I pitied them; their condition had already been set forth by the ancients as truly tragic; and, when I introduced them in the background of my "Iphigenia," I was indebted to them for a part of the effect which that piece had the good fortune to produce.

At this period I usually combined the art of design with poetical composition. I drew the portraits of my friends in profile on gray paper, in white and black chalk. Whenever I dictated or listened to reading, I sketched the positions of the writer and reader, with the surrounding objects: the resemblance could not be denied, and the drawings were well received. *Dilettanti* always have this advantage, because they give their labour for nothing. But, feeling the insufficiency of this copying, I betook myself once more to language and rhythm, which were once more at my command. How briskly, how joyously and eagerly, I went to work with them, will appear from the many poems which, enthusiastically proclaiming the *art* of nature, and the *nature* of art, infused, at the moment of their production, new spirit into me as well as into my friends.

I was at this epoch, and in the midst of these occupations, one evening, sitting, with a struggling light in my chamber, to which, at least, the air of an artist's studio was thus imparted, while the walls, stuck over and covered with half-finished works, gave the impression of great industry, when there entered a well-formed, slender man, whom at first, in the twilight, I took for Fritz Jacobi, but soon, discovering my mistake, greeted as a stranger. In his free and agreeable bearing a certain military air was perceptible. He announced himself by the name of Von Knebel; and from a brief introduction I gathered that he was in the Prussian service, and that, during a long residence at Berlin and Potsdam, he had actively cultivated an acquaintance with the literary men of those places, and with German literature in general. He had attached himself particularly to Ramler, and had adopted his mode of reciting poems. He was also familiar with all that Götz had written, who at that time had not as yet made a name among the Germans. Through his exertions the "Mädcheninsel" ("Isle of Maidens") of this poet had been printed at Potsdam, and had fallen into the hands of the king, who was said to have expressed a favourable opinion of it.

We had scarcely talked over these subjects of general interest in German literature, before I learned, much to my satisfaction, that he was at present stationed in Weimar, and was appointed the companion of Prince Constantin. Of matters there I had already heard much that was favourable; for several strangers, who had come from Weimar, assured us that the Duchess Amalia had gathered around her the best men to assist in the education of her sons; that the Academy of Jena, through its admirable teachers, had also contributed its part to this excellent purpose; and that the arts were not only protected by this princess, but were practised by her with great diligence and zeal. We also heard that Wieland was in especial favour. The *Deutsche Merkur*, too, which united the labours of so many scholars in other places, contributed not a little to the fame of the city in which it was published. There also was one of the best theatres in Germany, which was made famous by its actors, as well as by the authors who wrote for it. These noble institutions and plans seemed, however, to have received a sudden check, and to be threatened with a long interruption, in consequence of the terrible conflagration of the castle, which took place in the May of that year. But the confidence in the hereditary prince was so great that every one was convinced, not only that the damage would be repaired, but that, in spite of it, every other hope would be fully accomplished. As I inquired after these persons and things as if I were an old acquaintance, and expressed a wish to become more intimately acquainted with them, my visitor replied, in the most friendly manner possible, that nothing was easier; since the hereditary prince, with his brother, the Prince Constantin, had just arrived in Frankfort, and desired to see and know me. I at once expressed the greatest willingness to wait upon them; and my new friend told me that I must not delay, as their stay would not be long. In order to equip myself for the visit, I took Von Knebel to my father and mother, who were surprised at his arrival, and the message he bore, and conversed with him with great satisfaction. I then proceeded with him to the young princes, who received me in a very easy and friendly manner: Count Görtz also, the tutor of the hereditary prince, appeared not displeased to see me. Though there was no lack of literary subjects for our conversation, accident furnished the best possible introduction to it, and rendered it at once important and profitable.

Möser's "Patriotische Fantasien" ("Patriotic Fantasies"), that is to say, the first part, were lying on the table, fresh from the binder, with the leaves uncut. As I was familiar with them, whereas the rest were not, I had the advantage of being able to give a complete account of the work, and had here a favourable opportunity for speaking with a young prince, who was sincerely desirous, and also firmly determined, to make use of his station to do all the good in his power. Möser's book, both in its contents and its tone, could not but be highly interesting to every German. While, by other writers, division, anarchy, and impotence had been brought as a reproach against the German Empire, according to Möser this very number of small states was highly desirable, as affording room for the special cultivation of each, according to its necessities, which must vary with the site and peculiarities of such widely different provinces. In the same way, I remarked, that Möser, starting with the city and bishopric (*Stift*) of Osnaburg, and thence going over the circle of Westphalia, set forth its relation to the whole empire: and just as he, in the further examination of the subject, uniting the past with the present, deducted the latter from the former, and thus clearly showed what alterations were desirable or not; so might every ruler, by proceeding in the same way, obtain a thorough knowledge of the constitution of the state he governs, its connection with its neighbours and with the whole empire, and thus enable himself to judge both the present and the future.

In the course of our conversation, many remarks were made with regard to the difference between the states of Upper and Lower Saxony: not only their natural productions, it was observed, but also their manners, laws, and customs, had differed from the earliest times, and, according to the form of religion and government, had variously modified themselves. We endeavoured to obtain a clear view of the differences between the two regions; and, in this attempt, it soon appeared how useful it would be to have a good model, which if regarded, not in its individual peculiarities, but in the general method on which it had been based, might be applied to the most widely differing cases, and thereby might be highly serviceable in helping us to form a correct judgment.

This conversation, which was kept up when we were set down at table, made a better impression in my favour than I perhaps deserved. For instead of making such works as belonged to my own sphere of literature the subjects of discussion, instead of demanding an undivided attention for the drama and for romance, I appeared, while discussing Möser's book, to prefer those writers whose talents, proceeding from active life, returned to it with immediate benefit, whereas works properly poetical, as soaring above mere social and material interests, could only be indirectly and accidentally profitable. These discussions went on like the stories of the Arabian Nights; one important matter came up after another; many themes were only touched upon without our being able to follow them out; and accordingly, as the stay of the young princes in Frankfort was necessarily short, they made me promise to follow them to Mayence and spend a few days with them there. I gave this promise gladly enough, and hastened home to impart the agreeable intelligence to my parents.

My father, however, could not by any means be brought to approve of it. In accordance with his sentiments as a citizen of the empire, he had always kept aloof from the great; and, although constantly coming in contact with the "*chargés d'affaires*" of the neighbouring princes, he had, nevertheless, avoided all personal relations with them. In fact, courts were among the things about which he was accustomed to joke. He was not indeed displeased if any one opposed his opinions on this head, only he was not satisfied unless his opponent maintained his side with wit and spirit. If we allowed his "*Procul a Jove procul a fulmine*" to pass, but added, that with lightning the question was not so much whence it came as whither it went, he would bring up the old proverb, "With great lords it is not good to eat cherries." When to this we replied, that it was still worse to eat with dainty people out of one basket, he would not deny the truth of this; only he was sure to have another proverb ready at hand which was to put us to confusion. For since proverbs and rhyming apophthegms proceed from the people, who, while they are forced to obey, like at least to speak their ven-

geance, whereas their superiors indemnify themselves
by deeds; and since the poetry of the sixteenth
century is almost wholly of a nervous didactic character,—there is in our language no lack of jests and
serious adages, directed from below upwards. We
juniors, however, now began to aim from above downwards, fancying ourselves something great as we took
up the cause of the great. Of these sayings and
counter-sayings I will here insert a few.

A.

Long at court is long in hell,

B.

There many good folks warm them well.

A.

Such as I am, I'm still mine own :
To me shall favours ne'er be shown.

B.

Blush not a favour to receive,
For you must take if you would give.

A.

This trouble at the court you catch,
That, where you itch, you must not scratch.

B.

The sage, that would the people teach,
Must scratch a place that does not itch.

A.

Those who a slavish office choose,
One half of life are sure to lose ;
And, come what will, they may be sure
Old Nick the other will secure.

B.

Whoe'er with princes is at home,
Will some day find good fortune come:
Who courts the rabble, — to his cost
Will find that all his year is lost.

A.

Though wheat at court seems flourishing,
Doubt that great harvest it will bring:
When to your barn you deem it brought,
You'll find that after all 'tis naught.

B.

The wheat that blooms will ripen too,
For so of old it used to do;
And, if a crop is spoiled by hail,
The next year's harvest will not fail.

A.

He who would serve himself alone,
Should have a cottage of his own,
    Dwell with his children and his wife,
Regale himself with light new wine,
And on the cheapest viands dine:
    Then nothing can disturb his life.

B.

So, from a master thou'ldst be free?—
Whither dost thou mean to flee?
Dream not that freedom thou wilt get,
Thou hast a wife to rule thee yet.
She by her stupid boy is ruled,
Thus in thy cot thou still art schooled.

As I was lately looking up these rhymes in some
old memorandum-books, I fell in with many such
jeux d'esprit, in which we had amplified pithy old
German saws, in order to set them off against other
proverbs which are equally verified by experience.
A selection from them may perhaps hereafter, as an

epilogue to the "Puppenspiele" (puppet-shows), suggest some pleasant reflections.

But all these rejoinders could not move my father from his opinions. He was in the habit of saving his most stringent argument for the close of the discussion. This consisted of a minute description of Voltaire's adventure with Frederick the Second. He told us how the unbounded favour, familiarity, mutual obligations, were at once revoked and forgotten; how he had lived to see the comedy out in the arrest of that extraordinary poet and writer by the Frankfort civic guard, on the complaint of the Resident Freytag, and the warrant of the Burgomaster Fichard, and his confinement for some time in the tavern of the Rose, on the Zeil. To this we might have answered in many ways, — among others, that Voltaire was not free from blame himself; but from filial respect we always yielded the point. On the present occasion, when these things and others like them were alluded to, I hardly knew how to demean myself; for he warned me explicitly, maintaining that the invitation was given only to entice me into a trap, in order to take vengeance on me for my mischievous treatment of favoured Wieland. Fully as I was convinced of the contrary, yet as I saw but too plainly that a preconceived opinion, excited by hypochondriac fancies, afflicted my worthy father, I was unwilling to act in direct opposition to his convictions. Still I could not find any excuse for failing to keep my promise without appearing ungrateful and uncourteous. Unfortunately our friend Fräulein von Klettenberg, to whose advice we usually resorted in such cases, was confined to her bed. In her and my mother I had two incomparable companions. I called them Word and Deed: for, when the former cast her serene or rather blissful glance over earthly things, what was confusion to us children of earth at once grew plain before her; and she could almost always point out the right way, because she looked upon the labyrinth from above, and was not herself entangled in it. When a decision was once made, the readiness and energy of my mother could be relied on. While the former had Sight for her aid, the latter had Faith; and, as she maintained her serenity in all cases, she was never without the means of accomplishing what was proposed or desired. Accordingly she was now despatched to our sick friend to obtain her opinion; and, when this turned out in my favour, she was entreated to gain the consent of my father, who yielded, against his belief and will.

It was in a very cold season of the year that I arrived at the appointed hour in Mayence. My reception by the young princes and by their attendants was no less friendly than the invitation. The conversation in Frankfort was recalled, and resumed at the point where it had been broken off. When it touched upon the recent German literature and its audacities, it was perfectly natural that my famous piece, "Götter, Helden, und Wieland" ("Gods, Heroes, and Wieland"), should come up, at which I remarked with satisfaction that the thing was regarded with good humour. Being called on to give the real history of this *jeu d'esprit*, which had excited so great attention, I could not avoid confessing, first of all, that, as true fellows of the Upper Rhine, we had no bounds, either to our liking or disliking. With us, reverence for Shakespeare was carried to adoration. But Wieland, with his decided peculiarity of destroying the interest, both of himself and of his readers, had, in the notes to his translation, found much fault with the great author, and that in such a way as to vex us exceedingly, and to diminish, in our eyes, the value of the work. We saw that Wieland, whom we had so highly revered as a poet, and who, as a translator, had rendered such great service, was, as a critic, capricious, one-sided, and unjust. Besides this, he had deliberately spoken against our idols, the Greeks; and this sharpened our hostility yet more. It is well known that the Greek gods and heroes are eminent, not for moral, but for glorified physical, qualities; for which reason they afford such splendid subjects to artists. Now Wieland, in his " Alceste," had presented heroes and demi-gods after the modern fashion. Against this we had nothing to say, as every one is at liberty to mould poetic traditions to his own ends and way of thinking. But in the letters on this opera, which he inserted in the *Merkur*, he appeared to us unduly to exalt this mode of treating them; in short, to show too much of the partisan, and to commit an unpardonable sin against the good ancients and their higher style, by his absolute unwillingness to recognise the strong, healthy nature which is the basis of their productions. I told them we had hardly discussed these grievances with some vehemence in our little society, when my ordinary rage for dramatising everything came upon me one Sunday afternoon; and so at one sitting, over a bottle of good Burgundy, I wrote off the whole piece, just as it stands. It was no sooner read to those of my colleagues as were present, and received by them with exclamations of delight, than I sent the manuscript to Lenz at Strasburg, who appeared enraptured with it, and maintained that it must be printed without delay. After some correspondence, I at last consented; and he put it hastily to press at Strasburg. Some time afterward, I learned that this was one of the first steps which Lenz took in his design to injure me, and to bring me into disgrace with the public; but at that time I neither knew nor surmised anything of the kind.

In this way I had, with perfect candour, given my new patrons an account of the innocent origin of the piece, as well as I knew it myself, in order to convince them that it contained no personality, nor any ulterior motive. I also took care to let them understand with what gaiety and recklessness we were accustomed to banter and ridicule each other among ourselves. With this, I saw that they were quite content. They almost admired the great fear we had lest any one of ourselves should go to sleep upon his laurels. They compared such a society to those buccaneers who, in every moment of repose, are afraid of becoming effeminate, and whose leaders, when there are no enemies in sight, and there is no one to plunder, will let off a pistol under the mess-table, in order that even in peace there may be no want of wounds and horrors. After considerable discussion *pro* and *con* upon this subject, I was at last induced to write Wieland a friendly letter. I gladly availed myself of the opportunity; as, in the *Merkur*, he had spoken most liberally of this piece of youthful folly, and, as in literary feuds was almost always his custom, had ended the affair in the most skilful manner.

The few days of my stay at Mayence passed off very pleasantly; for, when my new patrons were abroad on visits and banquets, I remained with their attendants, drew the portraits of several, or went skating, for which the frozen ditches of the fortification afforded excellent opportunity. I returned home full of the kindness I had met with, and, as I entered the house, was on the point of emptying my heart by a minute account of it; but I saw only troubled faces, and the conviction was soon forced upon me that our friend Fräulein von Klettenberg was no more. At this I was greatly concerned; because, in my present situation, I needed her more than ever. They told me, for my consolation, that a pious death had crowned her happy life, and that the cheerfulness of her faith had remained undisturbed to the end. But there was also another obstacle in the way of a free communication

on the subject of my visit. My father, instead of
rejoicing at the fortunate issue of this little adventure,
persisted in his opinion, and maintained, on the other
hand, that it was nothing but dissimulation, and that
perhaps there was a danger of their carrying out in
the end something still worse against me. I was thus
driven to my younger friends with my narrative, and
to them I could not tell it circumstantially enough.
But their attachment and good will led to a result
which to me was most unpleasant. Shortly afterward
appeared a pamphlet, called "Prometheus and His
Reviewers," also in a dramatic form. In this the
comical notion was carried out, of putting little wood-
cut figures before the dialogue, instead of proper names,
and representing, by all sorts of satirical images, those
critics who had expressed an opinion upon my works,
or on works akin to them. In one place the Altona
courier, without his head, was blowing his horn; here
a bear was growling, and there a goose was cackling.
The *Merkur*, too, was not forgotten: and many wild
and tame animals were represented in the *atelier* of
the sculptor endeavouring to put him out; while he,
without taking particular notice of them, kept zealously
at his work, and did not refrain from expressing his
opinion about the matter in general. The appearance
of this *jeu d'esprit* surprised me much, and was as
unexpected as it was disagreeable. Its style and tone
evidently showed that it was by one of our society;
and, indeed, I feared it might be attributed to me.
But what was most annoying, was the circumstance
that "Prometheus" brought out some allusions to my
stay at Mayence, and to what was said there, which
nobody but myself could have known. To me this
was a proof that the author was one of those who
formed my most intimate circle of friends, where he
must have heard me relate these events in detail.
Accordingly we all looked at each other, and each

suspected the rest; but the unknown writer managed very well to keep his own secret. I uttered vehement reproaches against him; because it was exceedingly vexatious to me, after so gracious a reception and so important a conversation, and after the confiding letter I had written to Wieland, to see here an occasion for fresh distrust and disagreement. However, my uncertainty on this point was not of long duration. As I walked up and down my room reading the book aloud, I heard clearly, in the fancies and the turns of expression, the voice of Wagner — and it was he. When I had rushed down-stairs to impart my discovery to my mother, she confessed to me that she already knew it. Annoyed at the ill results of what had seemed to him a good and praiseworthy plan, the author had discovered himself to her, and besought her intercession with me, not to fulfil in his person my threat of holding no further intercourse with the writer who had so abused my confidence. The fact that I had found him out myself was very much in his favour, and the satisfaction always attending a discovery of one's own inclined me to be merciful. The fault which had given occasion for such a proof of my sagacity was forgiven. Nevertheless, it was not easy to convince the public that Wagner was the author, and that I had had no hand in the game. No one believed that he possessed such versatility of talent; and no one reflected, that it was very easy for him, though possessing no remarkable talents of his own, to notice, seize upon, and bring out in his own way, all that for some time had passed, either in jest and earnest, in an intellectual society. And thus on this occasion, as on many others afterward, I had to suffer, not only for my own follies, but also for the indiscretion and precipitancy of my friends.

As the remembrance of them is here suggested by many circumstances, I will speak of some distinguished men who, at different times on their passage through Frankfort, either lodged at our house or partook of our friendly hospitality. Once more Klopstock stands justly at the head. I had already exchanged several letters with him, when he announced to me that he was invited to go to Carlsruhe and to reside there; that he would be in Friedberg by a specified day, and wished that I would come there and fetch him. I did not fail to be there at the hour. He, however, had been accidentally detained upon the road; and, after I had waited in vain for some days, I went home, where he did not arrive till after some time, and then excused his delay, and received very kindly my readiness to come to meet him. His person was small, but well-built; his manners, without being stiff, were serious and precise; his conversation was measured and agreeable. On the whole, there was something of the diplomatist in his bearing. Such a man undertakes the difficult task of supporting, at the same time, his own dignity, and that of a superior to whom he is responsible; of advancing his own interest, together with the much more important interest of a prince, or even of a whole state; and of making himself, beyond all things, pleasing to other men while in this critical position. In this way Klopstock appeared to bear himself as a man of worth, and as the representative of other things, — of religion, of morality, and freedom. He had also assumed another peculiarity of men of the world; namely, not readily to speak on subjects upon which he was particularly expected and desired to discourse. He was seldom heard to mention poetic and literary subjects. But, as he found in me and my friends a set of passionate skaters, he discoursed to us at length on this noble art, on which he had thought much, having considered what in it was to be sought and what avoided. Still, before we could receive the instruction he proffered, we had to submit to be put right as to the word

itself, in which we blundered.[1] We spoke in good Upper
Saxon of *Schlittschuhen,* which he would not allow to
pass at all; for the word, he said, does not come from
Schlitten (sledge), as if one went on little runners, but
from *Schreiten* (to stride), because, like the Homeric
gods, the skater strides away on these winged shoes
over the sea frozen into a plain. Next we came to
the instrument itself. He would have nothing to do
with the high grooved skates, but recommended the
low, broad, smooth-bottomed Friesland steel skates as
the most serviceable for speed. He was no friend to
the tricks of art which are usually performed in this
exercise. I procured, according to his advice, a pair
of smooth skates, with long toes, and used them for
several years, though with some discomfort. He understood, too, the science of horsemanship and horsebreak-
ing, and liked to talk about it: thus, as if by design,
he avoided all conversation upon his own profession,
that he might speak with greater freedom about arts
quite foreign to it, which he pursued only as a pastime.
I might say much more of these and other peculiarities
of this extraordinary man, if those who lived longer
with him had not already informed us fully about
them. One observation, however, I will not suppress,
which is, that men whom nature, after endowing them
with uncommon advantages, has placed in a narrow
circle of action, or at least in one disproportioned to
their powers, generally fall into eccentricities, and,
as they have no opportunity of making direct use of
their gifts, seek to employ them in an extraordinary
or whimsical manner.

Zimmermann was also our guest for a time. He
was tall and powerfully built; of a vehement nature,

---

[1] There are two words used for "skate." One of them, *Schlitt-
schuh,* means "sledge-shoe;" the other, *Schrittschuh,* means
"stride-shoe." Goethe and his friends make use of the former;
Klopstock contends for the latter.

open to every impulse; yet he had his outward bearing and manners perfectly under control, so that in society he appeared as a skilful physician and polished man of the world. It was only in his writings and amongst his most confidential friends that he gave free course to his untamed inward character. His conversation was varied and highly instructive; and, for one who could pardon his keen sensitiveness to whatever grated on his own personal feelings and merits, no more desirable companion could be found. For myself, as what is called vanity never disturbed me, and I in return often presumed to be vain also, that is, did not hesitate to enlarge upon whatever in myself pleased me, I got on with him capitally. We mutually tolerated and scolded each other; and, as he showed himself thoroughly open and communicative, I learned from him a great deal in a short time.

To judge such a man with the indulgence of gratitude, nay, on principle, I cannot say that he was vain. We Germans misuse the word "vain" (citel) but too often. In a strict sense, it carries with it the idea of emptiness; and we properly designate by it only the man who cannot conceal his joy at his Nothing, his contentment with a hollow phantom. With Zimmermann it was exactly the reverse: he had great deserts, and no inward satisfaction. The man who cannot enjoy his own natural gifts in silence, and find his reward in the exercise of them, but must wait and hope for their recognition and appreciation by others, will generally find himself but badly off, because it is but too well known a fact, that men are very niggard of their applause; that they rather love to mingle alloy with praise, and, where it can in any degree be done, to turn it into blame. Whoever comes before the public without being prepared for this, will meet with nothing but vexation; since, even if he does not overestimate his own production, it still has for him an unlimited value; while the reception it meets with in the world is, in every case, qualified. Besides, a certain susceptibility is necessary for praise and applause, as for every other pleasure. Let this be applied to Zimmermann, and it will be acknowledged in his case, too, that no one can obtain what he does not bring with him.

If this apology cannot be allowed, still less shall we be able to justify another fault of this remarkable man, because it disturbed and even destroyed the happiness of others. I mean his conduct toward his children. His daughter, who travelled with him, stayed with us while he visited the neighbouring scenes. She might be about sixteen years old, slender and well formed, but without elegance; her regular features would have been agreeable, if there had appeared in them a trace of animation, but she was always as quiet as a statue; she spoke seldom, and in the presence of her father never. But she had scarcely spent a few days alone with my mother, receiving the cheerful and affectionate attentions of this sympathising woman, when she threw herself at her feet with an opened heart, and, with a thousand tears, begged to be allowed to remain with her. With the most passionate language she declared that she would remain in the house as a servant, as a slave all her life, rather than go back with her father, of whose severity and tyranny no one could form an idea. Her brother had gone mad under his treatment: she had hitherto borne it, though with difficulty, because she had believed that it was the same, or not much better, in every family; but now that she had experienced such a loving, mild, and considerate treatment, her situation at home had become to her a perfect hell. My mother was greatly moved as she related to me this passionate effusion; and, indeed, she went so far in her sympathy, as to give me pretty clearly to understand, that she would be content to keep the girl in the house, if I would make up my mind to marry her. If she were an orphan, I replied, I might think and talk it over; but God keep me from a father-in-law who is such a father! My mother took great pains with the poor girl, but this made her only the more unhappy. At last an expedient was found, by putting her to a boarding-school. She did not, however, live very long.

I should hardly mention this culpable peculiarity of a man of such great deserts, if it had not already become a matter of public notoriety, and especially had not the unfortunate hypochondria, with which, in his last hours, he tortured himself and others, been commonly talked of. For that severity toward his children was nothing less than hypochondria, a partial insanity, a continuous moral murder, which, after making his children its victims, was at last directed against himself. We must also remember, that, though apparently in such good health, he was a great sufferer, even in his best years; that an incurable disease troubled the skilful physician who had relieved, and still gave ease to, so many of the afflicted. Yes, this distinguished man, with all his outward reputation, fame, honour, rank, and wealth, led the saddest life; and whoever will take the pains to learn more about it from existing publications, will not condemn but pity him.

Should I be expected to give a more precise account of the effect this distinguished man had upon me, I must once more recall the general features of that period. The epoch in which we were living might be called an epoch of high requisitions, for every one demanded of himself and of others what no mortal had hitherto accomplished. On chosen spirits who could think and feel, a light had arisen, which enabled them to see that an immediate, original understanding of nature, and a course of action based upon it, was both the best thing a man could desire, and also not difficult to attain. Experience thus once more became the universal watchword, and every one opened his eyes as wide as he could. Physicians, especially, had a most pressing call to labour to this end, and the best opportunity for finding it. There shone upon them, out of antiquity, a star which could serve as an example of all that was to be desired. The writings which had come down to us under the name of Hippocrates, furnished a model of the way in which a man should both observe the world and relate what he had seen, without mixing up himself with it. But no one considered that we cannot see like the Greeks, and that we shall never become such poets, sculptors, and physicians as they were. Even granted that we could learn from them, still the results of experience already gone through were almost beyond number, and, besides, were not always of the clearest kind; moreover had too often been made to accord with preconceived opinions. All these were to be mastered, discriminated, and sifted. This, also, was an immense demand. Then, again, it was required that each observer, in his personal sphere and labours, should acquaint himself with the true, healthy nature, as if she were now for the first time noticed and attended, and thus only what was genuine and real was to be learned. But as, in general, learning can never exist without the accompaniment of a universal smattering and a universal pedantry, nor the practice of any profession without empiricism and charlatanry; so there sprung up a violent conflict, the purpose of which was to guard use from abuse, and place the kernel high above the shell in men's estimation. In the execution of this design, it was perceived that the shortest way of getting out of the affair, was to call in the aid of genius, whose magic gifts could settle the strife, and accomplish what was required. Meanwhile, however, the understanding meddled with the matter: all it alleged must be reduced to clear notions, and exhibited in a logical form, that every prejudice might be put aside, and all superstition destroyed. And since the achievements of some extraordinary men, such as Boerhaave and Haller, were actually incredible, people thought themselves justified in demanding even still more from their pupils and successors. It was maintained that the path was opened, forgetting that in earthly things a path can very rarely be spoken of: for, as the water that is dislodged by a ship instantly flows in again behind it; so by the law of its nature, when eminent spirits have once driven error aside, and made a place for themselves, it very quickly closes again upon them.

But of this the ardent Zimmermann could form no idea whatever: he would not admit that absurdity did, in fact, fill up the world. Impatient, even to madness, he rushed to attack everything that he saw and believed to be wrong. It was all the same to him whether he was fighting with a nurse or with Paracelsus, with a quack or a chemist. His blows fell alike heavily in either case; and, when he had worked himself out of breath, he was greatly astonished to see the heads of this hydra, which he thought he had trodden under foot, springing up all fresh again, and showing him their teeth from innumerable jaws.

Every one who reads his writings, especially his clever work "On Experience," will perceive more distinctly than I can express them, the subjects of discussion between this excellent man and myself. His influence over me was the more powerful, as he was twenty years my senior. Having a high reputation as a physician, he was chiefly employed among the upper classes; and the corruption of the times, caused by effeminacy and excess, was a constant theme of conversation with him. Thus his medical discourses, like those of the philosophers and my poetical friends, drove me again back to nature. In his vehement passion for improvement I could not fully participate: on the contrary, after we separated, I instantly drew back into my own proper calling, and endeavoured to employ the gifts nature had bestowed upon me, with moderate exertion, and by good-natured opposition to what I disapproved of, to gain a standing for myself, in perfect indifference how far my influence might reach or whither it might lead me.

Von Salis, who was setting up the large boarding-school at Marschlins, visited us also at that time. He was an earnest and intelligent man, and must have quietly made many humourous observations on the irregular though genial mode of life in our little society. The same was probably the case with Sulzer, who came in contact with us on his journey to the south of France: at least, a passage in his travels, where he speaks of me, seems to favour this opinion.

These visits, which were as agreeable as they were profitable, were, however, diversified by others, which we would rather have been spared. Needy and shameless adventurers fixed themselves on the confiding youth, supporting their urgent demands by real as well as fictitious relationships and misfortunes. They borrowed my money, and made it necessary for me to borrow in turn; so that I in consequence fell into the most unpleasant position with opulent and kind-hearted friends. If I wished that all these unfortunate folks were food for the crows, my father found himself in the situation of the *magician's apprentice*,[1] who was willing enough to see his house washed clean, but is frightened when the flood rushes in, without ceasing, over threshold and stairs. By an excessive kindness, the quiet and moderate plan of life which my father had designed for me was step by step interrupted and put off, and from day to day changed contrary to

[1] The allusion is to Goethe's own poem, "Der Zauberlehrling."

all expectation. All idea of a long visit to Ratisbon and Vienna was as good as given up; but still I was to pass through those cities on my way to Italy, so as at least to gain a general notion of them. On the other hand, some of my friends, who did not approve of taking so long a circuit in order to get into active life, recommended that I should take advantage of a moment which seemed in every way favourable, and think on a permanent establishment in my native city. Although I was excluded from the Council, first through my grandfather, and then through my uncle, there were yet many civil offices to which I could lay claim, where I could remain for a time and await the future. There were agencies of several kinds which offered employment enough, and the place of a *chargé-d'affaires* was highly respectable. I let them tell me about it, thinking that I was fit for the like without having previously asked myself whether a mode of life and business which requires, that, amid dissipation, we should most of all act for a certain end, would suit me. To these plans and designs there was now added a tender sentiment, which seemed to draw me toward a domestic life, and to accelerate my determination.

The society of young men and women already mentioned, which was kept together by, if it did not owe its origin to, my sister, still survived after her marriage and departure, because the members had grown accustomed to each other, and could not spend one evening in the week better than in this friendly circle. The eccentric orator also, whose acquaintance we made in the sixth book, had, after many adventures, returned to us, more clever and more perverse than ever, and once again played the legislator of the little state. As a sequel to our former diversions, he had devised something of the same kind : he enacted that every week lots should be drawn, not as before to decide what pairs should be lovers, but married couples.

How lovers should conduct themselves toward each other, he said, we knew well enough : but of the proper deportment of husbands and wives in society we were totally ignorant; and this, with our increasing years, we ought to learn before all things. He laid down general rules, which, of course, set forth that we must act as if we did not belong to each other; that we must not sit or speak often together, much less indulge in anything like caresses. And at the same time we were not only to avoid everything which would occasion mutual suspicion and discord, but, on the contrary, he was to win the greatest praises, who, with his free and open manners, should yet most endear to himself his wife.

The lots were at once drawn; some odd matches that they decided were laughed at and joked about; and the universal marriage comedy was begun in good humour and renewed every week.

Now, it fell out strangely enough, that, from the first, the same lady fell twice to me. She was a very good creature, just such a woman as one would like to think of as a wife. Her figure was beautiful and well-proportioned, her face pleasing, while in her manners there prevailed a repose which testified to the health of her mind and body. Every day and hour she was perfectly the same. Her domestic industry was in high repute. Though she was not talkative, a just understanding and natural talents could be recognised in her language. To meet the advances of such a person with friendliness and esteem was natural: on a general principle I was already accustomed to do it, and now I acted from a sort of traditional kindness as a social duty. But, when the lot brought us together for the third time, our jocose law-giver declared in the most solemn manner that Heaven had spoken, and we could not again be separated. We submitted to his sentence; and both of us adapted ourselves so well to our public conjugal duties, that we might really have served as a model. Since all the pairs who were severally united for the evening were obliged, by the general rules, to address each other for the few hours with *Du* (thou), we had, after a series of weeks, grown so accustomed to this confidential pronoun, that, even in the intervals, whenever we accidentally came together, the *Du* would kindly come out.[1] Habit is a strange thing: by degrees both of us found that nothing was more natural than this relation. I liked her more and more, while her manner of treating me gave evidence of a beautiful calm confidence; so that on many an occasion, if a priest had been present, we might have been united on the spot without much hesitation.

As at each of our social gatherings something new was required to be read aloud, I brought with me one evening a perfect novelty, "The Memoir of Beaumarchais against Clavigo," in the original. It gained great applause. The thoughts to which it gave occasion were freely expressed; and, after much had been spoken on both sides, my partner said, "If I were thy liege lady, and not thy wife, I would entreat thee to change this memoir into a play: it seems to me perfectly suited for it." "That thou mayst see, my love," I replied, "that liege lady and wife can be united in one person, I promise, that, at the end of a week, the subject-matter of this work, in the form of a piece for the theatre, shall be read aloud, as has just been done with these pages." They wondered at so bold a promise, but I did not delay to set about accomplishing it. What, in such cases, is called invention, was with me instantaneous. As I was escorting home my titulary wife, I was silent. She asked me what was the

---

[1] Members of the same family address each other with the second person singular "Du," instead of the more formal third person plural, "Sie." In the same way the French employ "Tu" instead of "Vous." — TRANS.

matter. "I am pondering on the play," I answered, "and have got already into the middle of it. I wished to show thee that I would gladly do anything to please thee." She pressed my hand; and, as I in return snatched a kiss, she said, "Thou must forget thy character! To be loving, people think, is not proper for married folks." "Let them think," I rejoined: "we will have it our own way."

Before I got home, — and, indeed, I took a very circuitous route, — the piece was pretty far advanced. Lest this should seem boastful, I will confess, that previously, on the first and second reading, the subject had appeared to me dramatic and even theatrical; but, without such a stimulus, this piece, like so many others, would have remained among the number of the merely possible creations. My mode of treating it is well enough known. Weary of villains, who, from revenge, hate, or mean purposes, attack a noble nature and ruin it, I wished, in Carlos, to show the working of clear good sense, associated with true friendship, against passion, inclination, and outward necessity, in order for once to compose a tragedy in this way. Availing myself of the example of our patriarch Shakespeare, I did not hesitate for a moment to translate, word for word, the chief scene, and all that was properly dramatic in the original. Finally, for the conclusion, I borrowed the end of an English ballad; and so I was ready before the Friday came. The good effect which I attained in the reading will easily be believed. My liege spouse took not a little pleasure in it; and it seemed as if, by this production, as an intellectual offspring, our union was drawn closer and dearer.

Mephistopheles Merck here did me, for the first time, a great injury. When I communicated the piece to him, he answered, "You must write hereafter no more such trifles; others can do such things." In this he was wrong. We should not, in all things, transcend the notions which men have already formed : it is good that much should be in accordance with the common way of thinking. Had I at that time written a dozen such pieces, which with a little stimulus would have been easy enough, three or four of them would perhaps have retained a place on the stage. Every theatrical manager who knows the value of a *répertoire*, can say what an advantage that would have been.

By these and other intellectual diversions, our whimsical game of marriage became a family story, if not the talk of the town, which did not sound disagreeably in the ears of the mothers of our fair ones. My mother, also, was not at all opposed to such an event : she had before looked with favour on the lady with whom I had fallen into so strange a relation, and did not doubt that she would make as good a daughter-in-law as a wife. The aimless bustle in which I had for some time lived was not to her mind ; and, in fact, she had to bear the worst of it. It was her part to provide abundant entertainment for the stream of guests, without any compensation for furnishing quarters to this literary army, other than the honour they did her son by feasting upon him. Besides, it was clear to her that so many young persons — all of them without property — united, not only for scientific and poetic purposes, but also for that of passing the time in the gayest manner, would soon become a burden and injury to themselves, and most certainly to me, whose thoughtless generosity, and passion for becoming security for others, she too well knew.

Accordingly she looked on the long-planned Italian journey, which my father once more brought forward, as the best means of cutting short all these connections at once. But, in order that no new danger might spring up in the wide world, she intended first of all to bind fast the union which had already been suggested, so as to make a return into my native country more desirable, and my final determination more decided. Whether I only attribute this scheme to her, or whether she had actually formed it with her departed friend, I am not quite sure: enough, that her actions seemed to be based on a well-digested plan. I had very often to hear from her a regret, that, since Cornelia's marriage, our family circle was altogether too small; it was felt that I had lost a sister, my mother an assistant, and my father a pupil: nor was this all that was said. It happened, as if by accident, that my parents met the lady on a walk, invited her into the garden, and conversed with her for a long time. Thereupon there was some pleasantry at supper; and the remark was made, with a certain satisfaction, that she had pleased my father, as she possessed all the chief qualities which he, being a judge, required of a woman.

One thing after another was now arranged in our first story as if guests were expected: the linen was reviewed, and some hitherto neglected furniture was thought of. One day I surprised my mother in a garret examining the old cradles, among which an immense one of walnut, inlaid with ivory and ebony, in which I had formerly been rocked, was especially prominent. She did not seem altogether pleased when I said to her, that such swing-boxes were quite out of fashion, and that now people put babies, with free limbs, into a neat little basket, and carried them about for show, by a strap over the shoulder, like other small wares.

In short, such prognostics of a renewal of domestic activity became frequent; and, as I was in every way submissive, the thought of a state which would last through life spread a peace over our house and its inhabitants such as had not been enjoyed for a long time.

Part Four

Nemo contra deum nisi deus ipse.

PREFACE

In a life history that proceeds on many levels, as does the one I have ventured to undertake here, to make certain events coherent and readable one is sometimes compelled to separate what in time was intertwined, and to draw together what in time was separated but can only be grasped as a sequence— thus putting together the whole in parts that one may thoughtfully examine, judge, and, to some extent, make one's own.

I place this observation at the opening of the present part as partial justification of my procedure, and I ask my readers to bear in mind that the story continued here does not connect precisely with the close of the previous book but has the aim of gradually gathering up the main threads again, setting forth persons, as well as moods and activities, in a meaningful sequence.

SIXTEENTH BOOK.

WHAT people commonly say of misfortunes, — that they never come alone, — may with almost as much truth be said also of good fortune, and, indeed, of other circumstances which often cluster around us in a harmonious way, whether it be by a kind of fatality, or whether it be that man has the power of attracting to himself all mutually related things.

At any rate, my present experience showed me everything conspiring to produce an outward and an inward peace. The former came to me while I resolved patiently to await the result of what others were meditating and designing for me : the latter, however, I had to attain for myself by renewing former studies.

I had not thought of Spinoza for a long time, and now I was driven to him by an attack upon him. In our library I found a little book, the author of which railed violently against that original thinker, and, to go the more effectually to work, had inserted for a frontispiece a picture of Spinoza himself, with the inscription, "*Signum reprobationis in vultu gerens*," bearing on his face the stamp of reprobation. This there was no gainsaying, indeed, so long as one looked at the picture ; for the engraving was wretchedly bad, a perfect caricature : so that I could not help thinking of those adversaries who, when they conceive a dislike to any one, first of all misrepresent him, and then assail the monster of their own creation.

This little book, however, made no impression upon

me: since generally I did not like controversial works, but preferred always to learn from the author himself how he did think, than to hear from another how he ought to have thought. Still, curiosity led me to the article "Spinoza" in Bayle's Dictionary, a work as valuable for its learning and acuteness as it is ridiculous and pernicious by its gossiping and scandal.

The article "Spinoza" excited in me displeasure and mistrust. In the first place, the philosopher is represented as an atheist, and his opinions as most abominable; but, immediately afterward, it is confessed that he was a calmly reflecting man, devoted to his studies, a good citizen, a sympathising neighbour, and a peaceable individual. The writer seemed to me to have quite forgotten the words of the gospel, "*By their fruits ye shall know them;*" for how could a life pleasing in the sight of God and man spring from corrupt principles?

I well remembered what peace of mind and clearness of ideas came over me when I first turned over the posthumous works of that remarkable man. The effect itself was still quite distinct to my mind, though I could not recall the particulars: I therefore speedily had recourse again to the works to which I had owed so much, and again the same calm air breathed over me. I gave myself up to this reading, and thought, while I looked into myself, that I had never before so clearly seen through the world.

As on this subject there always has been, and still is even in these later times, so much controversy, I would not wish to be misunderstood; and therefore I make here a few remarks upon these so much feared, nay, abhorred, views.

Our physical as well as our social life, manners, customs, worldly wisdom, philosophy, religion, and many an accidental event, all call upon us *to deny ourselves*. Much that is most inwardly peculiar to us we are not

allowed to develop; much that we need from without
for the completion of our character is withheld; while,
on the other hand, so much is forced upon us which is
as alien to us as it is burdensome. We are robbed of
all we have laboriously acquired for ourselves, or
friendly circumstances have bestowed upon us; and,
before we can see clearly what we are, we find ourselves compelled to part with our personality, piece by
piece, till at last it is gone altogether. Indeed, the
case is so universal, that it seems a law of society to
despise a man who shows himself surly on that account. On the contrary, the bitterer the cup we have
to drink, the more pleasant face we must put on, in
order that composed lookers-on may not be offended
by the least grimace.

To solve this painful problem, however, nature has
endowed man with ample power, activity, and endurance. But especially is he aided therein by his volatility (*Leichtsinn*), a boon to man which nothing can
take away. By means of it he is able to renounce the
cherished object of the moment, provided the next present him something new to reach at; and thus he goes
on unconsciously remodelling his whole life. We are
continually putting one passion in the place of another:
employments, inclinations, tastes, hobbies, — we try
them all, and end by exclaiming, *All is vanity!* No
one is shocked by this false and murmuring speech;
nay, every one thinks, while he says it, that he is uttering a wise and indisputable maxim. A few men there
are, and only a few, who anticipate this insupportable
feeling, and avoid all calls to such partial resignation
by one grand act of total self-renunciation.

Such men convince themselves of the Eternal, the
Necessary, and of Immutable Law, and seek to form
to themselves ideas which are incorruptible, nay, which
observation of the Perishable does not shake, but rather
confirms. But, since in this there is something super-

human, such persons are commonly esteemed *in*-human (monsters), without a God and without a World. People hardly know what sort of horns and claws to give them.

My confidence in Spinoza rested on the serene effect he wrought in me; and it only increased when I found my worthy mystics were accused of Spinozism, and learned that even Leibnitz himself could not escape the charge, — nay, that Boerhaave, being suspected of similar sentiments, had to abandon theology for medicine.

But let no one think that I would have subscribed to his writings, and assented to them, *verbatim et literatim*. For, that no one really understands another; that no one does attach to the same word the same idea which another does; that a dialogue, a book, excites in different persons different trains of thought, — this I had long seen all too plainly; and the reader will trust the assertion of the author of " Faust " and " Werther," that, deeply experienced in such misunderstandings, he was never so presumptuous as to think that he understood perfectly a man, who, as the scholar of Descartes, raised himself, through mathematical and rabbinical studies, to the highest reach of thought, and whose name, even at this day, seems to mark the limit of all speculative efforts.

How much I appropriated from Spinoza would be seen distinctly enough, if the visit of the " Wandering Jew " to Spinoza, which I had devised as a worthy ingredient for that poem, existed in writing. But it pleased me so much in the conception, and I found so much delight in meditating on it in silence, that I never could bring myself to the point of writing it out. Thus the notion, which would have been well enough as a passing joke, became expanded until it lost its charm; and I banished it from my mind as something troublesome. The chief points, however, of what I owed to my study of Spinoza, so far as they have remained indelibly impressed on my mind, and have exercised a great influence on the subsequent course of my life, I will now unfold as briefly and succinctly as possible.

Nature works according to such eternal, necessary, divine laws, that the Deity himself could alter nothing in them. In this belief, all men are unconsciously agreed. Think only how a natural phenomenon, which should intimate any degree of understanding, reason, or even of caprice, would instantly astonish and terrify us.

When in animals there is exhibited anything like reason, it is long before we can recover from our amazement; for, although they are so near to us, they nevertheless seem to be divided from us by an infinite gulf, and to belong altogether to the kingdom of necessity. It is therefore impossible to take it ill if some thinkers have pronounced the infinitely ingenious, but strictly limited, organisation of those creatures, to be thoroughly mechanical.

If we turn to plants, our position is still more strikingly confirmed. How unaccountable is the feeling which seizes an observer upon seeing the *Mimosa*, as soon as it is touched, fold together in pairs its downy leaves, and finally clap down its little stalk as if upon a joint (*Gewerbe*). Still higher rises that feeling, to which I will give no name, at the sight of the *Hedysarum Gyrans*, which, without any apparent outward occasion, moves up and down its little leaves, and seems to play with itself as with our thoughts. Let us imagine a *Banana* suddenly endowed with a similar capacity, so that of itself it could by turns let down and lift up again its huge leafy canopy: who would not, upon seeing it the first time, start back in terror ? So rooted within us is the idea of our own superiority, that we absolutely refuse to concede to the outward world any part or portion in it; nay, if we could, we would too often withhold such advantages from our fellows.

. On the other hand, a similar horror seizes upon us, when we see a man unreasonably opposing universally recognised moral laws, or unwisely acting against the interest of himself and others. To get rid of the repugnance we feel on such occasions, we convert it at once into censure or detestation; and we seek, either in reality or in thought, to get free from such a man.

This contrariety between Reason and Necessity, which Spinoza threw out in so strong a light, I, strangely enough, applied to my own being; and what has been said is, properly speaking, only for the purpose of rendering intelligible what follows.

I had come to look upon my indwelling poetic talent altogether as Nature; the more so, as I had always been impelled to regard outward Nature as its proper object. The exercise of this poetic gift could indeed be excited and determined by circumstances; but its most joyful, its richest, action was spontaneous, — nay, even involuntary.

> Through field and forest roaming,
> My little songs still humming,
> I spent the livelong day.

In my nightly vigils the same thing happened: I therefore often wished, like one of my predecessors, to get me a leathern jerkin made, and to accustom myself to write in the dark, so as to be able to fix down at once all such unpremeditated effusions. So frequently had it happened, that, after composing a little piece in my head, I could not recall it, that I would now hurry to the desk, and, at one standing, write off the poem from beginning to end; and, as I could not spare time to adjust my paper, however obliquely it might lie, the

lines often crossed it diagonally. In such a mood I
liked best to get hold of a lead pencil, because I could
write most readily with it; whereas the scratching and
spluttering of the pen would sometimes wake me from
my somnambular poetising, confuse me, and stifle a
little conception in its birth. For the poems thus
created I had a particular reverence; for I felt toward
them somewhat as the hen does toward her chickens,
which she sees hatched and chirping about her. My
old whim of making known these things only by means
of private readings, now returned to me: to exchange
them for money seemed to me detestable.

And this suggests to me to mention in the present
place a little incident, which, however, did not take
place till some time after. When the demand for my
works had increased, and a collected edition was much
called for, these feelings held me back from preparing
it myself: Himburg, however, took advantage of my
hesitation; and I unexpectedly received one day several
copies of my collected works in print. With cool audacity this unauthorised publisher even boasted of having
done me a public service, and offered to send me, if I
wished, some Berlin porcelain by way of compensation.
His offer served to remind me of the law which compelled the Jews of Berlin, when they married, to purchase a certain quantity of porcelain, in order to keep
up the sale of the Royal manufacture. The contempt
which was shown for the shameless pirate led me to
suppress the indignation which I could not but feel at
such a robbery. I gave him no reply; and, while he
was making himself very comfortable with my property, I revenged myself in silence with the following
verses:

> Records of the years once dreamed away,
> Long-fallen hairs, and flowers that show decay,
> Faded ribbons, veils so lightly wove,
> The mournful pledges of a vanished love;

Things that to the flames should long have gone, —
Saucy Sosias snatches every one.
Just as though he were the heir to claim
Lawfully the poets' works and fame.
And, to make the owner full amends,
Paltry tea and coffee cups he sends!
Take your china back, your gingerbread!
For all Himburgs living I am dead.

This very Nature, however, which thus spontaneously brought forth so many longer and smaller works, was subject to long pauses; and for considerable periods I was unable, even when I most wished it, to produce anything, and consequently often suffered from *ennui*. The perception of such contrasts within me gave rise to the thought whether it would not be my wisest course to employ on the other hand, for my own and others' profit and advantage, the human, rational, and intellectual part of my being, and so as I already had done, and as I now felt myself more and more called upon to do, devote the intervals, when Nature ceased to influence me, to worldly occupations, and thus to leave no one of my faculties unused. This course, which seemed to be dictated by those general ideas before described, was so much in harmony with my character, and my position in life, that I resolved to adopt it, and by this means to check the wavering and hesitation to which I had hitherto been subject. Very pleasant was it to me to reflect, that thus, for actual service to my fellow men, I might demand a substantial reward; while, on the other hand, I might go on disinterestedly spending that lovely gift of nature as a sacred thing. By this consideration I guarded against the bitterness of feeling which might have arisen when circumstances should force upon the remark that precisely this talent, so courted and admired in Germany, was treated as altogether beyond the pale of the law and of justice. For not only were piracies considered perfectly allowable, and even comical, in Berlin, but the estimable Margrave of Baden, so praised for his administrative virtues, and the Emperor Joseph, who had justified so many hopes, lent their sanction, one to his Macklot, and the other to his honourable noble *Von* Trattner; and it was declared, that the rights, as well as the property, of genius, should be left at the absolute mercy of the trade.

One day, when we were complaining of this to a visitor from Baden, he told us the following story : Her ladyship the margravine, being a very active lady, had established a paper manufactory; but the paper was so bad that it was impossible to dispose of it. Thereupon Mr. Bookseller Macklot proposed, if he were permitted to print the German poets and prose writers, he would use this paper, and thus enhance its value. The proposal was adopted with avidity.

Of course we pronounced this malicious piece of scandal to be a mere fabrication, but found our pleasure in it notwithstanding. The name of Macklot became a byword at the time, and was applied by us to all mean transactions. And a volatile youth, often reduced to borrowing himself, while others' meanness was enriching itself through his talents, felt sufficiently compensated by a couple of good jokes.

Children and youths wander on in a sort of happy intoxication, which betrays itself especially in the fact, that the good innocent creatures are scarcely able to notice, and still less to understand, the ever-changing state of things around them. They regard the world as raw material which they must shape, as a treasure which they must take possession of. Everything they seem to think belongs to them, everything must be subservient to their will; indeed, on this account, the greater part lose themselves in a wild, uncontrollable temper. With the better part, however, this tendency unfolds itself into a moral enthusiasm, which occasionally moves of its own accord after some actual or seeming good, but still oftener suffers itself to be prompted, led, and even misled.

Such was the case with the youth of whom we are at present speaking; and, if he appeared rather strange to mankind, still he seemed welcome to many. At the very first meeting, you found in him a freedom from reserve, a cheerful open-heartedness in conversation, and in action the unpremeditated suggestions of the moment. Of the latter trait a story or two.

In the close-built Jews' Street (*Judengasse*), a violent conflagration had broken out. My universal benevolence, which prompted me to lend my active aid to all, led me to the spot, full dressed as I was. A passage had been broken through from All Saints' Street (*Allerheiligengasse*), and thither I repaired. I found a great number of men busied with carrying water, rushing forward with full buckets, and back again with empty ones. I soon saw, that, by forming a lane for passing up and down the buckets, the help we rendered might be doubled. I seized two full buckets, and remained standing, and called others to me: those who came on were relieved of their load, while those returning arranged themselves in a row on the other side. The arrangement was applauded; my address and personal sympathy found favour; and the lane, unbroken from its commencement to its burning goal, was soon completed. Scarcely, however, had the cheerfulness which this inspired called forth a joyous, I might even say a merry, humour in this living machine, all of whose parts worked well together, when wantonness began to appear, and was soon succeeded by a love of mischief. The wretched fugitives, dragging off their miserable substance upon their backs, if they once got within the lane, must pass on without stopping, and, if they ventured to halt for a moment's rest, were immediately assailed. Saucy boys would sprinkle them with the water, and even add insult to misery. However, by means of gentle words and eloquent reproofs, prompted perhaps by a regard to my best clothes, which were in danger, I managed to put a stop to their rudeness.

Some of my friends had from curiosity approached, to gaze on the calamity, and seemed astonished to see their companion, in thin shoes and silk stockings, — for that was then the fashion, — engaged in this wet business. But few of them could I persuade to join us: the others laughed, and shook their heads. We stood our ground, however, a long while; for, if any were tired and went away, there were plenty ready to take their places. Many sightseers, too, came, merely for the sake of the spectacle; and so my innocent daring became universally known, and the strange disregard of etiquette became the town-talk of the day.

This readiness to do any action that a good-natured whim might prompt, which proceeded from a happy self-consciousness which men are apt to blame as vanity, made our friend to be talked of for other oddities.

A very inclement winter had completely covered the Main with ice, and converted it into a solid floor. The liveliest intercourse, both for business and pleasure, was kept up on the ice. Boundless skating-paths, and wide, smooth-frozen plains, swarmed with a moving multitude. I never failed to be there early in the morning, and once, being lightly clad, was well-nigh frozen by the time my mother arrived, who usually came at a later hour to visit the scene. She sat in the carriage, in her purple velvet and fur-trimmed cloak, which, held together on her breast by a strong golden cord and tassel, looked quite fine. " Give me your furs, dear mother!" I cried out on the instant, without a moment's thought: " I am terribly frozen." Nor did she stop to think, and so in a moment I was wrapped in her cloak. Reaching half-way below my knees with its purple colour, sable border, and gold trimmings, it contrasted not badly with the brown fur cap I wore. Thus clad, I carelessly went on skating up and down; the crowd was so great that no especial notice was taken of my strange appearance; still it was not unobserved, for often afterward it was brought up, in jest or in earnest, among my other eccentricities.

Leaving these recollections of happy and spontaneous action, we will now resume the sober thread of our narrative.

A witty Frenchman has said, If a clever man has once attracted the attention of the public by any meritorious work, every one does his best to prevent his ever doing a similar thing again.

It is even so: something good and spirited is produced in the quiet seclusion of youth; applause is won, but independence is lost; the concentrated talent is pulled about and distracted, because people think that they may pluck off and appropriate to themselves a portion of the personality.

It was owing to this that I received a great many invitations, or, rather, not exactly invitations: a friend, an acquaintance, would propose, with even more than urgency, to introduce me here or there.

The *quasi* stranger, now described as a bear on account of his frequent surly refusals, and then again like Voltaire's Huron, or Cumberland's West Indian, as a child of nature in spite of many talents, excited curiosity; and in various families negotiations were set on foot to see him.

Among others, a friend one evening entreated me to go with him to a little concert to be given in the house of an eminent merchant of the Reformed persuasion. It was already late; but, as I loved to do everything on the spur of the moment, I went with him, decently dressed, as usual. We entered a chamber on the ground-floor, — the ordinary but spacious sitting-room of the family. The company was numerous: a piano stood in the middle, at which the only daughter of the house sat down immediately, and played with considerable facility and grace. I stood at the lower end of the piano, that I might be near enough to observe her form and bearing: there was something childlike in her manner; the movements she was obliged to make in playing were unconstrained and easy.

After the sonata was finished, she stepped toward the end of the piano to meet me: we merely saluted, however, without further conversation; for a quartet had already commenced. At the close of it, I moved somewhat nearer, and uttered some civil compliment, telling her what pleasure it gave me that my first acquaintance with her should have also made me acquainted with her talent. She managed to make a very clever reply, and kept her position as I did mine. I saw that she observed me closely, and that I was really standing for a show; but I took it all in good part, since I had something graceful to look at in my turn. Meanwhile, we gazed at one another; and I will not deny that I was sensible of feeling an attractive power of the gentlest kind. The moving about of the company, and her performances, prevented any farther approach that evening. But I must confess that I was anything but displeased, when, on taking leave, the mother gave me to understand that they hoped soon to see me again; while the daughter seemed to join in the request with some friendliness of manner. I did not fail, at suitable intervals, to repeat my visit; since, on such occasions, I was sure of a cheerful and intellectual conversation, which seemed to prophesy no tie of passion.

In the meantime, the hospitality of our house once laid open caused many an inconvenience to my good parents and myself. At any rate, it had not proved in any way beneficial to my steadfast desire to notice the Higher, to study it, to further it, and, if possible, to imitate it. Men, I saw, so far as they were good, were pious, and, so far as they were active, were unwise and oftentimes unapt. The former could not help me, and the latter only confused me. One remarkable case I have carefully written down.

In the beginning of the year 1775, Jung, afterward called Stilling, from the Lower Rhine, announced to us that he was coming to Frankfort, being invited as an oculist, to treat an important case : the news was welcome to my parents and myself, and we offered him quarters.

Herr von Lersner, a worthy man advanced in years, universally esteemed for his success in the education and training of princely children, and for his intelligent manners at court and on his travels, had been long afflicted with total blindness : his strong hope of obtaining some relief of his affliction was not entirely extinct. Now, for several years past, Jung, with skilful boldness and a steady hand, had, in the Lower Rhine, successfully couched for the cataract, and thus had gained a widespread reputation. The candour of his soul, his truthfulness of character, and genuine piety, gained him universal confidence : this extended up the river through the medium of various parties connected by business. Herr von Lersner and his friends, upon the advice of an intelligent physician, resolved to send for the successful oculist; although a Frankfort merchant, in whose case the cure had failed, earnestly endeavoured to dissuade them. But what was a single failure against so many successful cases ! So Jung came, enticed by the hope of a handsome remuneration, which heretofore he had been accustomed to renounce ; he came, to increase his reputation, full of confidence and in high spirits : and we congratulated ourselves on the prospect of such an excellent and lively table-companion.

At last, after a preparatory course of medicine, the cataract upon both eyes was couched. Expectation was at its height. It was said that the patient saw the moment after the operation, until the bandage again shut out the light. But it was remarked that Jung was not cheerful, and that something weighed on his spirits; indeed, on further inquiry, he confessed to me that he was uneasy as to the result of the operation. Commonly, for I had witnessed several operations of the kind in Strasburg, nothing in the world seemed easier than such cases; and Stilling himself had operated successfully a hundred times. After piercing the insensible cornea, which gave no pain, the dull lens would, at the slightest pressure, spring forward of itself: the patient immediately discerned objects, and only had to wait with bandaged eyes, until the completed cure should allow him to use the precious organ at his own will and convenience. How many a poor man for whom Jung had procured this happiness, had invoked God's blessing and reward upon his benefactor, which was now to be realised by means of this wealthy patient!

Jung confessed to me that this time the operation had not gone off so easily and so successfully: the lens had not sprung forward; he had been obliged to draw it out, and indeed, as it had grown to the socket, to loosen it; and this he was not able to do without violence. He now reproached himself for having operated also on the other eye. But Lersner and his friends had firmly resolved to have both couched at the same time; and, when the emergency occurred, they did not immediately recover presence of mind enough to think what was best. Suffice it to say, the second lens also did not spontaneously spring forward, but had to be loosened and drawn out with difficulty.

How much pain our benevolent, good-natured, pious friend felt in this case, it is impossible to describe or to unfold: some general observations on his state of mind will not be out of place here.

To labour for his own moral culture is the simplest and most practicable thing which man can propose to himself; the impulse is inborn in him: while in social life both reason and love prompt or rather force him to do so.

Stilling could only live in a moral religious atmosphere of love; without sympathy, without hearty response, he could not exist; he demanded mutual attachment; where he was not known, he was silent; where he was only known, not loved, he was sad; accordingly he got on best with those well-disposed persons who can set themselves down for life in their assigned vocation, and go to work to perfect themselves in their narrow but peaceful sphere.

Such persons succeed pretty well in stifling vanity, in renouncing the pursuit of outward power, in acquiring a circumspect way of speaking, and in preserving a uniformly friendly manner toward companions and neighbours.

Frequently we may observe in this class traces of a certain form of mental character, modified by individual varieties: such persons, accidentally excited, attach great weight to the course of their experience; they consider everything a supernatural determination, in the conviction that God interferes immediately with the course of the world.

With all this there is associated a certain disposition to abide in his present state, and yet at the same time to allow themselves to be pushed or led on, which results from a certain indecision to act of themselves. The latter is increased by the miscarriage of the wisest plans, as well as by the accidental success brought about by the unforeseen concurrence of favourable occurrences.

Now, since a vigilant, manly character is much checked by this way of life, it is well worthy of reflection and inquiry, how men are most liable to fall into such a state.

The things sympathetic persons of this kind love most to talk of, are the so-called awakenings and conversions, to which we will not deny a certain psychological value. They are properly what we call in scientific and poetic matters, an " *aperçu;* " the perception of a great maxim, which is always a genius-like operation of the mind : we arrive at it by pure intuition, that is, by reflection, neither by learning nor tradition. In the cases before us, it is the perception of the moral power, which anchors in faith, and thus feels itself in proud security in the midst of the waves.

Such an *aperçu* gives the discoverer the greatest joy; because, in an original manner, it points to the infinite : it requires no length of time to work conviction; it leaps forth whole and complete in a moment : hence the quaint old French rhyme, —

> " En peu d'heure
> Dieu labeure."

Outward occasions often work violently in bringing about such conversions, and then people think they see in them signs and wonders.

Love and confidence bound me most heartily to Stilling : I had, moreover, exercised a good and happy influence on his life ; and it was quite in accordance with his disposition, to treasure up in a tender, grateful heart the remembrance of all that had ever been done for him : but, in my existing frame of mind and pursuits, his society neither benefited nor cheered me. I was glad to let every one interpret as he pleased and work out the riddle of his days : but this way of ascribing to an immediate, divine influence, all the good that after a rational manner occurs to us in our chanceful life, seemed to me too presumptuous; and the habit of regarding the painful consequences of the hasty acts and omissions of our own thoughtlessness or conceit, as a divine chastisement, did not at all suit me. I could, therefore, only listen to my good friend, but could not give him any very encouraging reply: still I readily suffered him, like so many others, to go his own way, and defended him since then, as well as before, when others, of too worldly a mind, did not hesitate to wound his gentle nature. Hence I never allowed to come to his ears a roguish remark made by a waggish man who once exclaimed quite seriously, "No! indeed, if I were as intimate with God as Jung is, I would never pray to the Most High for gold, but for wisdom and good counsel, that I might not make so many blunders which cost money, and draw after them wretched years of debt."

In truth, it was no time for such jests. Between hope and fear several more days passed away; with him the latter grew, the former waned, and, at last, vanished altogether : the eyes of the good patient man had become inflamed, and there remained no doubt that the operation had failed.

The state of mind to which our friend was reduced hereby, is not to be described : he was struggling against the deepest and worst kind of despair. For what was there now that he had not lost! In the first place, the warm thanks of one restored to sight, — the noblest reward which a physician can enjoy; then the confidence of others similarly needing help; then his worldly credit, while the interruption of his peculiar practice would reduce his family to a helpless state. In short, we played the mournful drama of Job through from beginning to end, since the faithful Jung took himself the part of the reproving friends. He chose to regard this calamity as the punishment of his former faults ; it seemed to him, that, in taking his accidental discovery of an eye-cure as a divine call to that business, he had acted wickedly and profanely ; he reproached himself for not having thoroughly studied this highly important department, instead of lightly trusting his cures to good fortune ; what his enemies had said of him recurred again to his mind ; he began to doubt whether perhaps it was not all true ; and it pained him the more deeply when he found, that, in the course of his life, he had been guilty of that levity which is so dangerous to pious men, and also of presumption and vanity. In such moments he lost himself ; and, in whatever light we might endeavour to set the matter, we at last elicited from him only the rational and necessary conclusion, — that the ways of God are unsearchable.

My unceasing efforts to be cheerful would have been more checked by Jung's visit, if I had not, according to my usual habit, subjected his state of mind to an earnest friendly examination, and explained it after my own fashion. It vexed me not a little to see my good mother so poorly rewarded for her domestic care and painstaking ; though she did not herself perceive it, with her usual equanimity and ever bustling activity. I was most pained for my father. On my account he, with a good grace, had enlarged what hitherto had been a strictly close and private circle : and at table especially, where the presence of strangers attracted familiar friends and even passing visitors, he liked to indulge in a merry, even paradoxical, conversation, in which I put him in good humour, and drew from him many an approving smile, by all sorts of dialectic pugilism ; for I had an ungodly way of disputing everything, which, however, I pertinaciously kept up in every case so long only as he, who maintained the right, was not yet made perfectly ridiculous. During the last few weeks, however, this procedure was not to be thought of; for many very happy and most cheering incidents, occasioned by some successful secondary cures on the part of our friend, who had been made so miserable by the failure of his principal attempt, did not affect him, much less did they give his gloomy mood another turn.

One incident in particular was most amusing. Among Jung's patients there was a blind old Jewish beggar, who had come from Isenburg to Frankfort, where, in the extremity of wretchedness, he scarcely found a shelter, scarcely the meanest food and attendance: nevertheless, his tough Oriental nature helped him through, and he was in raptures to find himself healed perfectly and without the least suffering. When asked if the operation pained him, he said, in his hyperbolical manner, "If I had a million eyes, I would let them all be operated upon, one after the other, for half a *Kopfstück*."[1] On his departure he acted quite as eccentrically in the *Fahrgasse* (or main thoroughfare): he thanked God, and, in good Old Testament style, praised the Lord, and the wondrous man whom he had sent. Shouting this, he walked slowly on through the long, busy street toward the bridge. Buyers and sellers ran out of the shops, surprised by this singular exhibition of pious enthusiasm, passionately venting itself before all the world; and he excited their sympathy to such a degree, that, without asking anything, he was amply furnished with gifts for his travelling expenses.

This lively incident, however, could hardly be mentioned in our circle; for though the poor wretch, with all his domestic misery, in his sandy home beyond the Main, could still be counted extremely happy, the man of wealth and dignity on this side of the river, for

---

[1] A coin, with the head of the sovereign stamped upon it, generally worth four and one-half good groschen. — TRANS.

whom we were most interested, had missed the price-less relief so confidently expected.

It was sickening, therefore, to our good Jung to receive the thousand guilders, which, being stipulated in any case, were honourably paid by the high-minded sufferer. This ready money was destined to liquidate, on his return, a portion of the debts which added their burden to other sad and unhappy circumstances.

And so he went off inconsolable; for he could not help thinking of his meeting with his careworn wife, the changed manner of her parents, who, as sureties for so many debts of this too confiding man, might, however well-wishing, consider they had made a great mistake in the choice of a partner for their daughter. In this and that house, from this and that window, he could already see the scornful and contemptuous looks of those who, even when he was prospering, had wished him no good; while the thought of a practice inter-rupted by his absence, and likely to be materially damaged by his failure, troubled him extremely.

And so we took our leave of him, not without all hope on our parts; for his strong nature, sustained by faith in supernatural aid, could not but inspire his friends with a quiet and moderate confidence.

SEVENTEENTH BOOK.

In resuming the history of my relation to Lilli, I have to mention the many very pleasant hours I spent in her society, partly in the presence of her mother, partly alone with her. On the strength of my writings, people gave me credit for knowledge of the human heart, as it was then called: and in this view our conversations were morally interesting in every way.

But how could we talk of such inward matters without coming to mutual disclosures? It was not long before, in a quiet hour, Lilli told me the history of her youth. She had grown up in the enjoyment of all the advantages of society and worldly comforts. She described to me her brothers, her relations, and all her nearest connections; only her mother was kept in a respectful obscurity.

Little weaknesses, too, were thought of; and among them she could not deny, that she had often remarked in herself a certain gift of attracting others, with which, at the same time, was united a certain peculiarity of letting them go again. By prattling on, we thus came at last to the important point, that she had exercised this gift upon me too, but had been punished for it, since she had been attracted by me also.

These confessions flowed forth from so pure and childlike a nature, that by them she made me entirely her own.

We were now necessary to each other, we had grown into the habit of seeing each other; but how many a day, how many an evening till far into the

night, should I have had to deny myself her company,
if I had not reconciled myself to seeing her in her own
circles! This was a source of manifold pain to me.

My relation to her was that of a character to a
character — I looked upon her as to a beautiful,
amiable, highly accomplished daughter: it was like
my earlier attachments, but was of a still higher kind.
Of outward circumstances, however, of the interchange
of social relations, I had never thought. An irresistible longing reigned in me; I could not be without her,
nor she without me; but from the circle which surrounded her, and through the interference of its individual members, how many days were spoiled, how
many hours wasted.

The history of pleasure-parties which ended in displeasure; a retarding brother, whom I was to accompany, who would, however, always be stopping to do
some business or other, which, perhaps, somewhat
maliciously, he was in no hurry to finish, and would
thereby spoil the whole well-concerted plan for a
meeting; and ever so much more of accident and
disappointment, of impatience and privation, — all
these little troubles, which, circumstantially set forth
in a romance, would certainly find sympathising
readers, I must here omit. However, to bring this
merely contemplative account nearer to a living experience to a youthful sympathy, I may insert some
songs, which are indeed well known, but are perhaps
especially impressive in this place.

> Heart, my heart, oh, what hath changed thee?
>   What doth weigh on thee so sore?
> What hath thus from me estranged thee,
>   That I know thee now no more?
> Gone is all which once seemed dearest,
> Gone the care which once was nearest,
>   Gone thy toils and tranquil bliss:
>   Ah! how couldst thou come to this?

Does that bloom so fresh and youthful,
  That divine and lovely form,
That sweet look, so good and truthful,
  Bind thee with unbounded charm?
If I swear no more to see her,
If I man myself to flee her,
    Soon I find my efforts vain:
    Back to her I'm led again.

She with magic thread has bound me,
  That defies my strength or skill:
She has drawn a circle round me,
  Holds me fast against my will.
Cruel maid, her charms enslave me:
I must live as she would have me.
    Ah! how great the change to me!
    Love! when wilt thou set me free?
                — Editor's Version.

Why dost draw me thus without resistance
  To that splendour bright?
Was not glad and happy my existence
  In the dreary night?

Secretly shut up within my chamber,
  I in moonshine lay:
In the showers of its light, sweet slumber
  Over me did sway.

There I of rich golden hours was dreaming,
  Of joy unalloyed:
Thy dear image with full beauty beaming
  In my breast I spied.

Is't still I, whom thou oft at card-table
  Hold'st 'midst many lights,
Seatest, as I scarce to bear am able,
  Opposite such frights?

Not more charming now to me spring's gladness
  Is when blossoms start:
Where thou, angel, art, is love and goodness;
  Nature where thou art.
                — Editor's Version.

Whoever reads these songs attentively to himself, or, better still, sings them with feeling, will certainly feel a breath of the fulness of those happy hours stealing over him.

But we will not take leave of that greater and more brilliant society, without adding some further remarks, especially to explain the close of the second poem.

She, whom I was accustomed to see only in a simple dress which was seldom changed, now stood before me on such occasions in all the splendour of elegant fashion; and still she was the same. Her usual grace and kindliness of manner remained, only I should say her gift of attracting shone more conspicuous, — perhaps, because brought into contact with several persons, she seemed called upon to express herself with more animation, and to exhibit herself on more sides, as various characters approached her. At any rate, I could not deny, on the one hand, that these strangers were annoying to me; while, on the other, I would not for a great deal have deprived myself of the pleasure of witnessing her talents for society, and of seeing that she was made for a wider and more general sphere.

Though covered with ornaments, it was still the same bosom that had opened to me its inmost secrets, and into which I could look as clearly as into my own: they were still the same lips that had so lately described to me the state of things amidst which she had grown up, and had spent her early years. Every look that we interchanged, every accompanying smile, bespoke a noble feeling of mutual intelligence; and I was myself astonished, here in the crowd, at the secret innocent understanding which existed between us in the most human, the most natural way.

But, with returning spring, the pleasant freedom of the country was to knit still closer these relations. Offenbach-on-the-Main showed even then the considerable beginnings of a promising city. Beautiful, and for the times splendid, buildings, were already conspicuous. Of these Uncle Bernard (to call him by his familiar title) inhabited the largest; extensive factories were adjoining; D'Orville, a lively young man of amiable qualities, lived opposite. Contiguous gardens and terraces, reaching down to the Main, and affording a free egress in every direction into the lovely surrounding scenery, put both visitors and residents into excellent humour. The lover could not find a more desirable spot for indulging his feelings.

I lived at the house of John André; and as I have here to mention this man, who afterward made himself well enough known, I must indulge in a short digression, in order to give some idea of the state of the opera at that time.

In Frankfort, Marchand was director of the theatre, and exerted himself in his own person to do all that was possible. In his best years he had been a fine, large, well-made man; the easy and gentle qualities appeared to predominate in his character; his presence on the stage, therefore, was agreeable enough. He had, perhaps, as much voice as was required for the execution of any of the musical works of that day: accordingly he endeavoured to adapt to our stage the large and smaller French operas.

The part of the father in Gretry's opera of "Beauty and the Beast" particularly suited him, and his acting was quite expressive in the scene of the Vision which was contrived at the back of the stage.

This opera, successful in its way, approached, however, the lofty style, and was calculated to excite the tenderest feelings. On the other hand, a demon of realism had got possession of the opera-house: operas founded upon different crafts and classes were brought out. "The Huntsmen," "The Coopers," and I know not what else, were produced: André chose "The Potter." He had written the words himself, and, upon that part of the text which belonged to him, had lavished his whole musical talent.

I was lodging with him, and will only say so much as occasion demands of this ever ready poet and composer.

He was a man of an innate lively talent, and was settled at Offenbach, where he properly carried on a mechanical business and manufacture: he floated between the chapel-master (or precentor) and the *dilettante*. In the hope of meriting the former title, he toiled very earnestly to gain a thorough knowledge of the science of music: in the latter character he was inclined to repeat his own compositions without end.

Among the persons who at this time were most active in filling and enlivening our circle, the pastor Ewald must be first named. In society an intellectual, agreeable companion, he still carried on in private quietly and diligently the studies of his profession, and in fact afterward honourably distinguished himself in the province of theology. Ewald, in short, was an indispensable member of our circle, being quick alike of comprehension and reply.

Lilli's pianoforte-playing completely fettered our good André to our society: what with instructing, conducting, and executing, there were few hours of the day or night in which he was not either in the family circle or at our social parties.

Bürger's "Leonore," then but just published, and received with enthusiasm by the Germans, had been set to music by him: this piece he was always forward to execute, however often it might be encored.

I too, who was in the habit of repeating pieces of poetry with animation, was always ready to recite it. Our friends at this time did not get weary of the constant repetition of the same thing. When the company had their choice which of us they would rather hear, the decision was often in my favour.

All this (however it might be) served to prolong the intercourse of the lovers. They knew no bounds; and, between them both, they easily managed to keep the good John André continually in motion, that, by repetitions, he might make his music last till midnight. The two lovers thus secured for themselves a precious and indispensable opportunity.

If we walked out early in the morning, we found ourselves in the freshest air, but not precisely in the country. Imposing buildings, which at that time would have done honour to a city; gardens, spreading before us and easily overlooked, with their smooth flower and ornamental beds; a clear prospect commanding the opposite banks of the river, over whose surface, even at an early hour, might be seen floating a busy line of rafts or nimble market-skiffs and boats, — these together formed a gently gliding, living world, in harmony with love's tender feelings. Even the lonely rippling of the waves and rustling of the reeds in a softly flowing stream was highly refreshing, and never failed to throw a decidedly tranquillising spell over those who approached the spot. A clear sky of the finest season of the year overarched the whole; and most pleasant was it to renew morning after morning her dear society, in the midst of such scenes.

Should such a mode of life seem too irregular, too trivial, to the earnest reader, let him consider, that, between what is here brought closely together for the sake of a convenient order, there intervened whole days and weeks of renunciation, other engagements and occupations, and indeed an insupportable tedium.

Men and women were busily engaged in their spheres of duty. I too, out of regard for the present and the future, delayed not to attend to all my obligations; and I found time enough to finish that to which my talent and my passion irresistibly impelled me.

The earliest hours of the morning I devoted to

poetry : the middle of the day was assigned to worldly business, which was handled in a manner quite peculiar. My father, a thorough and indeed finished jurist, managed himself such business as arose from the care of his own property, and a connection with highly valued friends : for, although his character as imperial councillor did not allow him to practise, he was at hand as legal adviser to many a friend ; while the papers he had prepared were signed by a regular advocate, who received a consideration for every such signature.

This activity of his had now become more lively since my return ; and I could easily remark, that he prized my talent higher than my practice, and on that account did what he could to leave me time for my poetical studies and productions. Sound and thoroughly apt, but slow of conception and execution, he studied the papers as private *Referendarius ;* and, when we came together, he would state the case, and left me to work it out, in which I showed so much readiness, that he felt a father's purest joy, and once could not refrain from declaring, " that, if I were not of his own blood, he should envy me."

To lighten our work we had engaged a scribe, whose character and individuality, well worked out, would have helped to adorn a romance. After his school-years, which had been profitably spent, and in which he had become fully master of Latin, and acquired some other useful branches of knowledge, a dissipated academic life had brought trouble on the remainder of his days. He, for a time, dragged on a wretched existence in sickness and in poverty, till at last he contrived to improve his circumstances by the aid of a fine handwriting and a readiness at accounts. Employed by some advocates, he gradually acquired an accurate knowledge of the formalities of legal business, and by his faithfulness and punctuality made every ɔne he served his patron. He had been frequently employed by our family, and was always at hand in matters of law and account.

He also was a useful assistant in our continually increasing business, which consisted, not only of law matters, but also of various sorts of commissions, orders, and transit agencies. In the city-hall he knew all the passages and windings; in his way, he was in tolerable favour at both burgomasters' audiences; and since from his first entrance into office, and even during the times of his equivocal behaviour, he had been well acquainted with many of the new senators, some of whom had quickly risen to the dignity of *Schoffen*, he had acquired a certain confidence, which might be called a sort of influence. All this he knew how to turn to the advantage of his patrons; and, since the state of his health forced him to limit his application to writing, he was always found ready to execute every commission or order with care.

His presence was not disagreeable; he was slender in person and of regular features; his manner was unobtrusive, though a certain expression betrayed his conviction that he knew all what was necessary to be done; moreover, he was cheerful and dexterous in clearing away difficulties. He must have been full forty, and (to say the same thing over again) I regret that I have never introduced him as the mainspring in the machinery of some novel.

Hoping that my more serious readers are now somewhat satisfied by what I have just related, I will venture to turn again to that bright point of time when love and friendship shone in their fairest light.

It was in the nature of such social circles that all birthdays should be carefully celebrated with every variety of rejoicing; it was in honour of the birthday of the pastor Ewald that the following song was written :

In every hour of pleasure,
   Enhanced by love and wine,
To sing this song's gay measure,
   Let ever us combine.
The god holds us united,
   Who hither brought us, who
Our flames he erst ignited,
   Now lighteth up anew.

— Editor's Version.

Since this song has been preserved until this day, and there is scarcely a merry party at which it is not joyfully revived, we commend it also to all that shall come after us; and to all who sing it or recite it we wish the same delight and inward satisfaction which we then had, when we had no thought of any wider world, but felt ourselves a world to ourselves in that narrow circle.

It will, of course, be expected that Lilli's birthday, which, on the 23d June, 1775, returned for the seventeenth time, was to be celebrated with especial honours. She had promised to come to Offenbach at noon; and I must observe that our friends, with a happy unanimity, had laid aside all customary compliments at this festival, and had prepared for her reception and entertainment nothing but such heartfelt tokens as were worthy of her.

Busied with such pleasant duties, I saw the sun go down, announcing a bright day to follow, and promising its glad, beaming presence at our feast, when Lilli's brother, George, who knew not how to dissemble, came somewhat rudely into the chamber, and, without sparing our feelings, gave us to understand that to-morrow's intended festival was put off; he himself could not tell how or why, but his sister had bid him say that it would be wholly impossible for her to come to Offenbach at noon that day, and take part in the intended festival; she had no hope of arriving before evening.

She knew and felt most sensibly how vexatious and disagreeable it must be to me and all her friends, but she begged me very earnestly to invent some expedient which might soften and perhaps do away the unpleasant effects of this news, which she left it to me to announce. If I could, she would give me her warmest thanks.

I was silent for a moment; but I quickly recovered myself, and, as if by heavenly inspiration, saw what was to be done. "Make haste, George!" I cried, "tell her to make herself easy, and do her best to come toward evening : I promise that this very disappointment shall be turned into a cause of rejoicing!" The boy was curious, and wanted to know how. I refused to gratify his curiosity, notwithstanding that he called to his aid all the arts and all the influence which a brother of our beloved can presume to exercise.

No sooner had he gone, than I walked up and down in my chamber with a singular self-satisfaction; and, with the glad, free feeling that here was a brilliant opportunity of proving myself her devoted servant, I stitched together several sheets of paper with beautiful silk, as suited alone such an occasional poem, and hastened to write down the title :

"SHE IS NOT COMING !

"A Mournful Family Piece, which, by the sore visitation of Divine Providence, will be represented in the most natural manner on the 23d of June, 1775, at Offenbach-on-the-Main. The action lasts from morning until evening."

I have not by me either the original or a copy of this *jeu d'esprit;* I have often inquired after one, but have never been able to get a trace of it; I must therefore compose it anew, a thing which, in the general way, is not difficult.

The scene is at D'Orville's house and garden in

Offenbach : the action opens with the domestics, of whom each one plays his special part; and evident preparations for a festival are being made. The children, drawn to the life, run in and out among them; the master appears, and the mistress, actively discharging her appropriate functions; then, in the midst of the hurry and bustle of active preparation, comes in neighbour Hans André, the indefatigable composer; he seats himself at the piano, and calls them all together to hear him try his new song, which he has just finished for the festival. He gathers around him the whole house, but all soon disperse again to attend to pressing duties; one is called away by another, this person wants the help of that; at last, the arrival of the gardener draws attention to the preparations in the grounds and on the water; wreaths, banners with ornamental inscriptions, in short, nothing is forgotten.

While they are all assembled around the most attractive objects, in steps a messenger, who, as a sort of humourous go-between, was also entitled to play his part, and who, although he has had plenty of drink-money, could still pretty shrewdly guess what was the state of the case. He sets a high value on his packet, demands a glass of wine and a wheaten roll, and after some roguish hesitation hands over his despatches. The master of the house lets his arms drop, the papers fall to the floor : he calls out, " Let me go to the table ! let me go to the bureau, that I may brush."

The spirited intercourse of vivacious persons is chiefly distinguished by a certain symbolical style of speech and gesture. A sort of conventional idiom arises, which, while it makes the initiated very happy, is unobserved by the stranger, or, if observed, is disagreeable.

Among Lilli's most pleasing particularities was the one which is here expressed by the word *brushing*, and which manifested itself whenever anything disagreeable was said or told, especially when she sat at table, or was near any flat surface.

It had its origin in a most fascinating but odd expedient, which she once had recourse to when a stranger, sitting near her at table, uttered something unseemly. Without altering her mild countenance, she brushed with her right hand, most prettily, across the table-cloth, and deliberately pushed off on to the floor everything she reached with this gentle motion. I know not what did not fall, — knives, forks, bread, saltcellar, and also something belonging to her neighbour; every one was startled; the servants ran up; and no one knew what it all meant, except the observing ones, who were delighted that she had rebuked and checked an impropriety in so pretty a manner.

Here now was a symbol found to express the repulsion of anything disagreeable, which still is frequently made use of in clever, hearty, estimable, well-meaning, and not thoroughly polished, society. We all adopted the motion of the right hand as a sign of reprobation: the actual brushing away of objects was a thing which afterward she herself indulged in only moderately and with good taste.

When, therefore, the poet gives to the master of the house, as a piece of dumb show, this desire for brushing (a habit which had become with us a second nature), the meaning and effect of the action and its tendency are at once apparent; for, while he threatens to sweep everything from all flat surfaces, everybody tries to hinder him and to pacify him, till finally he throws himself exhausted on a seat.

"What has happened?" all exclaimed. "Is she sick? Is any one dead?" "Read! read!" cries D'Orville: "there it lies on the ground." The despatch is picked up: they read it, and exclaim, "*She is not coming!*"

The great terror had prepared them for a greater; but she was well — nothing had happened to her! no one of the family was hurt: hope pointed still to the evening.

André, who in the meanwhile had kept on with his music, came running up at last, consoling, and seeking consolation. Pastor Ewald and his wife likewise came in quite characteristically, disappointed and yet reasonable, sorry for the disappointment, and yet quietly accepting all for the best. Everything now is at sixes and sevens, until the calm and exemplary uncle Bernard finally approaches, expecting a good breakfast and a comfortable dinner; and he is the only one who sees the matter from the right point of view. He, by reasonable speeches, sets all to rights, just as in the Greek tragedy a god manages with a few words to clear up the perplexities of the greatest heroes.

All this I had dashed off "*currente calamo*" through a part of the night, and given to a messenger with instructions to deliver it in Offenbach the next morning precisely at ten o'clock.

Next day when I awoke, it was one of the brightest mornings possible; and I set off just in time to arrive at Offenbach, as I purposed, precisely at noon.

I was received with the strangest *charivari* of salutations; the interrupted feast was scarcely mentioned; they scolded and rated me, because I had taken them off so well. The domestics were contented with being introduced on the same stage with their superiors: only the children, those most decided and indomitable realists, obstinately insisted that they had not talked so and so, that everything in fact went quite differently from the way in which it there stood written. I appeased them by some foretastes of the supper-table, and they loved me as much as ever. A cheerful dinner-party, with some though not all of our intended festivities, put us in the mood of receiving Lilli with less splendour, but perhaps the more affectionately. She came, and was welcomed by cheerful, nay, merry, faces, surprised to find that her staying away had not marred all our cheerfulness. They told her everything, they laid the whole thing before her; and she, in her dear, sweet way, thanked me as only she could thank.

It required no remarkable acuteness to perceive that her absence from the festival held in her honour was not accidental, but had been caused by gossiping about the intimacy between us. However, this had not the slightest influence, either on our sentiments or our behaviour.

At this season of the year there never failed to be a varied throng of visitors from the city. Frequently I did not join the company until late in the evening, when I found her apparently sympathising; and, since I commonly appeared only for a few hours, I was glad of an opportunity to be useful to her in any way, by attending to or undertaking some commission, whether trifling or not, in her behalf. And, indeed, this service is probably the most delightful a man can enter upon, as the old romances of chivalry contrive how to intimate in their obscure but powerful manner. That she ruled over me, was not to be concealed, and in this pride she might well indulge; for in this contest the victor and the vanquished both triumph, and enjoy an equal glory.

This my repeated, though often brief, coöperation, was always so much the more effective. John André had always store of music; I contributed new pieces, either by others or myself; so that poetical and musical blossoms showered down upon us. It was altogether a brilliant time: a certain excitement reigned in the company, and there were no insipid moments. Without further question, it seemed to be communicated to all the rest. For, where inclination and passion come out in their own bold nature, they encourage timid souls, who cannot comprehend why they should suppress their equally valid rights. Hence relations, which hitherto were more or less concealed, were now seen to intertwine themselves without reserve; while others, which did not confess themselves so openly, still glided on agreeably in the shade.

If, because of my multifarious avocations, I could not pass whole days out of doors with her, yet the clear evenings gave us opportunity for prolonged meetings in the open air. Loving souls will be pleased to read the following event.

Ours was a condition of which it is written, "I sleep, but my heart wakes;" the bright and the dark hours were alike; the light of the day could not outshine the light of love, and the night was made as the brightest day by the radiance of passion.

One clear starlight evening we had been walking about in the open country till it was quite late; and after I had seen her and her friends home to their several doors, and finally had taken leave of her, I felt so little inclined to sleep, that I did not hesitate to set off on another ramble. I took the highroad to Frankfort, giving myself up to my thoughts and hopes: here I seated myself on a bench, in the purest stillness of night, under the gleaming starry heavens, that I might belong only to myself and her.

My attention was attracted by a sound quite near me, which I could not explain; it was not a rattling nor a rustling noise; and on closer observation I discovered that it was under the ground, and caused by the working of some little animal. It might be a hedgehog or a weasel, or whatever creature labours in that way at such hours.

Having set off again toward the city, and got near to the Röderberg, I recognised, by their chalk-white gleam, the steps which lead up to the vineyards. I ascended them, sat down, and fell asleep.

When I awoke, dawn had already spread; and I found myself opposite the high wall, which in earlier times had been erected to defend the heights on this side. Saxenhausen lay before me, light mists marked out the course of the river: it was cool, and to me most welcome.

There I waited till the sun, rising gradually behind me, lighted up the opposite landscape. It was the spot where I was again to see my beloved, and I returned slowly back to the paradise which surrounded her yet sleeping.

On account of my increasing circle of business, which, from love to her, I was anxious to extend and to establish, my visits to Offenbach became more rare, and hence arose a somewhat painful predicament; so that it might well be remarked, that, for the sake of the future, one postpones and loses the present.

As my prospects were now gradually improving, I took them to be more promising than they really were; and I thought the more about coming to a speedy explanation, since so public an intimacy could not go on much longer without misconstruction. And, as is usual in such cases, we did not expressly say it to one another; but the feeling of being mutually pleased in every way, the full conviction that a separation was impossible, the confidence reposed in one another, — all this produced such a seriousness, that I, who had firmly resolved never again to get involved in any troublesome connection of the kind, and who found myself, nevertheless, entangled in this, without the certainty of a favourable result, was actually beset with a heaviness of mind, to get rid of which I plunged more and more in indifferent worldly affairs, from which, apart from my beloved, I had no care to derive either profit or pleasure.

In this strange situation, the like of which many, no doubt, have with pain experienced, there came to our aid a friend of the family, who saw through characters and situations very clearly. She was called Mlle. Delf: she presided with her elder sister over a little business in Heidelberg, and on several occasions had received many favours from the greater Frankfort commission-house. She had known and loved Lilli from her youth: she was quite a peculiar person, of an earnest, masculine look, and with an even, firm, hasty step. She had had peculiar reason to adapt herself to the world; and hence she understood it, in a certain sense at least. She could not be called intriguing; she was accustomed to consider distant contingencies, and to carry out her plans in silence: but then, she had the gift of seeing an opportunity; and, if she found people wavering betwixt doubt and resolution at the moment when everything depended upon decision, she skilfully contrived to infuse into their minds such a force of character, that she seldom failed to accomplish her purpose. Properly speaking, she had no selfish ends: to have done anything, to have completed anything, especially to have brought about a marriage, was reward enough for her. She had long since seen through our position, and, in repeated visits, had carefully observed the state of affairs, so that she had finally convinced herself that the attachment must be favoured; that our plans, honestly but not very skilfully taken in hand and prosecuted, must be promoted, and that this little romance be brought to a close as speedily as possible.

For many years she had enjoyed the confidence of Lilli's mother. Introduced by me to my parents, she had managed to make herself agreeable to them; for her rough sort of manner is seldom offensive in an imperial city, and, backed by cleverness and tact, is even welcome. She knew very well our wishes and our hopes; her love of meddling made her see in all this a call upon her good offices; in short, she had a conversation with our parents. How she commenced it, how she put aside the difficulties which must have stood in her way, I know not; but she came to us one evening, and brought the consent. "Take each other by the hand!" cried she, in her pathetic yet commanding manner. I stood opposite to Lilli, and offered her my hand: she, not indeed hesitatingly, but still slowly, placed hers in it. After a long and deep breath, we fell with lively emotion into each other's arms.

It was a strange decree of the overruling Providence that, in the course of my singular history, I should also have experienced the feelings of one who is betrothed.

I may venture to assert, that, for a truly moral man, it is the most agreeable of all recollections. It is pleasant to recall those feelings, which are with difficulty expressed and are hardly to be explained. For him the state of things is all at once changed; the sharpest oppositions are removed, the most inveterate differences are adjusted; prompting nature, ever-warning reason, the tyrannising impulses, and the sober law, which before kept up a perpetual strife within us, all are now reconciled in friendly unity; and at the festival, so universally celebrated with solemn rites, that which was forbidden is commanded, and that which was penal is raised to an inviolable duty.

The reader will learn with moral approval, that, from this time forward, a certain change took place in me. If my beloved had hitherto been looked upon as beautiful, graceful, and attractive, now she appeared to me a being of superior worth and excellence. She was, as it were, a double person: her grace and loveliness belonged to me, — that I felt as formerly; but the dignity of her character, her self-reliance, her confidence in all persons, remained her own. I beheld it, I looked through it, I was delighted with it as with a capital of which I should enjoy the interest as long as I lived.

There is depth and significance in the old remark, on the summit of fortune one abides not long. The consent of the parties on both sides, so gained in such a peculiar manner by Demoiselle Delf, was now ratified silently and without further formality. But as soon as we believe the matter to be all settled — as soon as the ideal, as we may well call it, of a betrothal is over, and it begins to pass into the actual, and to enter soberly into facts, then too often comes a crisis. The outward world is utterly unmerciful, and it has reason; for it must maintain its authority at all costs; the confidence of passion is very great, and we see it too often wrecked upon the rocks of opposing realities. A young married couple who enter upon life unprovided with sufficient means, can promise themselves no honeymoon, especially in these latter times: the world immediately presses upon them with incompatible demands, which, if not satisfied, make the young couple appear ridiculous.

Of the insufficiency of the means which, for the attainment of my end, I had anxiously scraped together, I could not before be aware, because they had held out up to a certain point; but, now the end was drawing nearer, I saw that matters were not quite what they ought to be.

The fallacy, which passion finds so convenient, was now exposed in all its inconsistency. My house, my domestic circumstances, had to be considered in all their details, with some soberness. The consciousness that his house would one day contain a daughter-in-law, lay indeed at the bottom of my father's design; but then, what sort of a lady did he contemplate?

At the end of our third part, the reader made the acquaintance of the gentle, dear, intelligent, beautiful, and talented maiden, so always like herself, so affectionate, and yet so free from passion: she was a fitting keystone to the arch already built and curved. But here, upon calm, unbiassed consideration, it could not be denied, that, in order to establish the newly acquired treasure in such a function, a new arch would have to be built!

However, this had not yet become clear to me; and still less was it so to her mind. But now, when I tried to fancy myself bringing her to my home, she did not seem somehow to suit it exactly. It appeared to me something like what I had myself experienced, when I first joined her social circle: in order to give no offence to the fashionable people I met there, I found it necessary to make a great change in my style of dress. But this could not be so easily done with the domestic arrangement of a stately burgher's house, which, rebuilt in the olden style, had, with its antique ornaments, given an old-fashioned character to the habits of its inmates.

Moreover, even after our parents' consent had been gained, it had not been possible to establish friendly relations or intercourse between our respective families. Different religious opinions produced different manners; and, if the amiable girl had wished to continue in any way her former mode of life, it would have found neither opportunity nor place in our moderate-sized house.

If I had never thought of all this until now, it was because I had been quieted by the opening of fine prospects from without, and the hope of getting some valuable appointment. An active spirit gets a footing everywhere; capacities, talents, create confidence; every one thinks that a change of management is all that is needed. The earnestness of youth finds favour: genius is trusted for everything, though its power is only of a certain kind.

The intellectual and literary domain of Germany

was at that time regarded as but newly broken ground. Among the business people there were prudent men, who desired skilful cultivators and prudent managers for the fields about to be turned up. Even the respectable and well-established Free-Mason's lodge, with the most distinguished members of which I had become acquainted through my intimacy with Lilli, contrived in a suitable manner to get me introduced to them; but I, from a feeling of independence, which afterward appeared to me madness, declined all closer connection with them, not perceiving that these men, though already bound together in a higher sense, would yet do much to further my own ends, so nearly related to theirs.

I return to more personal matters.

In such cities as Frankfort, men often hold several situations together, such as residentships and agencies, the number of which may by diligence be indefinitely increased. Something of this sort now occurred to me, and at first sight it seemed both advantageous and honourable. It was assumed that I should suit the place; and it would, under the conditions, certainly have succeeded, if it could have commanded the co-operation of the Chancery triad already described. We thus suppress our doubts; we dwell only on what is favourable; by powerful activity we overcome all wavering, whence there results a something untrue in our position, without the force of passion being in the least subdued.

In times of peace there is no more interesting reading for the multitude than the public papers, which furnish early information of the latest doings in the world. The quiet, opulent citizen exercises thus in an innocent way a party spirit, which, in our finite nature, we neither can nor should get rid of. Every comfortable person thus gets up a factitious interest, like that which is often felt in a bet, experiences an unreal gain or loss, and, as in the theatre, feels a very lively, though imaginary, sympathy in the good or evil fortune of others. This sympathy seems often arbitrary, but it rests on moral grounds. For now we give to praiseworthy designs the applause they deserve; and now again, carried away by brilliant successes, we turn to those whose plans we should otherwise have blamed. For all this there was abundant material in those times.

Frederick the Second, resting on his victories, seemed to hold in his hand the fate of Europe and of the world: Catherine, a great woman, who had proved herself every way worthy of a throne, afforded ample sphere of action to able and highly gifted men, in extending the dominion of their empress; and as this was done at the expense of the Turks, whom we are in the habit of richly repaying for the contempt with which they look down upon us, it seemed as if it was no sacrifice of human life, when these infidels were slain by thousands. The burning of the fleet in the harbour of Tschesme caused a universal jubilee throughout the civilised world; and every one shared the exultation of a victory when, in order to preserve a faithful picture of that great event, a ship-of-war was actually blown up on the roads of Livorno, before the studio of an artist. Not long after this, a young Northern king, to establish his own authority, seized the reins of government out of the hands of an oligarchy. The aristocrats he overthrew were not lamented, for aristocracy finds no favour with the public, since it is in its nature to work in silence, and it is the more secure the less talk it creates about itself; and in this case the people thought all the better of the young king, since, in order to balance the enmity of the higher ranks, he was obliged to favour the lower, and to conciliate their good will.

The lively interest of the world was still more

excited when a whole people prepared to effect their independence. Already had it witnessed a welcome spectacle of the same effort on a small scale: Corsica had long been the point to which all eyes were directed; Paoli, when, despairing of ever being able to carry out his patriotic designs, he passed through Germany to England, attracted and won all hearts; he was a fine man, slender, fair, full of grace and friendliness. I saw him in the house of Bethmann, where he stopped a short time, and received with cheerful cordiality the curious visitors who thronged to see him. But now similar events were to be repeated in a remote quarter of the globe: we wished the Americans all success; and the names of Franklin and Washington began to shine and sparkle in the firmament of politics and war. Much had been accomplished to improve the condition of humanity; and now when, in France, a new and benevolent sovereign evinced the best intentions of devoting himself to the removal of so many abuses, and to the noblest ends, — of introducing a regular and efficient system of political economy, of dispensing with all arbitrary power, and of ruling alone by law and justice — the brightest hopes spread over the world; and confident youth promised itself and to all mankind a bright and noble future.

In all these events, however, I only took part so far as they interested society in general; I myself and my immediate circle did not meddle with the news of the day: our affair was to study men; men in general we allowed to have their way.

The quiet position of the German Fatherland, to which also my native city had now conformed for upwards of a hundred years, had been fully preserved in spite of many wars and convulsions. A highly varied gradation of ranks, which, instead of holding the several classes apart, seemed to bind them the more closely together, had promoted the interest of all, from the highest to the lowest, — from the emperor to the Jew. If the sovereign princes stood in a subordinate relation to the emperor, still their electoral rights and immunities, thereby acquired and maintained, were a full compensation. Moreover, the highest nobility belonged exclusively to the agnates of the royal houses; so that, in the enjoyment of their distinguished privileges, they could look upon themselves as equal with the highest, and even superior to them in some sense, since, as spiritual electors, they might take precedence of all others, and, as branches of the sacred heirarchy, hold an honourable and uncontested rank.

If, now, we think of the extraordinary privileges which these ancient houses enjoyed, not only in their old patrimonial estates, but also in the ecclesiastical endowments, the knightly orders, the official administration of the empire, and the old brotherhoods and alliances for mutual defence and protection, we can vainly conceive that this great body of influential men, feeling themselves at once subordinated to and coördinate with the highest, and occupying their days with a regular round of employments, might well be contented with their situation, and would without further anxiety seek only to secure and transmit to their successors the same comforts and prerogatives. Nor was this class deficient in intellectual culture. Already for more than a century the decided proofs of high training in military and political science had been discernible in our noble soldiers and diplomatists. But at the same time there were many minds, who, through literary and philosophical studies, had arrived at views not over favourable to the existing state of things.

In Germany scarcely any one had as yet learned to look with envy on that monstrous privileged class, or to grudge its fortunate advantages. The middle class had devoted themselves undisturbed to commerce and the sciences, and by these pursuits, as well as by the practice of the mechanic arts, so closely related to them, had raised themselves to a position of importance, which fully balanced its political inferiority : the free or half-free cities favoured this activity, while individuals felt a certain quiet satisfaction in it. The man who increased his wealth, or enhanced his intellectual influence, especially in matters of law or state, could always be sure of enjoying both respect and authority. In the supreme courts of the empire, and, indeed, in all others, a learned bench stood parallel with the noble; the uncontrolled oversight of the one managed to keep in harmony with the deepest insight of the other, and experience could never detect a trace of rivalry between them; the noble felt secure in his exclusive and time-hallowed privileges, and the burgher felt it beneath his dignity to strive for a semblance of them by a little prefix to his name.[1] The merchant, the manufacturer, had enough to do to keep pace with those of other nations in progress and improvement. Leaving out of the account the usual temporary fluctuations, we may certainly say that it was on the whole a time of pure advance, such as had not appeared before, and such as, on account of another and greater progress, both of mind and things, could not long continue.

My position with regard to the higher classes at this time was very favourable. In "Werther," to be sure, the disagreeable circumstances which arise just at the boundary between two distinct positions, were descanted upon with some impatience; but this was overlooked in consideration of the generally passionate

[1] The "von," which in Germany those who are ennobled prefix to their surnames.

character of the book, since every one felt that it had no reference to any immediate effect.

But "Götz von Berlichingen" had set me quite right with the upper classes: whatever improprieties might be charged upon my earlier literary productions, in this work I had with great learning and much felicity depicted the old German constitution, with its inviolable emperor at the head, with its many degrees of nobility, and a knight who, in a time of general lawlessness, had determined as a private man to act uprightly, if not lawfully, and thus fell into a very sorry predicament. This complicated story, however, was not snatched from the air, but founded on fact; it was cheerful, lively, and consequently here and there a little modern; but it was, nevertheless, on the whole, in the same spirit as the brave and capable man had with some degree of skill set it forth in his own narrative.

The family still flourished: its relation to the Frankish knighthood had remained in all its integrity; although that relation, like many others at that time, might have grown somewhat faint and nominal.

Now all at once the little stream of Jaxt, and the castle of Jaxthausen, acquired a poetical importance: they, as well as the city-hall of Heilbronn, were visited by travellers.

It was known that I had a mind to write of other points of that historical period; and many a family, which could readily deduce their origin from that time, hoped to see their ancestors brought to the light in the same way.

A strange satisfaction is generally felt, when a writer felicitously brings a nation's history to its recollection: men rejoice in the virtues of their ancestors, and smile at the failings, which they believe they themselves have long since got rid of. Such a delineation never fails to meet with sympathy and applause, and in this respect I enjoyed an envied influence.

Yet it may be worth while to remark, that among the numerous advances, and in the multitude of young persons who attached themselves to me, there was found no nobleman: on the other hand, many who had already arrived at the age of thirty came in search of, and visited me; and of these the willing and striving were pervaded by a joyful hope of earnestly developing themselves in a national and even more universally humane sense.

At this time a general curiosity about the epoch between the fifteenth and sixteenth century had commenced, and was very lively. The works of Ulrich von Hutten had fallen into my hands; and I was not a little struck to see something so similar to what had taken place in his time, again manifesting itself in our later days.

The following letter of Ulrich von Hutten to Billibald Pyrkheymer may therefore suitably find place here:

" What fortune gives us, it generally takes away again; and not only that — everything else which accrues to man from without, is, we see, liable to accident and change. And yet, notwithstanding, I am now striving for honour, which I should wish to obtain, if possible, without envy, but still at any cost; for a fiery thirst for glory possesses me, so that I wish to be ennobled as highly as possible. I should make but a poor figure in my own eyes, dear Billibald, if, born in the rank, in the family I am, and of such ancestors, I could be content to hold myself to be noble, though I never ennobled myself by my own exertions. So great a work have I in my mind! My thoughts are higher! It is not that I would see myself promoted to a more distinguished and more brilliant rank; but I would fain seek a fountain elsewhere,

out of which I might draw a peculiar nobility of my
own, and not be counted among the factitious nobility,
contented with what I have received from my ancestors. On the contrary, I would add to those advantages something of my own, which may, from me, pass
over to my posterity.

"Therefore, in my studies and efforts, I proceed in
opposition to the opinion of those who consider that
what actually exists is enough; for to me nothing of
that sort is enough, according to what I have already
confessed to you of my ambition in this respect. And
I here avow that I do not envy those who, starting
from the lowest stations, have climbed higher than I;
for on this point I by no means agree with those of
my own rank, who are wont to sneer at persons, who,
of a lower origin, have, by their own talents, raised
themselves to eminence. For those with perfect right
are to be preferred to us, who have seized for themselves and taken possession of the material of glory,
which we ourselves neglected: they may be the sons
of fullers or of tanners; but they have contrived to
attain their ends, by struggling with greater difficulties
than we should have had against us. The ignorant
man, that envies him who by his knowledge has distinguished himself, is not only to be called a fool, but
is to be reckoned among the miserable — indeed, among
the most miserable; and with this disease are our
nobles especially affected, that they look with an evil
eye upon such accomplishments. For what, in God's
name! Is it to envy one who possesses that which we
have despised? Why have we not applied ourselves
to the law? Why have we not ourselves this excellent
learning, the best arts? And now fullers, shoemakers,
and wheelwrights have got ahead of us. Why have
we forsaken our post, why left the most liberal studies
to hired servants and (shamefully for us!) to the very
lowest of the people ? Most justly has that inheritance

of nobility which we have thrown away been taken possession of by every clever and diligent plebeian who makes it profitable by its own industry. Wretched beings that we are, who neglect that which suffices to raise the very humblest above us: let us cease to envy, and strive also to obtain what others, to our deep disgrace, have claimed for themselves.

"Every longing for glory is honourable: all striving for the excellent is praiseworthy. To every rank may its own honour remain, may its own ornaments be secured to it! Those statues of my ancestors I do not despise any more than the richly endowed pedigree: but, whatever their worth may be, it is not ours, unless by our own merits we make it ours; nor can it endure, if the nobility do not adopt the habits which become them. In vain will yonder fat and corpulent head of a noble house point to the images of his ancestors, whilst he himself, inactive, resembles a clod rather than those whose virtues throw a halo upon his name from bygone days.

"So much have I wished most fully and most frankly to confide to you respecting my ambition and my nature."

Although, perhaps, not exactly in the same train of ideas, yet the same excellent and strong sentiments had I to hear from my more distinguished friends and acquaintances, of which the results appeared in an honest activity. It had become a creed, that every one must earn for himself a personal nobility; and, if any rivalry appeared in those fine days, it was from above downwards.

We others, on the contrary, had what we wished, — the free and approved exercise of the talents lent to us by nature, as far as could consist with all our civil relations.

For my native city had in this a very peculiar position, and one which has not been enough considered.

While, of the free imperial cities, the northern could boast of an extended commerce, but the southern, declining in commercial importance, cultivated the arts and manufactures with more success, Frankfort-on-the-Main exhibited a somewhat mixed character, combining the results of trade, wealth, and capital with the passion for learning, and its collection of works of art.

The Lutheran Confession controlled its government: the ancient lordship of the *Gan*, now bearing the name of the house of Limburg; the house of Frauenstein, originally only a club, but, during the troubles occasioned by the lower classes, faithful to the side of intelligence; the jurist, and others well to do and well disposed, — none was excluded from the magistracy: even those mechanics who had upheld the cause of order at a critical time were eligible to the council, though they were only stationary in their place. The other constitutional counterpoises, formal institutions, and whatever else belongs to such a constitution, afforded employment to the activity of many persons; while trade and manufacture, in so favourable a situation, found no obstacle to their growth and prosperity.

The higher nobility kept to itself, unenvied and almost unnoticed: a second class pressing close upon it was forced to be more active, and, resting upon old wealthy family foundations, sought to distinguish itself by political and legal learning.

The members of the so-called Reformed persuasion (Calvinists) composed, like the refugees in other places, a distinguished class, and, when they rode out in fine equipages on Sundays to their service in Bockenheim, seemed almost to celebrate a sort of triumph over the citizen's party, who had the privilege of going to church on foot in good weather and in bad.

The Roman Catholics were scarcely noticed, but they also were aware of the advantages which the other two confessions had appropriated to themselves.

EIGHTEENTH BOOK.

RETURNING to literary matters, I must bring forward a circumstance which had great influence on the German poetry of this period, and which is especially worthy of remark, because this very influence has lasted through the history of our poetic art to the present day, and will not be lost even in the future.

From the earlier times, the Germans were accustomed to rhyme: it had this advantage in its favour, that one could proceed in a very *naïve* manner, scarcely doing more than count the syllables. If, with the progress of improvement, attention began more or less instinctively to be paid also to the sense and signification of the syllables, this was highly praiseworthy, and a merit which many poets contrived to make their own. The rhyme was made to mark the close of the poetical proposition: the smaller divisions were indicated by shorter lines, and a naturally refined ear began to make provision for variety and grace. But now all at once rhyme was rejected before it was considered that the value of the syllables had not as yet been decided, indeed that it was a difficult thing to decide. Klopstock took the lead. How earnestly he toiled, and what he has accomplished, is well known. Every one felt the uncertainty of the matter; many did not like to run a risk; and, stimulated by this natural tendency, they snatched at a poetic prose. Gessner's extremely charming Idylls opened an endless path. Klopstock wrote the dialogue of "Hermann's Schlacht" ("Hermann's Fight") in prose, as well as

"Der Tod Adams" ("The Death of Adam"). Through the domestic tragedies as well as the more classic dramas, a style more lofty and more impassioned gained possession of the theatre; while, on the other hand, the iambic verse of five feet, which the example of the English had spread among us, was reducing poesy to prose. But in general the demand for rhythm and for rhyme could not be silenced. Ramler, though proceeding on vague principles (as he was always severe with respect to his own productions), could not help exercising the same severity upon those of others. He transformed prose into verse, altered and improved the works of others, by which means he earned little thanks, and only confused the matter still more. Those succeeded best who still conformed to the old custom of rhyme with a certain observance of syllable quantity, and who, guided by a natural taste, observed laws though unexpressed and undetermined; as, for example, Wieland, who, although inimitable, for a long time served as a model to more moderate talents.

But still in any case the practice remained uncertain; and there was no one, even among the best, who might not for the moment have gone astray. Hence the misfortune, that this epoch of our poetic history, so peculiarly rich in genius, produced little which, in its kind, could be pronounced correct: for here also the time was stirring, advancing, active, and calling for improvement, but not reflective, and satisfying its own requirements.

In order, however, to find a firm soil on which poetic genius might find a footing — to discover an element in which they could breathe freely, they had gone back some centuries, where earnest talents were brilliantly prominent amid a chaotic state of things; and thus they made friends with the poetic art of those times. The Minnesingers lay too far from us; it would have been necessary first to study the language, and that was not our object: we wanted to live and not to learn.

Hans Sachs, the really masterly poet, was nearest to our sympathy. A man of true talent, not indeed like the Minnesinging knights and courtiers, but a plain citizen, such as we also boasted ourselves to be. A didactic realism suited us; and on many occasions we made use of the easy rhythm, of the readily occurring rhyme. His manner seemed so suitable to mere poems of the day, and such we needed at every hour.

If important works, which required the attention and labour of a year or a whole life, were built, more or less, upon such hazardous grounds on trivial occasions, it may be imagined how wantonly all other ephemeral productions took their rise and shape ; for example, the poetical epistles, parables, and invectives of all forms, with which we went on making war within ourselves, and seeking squabbling abroad.

Of this kind, besides what has already been printed, something, though very little, survives : it may be laid up somewhere. Brief allusions will suffice to reveal to thinking men their origin and purposes. Persons of more than ordinary penetration, to whose sight these may hereafter be brought, will be ready to observe that an honest purpose lay at the bottom of all such eccentricities. An upright will revolts against presumption, nature against conventionalities, talent against forms, genius with itself, energy against indecision, undeveloped capacity against developed mediocrity ; so that the whole proceeding may be regarded as a skirmish which follows a declaration of war, and gives promise of a violent contest. For, strictly considered, the contest is not yet fought out, in these fifty years : it is still going on, only in a higher region.

I had, in imitation of an old German puppet-play, invented a wild *extravaganza*, which was to bear the title of "Hanswurst's Hochzeit" ("Jack Pudding's Wedding").[1] The scheme was as follows: Hanswurst, a rich young farmer and an orphan, has just come of age, and wishes to marry a rich maiden, named Ursel Blandine. His guardian, Kilian Brustfleck (*Leather-apron*), and her mother, Ursel, are highly pleased with the purpose. Their long-cherished plans, their dearest wishes, are at last fulfilled and gratified. There is not the slightest obstacle; and properly the whole interest turns only upon this, that the young people's ardour for their union is delayed by the necessary arrangements and formalities of the occasion. As prologue, enters the inviter to the wedding festivities, who proclaims the banns after the traditional fashion, and ends with the rhymes,

> The wedding-feast is at the house
> Of mine host of the Golden Louse.

To obviate the charge of violating the unity of place, the aforesaid tavern, with its glittering insignia, was placed in the background of the theatre, but so that all its four sides could be presented to view by being turned upon a peg; and, as it was moved around, the front scenes of the stage had to undergo corresponding changes.

In the first act the front of the house facing the street was turned to the audience, with its golden sign magnified as it were by the solar microscope; in the second act, the side toward the garden. The third was toward a little wood; the fourth toward a neighbouring lake, which gave rise to a prediction, that in after-times the decorator would have little difficulty in carry-

---

[1] Hanswurst is the old German buffoon, whose name answers to the English "Jack Pudding." — TRANS.

ing a wave over the whole stage up to the prompter's box.

But all this does not as yet reveal the peculiar interest of the piece. The principal joke which was carried out, even to an absurd length, arose from the fact that the whole *dramatis personœ* consisted of mere traditional German nicknames, which at once brought out the characters of the individuals, and determined their relations to one another.

As we would fain hope that the present book will be read aloud in good society, and even in decent family circles, we cannot venture, after the custom of every playbill, to name our persons here in order, nor to cite the passages in which they most clearly and prominently showed themselves in their true colours; although, in the simplest way possible, lively, roguish, broad allusions, and witty jokes, could not but arise. We add one leaf as a specimen, leaving our editors the liberty of deciding upon its admissibility.

Cousin Schuft (scamp), through his relationship to the family, was entitled to an invitation to the feast; no one had anything to say against it; for though he was a thoroughly good-for-nothing fellow, yet there he was; and, since he was there, they could not with propriety leave him out; on such a feast-day, too, they were not to remember that they had occasionally been dissatisfied with him.

With Master Schurke (knave), it was a still more serious case: he had, indeed, been useful to the family, when it was to his own profit; on the other hand, again, he had injured it, perhaps, in this case, also with an eye to his own interests, perhaps, too, because he found an opportunity. Those who were anyways prudent voted for his admission: the few who would have excluded him were out-voted.

But there was a third person, about whom it was still more difficult to decide; an orderly man in society, no less than others, obliging, agreeable, useful in many ways: he had a single failing, that he could not bear his name to be mentioned, and, as soon as he heard it, was instantaneously transported into a heroic fury, like that which the Northmen call " Berserker-rage," attempted to kill all right and left, and in his frenzy hurt others and received hurt himself; indeed, the second act of the piece was brought, through him, to a very perplexed termination.

Here was an opportunity, which I could not allow to pass, for chastising the piratical publisher Macklot. He is introduced going about hawking his Macklot wares; and, when he hears of the preparation for the wedding, he cannot resist the impulse to go sponging for a dinner, and to stuff his ravening maw at other people's expense. He announces himself: Kilian Brustfleck inquires into his claims, but is obliged to refuse him, since it was an understanding that all the guests should be well-known public characters, to which recommendation the applicant can make no claim. Macklot does his best to show that he is as renowned as any of them. But when Kilian Brustfleck, as a strict master of ceremonies, shows himself immovable, the nameless person, who has recovered from his Berserker-rage at the end of the second act, espouses the cause of his near relative, the book-pirate, so urgently, that the latter is finally admitted among the guests.

About this time the Counts Stolberg arrived at Frankfort: they were on a journey to Switzerland, and wished to make us a visit. The earliest productions of my dawning talent, which appeared in the *Göttingen Musenalmanach*, had led to my forming a friendly relation with them, and with all those other young men whose characters and labours are now well known. At that time rather strange ideas were entertained of friendship and love. They applied themselves to nothing more, properly speaking, than a certain vivacity of youth, which led to a mutual association and to an interchange of minds, full indeed of talent, but nevertheless uncultivated. Such a mutual relation, which looked indeed like confidence, was mistaken for love, for genuine inclination: I deceived myself in this as well as others, and have, in more than one way, suffered from it many years. There is still in existence a letter of Bürger's belonging to that time, from which it may be seen, that, among these companions, there was no question about the moral æsthetic. Every one felt himself excited, and thought that he might act and poetise accordingly.

The brothers arrived, bringing Count Haugwitz with them. They were received by me with open heart, with kindly propriety. They lodged at the hotel, but were generally with us at dinner. The first joyous meeting proved highly gratifying, but troublesome eccentricities soon manifested themselves.

A singular position arose for my mother. In her ready, frank way, she could carry herself back to the Middle Ages at once, and take the part of Aja with some Lombard or Byzantine princess. They called her nothing else than Tian Aja, and she was pleased with the joke; entering the more heartily into the fantasies of youth, as she believed she saw her own portrait in the lady of Götz von Berlichingen.

But this could not last long. We had dined together but a few times, when once, after enjoying glass after glass, our poetic hatred for tyrants showed itself; and we avowed a thirst for the blood of such villains. My father smiled, and shook his head: my mother had scarcely heard of a tyrant in her life; however, she recollected having seen the copperplate engraving of such a monster in Gottfried's Chronicles, viz., King Cambyses, whom he describes as having shot with an arrow the little son of an enemy through the heart, and boasting of his deed to the father's face: this still stood in her memory. To give a cheerful turn to the conversation, which continually grew more violent, she betook herself to her cellar, where her oldest wines lay carefully preserved in large casks. There she had in store no less treasure than the vintages of 1706, '19, '26, and '48, all under her own especial watch and ward, which were seldom broached except on solemn festive occasions.

As she set before us the rich-coloured wine in the polished decanter, she exclaimed, " Here is the true tyrant's blood ! Glut yourselves with this, but let all murderous thoughts go out of my house ! "

" Yes, tyrant's blood indeed ! " I cried : " there is no greater tyrant than the one whose heart's blood is here set before you. Regale yourselves with it, but use moderation ; for beware lest he subdue you by his spirit and agreeable taste ! The vine is the universal tyrant, who ought to be rooted up : let us therefore choose and reverence as our patron saint the holy Lycurgus, the Thracian ; he set about the pious work in earnest ; and, though at last blinded and corrupted by the infatuating demon Bacchus, he yet deserves to stand high in the army of martyrs above.

" This vine is the very vilest tyrant, at once an oppressor, a flatterer, and a hypocrite. The first draughts of his blood are sweetly relishing, but one drop incessantly entices another after it : they succeed each other like a necklace of pearls, which one fears to pull apart."

If I should be suspected here of substituting, as the best historians have done, a fictitious speech for the actual address, I can only express my regret that no shorthand writer had taken down this peroration at once, and handed it down to us. The thoughts would be found the same, but the flow of the language perhaps more graceful and attractive. Above all, however, in the present sketch, as a whole, there is a want of that diffuse eloquence and fulness of youth, which feels itself, and knows not whither its strength and faculty will carry it.

In a city like Frankfort, one is placed in a strange position: strangers, continually crossing each other, point to every region of the globe, and awaken a passion for travelling. On many an occasion before now I had shown an inclination to be moving; and now at the very moment when the great point was, to make an experiment whether I could renounce Lilli — when a certain painful disquiet unfitted me for all regular business, the proposition of the Stolbergs, that I should accompany them to Switzerland, was welcome. Stimulated, moreover, by the exhortations of my father, who looked with pleasure on the idea of my travelling in that direction, and who advised me not to omit to pass over into Italy if a suitable occasion should offer itself, I at once decided to go, and soon had everything packed for the journey. With some intimation, but without leave-taking, I separated myself from Lilli: she had so grown into my heart, that I did not believe it possible to part myself from her.

In a few hours I found myself with my merry fellow travellers in Darmstadt. Even at court we should not always act with perfect propriety: here Count Haugwitz took the lead. He was the youngest of us all, well formed, of a delicate but noble appearance, with soft, friendly features, of an equable disposition, sympathising enough, but with so much moderation, that, contrasted with us, he appeared quite impassible. Consequently, he had to put up with all sorts of jibes and nicknames from them. This was all very well, so long as they believed that they might act like children of nature; but as soon as occasion called for propriety, and when one was again obliged, not unwillingly, to put on the reserve of a count, then he knew how to introduce and to smooth over everything; so that we always came off with tolerable credit, if not with *éclat.*

I spent my time, meanwhile, with Merck, who, in his Mephistopheles manner, looked upon my intended journey with an evil eye, and described my companions, who had also paid him a visit, with a discrimination that listened not to any suggestions of mercy. In his way he knew me thoroughly; the *naïve* and indomitable good nature of my character was painful to him; the everlasting purpose to take things as they are, the live and let live, was his detestation. "It is a foolish trick," he said, "your going with these Burschen;" and then he would describe them aptly, but not altogether justly. Throughout there was a want of good feeling, and here I could believe that I could see farther than he did; although I did not in fact do this, but only knew how to appreciate those ideas of their character which lay beyond the circle of his vision.

"You will not stay long with them!" was the close of all his remarks. On this occasion I remember a remarkable saying of his, which he repeated to me at a later time, which I had often repeated to myself, and frequently found confirmed in life. "Thy striving," said he, "thy unswerving effort is, to give a poetic form to the real: others seek to give reality to the so-called poetic, to the imaginative; and of that nothing will ever come but stupid stuff." Whoever apprehends the immense difference between these two modes of action, whoever insists and acts upon this conviction, has reached the solution of a thousand other things.

Unluckily, before our party left Darmstadt, an incident happened which tended to verify beyond dispute the opinion of Merck.

Among the extravaganzas which grew out of the notion that we should try to transport ourselves into a state of nature, was that of bathing in public waters in the open air; and our friends, after violating every other law of propriety, could not forego this additional unseemliness. Darmstadt, situated on a sandy plain, without running water, had, it appeared, a pond in the neighbourhood, of which I only heard on this occasion. My friends, who were hot by nature, and moreover kept continually heating themselves, sought refreshment in this pond. The sight of naked youths in the clear sunshine might well seem something strange in this region: at all events scandal arose. Merck sharpened his conclusions, and I do not deny that I was glad to hasten our departure.

Already on the way to Mannheim, in spite of all good and noble feelings which we entertained in common, a certain difference in sentiment and conduct exhibited itself. Leopold Stolberg told us, with much of feeling and passion, that he had been forced to renounce a sincere attachment to a beautiful English lady, and on that account had undertaken so long a journey. When he received in return the sympathising confession that we, too, were not strangers to such experiences, then he gave vent without respect to the feelings of youth, declaring that nothing in the world could be compared with his passion, his sufferings, or with the beauty and amiability of his beloved. If by moderate observations we tried, as is proper among good companions, to bring him duly to qualify his assertion, it only made matters worse; and Count Haugwitz, as well as I, were inclined at last to let the matter drop. When we had reached Mannheim, we occupied pleasant chambers in a respectable hotel; and after our first dinner there, during the dessert, at which the wine was not spared, Leopold challenged us to drink to the health of his fair one, which was done noisily enough. The glasses having been drained, he cried out, " But now, out of goblets thus consecrated, no more drinking must be permitted; a second health would be a profanation; therefore, let us annihilate these vessels!" and with these words he dashed the wine-glass against the wall behind him. The rest of us followed his example; and I imagined, at the moment, that Merck pulled me by the collar.

But youth still retains this trait of childhood, that it harbours no malice against good companions; that its unsophisticated good nature may be brushed somewhat roughly indeed, to be sure, but cannot be permanently injured.

The glasses thus proclaimed angelical had considerably swelled our reckoning: comforting ourselves, however, and determined to be merry, we hastened for Carlsruhe, there to enter a new circle, with all the confidence of youth and its freedom from care. There we found Klopstock, who still maintained, with dignity, his ancient authority over disciples who held him in reverence. I also gladly did homage to him; so that, when bidden to his court with the others, I probably conducted myself tolerably well for a novice. One felt too, in a certain manner, called upon to be natural and sensible at the same time.

The reigning margrave, highly honoured among the German sovereigns as one of their princely seniors, but more especially on account of the excellent aims of his government, was glad to converse about matters of political economy. The margravine, active and well versed in the arts and various useful branches of knowledge, was also pleased by some graceful speeches to manifest a certain sympathy for us, for which we were duly grateful, though when at home we could not refrain from venting some severe remarks upon her miserable paper-manufactory, and the favour she showed to the piratical bookseller Macklot.

The circumstance, however, of importance for me, was, that the young duke of Saxe-Weimar had arrived here to enter into a formal matrimonial engagement with his noble bride, the Princess Louisa of Hesse-

Darmstadt : President von Möser had already arrived
on the same business, in order to settle this important
contract with the court-tutor, Count Görtz, and fully
to ratify it. My conversations with both the high
personages were most friendly ; and, at the farewell
audience, they both made me repeated assurances that
it would be pleasant to them to see me at Weimar.

Some private conversations with Klopstock won me
by the friendliness they showed, and led me to use
openness and candour with him. I communicated to
him the latest scenes of "Faust," which he seemed
to approve of. Indeed, as I afterward learned, he had
spoken of them to others with marked commendation,
a thing not usual with him, and expressed a wish to
see the conclusion of the piece.

Our former rudeness, though sometimes, as we called
it, our genius-like demeanour, was kept in something
like a chaste restraint in Carlsruhe, which is decent
and almost holy ground. I parted from my companions, as I had resolved to take a wide round and go
to Emmendingen, where my brother-in-law was high
bailiff. I looked upon this visit to my sister as a real
trial. I knew that her married life was unhappy ;
while there was no cause to find fault with her, with
her husband, or with circumstances. She was of a
peculiar nature, of which it is difficult to speak : we
will endeavour, however, to set down here whatever
admits of being described.

A fine form was in her favour ; but not so her
features, which, although expressing, clearly enough,
goodness, intelligence, and sensibility, were nevertheless wanting in regularity and grace.

Add to this, that a high and strongly arched forehead, exposed still more by the abominable fashion of
dressing the hair back on the head, contributed to
leave a certain unpleasant impression, although it bore
the best testimony to her moral and intellectual quali-

ties. I can fancy, that if, after the modern fashion, she had surrounded the upper part of her face with curls, and clothed her temples and cheeks with ringlets, she would have found herself more agreeable before the mirror, without fear of displeasing others as well as herself. Then, there was the grave fault, that her skin was seldom clean, an evil which from her youth up, by some demoniacal fatality, was most sure to show itself on all festal occasions, and at concerts, balls, and other parties.

In spite of these drawbacks, she gradually made her way, however, as her better and nobler qualities showed themselves more distinctly.

A firm character not easily controlled, a soul that sympathised and needed sympathy, a highly cultivated mind, fine acquirements and talents, some knowledge of languages and a ready pen, — all these she possessed; so that, if she had been more richly favoured with outward charms, she would have been among the women most sought after in her day.

Besides all this, there is one strange thing to be mentioned: there was not the slightest touch of sensual passion in her nature. She had grown up with me, and had no other wish than to continue and pass her life in this fraternal union. Since my return from the academy we had been inseparable: with the most unreserved confidence we shared all our thoughts, feelings, and humours, and even the most incidental and passing impressions of every accidental circumstance. When I went to Wetzlar, the loneliness of the house without me seemed insupportable: my friend Schlosser, neither unknown nor repugnant to the good girl, stepped into my place. In him, unfortunately, the brotherly affection changed into a decided, and, to judge from his strictly conscientious character, probably a first, passion. Here there was found what people call as good a match as could be wished; and my sister, after having steadfastly rejected several good offers, but from insignificant men, whom she always had an aversion to, allowed herself to be, I may well say, talked into accepting him.

I must frankly confess that I have frequently indulged in fancies about my sister's destiny : I did not like to think of her as the mistress of a family, but rather as an abbess, as the lady superior of some noble community. She possessed every requisite for such a high position, while she was wanting in all that the world deems indispensable in its members. Over feminine souls she always exercised an irresistible influence : young minds were gently attracted toward her, and she ruled them by the spirit of her inward superiority. As she had in common with me a universal tolerance for the good, the human, with all its eccentricities, provided they did not amount to perversity, there was no need for seeking to conceal from her any idiosyncrasy which might mark any remarkable natural talents, or for its owner feeling any constraint in her presence : hence our parties, as we have seen before, were always varied, free, ingenuous, and sometimes, perhaps, bordering on boldness. My habit of forming intimacies of a respectful and obliging nature with young ladies, without any closer engagement or relations being the result, was mainly owing to my sister's influence over me. And now the sagacious reader, who is capable of reading into these lines what does not stand written in them, but is nevertheless implied, will be able to form some conception of the serious feelings with which I then set foot in Emmendingen.

But at my departure, after a short visit, a heavier load lay on my heart; for my sister had earnestly recommended, not to say enjoined, me, to break off my connection with Lilli. She herself had suffered much from a long-protracted engagement : Schlosser, with his spirit of rectitude, did not betroth himself to her

until he was sure of his appointment under the Grand
Duke of Baden, — indeed, if one would take it so, until
he was actually appointed. The answer to his application, however, was delayed in an incredible manner.
If I may express my conjecture on the matter, the
brave Schlosser, able man of business as he was, was
nevertheless, on account of his downright integrity,
desirable neither to the prince as a servant, immediately in contact with himself, nor to the minister, who
still less liked to have so honest a coadjutor near to
him. His expected and earnestly desired appointment
at Carlsruhe was never filled up. But the delay was
explained to me when the place of upper bailiff in
Emmendingen became vacant and he was instantly
selected for it. Thus an office of much dignity and
profit was now entrusted to him, for which he had
shown himself fully competent. It seemed entirely
suited to his taste, his mode of action, to stand here
alone, to act according to his own conviction, and to be
held responsible for everything, whether for praise or
blame.

As no objections could be raised to his accepting
this place, my sister had to follow him, not indeed to a
court-residence, as she had hoped, but to a place which
must have seemed to her a solitude, a desert; to a
dwelling, spacious to be sure, with an official dignity,
and stately, but destitute of all chance of society.
Some young ladies, with whom she had cultivated an
early friendship, followed her there: and, as the Gerock
family was blessed with many daughters, these contrived to stay with her in turn; so that, in the midst
of such privation, she always enjoyed the presence of
at least one long-trusted friend.

These circumstances, these experiences, made her
feel justified in recommending to me, most earnestly,
a separation from Lilli. She thought it hard to take
such a young lady (of whom she had formed the

highest opinion) out of the midst of a lively, if not splendid, circle, and to shut her up in our old house, which, although very passable in its way, was not suited for the reception of distinguished society, sticking her, as it were, between a well-disposed, but unsociable, precise, and formal, father, and a mother extremely active in her domestic matters, who, after the household business of the day was over, would not like to be disturbed over some notable bit of work by a friendly conversation with forward and refined young girls. On the other hand, she in a lively manner set Lilli's position before me; for partly in my letters, partly in a confidential but impassioned conversation, I had told her everything to a hair.

Unfortunately her description was only a circumstantial and well-meant completion of what a gossiping friend, in whom, by degrees, all confidence ceased to be placed, had contrived, by mentioning a few characteristic traits, to insinuate into her mind.

I could promise her nothing, although I was obliged to confess that she had convinced me. I went on with that enigmatic feeling in my heart, with which passion always nourishes itself; for the child Cupid clings obstinately to the garment of Hope, even when she is preparing with long steps to flee away.

The only thing between this place and Zurich which I now clearly remember is the falls of the Rhine at Schaffhausen. A mighty cascade here gives the indication of the mountainous region which we designed to enter, where, each step becoming steeper and more difficult, we should have laboriously to clamber up the heights.

The view of the lake of Zurich, which we enjoyed from the gate of the " *Sword*," is still before me: I say from the gate of the tavern; for, without stopping to enter it, I hastened to Lavater. He gave me a cheerful and hearty reception, and was, I must confess, extremely gracious: confiding, considerate, kind, and elevating was his bearing; indeed, it would be impossible to expect anything else of him. His wife, with somewhat singular, but serene, tenderly pious, expression of countenance, fully harmonised, like everything else about him, with his way of thinking and living.

Our first and perhaps only theme of conversation was his system of physiognomy. The first part of this remarkable work was, if I mistake not, already printed, or at least near its completion. It might be said to be at once stamped with genius, and yet empirical; methodical, but still in its instances incomplete and partial. I was strangely connected with it: Lavater wanted all the world for coöperators and sympathisers. During his travels up the Rhine, he had portraits taken of a great many distinguished men, in order to excite their personal interest in a work in which they were to appear. He proceeded in the same way with artists: he called upon every one to send him drawings for illustrations. The latter came, and many were not exactly suited for his purpose. So, too, he had copperplates engraved in all parts, which seldom turned out characteristic copies. Much labour had been bestowed on his part: with money and exertions of all kinds, an important work was now ready, and full honour was done to physiognomy. But when in a great volume, illustrated by examples, physiognomy, founded on doctrine, was to set up its claims to the dignity of science, it was found that not a single picture said what it ought to say: all the plates had to be censured or to be taken with exceptions, none to be praised, but only tolerated; many, indeed, were quite altered by the explanations. For me, who in all my studies sought a firm footing before I went farther, I had now to perform one of the most painful tasks which industry could be set to. Let the reader judge. The manuscript, with impressions of the plates in-

serted, was sent to me at Frankfort. I was authorised
to strike out whatever displeased me, to change and
put in what I liked. However, I made a very moderate use of this liberty. In one instance he had introduced a long and violent piece of controversy against
an unjust orator, which I left out, and substituted a
cheerful poem about nature; for this he scolded me,
but afterward, when he had cooled down, approved of
what I had done.

Whoever turns over the four volumes of physiognomy, and (what he will not repent of) reads them,
may conceive the interest there was in our interviews,
during which, as most of the plates contained in it
were already drawn, and part of them had been engraved, we examined, and decided on those fit to be
inserted in the work, and considered the ingenious
means by which those, which did not exactly tally
with its principles, might be made instructive and
suitable.

Whenever at present I look through the work of
Lavater, a comic, merry feeling comes over me: it
seems as if I saw before me the shadows of men
formerly known to me, over whom I once fretted, and
in whom I find little satisfaction now.

The possibility, however, of retaining, in some sort,
much that otherwise would have been unsuitable, was
owing to the fine and decided talent of the sketcher
and engraver, Lips. He was, in fact, born for the free
prosaic representation of the actual, which was precisely the thing wanted in this case. He worked
under a singularly exacting physiognomist, and therefore was obliged to look sharp to approximate to the
demands of his master: the clever peasant boy felt the
whole responsibility of working for a clerical gentleman
from a city so highly privileged, and gave his best care
to the business.

Living in a separate house from my companions, I

became every day more of a stranger to them, without the least unpleasant feeling having arisen: our rural excursions were no longer made together, although in the city we still kept up some intercourse. With all the arrogance of young counts, they had honoured Lavater with a visit, and appeared to the skilful physiognomist somewhat different from what they did to the rest of the world. He spoke to me about them; and I remember quite well, that, speaking of Leopold Stolberg, he exclaimed, " I know not what you all mean: he is a noble, excellent youth, and full of talent; but you have described him to me as a hero, as a Hercules; and I have never in my life seen a softer and more sensitive young man, nor, if need be, one more easily influenced. I am still far from having formed a clear physiognomical judgment of him; but as for you and all the rest, you are in a fog altogether."

Since Lavater's journey on the Lower Rhine, the public interest in him and his physiognomical studies had greatly increased: visitors of all sorts crowded upon him; so that he felt in some sort embarrassed at being looked upon as the first of spiritual and intellectual men, and the chief point of attraction for strangers. Hence, to avoid envy and all unpleasant feelings, he managed to remind and warn his visitors that they must treat other distinguished men with friendship and respect.

In this, especial regard was had to the aged Bodmer; and, accordingly, we were compelled to visit him and pay our youthful respects to him. He lived on a hill, above the large or old town, which lay on the right bank, where the lake contracts its waters into the Limmat. We crossed the old town, and, by a path that became steeper and steeper, at last ascended the height behind the walls, where, between the fortifications and the old wall, a pleasant suburb had sprung up, partly in continuous and partly in detached houses, with a half-country look. The house where Bodmer had passed his whole life stood in the midst of an open and cheerful neighbourhood, which, the day being beautiful and clear, we often paused on our road to survey with the greatest pleasure.

We were conducted up a flight of steps into a wainscoted chamber, where a brisk old man, of middle stature, came to meet us. He received us with the greeting he usually addressed to young visitors, telling us that we must consider it an act of courtesy on his part to have delayed so long his departure from this world, in order that he might receive us kindly, form our acquaintance, refresh himself with our talents, and wish us joy in our future career.

We, on the other hand, congratulated him, that as a poet, belonging to the patriarchal world, he had yet, in the neighbourhood of the most highly cultivated city, possessed during his whole life a truly idyllic dwelling, and, in the high, free air, had enjoyed for so many long years such a wide and beautiful prospect to feed his eyes with unfading delight.

It seemed anything but displeasing to the old man when we asked permission to take a view from his window of the neighbouring scenery; and truly the prospect in the cheerful sunshine, and in the best season of the year, appeared quite incomparable. The prospect commanded much of the slope, from the great town down to the water's edge, as well as the smaller town across the Limmat, and the whole of the fertile Sihl-feld, toward the west. Behind us, on the left, was a part of the lake of Zurich, with its bright, rippled surface, and its shores endlessly varying with alternating hill and valley and height after height in greater variety than the eye could take in, which, dazzled by this splendour, delighted to rest on the blue range of the loftier mountains in the distance,

whose snowy summits man has been so far intimate
with as to give names to.

The rapture of young men at sight of the mar-
vellous beauty, which, for so many years, had daily
been before him, appeared to please the old poet; he
became, so to speak, ironically sympathising: and we
parted the best of friends, but not before a yearning for
those blue mountain heights had taken possession of
our souls.

Now that I am on the point of leaving our worthy
patriarch, I remark, for the first time, that I have as
yet said nothing of his form and countenance, of his
movements, and his carriage and bearing.

In general, I do not think it quite right for travellers to describe every distinguished man whom they
visit, as if they wanted to furnish materials for adver-
tising a runaway. No one sufficiently considers that
he has only looked at the great man during the moment of introduction, and then only in his own way;
and that, according to the circumstances of the moment, the host may or not be what he seemed, proud
or meek, silent or talkative, cheerful or morose. In
this particular case, however, I may excuse myself
from the attempt, by saying that no verbal description
of Bodmer's venerable person would convey an ade-
quate impression. Fortunately, there exists a picture
of him by Count von Bause, which perfectly represents
the man as he appeared to us, and, indeed, exactly
preserves his peculiar penetrating and reflective look.

A great, not indeed unexpected, but still highly
coveted, gratification awaited me in Zurich, where I
met my young friend Passavant. Of a respectable
family of the Reformed persuasion, and born in my
native city, he lived in Switzerland, at the fountain-
head of the doctrine which he was afterward to pro-
claim as a preacher. With a frame not large, but
active, his face and his whole manner promised a quick

and agreeable resoluteness of character. His hair and beard were black, his eyes lively. On the whole, you saw in him a man of some sensitiveness, but of moderate energy.

Scarcely had we embraced one another, and exchanged the first greeting, when he immediately proposed to me to visit the smaller cantons. Having himself already walked through them with great delight, he wished, with the sight of them, to awaken my rapture and enthusiasm.

While I was talking over, with Lavater, the most interesting and important points of our common business, until we had nearly exhausted them, my lively fellow travellers had already sallied forth in various directions, and, in their own fashion, had examined the country. Passavant, receiving and welcoming me with hearty friendship, believed that he had gained thereby a right to the exclusive possession of my society, and therefore, in the absence of my companions, contrived to entice me to the mountains, the more easily, since I was decidedly inclined to accomplish the long-desired ramble in quiet, and at liberty to follow my own whims. Without further deliberation, therefore, we stepped into a boat, and sailed up the glorious lake on a fine clear morning.

A poem inserted here may give the reader some intimation of those happy moments:

> And here I drink new blood, fresh food,
>   From world so free, so blest:
> How sweet is Nature, and how good,
>   Who holds me to her breast!
> The waves are cradling up our boat,
>   The oars are beating time;
> Mountains we meet that seem afloat
>   In heavenly clouds sublime.
>
> Why, my eye, art downward turning?
> Golden dreams, are ye returning?

Dream, though gold, I thee repel:
Love and life here also dwell.

'Neath the wave are sinking
Stars from heaven sparkling;
Soft white mists are drinking
Distance towering, darkling;
Morning wind is fanning
Trees, by the bay that root;
And its image scanning
Is the ripening fruit.

— *Editor's Version.*

We landed in Richterswyl, where we had an introduction from Lavater to Doctor Hotze. As a physician,
and a highly intelligent and benevolent man, he enjoyed
great esteem in his immediate neighbourhood and in
the whole country; and we can do no better honour to
his memory than by referring to a passage in Lavater's
" Physiognomy," which describes him.

After a very hospitable entertainment, which he
relieved with a highly agreeable and instructive conversation, describing to us the next halting-places in our
journey, we ascended the mountains which lay before
us. When we were about to descend again into the
vale of Schindellegi, we turned round to take in once
more the charming prospect over the lake of Zurich.

Of my feelings at that moment some idea may be
gathered from the following lines, which, just as I
wrote them down, are still preserved in a little memo-
randum-book :

If I, dearest Lilli, did not love thee,
What delight I should have in this view!
And yet were I, Lilli, not to love thee,
Could here, could true bliss to me accrue?

— *Editor's Version.*

This little impromptu reads to me more expressive
in its present context than as it stands by itself in the
printed collection of my poems.

The rough roads which led to St. Mary's hermitage did not wear out our good spirits. A number of pilgrims, whom we had remarked below upon the lake, now overtook us, and asked the aid of our prayers in behalf of their pious object. We saluted them, and let them pass; and, as they moved regularly with their hymns and prayers, they lent a characteristic graceful animation to the dreary heights. We saw livingly marked out the serpentine path which we, too, had to travel, and seemed to be joyously following. The customs of the Romish Church are altogether significant and imposing to the Protestant, inasmuch as he only recognises the inmost principle by which they were first called forth, the human element by which they are propagated from race to race; thus penetrating at once to the kernel, without troubling himself, just at the moment, with the shell, the rind, or even with the tree itself, its twigs, leaves, bark, and roots.

We now saw rising a dreary, treeless vale, the splendid church, the cloister, of broad and stately compass, in the midst of a neat place of sojourn for a large and varied assembly of guests.

The little church within the church, the former hermitage of the saint, encrusted with marble, and transformed as far as possible into a regular chapel, was something new to me, something that I had not seen, — this little vessel, surrounded and built over with pillars and vaults. It could not but excite sober thoughts to reflect how a single spark of goodness, and of the fear of God, had here kindled a bright and burning flame, so that troops of believers never ceased to make painful pilgrimages in order to light their little tapers at this holy fire. However the fact is to be explained, it plainly points at least to an unbounded craving in man for equal light, for equal warmth, with that which this old hermit cherished and enjoyed in the deepest feeling and the most secure conviction.

We were shown into the treasure-chamber, which was rich and imposing enough, and offered to the astonished eye busts of the size of life, not to say colossal, of the saints and founders of different orders.

A very different sort of feeling was awakened at the sight of a closet opening upon this. It was filled with antique valuables, here dedicated and honoured. My attention was fixed by various golden crowns of re-markable workmanship, out of which I contemplated one exclusively. It was a pointed crown in the style of former days, such as one may have seen in pictures on the heads of ancient queens, but of a most tasteful design and of highly elaborate execution. The coloured stones with which it was studded were distributed over it or set opposite to each other with great effect and judgment: it was, in short, a work of that kind which one would pronounce perfect at the first glance, with-out waiting to bring out this impression by an appeal to the laws of art.

In such cases, where the art is not recognised, but felt, heart and soul are turned toward the object: one would like to possess the jewel, that one might impart pleasure to others with such a gift. I begged permis-sion to handle the little crown ; and, as I held it up respectfully in my hand, I could not help thinking that I should like to press it upon the bright, glittering locks of Lilli, lead her before the mirror, and witness her own joy in it, and the happiness which she spread around her. I have often thought since, that this scene, if realised by a skilful painter, would be highly touch-ing and full of meaning. It were worth one's while to be the young king to receive a bride and a new king-dom in this way.

In order to show us all the treasures of the cloister, they led us into a cabinet of natural and artificial curiosities. I had then but little idea of the value of such things : at that time geognosy, which is so commendable in itself, but which fritters away the impression produced by the earth's beautiful surface on the mind's eye, had not begun to entice me, still less had a fantastic geology entangled me in its labyrinths. Nevertheless, the monk who acted as our guide compelled me to bestow some attention on a fossil, much prized as he said by connoisseurs, — a small wild-boar's head well preserved in a lump of blue fuller's clay, which, black as it was, has dwelt in my imagination ever since. They had found it in the country of Rapperswyl, a district which, ever since the memory of man, was so full of morasses that it could well receive and keep such mummies for posterity.

Far different attractions were presented to me by a copperplate engraving of Martin Schön, which was kept under a glass frame, and represented the Assumption of the Virgin. True, only a perfect specimen could give an idea of the art of such a master; but then, we are so affected by it, as with the perfect in every branch of art, that we cannot get rid of the wish to possess something in some way like it, to be able constantly to repeat the sight of it, however long a time may intervene. Why should I not anticipate and confess here, that afterward I could not rest until I had succeeded in obtaining an excellent copy of this plate.

On the 16th of July, 1775 (for here I find a date first set down), we entered upon a toilsome journey; wild, stony heights were to be surmounted, and that, too, in a perfect solitude and wilderness. At a quarter before eight in the evening, we stood before the Schwyzer-Haken, two mountain peaks which jut out boldly, side by side, into the sky. For the first time we found snow upon our path, where on the jagged rocks it had been hanging since the winter. A primeval forest, with its solemn awe, filled the immense valleys into which we were about to descend. Refreshed, after a short rest, we sprang, with bold and light step, from cliff to cliff, from ledge to ledge, down the precipitous foot-path, and arrived by ten o'clock at Schwyz. We had become at once weary yet cheerful, exhausted yet excited: we eagerly quenched our violent thirst, and felt ourselves still more inspired. Imagine the young man who but two years before had written "Werther," and his still younger friend who still earlier had read that remarkable work in manuscript, and had been strangely excited by it, transported, in some respect without their knowing it or wishing it, into a state of nature, and there, in the consciousness of rich powers, vividly recalling past passions, clinging to those of the present, shaping fruitless plans, rioting through the realm of fancy, and you will be able to form some conception of our situation then, which I should not know how to describe if it did not stand written in my journal, " Laughing and shouting lasted until midnight."

On the morning of the 17th we saw the Schwyzer-Haken from our windows. Around these vast and irregular natural pyramids, clouds rose upon clouds. At one in the afternoon we left Schwyz, on our way to the Rigi: at two we were on the Lawerzer lake, the sun shining brilliantly on it and on us all the while. For sheer delight we saw nothing   Two stout maidens guided the boat: that looked pretty, and we made no objection. We arrived upon the island, on which they say once lived the former lord of the castle : be this as it may, the hut of the anchorite has now planted itself amidst the ruins.

We climbed the Rigi; at half-past seven we stood at the foot of the " Mother of God " covered in snow; then passed the chapel and the nunnery, and rested at the hotel of the Ox.

On the 18th, Sunday morning early, we took a sketch of the chapel from the Ox. At twelve we went to Kaltenbad, or the fountain of the Three Sisters. By a quarter after two we had reached the summit: we found ourselves in the clouds, this time doubly disagreeable to us, since they both hindered the prospect and drenched us with mist. But when, here and there, they opened and showed us, framed as it were by their ever-varying outline, a clear, majestic, sun-lit world, with the changing scenes of a diorama, we no longer lamented these accidents; for it was a sight we had never seen before and should never behold again: and we lingered long in this somewhat inconvenient position, to catch, through the chinks and crevices of the ever-shifting masses of cloud, some little point of sunny earth, some little strip of shore, or pretty nook of the lake.

By eight in the evening we were back again at the door of the inn, and refreshed ourselves with baked fish and eggs, and plenty of wine.

As the twilight and the night gradually came on, our ears were filled with mysteriously harmonising sounds, — the tinkling of the chapel bells, the splashing of the fountain, the rustling of changeful breezes, with the horns of the foresters in the distance: these were blest, soothing, tranquillising moments.

At half-past six, on the morning of the 19th, first ascending,. then going down by the Waldstätter Lake, we came to Fitznau; from thence, by water, to Gersau. At noon we were in the hotel on the lake. About two o'clock we were opposite to Grutli, where the three Tells conspired; then upon the flat rock where the hero sprang from his boat, and where the legend of his life and deeds is recorded and immortalised by a painting. At three we were at Flüelen, where he embarked; and at four in Altorf, where he shot the apple.

Aided by this poetic thread, one winds conveniently through the labyrinth of these rocky walls, which, descending perpendicularly to the water, stand silently before us. They, the immovable, stand there as quietly as the side-scenes of a theatre: success or failure, joy or sorrow, merely pertain to the persons who for the day successively strut upon the stage.

Such reflections, however, were wholly out of the circle of the vision of the youths who then looked upon them: what had recently passed had been dismissed from their thoughts, and the future lay before them as strangely inscrutable as the mountain region which they were laboriously penetrating.

On the 20th we breakfasted at Amstäg, where they cooked us a savoury dinner of baked fish. Here now, on this mountain ledge, where the Reuss, which was at all times wild enough, was rushing from rugged clefts, and dashing the cool snow-water over the rocky channels, I could not help enjoying the longed-for opportunity, and refreshing myself in the foaming waves.

At three o'clock we proceeded onward: a row of sumpter-horses went before us; we marched with them over a broad mass of snow, and did not learn till afterward that it was hollow underneath. The snows of winter, that had deposited themselves here in a mountain gorge, which at other seasons it was necessary to skirt circuitously, now furnished us with a shorter and more direct road. But the waters which forced their way beneath had gradually undermined the snowy mass, and the mild summer had melted more and more of the lower side of the vault; so that now, like a broad, arched bridge, it formed a natural connection between the opposite sides. We convinced ourselves of this strange freak of nature by venturing more than half-way down into the broader part of the gorge. As we kept ascending, we left pine forests in the chasm, through which the Reuss from time to time appeared, foaming and dashing over rocky precipices.

At half-past seven we arrived at Wasen, where, to

render palatable the red, heavy, sour Lombardy wine, we were forced to have recourse to water, and to supply, by a great deal of sugar, the ingredient which nature had refused to elaborate in the grape. The landlord showed us some beautiful crystals; but I had at that time so little interest in the study of nature and such specimens, that I did not care to burden myself with these mountain products, however cheaply they might be bought.

On the 21st, at half-past six, we were still ascending; the rocks grew more and more stupendous and awful; the path to the *Teufelstein* (Devil's Stone), from which we were to gain a view of the Devil's Bridge, was still more difficult. My companion, being disposed for a rest, proposed to me to sketch the most important views. My outlines were, perhaps, tolerably successful: but nothing seemed to stand out, nothing to retire into the distance; for such objects I had no language. We toiled on farther: the horrors of the wilderness seemed continually to deepen, plains became hills and hollows chasms. And so my guide conducted me to the cave of Ursern, through which I walked in somewhat of an ill humour: what we had seen thus far was, at any rate, sublime; this darkness took everything away.

But the roguish guide anticipated the joyful astonishment which would overwhelm me on my egress. There the moderately foaming stream wound mildly through a level vale surrounded by mountains, but wide enough to invite habitation. Above the clean little village of Ursern and its church, which stood opposite to us on a level plot, rose a pine grove, which was held sacred because it protected the inhabitants at its foot from the rolling of the avalanches. Here we enjoyed the sight of long-missed vegetation. The meadows of the valley, just beginning to look green, were adorned along the river side with short willows. The tranquillity was great: upon the level paths we felt our powers revive again, and my fellow traveller was not a little proud of the surprise which he had so skilfully contrived.

The meadows produce the celebrated Ursern cheese; and the youthful travellers, high in spirits, pronounced very tolerable wine not to be surpassed, in order to heighten their enjoyment, and to give a more fantastic impulse to their projects.

On the 22d, at half-past three, we left our quarters, that from the smooth Ursern valley we might enter upon the stony valley of Liviner. Here, too, we at once missed all vegetation: nothing was to be seen or heard but naked or mossy rocks covered with snow, fitful gusts blowing the clouds backwards and forwards, the rustling of waterfalls, the tinkling of sumpter-horses in the depth of solitude, where we saw none coming and none departing. It did not cost the imagination much to see dragons' nests in the clefts. But, nevertheless, we felt inspired and elevated by one of the most beautiful and picturesque waterfalls, sublimely various in all its rocky steps, which, being at this time of the year enriched by melted snows, and now half hidden by the clouds, now half revealed, chained us for some time to the spot.

Finally, we came to little mist-lakes, as I might call them, since they were scarcely to be distinguished from the atmospheric streaks. Before long, a building loomed toward us out of the vapour: it was the Hospice, and we felt great satisfaction at the thoughts of sheltering ourselves under its hospitable roof.

NINETEENTH BOOK.

Announced by the low barking of a little dog which ran out to meet us, we were cordially received at the door by an elderly but active female. She apologised for the absence of the Pater, who had gone to Milan, but was expected home that evening; and immediately, without any more words, set to work to provide for our comfort and wants. We were shown into a warm and spacious room, where bread, cheese, and some passable wine, were set before us, with the promise of a more substantial meal for our supper. The surprise of the day was now talked over; and my friend was not a little proud that all had gone off so well, and that we had passed a day the impressions of which neither poetry nor prose could ever reproduce.

At length with the twilight, which did not here come on till late, the venerable father entered the room, greeted his guests with dignity but in a friendly and cordial manner, and in a few words ordered the cook to pay all possible attention to our wishes. When we expressed the wonder we could not repress, that he could like to pass his life up here, in the midst of such a perfect wilderness, out of the reach of all society, he assured us that society was never wanting, as our own welcome visit might testify. A lively trade, he told us was, kept up between Italy and Germany. This continual traffic brought him into relation with the first mercantile houses. He often went down to Milan, and also to Lucerne, though not so frequently, from which place, however, the houses which had charge of the posting on the main route frequently sent young people to him, who, here at the point of passage between the two countries, required to be made acquainted with all the circumstances and events connected with such affairs.

Amid such varied conversation the evening passed away; and we slept a quiet night on somewhat short sleeping - places, fastened to the wall, and more like shelves than bedsteads.

Rising early, I soon found myself under the open sky, but in a narrow space surrounded by tall mountain tops. I sat down upon the foot-path which led to Italy, and attempted, after the manner of *dilettanti*, to draw what could not be drawn, still less make a picture; namely, the nearest mountain tops, whose sides, with their white furrows and black ridges, were gradually made visible by the melting of the snow. Nevertheless, that fruitless effort has impressed the image indelibly on my memory.

My companion stepped briskly up to me, and began, " What say you of the story of our spiritual host last evening? Have not you, as well as myself, felt a desire to descend from this dragon's height into those charming regions below? A ramble through these gorges must be glorious and not very toilsome; and, when it ends with Bellinzona, what a pleasure that must be! The words of the good father have again brought a living image before my soul of the isles of the Lago Maggiore. We have heard and seen so much of them since Keyssler's travels, that I cannot resist the temptation."

" Is it not so with you too ? " he resumed : " you are sitting on exactly the right spot; I stood there once, but had not the courage to jump down. You can go on without ceremony, wait for me at Airolo: I will follow with the courier when I have taken leave of the good father, and settled everything."

" Such an enterprise," I replied, " so suddenly undertaken, does not suit me." " What's the use of deliberating so much?" cried he: "we have money enough to get to Milan, where we shall find credit; through our fair, I know more than one mercantile friend there." He grew still more urgent. "Go!" said I, "and make all ready for the departure: then we will decide."

In such moments it seems to me as if a man feels no resolution in himself, but is rather governed and determined by earlier impressions. Lombardy and Italy lay before me, altogether foreign land; while Germany, as a well-known dear home, full of friendly, domestic scenes, and where, let me confess it, — was that which had so long entirely enchained me, and on which my existence was centred, remained even now the most indispensable element, beyond the limits of which I felt afraid to step. A little golden heart, which, in my happiest hours, I had received from *her*, still hung love-warmed about my neck, suspended by the same ribbon to which she had tied it. Snatching it from my bosom, I loaded it with kisses. This incident gave rise to a poem, which I here insert:

Thou, of joy that died away, the token,
Which as yet I on my neck am wearing,
Longer hold'st us twain, than mental tie that's broken.
Art thou the length of love's short days repairing?

Flee I, Lilli, from thee! Must still, tied to thy fetter,
Like unto a debtor,
Roam in strange lands, through vales and forests darting!
Ah! not so soon could this my heart from
My Lilli's heart be parting.

Like a bird that erst did break his string,
And to the wood returns,
He drags of his prison the disgrace,
Still some bit of the string on his trace;
No longer the old bird, once born with freedom's wing;
Has been a slave where'er he turns.

— *Editor's Version.*

Seeing my friend with the guide, who carried our knapsack, come storming up the heights, I rose hastily, and removed from the precipice, where I had been watching his return, lest he should drag me down into the abyss with him. I also saluted the pious father, and turned, without saying a word, to the path by which we had come. My friend followed me, somewhat hesitating, and, in spite of his love and attachment to me, kept for a long time at a distance behind, till at last a glorious waterfall brought us again together for the rest of our journey; and what had been once decided was from henceforth looked upon as the wisest and the best.

Of our descent I will only remark that we now found the snow-bridge, over which we had securely travelled with a heavy laden train a few days before, all fallen in, and that now, as we had to make a circuit around the opened thicket, we were filled with astonishment and admiration by the colossal fragments of that piece of natural architecture.

My friend could not quite get over his disappointment at not returning into Italy: very likely he had thought of the plan some time before, and with amiable cunning had hoped to surprise me on the spot. On this account our return did not proceed so merrily as our advance; but I was occupied all the more constantly on my silent route, with trying to fix, at least in its more comprehensible and characteristic details, that sense of the sublime and vast, which, as time advances, usually grows contracted in our minds.

Not without many both new and renewed emotions and reflections did we pass over the remarkable heights about the Vierwaldstätter Lake, on our way to Küssnacht, where, having landed, and pursued our ramble, we had to greet Tell's chapel, which lay on our route, and to reflect upon that assassination, which, in the eyes of the whole world, is so heroical, patriotic, and glorious. So, too, we sailed over the Zuger Lake, which we had seen in the distance as we looked down from Rigi. In Zug, I only remember some painted glass, inserted into the casement of a chamber of the inn, not large to be sure, but excellent in its way. Our route then led over the Albis into the Sihl valley, where, by visiting a young Hanoverian, Von Lindau, who delighted to live there in solitude, we sought to mitigate the vexation which he had felt some time before in Zurich, at our declining the offer of his company not in the most friendly or polite manner. The jealous friendship of the worthy Passavant was really the reason of my rejecting the truly dear but inconvenient presence of another.

But, before we descend again from these glorious heights to the lake and to the pleasantly situated city, I must make one more remark upon my attempts to carry away some idea of the country by drawing and sketching. A habit from youth upward of viewing a landscape as a picture led me, whenever I observed any picturesque spot in the natural scenery, to try and fix it, and so to preserve a sure memorial of such moments. But, having hitherto only exercised myself on confined scenes, I soon felt the incompetency of my art for such a world.

The haste I was in at once compelled me to have recourse to a singular expedient: scarcely had I noticed an interesting object, and with light and very sketchy strokes drawn the outlines on the paper, than I noted down, in words, the particular objects which I had no time to catch and fill up with the pencil, and, by this means, made the scenes so thoroughly present to my mind, that every locality, whenever I afterward wanted it for a poem or a story, floated at once before me, and was entirely at my command.

On returning to Zurich, I found the Stolbergs were

gone: their stay in this city had been cut short in a singular manner.

It must be confessed that travellers, upon removing to a distance from the restraints of home, are only too apt to think they are stepping, not only into an unknown, but into a perfectly free, world,— a delusion which it was the more easy to indulge in at this time, as there was not as yet any passports to be examined by the police, or any tolls and such like checks and hinderances on the liberties of travellers, to remind men that abroad they are subject to still worse and more painful restraints than at home.

If the reader will only bear in mind this decided tendency to realise the freedom of nature, he will be able to pardon the young spirits who regarded Switzerland as the very place in which to "idyllise" the fresh independence of youth. The tender poems of Gessner, as well as his charming sketches, seemed decidedly to justify this expectation.

In fact, bathing in wide waters seems to be one of the best qualifications for expressing such poetic talents. Upon our journey thus far, such natural exercises had not seemed exactly suitable to modern customs; and we had, in some degree, abstained from them. But, in Switzerland, the sight of the cool stream — flowing, running, rushing, then gathering on the plain, and gradually spreading out to a lake — presented a temptation that was not to be resisted. I cannot deny that I joined my companions in bathing in the clear lake; but we chose a spot far enough, as we supposed, from all human eyes. But naked bodies shine a good way, and whoever chanced to see us doubtless took offence.

The good, innocent youths who thought it nowise shocking to see themselves half naked, like poetic shepherds, or entirely naked, like heathen deities, were admonished by their friends to leave off all such practices. They were given to understand that they were living, not in primeval nature, but in a land where it was esteemed good and salutary to adhere to the old institutions and customs, which had been handed down from the Middle Ages. They were not disinclined to acknowledge the propriety of all this, especially as the appeal was made to the Middle Ages, which to them seemed venerable as a second nature. Accordingly, they left the more public lake-shores; but when, in their walks through the mountains, they fell in with the clear, rustling, refreshing streams, it seemed to them impossible, in the middle of July, to abstain from the refreshing exercise. Thus, on their wide-sweeping walks, they came also to the shady vale where the Sihl, streaming behind the Albis, shoots down to empty itself into the Limmat below Zurich. Far from every habitation, and even from all trodden foot-paths, they thought there could be no objection here to their throwing off their clothes and boldly meeting the foaming waves. This was not indeed done without a shriek, without a wild shout of joy, excited partly by the chill and partly by the satisfaction, by which they thought to consecrate these gloomy, wooded rocks into an idyllic scene.

But whether persons previously ill-disposed had crept after them, or whether this poetic tumult called forth adversaries even in the solitude, cannot be determined. Suffice it to say, stone after stone was thrown at them from the motionless bushes above, whether by one or more, whether accidentally or purposely, they could not tell: however, they thought it wisest to renounce the quickening element, and look after their clothes.

No one got hit: they sustained no injury but the moral one of surprise and chagrin; and, full of young life as they were, they easily shook off the recollection of this awkward affair.

But the most disagreeable consequences fell upon Lavater, who was blamed for having given so friendly a welcome to such saucy youths, as even to have arranged walks with them, and otherwise to show attention to persons whose wild, unbridled, unchristian, and even heathenish, habits, had caused so much scandal to a moral and well-regulated neighbourhood.

Our clever friend, however, who well knew how to smooth over such unpleasant occurrences, contrived to hush up this one also; and, after the departure of these meteoric travellers, we found, on our return, peace and quiet restored.

In the fragment of Werther's travels, which has lately been reprinted in the sixteenth volume of my works, I have attempted to describe this contrast of the commendable order and legal restraint of Switzerland, with that life of nature which youth in its delusions so loudly demands. But as people generally are apt to take all that the poet advances without reserve for his decided opinions, or even didactic censure, so the Swiss were very much offended at the comparison; and I, therefore, dropped the intended continuation, which was to have represented, more or less in detail, Werther's progress up to the epoch of his sorrows, and which, therefore, would certainly have been interesting to those who wish to study mankind.

Arrived at Zurich, I devoted my time almost exclusively to Lavater, whose hospitality I again made use of. The "Physiognomy," with all its portraits and monstrous caricatures, weighed heavily and with an ever-increasing load on the shoulders of the worthy man. We arranged all as well as we could under the circumstances; and I promised him, on my return home, to continue my assistance.

I was led to give this promise by a certain youthful unlimited confidence in my own quickness of comprehension, and still more by a feeling of my readiness of adaptation to any subject; for, in truth, the way in which Lavater dissected physiognomies was not at all in my vein. The impression which, at our first meeting, he had made upon me, determined, in some degree, my relation to him; although a general wish to oblige, which was always strong, joined to the light-heartedness of youth, had a great share in all my actions, by causing me to see things in a certain twilight atmosphere.

Lavater's mind was altogether an imposing one: in his society it was impossible to resist his decided influence; and I had no choice but to submit to it at once, and set to work observing foreheads and noses, eyes and mouths, in detail, and weighing their relations and proportions. My fellow observer did this from necessity, as he had to give a perfect account of what he himself had discerned so clearly; but to me it always seemed like a trick, a piece of espionage, to attempt to analyse a man into his elements before his face, and so to get upon the track of his hidden moral peculiarities. I had more pleasure in listening to his conversation, in which he unveiled himself at will. And yet, I must confess, I always felt a degree of constraint in Lavater's presence; for while, by his art of physiognomy, he possessed himself of our peculiarities, he also made himself, by conversation, master of our thoughts, which, with a little sagacity, he would easily guess from our variety of phrases.

He who feels a pregnant synthesis in himself has peculiarly a right to analyse, since by the outward particulars he tests and legitimises his inward whole. How Lavater managed in such cases, a single example will suffice to show.

On Sundays, after the sermon, it was his duty, as an ecclesiastic, to hold the short-handled velvet alms-bag before each one who went out, and to bless as he received the pious gift. Now, on a certain Sunday, he proposed to himself, without looking at the several persons as they dropped in their offerings, to observe only their hands, and by them, silently, to judge of the forms of their owner. Not only the shape of the finger, but its peculiar action in dropping the gift, was attentively noted by him; and he had much to communicate to me on the conclusions he had formed. How instructive and exciting must such conversations have been to one who also was seeking to qualify himself for a painter of men!

Often, in my after life, had I occasion to think of Lavater, who was one of the best and worthiest men that I ever formed so intimate a relation with. These notices of him that I have introduced in this work were accordingly written at various times. Following our divergent tendencies, we gradually became strangers to each other; and yet I never could bring myself to part with the favourable idea which his worth had left upon my mind. In thought, I often brought him before me; and thus arose these leaves, which, as they were written without reference to and independently of each other, may contain some repetitions, but, it is hoped, no contradictions.

By his cast of mind, Lavater was a decided realist, and knew of nothing ideal except in a moral form: by keeping this remark steadily in mind, you will most readily understand this rare and singular man.

His " Prospects of Eternity " look merely for a continuance of the present state of existence under easier conditions than those which we have now to endure. His " Physiognomy " rests on the conviction that the sensible corresponds throughout with the spiritual, and is not only an evidence of it, but indeed its representative.

The ideals of art found little favour with him, because with his sharp look he saw too clearly the impossibility of such conceptions ever being embodied in a living organisation; and he therefore banished them into the realm of fable, and even of monstrosity.

His incessant demand for a realisation of the ideal gained him the reputation of a visionary, although he maintained and felt convinced that no man insisted more strongly on the actual than he did: accordingly, he never could detect the error in his mode of thinking and acting.

Seldom has there been a man who strove more passionately than he did for public recognition, and thus he was particularly fitted for a teacher; but, if all his labours tended to the intellectual and moral improvement of others, this was by no means their ultimate aim.

To realise the character of Christ was what he had most at heart: hence that almost insane zeal of his, to have pictures of Christ drawn, copied, moulded, one after another; none of which, however, as to be expected, ever satisfied him.

His writings are hard to understand, even now; for it is far from easy to penetrate into his precise meaning. No one ever wrote so much of the times and for the times, as Lavater: his writings are veritable journals, which, in an especial manner, require to be explained by the history of the day; they, moreover, are written in the language of a coterie, which one must first acquaint one's self with before we can hold communion with them, otherwise many things will appear stupid and absurd, even to the most intelligent reader. Indeed, objections enough of the kind have been made against this author, both in his lifetime and since.

Thus, for example, with our rage for dramatising and representing under this form all that struck us, and caring for no other, we once so warmed his brain with a dramatic ardour, that, in his "Pontius Pilate," he laboured very hard to show that there is no more dramatic work than the Bible, and, especially, that the history of Christ's passion must be regarded as the drama of all dramas.

In this chapter, and, indeed, throughout the work, Lavater appears greatly to resemble Father Abraham of Santa Clara; for into this manner every richly gifted mind necessarily falls who wishes to work upon his contemporaries. He must acquaint himself with existing tendencies and passions, with the speech and terminology of the day, and adapt them to his ends, in order to approach the mass whom he seeks to influence.

Since Lavater took Christ literally, — as described by the Scriptures and by most commentators, — he let this representation serve so far for the supplement of his own being, that he ideally incorporated the God-man into his own individual humanity, until he finally was able to imagine himself melted into one and united with him, and, indeed, to have become the same person.

This decidedly literal faith had also worked in him a perfect conviction that miracles can be wrought to-day as well as heretofore. Accordingly, since in some important and trying emergencies of his earlier days, he had, by means of earnest and indeed violent prayer, succeeded in procuring an instantaneous and favourable turn of the impending calamity, no mere cold objections of the reasoning intellect would make him for a moment waver in this faith. Penetrated, moreover, by the idea of the greatness and excellence of Humanity as restored by Christ, and through him destined to a blissful immortality, but, at the same time, fully sensible of the manifold requisitions of man's heart and mind, and of his insatiable yearnings after knowledge, and, moreover, feeling in himself that desire of expanding himself into the infinite to which the starry heavens seem so sensibly to invite us, he wrote under these feelings his " Prospects of Eternity," which must have appeared a very strange book indeed to the greater part of his contemporaries.

All this striving, however, all wishes, all undertakings, were overborne by the genius for physiognomy, which Nature had bestowed upon him. For as the touchstone, by its blackness and peculiar roughness of surface, is eminently fitted to distinguish between the metals which are applied to it; so that pure idea of humanity, which Lavater carried within himself, and that sharp yet delicate gift of observation, which at first he exercised from natural impulse occasionally only and accidentally, but afterward with deliberate reflection and regularly, qualified him in the highest degree to note the peculiarities of individual men, and to understand, distinguish, and express them.

Every talent which rests on a decided natural gift seems, from our inability to subordinate either it or its operations to any idea, to have something of magic about it. And, in truth, Lavater's insight into the characters of individuals surpassed all conception : one was utterly amazed at his remarks, when in confidence we were talking of this or that person; nay, it was frightful to live near a man who clearly discerned the nicest limits by which nature had been pleased to modify and distinguish our various personalities.

Every one is apt to believe that what he possesses himself may be communicated to others; and so Lavater was not content to make use of this great gift for himself alone, but insisted that it might be found and called forth in others, — nay, that it might even be imparted to the great mass. The many dull and malicious misinterpretations, the stupid jests in abundance, and detracting railleries, this striking doctrine gave rise to, may still be remembered by some men : however, it must be owned that the worthy man himself was not altogether without blame in the matter. For though a high moral sense preserved the unity of his inner being, yet, with his manifold labours, he was unable to attain to outward unity, since he did not possess the slightest capacity for philosophical method, nor for artistic talent.

He was neither Thinker nor Poet; indeed, not even an orator, in the proper sense of the term. Utterly unable to take a comprehensive and methodical view, he nevertheless formed an unerring judgment of individual cases; and these he noted down boldly side by side. His great work on physiognomy is a striking proof and illustration of this. In himself, the idea of the moral or of the sensual man might form a whole; but out of himself he could not represent this idea, except practically by individual cases, in the same way as he himself had apprehended them in life.

That very work sadly shows us how, in the commonest matter of experience, so sharp-sighted a man may go groping about him. For after spending an immense sum, and employing every artist and botcher living, he procured at last drawings and engravings which were so far without character, that he is obliged in his work to say after each one that it is more or less a failure, unmeaning and worthless. True, by this means he sharpened his own judgment, and the judgment of others; but it also proves that his mental bias led him rather to heap up cases of experience, than to draw from them any clear and sober principle. For this reason he never could come to results, though I often pressed him for them. What in later life he confided as such to his friends, were none to me; for they consisted of nothing more than a collection of certain lines and features, nay, warts and freckles, with which he had seen certain moral, and frequently immoral, peculiarities associated. There were certainly among them some remarks causing surprise and disgust, but they formed no series; one thing followed another accidentally; there was no gradual advance toward any general deductions, and no reference to any principles previously established. And, indeed, there was just as little of literary method or artistic feeling to be found in his other writings, which invariably contained passionate and earnest expositions of his thoughts and objects, and supplied by the most affecting and appropriate instances, what they could not accomplish by the general conception.

The following reflections, as they refer to those circumstances, may be aptly introduced here.

No one willingly concedes superiority to another, so long as he can in any way deny it. Natural gifts of every kind can the least be denied; and yet, by the phraseology common in those times, genius was ascribed to the poet alone. But another world seemed all at once to rise up: genius was looked for in the physician, in the general, in the statesman, and before long in all men who thought to make themselves eminent either in theory or practice. Zimmermann, especially, had advanced these claims. Lavater, by his views of physiognomy, was compelled to assume a more general distribution of mental gifts by nature: the word *genius* became a universal symbol; and, because men heard it uttered so often, they thought that what was meant by it was habitually at hand. But then, since every one felt himself justified in demanding genius of others, he finally believed that he also must possess it himself. The time was yet far distant when it could be affirmed that genius is that power of man which, by its deeds and actions, gives laws and rules. At this time it was thought to manifest itself only by overstepping existing laws, breaking established rules, and declaring itself above all restraint. It was, therefore, an easy thing to be a genius; and nothing was more natural than that extravagance, both of word and deed, should provoke all orderly men to oppose themselves to such a monster.

When anybody rushed into the world on foot, without exactly knowing why or whither, it was called a pass of genius; and, when any one undertook an aimless and useless absurdity, it was a stroke of genius. Young men, of vivacious and true talents, too often lost themselves in the limitless; and then older men of understanding, wanting perhaps in talent and in soul, found a most malicious gratification in exposing to the public gaze their manifold and ludicrous miscarriages.

For my part, in the development and the expression of my own ideas, I perhaps experienced far more hinderance and checks from the false coöperation and interference of the like-minded, than by the opposition of those whose turn of mind was directly contrary to my own.

With a strange rapidity, words, epithets, and phrases, which have once been cleverly employed to disparage the highest intellectual gifts, spread by a sort of mechanical repetition among the multitude; and in a short time they are to be heard everywhere, even in common life, and in the mouths of the most uneducated; indeed, before long they even creep into dictionaries. In this way the word genius had suffered so much from misrepresentation, that it was almost desired to banish it entirely from the German language.

And so the Germans, with whom the common voice is more apt to prevail than with other nations, would perhaps have sacrificed the fairest flower of speech, the word which, though apparently foreign, really belongs to every people, had not the sense for what is highest and best in man been happily restored and solidly established by a profounder philosophy.

In the preceding pages mention has been frequently made of the youthful times of two men whose memory will never fade from the history of German literature and morals. At this period, however, we came to know them, as it were, only by the errors into which they were misled by a false maxim which prevailed among their youthful contemporaries. Nothing, therefore, can be more proper than with due appreciation and respect to paint their natural form, their peculiar individuality, just as it appeared at that time, and as their immediate presence exhibited itself to the penetrating eye of Lavater. Consequently, since the heavy and expensive volumes of the great work on physiognomy are probably accessible to a few only of our readers, I have no scruple in inserting here the remarkable passages of that work which refer to both the Stolbergs in the second part, and its thirtieth fragment, p. 224:

" The young men, whose portraits and profiles we have here before us, are the first men who ever sat and stood to me for physiognomical description, as another would sit to a painter for his portrait.

" I knew them before, the noble ones — and I made the first attempt, in accordance with nature and with all my previous knowledge, to observe and to describe their character.

" Here is the description of the whole man:

" FIRST, OF THE YOUNGER.

" See the blooming youth of twenty-five! The lightly floating, buoyant, elastic creature! It does not lie, it does not stand, it does not lean, it does not fly: it floats or swims. Too full of life to rest, too supple to stand firm, too heavy and too weak to fly.

" A floating thing, then, which does not touch the earth! In its whole contour not a single slack line, but, on the other hand, no straight one, no tense one, none firmly arched or stiffly curved; no sharp-entering angles, no rock-like projection of the brow; no hardness; no stiffness; no defiant roughness; no threatening insolence; no iron will — all is elastic, winning, but nothing iron; no steadfast and searching profundity; no slow reflection or prudent thoughtfulness; nowhere the reasoner with the scales held firmly in the one hand, and the sword in the other; and yet not the least formality in look or judgment! But still the most perfect straightforwardness of intellect, or rather the most immaculate sentiment of truth! Always the inward feeler, never the deep thinker; never the discoverer, the testing unfolder of truth so quickly seen, so quickly known, so quickly loved, and quickly grasped. . . . Perpetual soarer, a seer; idealiser; beautifier; — that gives a shape and form to all his ideas! Ever the half-intoxicated poet, seeing only what he will see; — not the sorrowfully languishing; not the sternly crushing; but the lofty, noble, powerful! Who with 'thirst for the sun' (*Sonnendurst*), hovers to and fro in the regions of air, strives aloft, and again — *sinks* not to earth! but throws himself headlong to earth, bather in the floods of the 'Rock-stream' (*Felsenstrom*), and cradles himself 'in the thunder of the echoing rocks around' (*im Donner der hallenden Felsen umher*). His glance — not the fire-glance of the eagle. His brow and nose — not the courage of the lion. His breast — not the steadfastness of the steed that neighs for battle! In the whole, however, there is much of the tearing activity of the elephant. . . .

"The projecting upper lip slightly drawn up toward the overhanging nose, which is neither sharply cut nor angular, evinces, with such a closing of the mouth, much taste and sensibility; while the lower part of the face bespeaks much sensuality, indolence, and thoughtlessness. The whole outline of the profile shows openness, honesty, humanity, but at the same time a liability to be led astray, and a high degree of that good-hearted indiscretion which injures no one but himself. The middle line of the mouth bespeaks, in its repose, a downright, planless, weak, good-natured disposition; when in motion, a tender, finely feeling, exceedingly susceptible, benevolent, noble man. In the arch of the eyelids, and in the glance of the eyes, there sits not Homer, but the deepest, most thorough, and most quick, feeling, and comprehension of Homer; not the epic, but the lyric, poet; genius, which fuses, moulds, creates, glorifies, hovers, transforms all into a heroic form — which deifies all. The half-closed eyelids, from such an arch, indicate the keenly sensitive poet, rather than the slowly labouring artist, who creates after a plan; the whimsical rather than the severe. The full face of the youth is much more taking and attractive than the somewhat too loose, too protracted, half-face; the fore-part of the face, in its slightest motion, tells of a highly sensitive, thoughtful, inventive, untaught, inward goodness, of a softly tremulous, wrong-abhorring love of liberty — an eager vivacity. It cannot conceal from the commonest observer the slightest impression which it receives for the moment, or adopts for ever. Every object, which nearly concerns or interests him, drives the blood into the cheeks and nose; where honour is concerned, the most maidenly blush of shame spreads like lightning over the delicately sensitive skin.

" The complexion is not the pale one of all-creating, all-consuming genius; not the wildly glowing one of the contemptuous destroyer; not the milk-white one of the blond; not the olive one of the strong and hardy; not the brownish one of the slowly plodding peasant; but the white, the red, and the violet, running one into another, and so expressively, and so happily, blended together like the strength and weakness of the whole character. The soul of the whole and of each single feature is freedom, and elastic activity, which springs forth easily and is as easily repulsed. The whole fore-face, and the way the head is carried, promise magnanimity and upright cheerfulness. Incorruptible sensibility, delicacy of taste, purity of mind, goodness and nobleness of soul, active power, a feeling of strength and of weakness, shine out so transparently through the whole face, that what were otherwise a lively self-complacency dissolves itself into a noble modesty; and most artlessly and unconstrainedly the natural pride and vanity of youth melt with the loveliness of twilight into the easy majesty of the whole man. The whitish hair, the length and awkwardness of form, the softness and lightness of step, the hesitating gait, the flatness of the breast, the fair, unfurrowed brow, and various other features, spread over the whole man a certain feminine air, by which the inward quickness of action is moderated, and every intentional offence and every meanness made for ever impossible to the heart; but at the same time clearly evincing that the spirited and fiery poet, with all his unaffected thirst for freedom and for emancipation, is neither destined to be a man of business, thoroughly persistent, who steadily and resolutely carries out his plans, or to become immortal in the bloody strife. And now, in conclusion, I remark, for the first time, that I have as yet said nothing of the most striking trait, — the noble simplicity, free from all affectation! Nothing of his childlike openness of heart! Nothing of the entire unconsciousness of his outward nobility! Nothing of the inexpressible *bonhommie* with which he accepts and bears reproaches or warnings, nay, even accusations and wrongful charges.

"But who can find an end, who will undertake to tell all that he sees or feels in a good man, in whom there is so much pure humanity?

"DESCRIPTION OF THE ELDER STOLBERG.

"What I have said of the younger brother — how much of it may be said also of the elder! The principal thing I have to remark is the following:

"This figure and this character are more compact and less diffuse than the former. There all was longer or flatter; here all is shorter, broader, more arched, and rounded: there all was vague; here everything is more precise and sharply defined. So the brow; so the nose; so the breast: more compressed, more active, less diffuse, more of concentrated life and power! For the rest, the same amiableness and *bonhommie!* Not that striking openness, rather more of reserve, but in principle, or rather in deed, the same honourable tone. The same invincible abhorrence of injustice and baseness; the same irreconcilable hatred of all that is called cunning and trickery; the same unyielding opposition to tyranny and despotism; the same pure, incorruptible sensibility to all that is noble and great and good; the same need of friendship and of freedom; the same sensitiveness and noble thirst for glory; the same catholicity of heart for all good, wise, sincere, and energetic men, renowned or unrenowned, known or misunderstood, — and the same light-hearted inconsiderateness. No! not exactly the same. The face is sharper, more contracted, firmer; has more inward, self-developing capacity for business and practical counsels; more of enterprising spirit — which is shown especially by the strongly prominent and fully rounded bones of the eye-sockets. Not the all-blending, rich, pure, lofty poet's feeling — not the ease and rapidity of the productive power which marks the other — but yet he is, and that in profounder depths, vivacious, upright, ardent. Not the airy genius of light floating away in the morning red of heaven, and fashioning huge shapes therein — but more of inward power, though perhaps less of expression! more powerful and terrible — less of elegance and finish; though his pencil, nevertheless, wants neither colouring nor enchantment. More wit and riotous humour; droll satire; brow, nose, look — all so downward, so overhanging — decidedly what it should be for original and all-enlivening wit, which does not gather from without, but brings forth from within. Above all, in this character every trait more prominent, more angular, more aggressive, more storming! No passive dulness, no relaxation, except in the sunken eyes, where, as well as in the brow and nose, pleasure evidently sits. In all besides — and even in this very brow, this concentration of all — in this look indeed — there is an unmistakable expression of natural, unacquired greatness; strength, impetuosity of manliness: constancy, simplicity, precision!"

After having in Darmstadt conceded to Merck the justice of his opinions, and allowed him to triumph, in his having predicted my speedy separation from these gay companions, I found myself again in Frankfort, well received by every one, including my father; although the latter could not conceal his disappointment that I had not descended by the pass to Airolo, and announced to him from Milan my arrival in Italy. All this was expressed by his silence rather than by his words; but above all he did not show the slightest sympathy with those wild rocks, those lakes of mist and dragon's nests.

At last, however, by an incidental remark, by no means intended for a reproach, he gave me to understand how little all such sights were worth: he who has not seen Naples, he observed, has lived to no end.

On my return I did not, I could not, avoid seeing Lilli: the position we maintained toward each other was tender and considerate. I was informed that they had fully convinced her, in my absence, that she must break off her intimacy with me, and that this was the more necessary, and indeed more practicable, since, by my journey and voluntary absence, I had given a sufficiently clear intimation of my own intentions. Nevertheless, the same localities in town and country, the same friends, confidentially acquainted with all the past, could scarcely be seen without emotion by either of us — still and for ever lovers, although drawn apart in a mysterious way. It was an accursed state, which in a certain sense resembled Hades, or the meeting of the happy with the unhappy dead.

There were moments when departed days seemed to revive, but instantly vanished again, like ghosts.

Some kind people had told me in confidence, that Lilli, when all the obstacles to our union were laid before her, had declared, that for my love she was ready to renounce all present ties and advantages, and to go with me to America. America was then perhaps, still more than now, the Eldorado of all who found themselves crossed in the wishes of the moment.

But the very thing which should have animated my hopes depressed them only the more. My handsome paternal house, only a few hundred steps from hers, offered certainly a more tolerable and more attractive habitation than an uncertain and remote locality beyond the ocean; still I do not deny, that in her presence all hopes, all wishes, sprang to life again, and irresolution was stirring within me.

True, my sister's injunctions were very peremptory and precise: not only had she, with all the shrewd penetration of which she was mistress, explained the situation of things to me, but she had also, with painfully cogent letters, harped upon the same text still more powerfully. "It were very well," said she, "if you could not help it: then you would have to put up with it; such things one must *suffer* but not *choose*."

Some months passed away in this most miserable of all conditions; every circumstance had conspired against the union; in her alone I felt, I knew, lay the power which could have overcome every difficulty.

Both lovers, conscious of their position, avoided all solitary interviews; but, in company, they could not help meeting in the usual formal way. It was now that I had to undergo the hardest trial, as every noble and feeling soul will acknowledge, when I shall have explained myself more fully.

It is generally allowed, that in a new acquaintance, in the formation of a new attachment, the lover gladly draws a veil over the past. Growing affection troubles itself about no antecedents; and as it springs up like genius, with the rapidity of lightning, it knows nothing either of past or future. It is true, my closer intimacy with Lilli had begun by her telling me the story of her early youth: how, from a child up, she had excited in many both a liking and devotion to herself, especially in strangers visiting her father's gay and lively house, and how she had found her pleasure in all this, though it had been attended with no further consequences, and had led to no permanent tie.

True, lovers consider all they have felt before only as preparation for their present bliss, only as the foundation on which the structure of their future life is to be reared. Past attachments seem like spectres of the night, which glide away before the break of day.

But what occurred! The fair came on, and with it appeared the whole swarm of those spectres in their reality: all the mercantile friends of the eminent house came one by one; and it was soon manifest, that not a man among them was willing or able wholly to give up a certain claim to the lovely daughter. The younger ones, without being obtrusive, still seemed to claim the rights of familiar friends; the middle-aged, with a certain obliging dignity, like those who seek to make themselves beloved, and who, in all probability, might come forward with higher claims. There were fine men among them, with the additional recommendation of a substantial fortune.

The older gentlemen, with their *uncle's* ways and manners, were altogether intolerable: they could not bridle their hands, and, in the midst of their disagreeable twaddle, would demand a kiss, for which the cheek was not refused. It was so natural to her, gracefully to satisfy every one. The conversation, too, excited many a painful remembrance. Allusion was constantly made to pleasure-parties by water and by land, to perils of all kinds with their happy escapes, to balls and evening promenades, to the amusement afforded by ridiculous wooers, and to whatever could excite an uncomfortable jealousy in the heart of an inconsolable lover, who had, as it were, for a long time drawn to himself the sum of so many years. But amid all this crowd and gaiety, she did not push aside her friend; and, when she turned to him, she contrived, in a few words, to express all the tenderness which seemed allowable to their present position.

But let us turn from this torture, of which the memory even is almost intolerable, to poesy, which afforded, at least, an intellectual and heartfelt alleviation of my sufferings.

" Lilli's Menagerie " belongs somewhere to this period : I do not adduce the poem here, because it does not reveal the softer sentiment, but seeks only, with genial earnestness, to exaggerate the disagreeable, and, by comical and provoking images, to change renunciation into despair.

The following song expresses rather the sweeter side of that misery, and on that account is here inserted :

O sweet roses, ye are going!
For my love ye did not grow;
For a sad heart ye were blowing,
Which did hope no longer know.

Of those days I think with weeping,
When I, angel, clung to thee,
To my garden went out, peeping
Early, first small buds to see.

Every fruit and every flower
Still was laying at thy feet;
Hope not yet had lost all power,
At thy sight in me did beat.

O sweet roses, ye are going!
For my love ye did not grow;
For a sad heart ye were blowing,
Which did hope no longer know.
— *Editor's Version.*

The opera of "Erwin and Elvira" was suggested by the pretty little romaunt or ballad introduced by Goldsmith in his "Vicar of Wakefield," which had given us so much pleasure in our happiest days, when we never dreamed that a similar fate awaited us.

I have already introduced some of the poetical productions of this epoch, and I only wish they had all been preserved. A never-failing excitement in the happy season of love, heightened by the beginning of care, gave birth to songs, which, throughout, expressed no overstrained emotion, but always the sincere feeling of the moment. From social songs for festivals, down to the most trifling of presentation-verses, all was living and real, and what a refined company had sympathised in; first glad, then sorrowful, till, finally, there was no height of bliss, no depth of woe, to which a strain was not devoted.

All these internal feelings and outward doings, so far as they were likely to vex and pain my father, were, by my mother's bustling prudence, skilfully kept from him. Although his hope of seeing me lead into his house that first one (who had so fully realised his ideas of a daughter-in-law) had died away, still this "state-lady," as he used to call her in his confidential conversations with his wife, would never suit him.

Nevertheless, he let matters take their course, and diligently occupied himself with his little Chancery. The young juristic friend, as well as the dexterous amanuensis, gained continually more and more of influence under his firm hand. As the absentee was now no longer missed there, they let me take my own way, and sought to establish themselves firmly upon a ground on which I was not destined to thrive.

Fortunately, my own tendencies corresponded with the sentiments and wishes of my father. He had so great an idea of my poetic talents, and felt so personal a pleasure in the applause which my earliest efforts had obtained, that he often talked to me on the subject of new and further attempts. On the other hand, I did not venture to communicate to him any of these social effusions and poems of passion.

As, in "Götz von Berlichingen," I had, in my own way, mirrored forth the image of an important epoch of the world, I now again carefully looked round for another crisis in political history of similar interest. Accordingly, the Revolt of the Netherlands attracted my attention. In Götz I had depicted a man of parts and energy, sinking under the delusion, that in times of anarchy, ability, and honesty of purpose, must have their weight and influence. The design of Egmont was to show that the most firmly established institutions cannot maintain themselves against a powerful and shrewdly calculating despotism. I had talked so earnestly with my father about what the play ought to be, and what I wanted to do, that it inspired him with an invincible desire to see the plan which I had already worked out in my head, fairly set down on paper, in order to its being printed and admired.

In earlier times, while I still hoped to gain Lilli's hand, I had applied myself with the utmost diligence to the study and practice of legal business; but now I sought to fill the fearful gulf which separated me from her, with occupations of more intellect and soul. I therefore set to work in earnest with the composition of "Egmont." Unlike the first, "Götz von Berlichingen," however, it was not written in succession and in order; but, immediately after the first introduction, I went at once to the main scenes, without troubling myself about the various connecting links. I made rapid progress, because my father, knowing my fitful way of working, spurred me on (literally and without exaggeration) day and night, and seemed to believe that the plan, so easily conceived, might as easily be executed.

TWENTIETH BOOK.

AND so I got on rapidly with my "Egmont;" and, while I found in this some alleviation of my wounded passion, the society of a clever artist also helped me through many wearisome hours. And thus, as had often before been the case, a vague desire of practical improvement brought me a secret peace of mind at a time when it could scarcely be hoped for.

John Melchior Kraus, who had been born at Frankfort, but educated in Paris, having just returned from a short tour to the north of Germany, paid me a visit; and I immediately felt an impulse and a need to attach myself to him. He was a cheerful, merry fellow, whose light, joyous disposition had found its right sphere in Paris.

At that time Paris promised a pleasant welcome for Germans: Philip Hackert was residing there in credit and opulence; the true German style in which, both in oil and water-colours, he faithfully executed landscapes after nature, met with great favour, as contrasted with the formal "*mannerism*" into which the French had fallen. Wille, in high esteem as a copperplate engraver, supported and made German excellence more widely known. Grimm, already an artist of some influence, rejoiced to help his countrymen. Pleasant excursions, in order to take original sketches from nature, were constantly undertaken, in which much of undoubted excellence was either executed or designed.

Boucher and Watteau, both of them artists born, whose works, though fluttering in the style and spirit of the time, were always highly respectable, were favourably inclined to the new school, and even took an active part in their excursions, though only for the sake of amusement and experiment. Greuze, living quietly by himself in his family circle, and fond of representing such domestic scenes, seemed delighted with his own works, held an honoured and easy pencil.

All these several styles our townsman Kraus was able to take up and blend with his own particular talent; he formed himself in school after school, and was skilful in his portrait-like delineations of family and friendly gatherings; equally happy was he in his landscape sketches, which cordially commended themselves to the eye by their clear outlines, massive shadows, and agreeable colouring. The inward sense was satisfied by a certain *naïve* truth, while the admirer of artistic skill was especially pleased with the tact by which he arranged and grouped into a picture what he had copied singly from nature.

He was a most agreeable companion; a cheerful equanimity never failed him; obliging without obsequiousness, reserved without pride; he was everywhere at home, everywhere beloved, the most active, and, at the same time, the most manageable, of all mortals. With such talents, and of such a disposition, he soon won the favour of the higher circles; but he was especially well received at the castle of the Baron von Stein, at Nassau on the Lahn, whose accomplished and lovely daughter he assisted in her artistic studies, and in many ways enlivened the whole circle.

Upon the marriage of this excellent lady to the Count von Werther, the newly wedded couple took the artist with them to Thuringia, where the count possessed a large estate; and thus he got to Weimar. His acquaintance was immediately sought, his talents were appreciated — and a wish expressed that he would fix his permanent abode there.

Obliging as he was to everybody, upon his return at this time to Frankfort, he stimulated my love of art, which had been contented with merely collecting, and to making practical essays. The neighbourhood of the artist is indispensable to the *dilettante*, for the latter sees all that is wanting in himself supplied by the former: the wishes of the amateur are fulfilled in the artist.

By a certain natural talent, assisted by practice, I succeeded pretty well in an outline, and I could give the shape of all that I saw before me in nature; but I wanted the peculiar plastic power, the skilful industry, which lends a body to the outline by well-graduated light and shade. My copies were rather remote suggestions of the real form, and my figures like those light, airy beings in Dante's "Purgatory," which, casting no shadow themselves, fled affrighted at the shadows of actual bodies.

Lavater's fishing for physiognomical treasures — for so we may well designate the importunate urgency with which he called upon all men, not only to observe physiognomies, but also practically to make, be it artistic or most bungling, attempts at copying faces — led me into the habit of taking the portraits of all my friends on gray paper, with black and white chalk. The likeness was not to be mistaken, but it required the hand of my artistic friend to make them stand out from the dark background.

In turning over and looking through the rich portfolio of drawings which the good Kraus had taken during his travels, we had most pleasant talk together when he came to the sketches of scenes and persons in and about Weimar. On such paintings I, too, was glad to dwell; and you may imagine that it must have been flattering to the young man, to see in so many pictures only the text which was to lead to a circumstantially repeated exclamation, they would be glad to see *him* there! With much grace he would imitate the different persons whose portraits he had taken, and impersonate the greetings and invitations he had received. One very successful oil-painting represented the chapel-master, Wolf, at the piano, with his wife behind him preparing to sing; and this gave the artist opportunity to assure me, in earnest terms, of the warm welcome this worthy pair would give me. Among his sketches were several of the wood and mountain scenery around Bürgel. Here an honest forester, more, perhaps, to please his pretty daughters than himself, had, by means of bridges, railings, and mossy paths, opened pleasant and sociable walks through the rough masses of rocks, thickets, and plantations. In one of these beautiful promenades he had painted the fair damsels in white dresses, and not without their attendant cavaliers. In one of these you immediately recognised Bertuch, whose serious designs upon the oldest daughter were openly avowed; and Kraus was not offended if you ventured to refer a second youth to himself, and guessed his growing attachment to the sister.

Bertuch, as the pupil of Wieland, had so distinguished himself in science and in business, that, already appointed private secretary of the duke, he had the best possible prospects before him. From him we passed to Wieland, and talked at length of his rectitude and cheerfulness and kindly disposition; his fine literary and poetical designs were dwelt upon, and allusions were made to the influence of the *Merkur* throughout Germany: many other names of literary, political, or social distinction were also mentioned, and, among them, Musæus, Kirms, Berendis, and Ludecus. Of women, the wife of Wolf, and a widow Kotzebue with a lovely daughter and a bright boy, were, among many others, characterised and extolled. Everything seemed to point to a fresh and active life of literature and art.

And so, by degrees, was exhibited the element which,

on his return, the young duke was to fashion. His mother and guardian had prepared this state of things; while, as regarded the introduction of more important measures, all that, in accordance with the duty of such provisional governments, was left to the judgment and decision of the future sovereign. The sad ruin caused by the burning of the palace was already looked upon as furnishing occasion for new improvements. The mines at Ilmenau, which had stopped working, but which, it was asserted, might again be made profitable by going to the great expense of repairing the deep shaft; the academy at Jena, which was somewhat behind the spirit of the age, and was consequently threatened with the loss of some of its most able teachers; and many other matters, — roused a noble common interest. Already were looks cast around for persons, who, in the upward struggle of Germany, might be qualified to further such various designs for good; and the prospect seemed as fresh as the vivacity and energy of youth could desire. And if it seemed sad to bring a young princess, not to a home of a suitable princely dignity, but to a very ordinary dwelling built for quite a different object, still such beautifully situated and well contrived country-houses as Ettenburg, Belvedere, and other delightful pleasure-seats, gave enjoyment for the present, and also a hope that the life of nature thus rendered necessary might lead to profitable and agreeable occupations.

In the course of this biography we have circumstantially exhibited the child, the boy, the youth, seeking by different ways to approach to the Suprasensible, first looking with strong inclination to a religion of nature, then clinging with love to a positive one, and, finally, concentrating himself in the trial of his own powers, and joyfully giving himself up to the general faith. Whilst he wandered to and fro space which lay intermediate between the sensible and suprasensible regions, seeking and looking about him, much came in his way which did not appear to belong to either; and he seemed to see, more and more distinctly, that it is better to avoid all thought of the immense and incomprehensible.

He thought he could detect in nature — both animate and inanimate, with soul or without soul — something which manifests itself only in contradictions, and which, therefore, could not be comprehended under any idea, still less under one word. It was not godlike, for it seemed unreasonable; not human, for it had no understanding; nor devilish, for it was beneficent; nor angelic, for it often betrayed a malicious pleasure. It resembled chance, for it evolved no consequences: it was like Providence, for it hinted at connection. All that limits us it seemed to penetrate; it seemed to sport at will with the necessary elements of our existence; it contracted time and expanded space. In the impossible alone did it appear to find pleasure, while it rejected the possible with contempt.

To this principle, which seemed to come in between all other principles to separate them, and yet to link them together, I gave the name of Demoniac, after the example of the ancients, and of those who, at any rate, had perceptions of the same kind. I tried to screen myself from this fearful principle, by taking refuge, according to my usual habits, in an imaginary creation.

Among the parts of history which I had particularly studied with some care were the events which have made the United Netherlands so famous. I had diligently examined the original sources, and had endeavoured as far as possible to get my facts at first hand, and to bring the whole period vividly before my mind's eye. The situations it presented appeared to me to be in the highest degree dramatic; while for a principal figure, around whom the others might be grouped with the happiest effect, there was Count

Egmont, whose greatness as a man and a hero was most captivating.

But for my purpose it was necessary to convert him into a character marked by such peculiarities as would grace a youth better than a man in years, and an unmarried man better than the father of a family; and one independent rather than one who, however freely disposed, is nevertheless restrained by the various relations of life.

Having thus, in my conception of Egmont's character, made him youthful, and set him free from all domestic restraints, I ascribed to him unlimited enjoyment of life and its pleasures, boundless self-reliance, a gift of drawing all men to himself, and consequently also of winning the favour of the people, and which, while it inspired a princess with a silent, and a young child of nature with an avowed, passion, won for him the sympathy of a shrewd statesman, and even the loving admiration of the son of his great adversary.

The personal courage which distinguishes the hero is the foundation upon which his whole character rests, the ground and soil from which it sprung. He knows no danger, and willingly is blind to the greatest when it is close at hand. Surrounded by enemies, we may at any rate cut our way through them: the meshes of state policy are harder to break through. The demoniacal element, which is in play on both sides, and in conflict with which the lovely falls while the hated triumphs; and above all the prospect that out of this conflict will spring a third element which will answer to the wishes of all men, — this perhaps is what has gained for the piece (not indeed immediately on its first appearance, but later, and at the right time) the favour which it now enjoys. Here, therefore, for the sake of many beloved readers, I will anticipate myself, and, as I know not whether I shall soon have another opportunity, will express a conviction which, however, I did not form till a considerable period subsequent to that of which I am now writing.

Although this demoniacal element can manifest itself in all corporeal and incorporeal things, and even expresses itself most distinctly in animals, yet with man especially has it a most wonderful connection, forming in him a power, which, if it be not opposed to the moral order of the world, nevertheless does often so cross it that one may be regarded as the warp and the other as the woof.

For the phenomena which it gives rise to, there are innumerable names; for all philosophies and religions have tried in prose and poetry to solve this enigma, and to read once for all the riddle, an employment which they are welcome to continue.

But the most fearful manifestation of the demoniacal is when it is seen predominating in some individual character. During my life I have observed several instances of this, either more closely or remotely. Such persons are not always the most eminent men, either morally or intellectually; and it is seldom that they recommend themselves to our affections by goodness of heart: a tremendous energy seems to be seated in them; and they exercise a wonderful power over all creatures, and even over the elements; and, indeed, who shall say how much farther such influence may extend? All the moral powers combined are of no avail against them: in vain does the more enlightened portion of mankind attempt to throw suspicion upon them as deceived if not deceivers, — the mass is still drawn on by them. Seldom if ever do the great men of an age find their equals among their contemporaries, and they are to be overcome by nothing but by the universe itself; and it is from observation of this fact that the strange but most striking proverb must have risen, *Nemo contra Deum nisi Deus ipse.*

From these lofty recollections I return to the littleness of my own life, for which strange events, clothed at least with a demoniacal appearance, were in store. From the summit of Mont Gotthard I had turned my back upon Italy, and returned home; because I could not make up my mind to go to a distance from Lilli. An affection founded on the hope of possessing for life one dearly beloved in an intimate and cordial union does not die away all at once: on the contrary, it is nourished by a consideration of the reasonable desires and honest hopes we are conscious of cherishing.

It is in the nature of the thing, that in such cases the maiden is much more ready to restrict herself than the youth. To these beautiful children, as descendants of Pandora, is granted the enviable gift to charm, attract, and (more through nature and of half-purpose than through design or of malice) to gather admirers around them; and thus, like the Magician's Apprentice, they are often in danger of being frightened by the crowd of their adorers. And then at last a choice must be made from among them all, one must be exclusively preferred, one must carry off the bride.

And how often does accident determine the choice, and sway the mind of her who has to make the selection! I had renounced Lilli from conviction, but love made me suspect my own reason. Lilli had taken leave of me with the same feelings; and I had set out on a beautiful tour in order to distract my mind, but it had produced the opposite effect.

As long as I was absent, I believed in the separation, but did not believe in the renunciation. Recollections, hopes, and wishes all had free play. Now I came back; and as the reunion of those whose happy love is unopposed is a heaven, so the meeting again of two lovers who are kept apart by cold calculations of reason is an intolerable purgatory, a forecourt of hell. When I again entered the circle in which Lilli still moved, all the dissonances which tended to oppose our union seemed to have gained double force: when I stood once more before her, the conviction that she was lost to me fell heavy upon my heart.

Accordingly I resolved at once on flight; and under this impression there was nothing which I desired more than that the young ducal pair of Weimar should come from Carlsruhe to Frankfort, in order that, complying with old and new invitations, I might follow them to Weimar. Their Highnesses had always maintained toward me a gracious and confidential manner, for which I on my part returned the warmest thanks. My attachment to the duke from the first moment I saw him; my respect for the princess, whom by reputation I had so long known; a desire to render personally some friendly service to Wieland, whose conduct had been so liberal; and to atone upon the spot for my half-wilful, half-unintentional, improprieties,— were motives enough to induce and even to force the assent of a youth who now had no attachment to detain him. Moreover, from Lilli I must fly, whether to the south, where my father's enthusiasm was daily depicting to me a most glorious heaven of art and nature, or to the north, whither so distinguished a circle of eminent men invited me.

The young princely pair now reached Frankfort on their way home. The suite of the Duke of Meiningen was there at the same time; and by him, as well as by the Privy Counsellor von Dürkheim, who accompanied the young prince, I was received in the most friendly manner possible. But now, to keep up the fashion of my youth, a strange incident was not wanting: a little misunderstanding arose to throw me into an incredible but rather laughable perplexity.

Their Highnesses of Weimar and Meiningen were living in the same hotel. I received one day an invitation to dinner. My mind was so preoccupied with the court of Weimar, that I did not think it necessary

more particularly to inform myself, especially as I had
not the presumption to imagine that any notice would
be taken of me by the Duke of Meiningen. Accordingly I go in full dress to the " Roman Emperors," and,
making my way to the apartments of the Weimar
family, find them empty; being informed that the
duke and his suite are with his Highness of Meiningen, I betake myself thither, and am kindly received. Supposing that this is only a morning visit, or
that perhaps the two dukes are to dine together, I
await the issue. Suddenly, however, the Weimar suite
sets itself in motion; and I, of course, follow : but, instead of returning to their own apartments, they go
straight down-stairs, and into their chariots; and I
am left alone in the street.

Now, instead of inquiring into the matter, and
adroitly and prudently seeking some solution of it, I,
with my usual precipitancy, went straight home, where
I found my parents at supper. My father shook his
head, while my mother made every possible excuse for
me. In the evening she told me in confidence, that,
after I had left the table, my father had said, that he
wondered very much how I, generally acute enough,
could not see that in that quarter they only wished to
make a fool of me and to laugh at me. But this did
not move me; for meanwhile I had met with Herr von
Dürkheim, who, in his mild way, brought me to book
with sundry graceful and humourous reproaches. I
was now awakened from my dream, and had an opportunity to express my most sincere thanks for the
favour intended me contrary to my hope and expectation, and to ask forgiveness for my blunder.

After I had on good grounds determined to accept
their friendly offers, the following arrangement was
made. A gentleman of the duke's suite, who had
stayed behind in Carlsruhe to wait for a landau which
was building in Strasburg, was to be by a certain day

in Frankfort; and I was to hold myself in readiness to set off directly with him for Weimar. The cheering and gracious farewell with which the young sovereigns took their leave of me, the kind behaviour of the courtiers, made me look forward most anxiously to this journey, for which the road seemed so pleasantly to smooth itself.

But here, too, accidents came in to complicate so simple an arrangement, which through passionate impatience became still more confused, and was almost quite frustrated. Having announced the day of my departure, I had taken leave of everybody; and after packing up in haste my chattels, not forgetting my unprinted manuscripts, I waited anxiously for the hour which was to bring the aforesaid friend in the new landau, and to carry me into a new country and into new circumstances. The hour passed, and the day also; and since, to avoid a second leave-taking and the being overrun with visits, I had given out that I was to depart early in the morning, I was obliged to keep close to the house, and to my own room, and had thus placed myself in a peculiar situation.

But since solitude and a narrow space were always favourable to me, and I was now compelled to find some employment for these hours, I set to work on my "Egmont," and brought it almost to a close. I read over what I wrote to my father, who had acquired a peculiar interest in this piece, and wished nothing more than to see it finished and in print, since he hoped that it would add to his son's reputation. He needed something of this sort to keep him quiet, and to make him contented; for he was inclined to make very grave comments on the non-arrival of the carriage. He maintained that the whole affair was a mere fiction, would not believe in any new landau, and pronounced the gentleman who stayed behind to be a phantom of the air. It was, however, only indirectly that he gave me to understand all this ; but he only tormented himself and my mother the more openly, insisting that the whole thing was a mere piece of court pleasantry, which they had practised upon me in consequence of my former escapades, and, in order to sicken and to shame me, had put upon me a disgraceful mockery instead of the expected honour.

As to myself, I held fast to my first faith, and congratulated myself upon these solitary hours, disturbed by neither friends nor strangers, nor by any sort of social distraction. I therefore vigorously proceeded with "Egmont," though not without inward mortification. And this frame of mind may perhaps have benefited the play itself, which, agitated by so many passions, could not very well have been written by one entirely passionless.

Thus passed a week, and I know not how many more days, when such perfect imprisonment began to prove irksome. Accustomed for many years to live in the open air, and to enter into society on the most frank and familiar terms, in the neighbourhood, too, of one dearly beloved, from whom, indeed, I had resolved to part, but from whom, so long as I was within the circle of her attraction, I found it difficult to absent myself, — all this began to make me so uneasy, that there was danger lest the interest of my tragedy should suffer, and my inventive powers be suspended through my impatience. Already for several evenings I had found it impossible to remain at home. Disguised in a large mantle, I crept round the city, passing the houses of my friends and acquaintances, and not forbearing to walk up to Lilli's window. She was living on the ground floor of a house at the corner of the street : the green shades were down, but I could easily remark that the lights stood in their usual places. Soon I heard her singing at the piano : it was the song, "Why dost draw me thus without resistance?"

which I had written for her hardly a year before. She seemed to me to sing with more expression than ever: I could make out every word distinctly, for I had placed my ear as close as the convex lattice would permit. After she had finished her song, I saw by the shadow which fell upon the curtain that she got up and walked backward and forward; but I tried in vain to catch the outline of her lovely person through the thick curtains. Nothing but the firm resolve to tear myself away, and not to afflict her with my presence, but actually to renounce her, and the thought of the strange impression which would be made by my re-appearance, could have determined me to leave so dear a neighbourhood.

Several more days passed; and my father's suggestions seemed daily to become more probable, since not even a letter arrived from Carlsruhe to explain the reasons of the delay. I was unable to go on with my poetic labours; and now, in the uneasiness with which I was internally distracted, my father had the game to himself. He represented to me, that it was now too late to change matters, that my trunk was packed, and he would give me money and credit to go to Italy; but I must decide quickly. In such a weighty affair, I naturally doubted and hesitated. Finally, however, I agreed, that if, by a certain hour, neither carriage nor message came, I would set off, directing my steps first of all to Heidelberg, and from there over the Alps, not, however, going through Switzerland again, but rather taking the route through the Grisons or the Tyrol.

Strange things indeed must happen, when a planless youth, who of himself is so easily misled, is also driven into a false step by a passionate error of age. But so it is both with youth and the whole of life. It is not till the campaign is over that we learn to see through its tactics. In the ordinary course of things, such an accident could have been explained easily enough; but we are always too ready to conspire with error against what is naturally probable, just as we shuffle the cards before we deal them round, in order that chance may not be deprived of its full share in the game. It is precisely thus that the element arises in and upon which the demoniacal so loves to work; and it even sports with us the more fearfully, the clearer are the inklings we have of its approach.

The last day for my waiting had arrived, and the next morning was fixed for my setting out on my travels; and now I felt extremely anxious to see my friend Passavant again, who had just· returned from Switzerland, and who would really have had cause to be offended if, by keeping my plans entirely to myself, I had violated the intimate confidence which subsisted between us. I therefore sent him an anonymous note, requesting a meeting by night at a certain spot, where I was the first to arrive enveloped in my mantle: but he was not long after me; and if he wondered at the appointment, he was still more surprised to meet the person he did. His joy, however, was equal to his astonishment: conversation and counsel were not to be thought of; he could only wish me well through my Italian journey, and so we parted. The next day I saw myself by good time advancing along the mountain-road.

I had several reasons for going to Heidelberg: one was very sensible and prudent, for I had heard that my missing Weimar friend must pass through Heidelberg from Carlsruhe; and so, when we reached the post-house, I left a note which was to be handed to a cavalier who should pass through in the carriage described; the second reason was one of passion, and had reference to my late attachment to Lilli. In short, Mlle. Delf who had been the confidante of our love, and indeed the mediator with our respective parents for their approval of our marriage, lived there;

and I prized it as the greatest happiness to be able, before I left Germany, to talk over those happy times with a worthy, patient, and indulgent friend.

I was well received, and introduced into many families: among others, the family of the high warden of the forests, Von W——, particularly pleased me. The parents were dignified and easy in their manners, and one of the daughters resembled Frederica. It was just the time of vintage, the weather beautiful, and all my Alsatian feelings revived in the beautiful valley of the Rhine. At this time, however, my experience, both of myself and others, seemed very strange : it was as yet quite vague and undigested in my mind, no deliberate judgment upon life had shaped itself before me, and whatever sense of the infinite had been awakened within me served only to confuse and perplex me the more. In society, nevertheless, I was as agreeable and entertaining as ever, and possibly even still more so. Here, under this free air of heaven, among joyous men, I sought again the old sports which never lose their novelty and charm for youth. With an earlier and not yet extinguished love in my heart, I excited sympathy without seeking it, even though it sought no utterance of itself; and thus I soon became at home in this circle, and indeed necessary to it; and I forgot that I had resolved, after talking away a couple of evenings, to continue my journey.

Mlle. Delf was one of those persons, who, without exactly intriguing, always like to have some business in hand, and to keep others employed, and to carry through some object or other. She had conceived a sincere friendship for me, and prevailed the more easily on me to prolong my visit, as I lived in her house, where she suggested all manner of inducements for my stay, and raised all manner of obstacles to my journey. When, however, I wanted to turn the conversation to Lilli, she was not so well pleased or so sympathising as I had hoped. On the contrary, she said, that, under the circumstances, nothing could be wiser than our resolution to part, and maintained that one must submit to what is unavoidable, banish the impossible from the mind, and look around for some new object of interest in life. Full of plans as she always was, she had not intended to leave this matter to accident, but had already formed a project for my future conduct: from which I clearly saw that her recent invitation to Heidelberg had not been so disinterested as it sounded.

She reminded me that the Electoral Prince, Charles Theodore, who had done so much for arts and sciences, was still residing at Mannheim, and that as the court was Roman Catholic, while the country was Protestant, the latter party was extremely anxious to strengthen itself by enlisting the services of able and hopeful men. I was now to go, in God's name, to Italy, and there mature my views of art: meanwhile they would work for me. It would, on my return, soon be seen whether the budding affection of Fräulein von W—— had expanded, or had been nipped, and whether it would be politic, through an alliance with a respectable family, to establish myself and my fortunes in a new home.

All these suggestions I did not, to be sure, reject; but my planless nature could not wholly harmonise with the scheming spirit of my friend: I was gratified, however, with the kind intentions of the moment; while Lilli's image floated before me, waking and dreaming, and mingled with everything else which afforded me pleasure or distraction. But now I summoned before my soul the serious import of my great project of travel; and I resolved to set myself free, gently and with propriety, and in a few days to make known to her my determination of taking leave of her, and to continue on my way.

One night Mlle. Delf had gone on until late unfolding to me her plans, and all that certain parties were disposed to do for me; and I could not but feel grateful for such sentiments, although the scheme of strengthening a certain circle, through me and my possible influence at court, was manifest enough. It was about one o'clock when we separated. I soon fell into a sound sleep; but before very long I was awakened by the horn of a postilion, who was stopping and blowing it before the house. Very soon Mlle. Delf appeared with a light, and a letter in her hands, and, coming up to my bedside, she exclaimed, "Here's the letter! read and tell me what it says. Surely it comes from the Weimar people. If it is an invitation, do not follow it, but call to mind our conversation." I asked her to give me a light, and leave me for a quarter of an hour to myself. She went away very reluctantly. I remained thinking for some time without opening the letter. The express, then, has come from Frankfort, — I know both the seal and hand; the friend, then, has arrived there; he is still true to his invitation, and our own want of faith and incredulity had made us act prematurely. Why could one not wait, in a quiet, civilised place, for a man who had been announced distinctly, but whose arrival might be delayed by so many accidents? The scales fell from my eyes. All the kindness, the graciousness, the confidence, of the past came up livingly before me; and I was almost ashamed of the strange, wilful step I had taken. I opened the letter, and found all that had happened explained naturally enough. My missing guide had waited for the new landau, which was to come from Strasburg, day after day, hour after hour, as we had waited for him; then, for the sake of some business, he had gone round by way of Mannheim to Frankfort, and to his dismay had not found me there. He sent the hasty letter by express, proposing, that now the mistake was explained, I should instantly return, and save him the shame of going to Weimar without me.

Much as my understanding and my feeling inclined me to this side, there was still no lack of weighty arguments in favour of my new route. My father had laid out for me a fine plan of travel, and given me a little library, which might prepare me for the scenes I was to visit, and also guide me on the spot. In my leisure hours I had had no other entertainment than to reflect on it; and, indeed, during my last short journey I had thought of nothing else in the coach. Those glorious objects with which, from my youth up, I had become acquainted, histories, and all sorts of tales, gathered before my soul; and nothing seemed to me so desirable as to visit them, while I was parting from Lilli for ever.

As these thoughts passed through my mind, I had dressed, and was walking up and down my chamber. My anxious hostess entered. "What am I to hope?" she cried. "Dearest madam," I answered, "say no more on the subject: I have made up my mind to return; the grounds of that conclusion I have well weighed, and to repeat them to you would be wasting time. A resolution must be taken sooner or later, and who should take it but the person whom it most concerns?"

I was moved, and so was she; and we had an excited scene, which I cut short by ordering my servant to engage a post-coach. In vain I begged my hostess to calm herself, and to turn the mock-departure which I took of the company the evening before into a real one; to consider that it was only a temporary visit, a postponement for a short time; that my Italian journey was not given up, and my return that way was not precluded. She would listen to nothing, and disquieted her friend, already deeply excited, still more. The coach was at the door; everything was packed, and the postilion gave the usual signs of impatience; I tore myself away; she would not let me go, and, with so much art, brought up all the arguments of the present, that finally, impassioned and inspired, I shouted out the words of Egmont, —

"Child! child! no more! The coursers of time, lashed, as it were, by invisible spirits, hurry on the light car of our destiny; and all that we can do is in cool self-possession to hold the reins with a firm hand, and to guide the wheels, now to the left, now to the right, avoiding a stone here, or a precipice there. Whither it is hurrying, who can tell? and who, indeed, can remember whence he came?"

THE END

THE
EASTERN
EUROPE
COLLECTION

THE
LABYRINTH OF THE WORLD
AND THE
PARADISE OF THE HEART

John Amos Komensky

ARNO PRESS & THE NEW YORK TIMES

New York · 1971

122133

Reprint Edition 1971 by Arno Press Inc.

Reprinted from a copy in
The Pennsylvania State University Library

LC# 73-135812

ISBN 0-405-02754-0

The Eastern Europe Collection
ISBN for complete set: 0-405-02730-3

Manufactured in the United States of America

THE LABYRINTH OF THE WORLD

THE
LABYRINTH OF THE WORLD

AND THE

PARADISE OF THE HEART

BY

JOHN AMOS KOMENSKY

(COMENIUS)

EDITED AND TRANSLATED BY

COUNT LÜTZOW

Member of the Bohemian Society of Sciences, and of the Bohemian Academy ;
formerly Deputy for Bohemia in the Austrian Parliament ; Author of
" A History of Bohemian Literature," " Bohemia : an Historical
Sketch," " Prague" (Mediæval Towns Series)

NEW YORK
E. P. DUTTON & CO.
1901

" Nevzali jsme ssebou
  Nic, po vsem veta
  Jen bibli Kralickou
  Labyrint sveta."

" Nothing have we taken with us,
  Everything is lost ;
  We have but our bible of Kralice,
  Our ' Labyrinth of the World.' "

—*Song of the Bohemian Exiles.*

Printed in Great Britain